THE WORLD OF MALUKU

THE WORLD OF MALUKU

Eastern Indonesia in the Early Modern Period

LEONARD Y. ANDAYA

UNIVERSITY OF HAWAII PRESS

HONOLULU

To my parents, Doris and Alejo

98 97 96 95 94 93   5 4 3 2 1

Library of Congress Cataloging-in-Publication Data

Andaya, Leonard Y.
The world of Maluku : eastern Indonesia in the early modern period
/ Leonard Y. Andaya.
p.   cm.
Includes bibliographical references and index.
ISBN 0-8248-1490-8 (acid-free paper)
1. Maluku (Indonesia)—History.   I. Title.
DS646.67.A54   1993
959.8'5—dc20   93-18245
CIP

Designed by Paula Newcomb

CONTENTS

MAPS

Acknowledgments

The process of conceiving and writing this book has involved a large number of people and institutions throughout the world. It would have been an almost impossible task had it not been for the assistance and kindness shown to me throughout this endeavor.

The generous leave provisions of the University of Auckland, where I have been teaching for the last fifteen years, enabled me to undertake the necessary research in Europe, America, and Asia. It is indeed gratifying to work for an institution which values original research and continues to fund such activity. In Holland I have only praise for the highly efficient archival and library system at the General State Archives in The Hague and the Royal Institute of Linguistics and Anthropology in Leiden. The helpfulness of the staff of these institutions made research pleasant and enjoyable, and I would like to express my gratitude to all of them.

My lack of familiarity with the Portuguese archival sources was compensated by the excellent advice I received from Dr. George Winius, Dr. Luis Felipe Thomaz, and Dr. Pierre-Yves Manguin. Without their help I would not have been able to use my time as profitably as I did. I also would like to thank the staff members of the Archivo Nacional da Torre do Tombo, the Bibliotéca Ajuda de Lisboa, the Bibliotéca Nacional Lisboa, and especially the Centro de Estudos Históricos Ultramarinos, for making the relevant documents available to me. In Spain I wish to thank the staff of the Arquivo General de Indias (Casa de India) in Seville for their assistance.

To the members of Kyoto University's Center for Southeast Asian Studies, I would like to express my appreciation for providing financial support and facilities to complete my research and for the opportunity to discuss my preliminary findings. The atmosphere at the Center was always pleasant and the discussions with my colleagues exhilarating. I would especially like to single out the Center's former director, Professor Yoneo Ishii, and my sponsor, Professor Narifumi Maeda, for their support and intellectual stimulation. I could not have spent a more enjoyable and profitable eight months with my Japanese colleagues in the Center, and for that I am grateful. During this period in Kyoto, Michael and Maria Aung-Thwin were wonderful companions and neighbors and helped make research fun.

In Indonesia I would first of all like to express my gratitude once again to the Indonesian Institute of Social Sciences (LIPI) for their sponsorship of my project. In particular I would like to mention Dr. Eddy Masinambow, Dr. Adriaan Lapian, the late Dra. Paramita Abdurrachman, Dr. Taufik Abdullah, and Luwarsih Pringgoadisurjo for their suggestions and hospitality. A special thank you to Heather Baigent, then serving in the New Zealand Embassy in Jakarta, for her most gracious and wonderful hospitality at a time when I most needed it.

There were many individuals in Maluku who were generous with their time, knowledge, and hospitality. In Ternate I am especially indebted to Abdul Hamid Hasan, whose understanding of Ternaten culture and history was impressive indeed. I appreciated also his willingness to take me to historic places and to share with me the research he had done on the area. In Tidore I would like to thank Abdul Wahab Togubu for the assistance with documents held in the office of the Department of Education and Culture in Soa Sio. In Bacan Hasanuddin Adam proved to be an enjoyable and informative companion. There were many others in north Maluku without whose assistance I would never have been able to do my research as profitably as I did. To these I am deeply grateful. I would also like to thank the government officials and the members of the various departments of education and culture in Ternate, Tidore, Makian, Bacan, Jailolo, Sahu, Galela, Tobelo, Kau, Payahe, Patani, Weda, and Gebe who were helpful and hospitable to this stranger asking oftentimes difficult questions about their past and their society. To all of them, a very sincere *terima kasih*.

The final stages of the writing of this manuscript occurred at the University of Hawaii. To Professor Robert van Niel, head of the Department of History, and Professor Mark Juergensmeyer, dean of the School of Hawaiian, Asian, and Pacific Studies, I would like to express my appreciation for the opportunity to spend time in Hawaii and for the facilities to complete my manuscript. I would especially like to thank Professor Jim Collins for his helpful comments on the manuscript and his infectious enthusiasm for Malukan studies. To Martin Leicht I owe my gratitude for helping me overcome computer hitches in the preparation of the manuscript; I am grateful to Pamela Kelley for her useful suggestions for revisions of the text.

In Auckland, I would like to thank Jan Kelly of the Cartography

Section of the Geography Department in the University of Auckland for her patience in my ever-expanding list of names to be included in the maps; to Diana Holmes, the administrative assistant of the History Department, for the technical assistance in the final revision of the manuscript on a Macintosh; and to Barbara Batt of the History Department for correcting some of the typescript for publication.

Throughout the many experimentations and drafts, it was comforting to know that there was one colleague nearby who was always on tap for advice and comfort. As anyone knows who has ever attempted to write a book, the process is a long one with periods of highs and lows. Throughout it all Barbara Watson Andaya has helped me overcome both emotional and intellectual lows to see this work to completion. To her I owe a tremendous *utang na loob*.

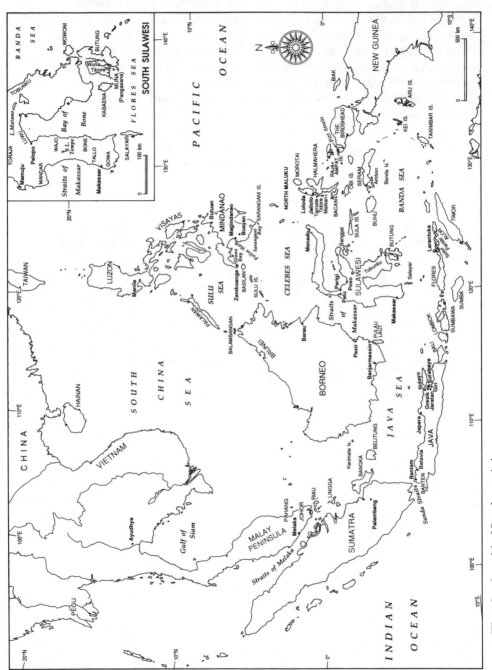

MAP I. The island world of Southeast Asia

Introduction

The very mention of the name "the spice islands" evokes a romantic image of the days of early European adventurers in the waters of the Pacific. It was the highly desired trinity of spices—clove, nutmeg, and mace—which lured the Europeans and other foreigners to the Moluccas or Maluku in eastern Indonesia. The clove tree (*Eugenia aromatica*, Kuntze) is native to the five small northern Malukan islands of Ternate, Tidore, Moti, Makian, and Bacan. These magnificent volcanic islands rise almost vertically out of the water and are in fact the peaks of some of the highest mountains in the world anchored to the ocean shelf just off the starfish-shaped island of Halmahera. Nutmeg and its red filament mace come from the nutmeg tree (*Myristica fragrans*, Linn.), whose origins are in the equally tiny volcanic and coral islands of Banda located to the south of the large island of Seram.

Of these spices it was the clove which was highest valued. Among the local inhabitants it was both a delicacy and a remedy. When the fruit was green it was sugared and made into conserves, or salted and pickled in vinegar. In powdered form it was used for medicinal purposes. But it was the applications found for this spice/drug among foreign nations, especially the Chinese and the Europeans, which contributed to the clove's considerable appeal. The Chinese used it for medicine, to sweeten the breath, and in the T'ang dynasty to flavor food.[1] In Europe the sweet-smelling essence distilled from the clove was said to strengthen one's vision if applied to the eye. The powder was rubbed on the forehead to relieve head colds, and when added to food and drink it was said to stimulate the appetite and assist in the clearing of the bladder and the intestines. An added inducement was the belief that when drunk with milk it enhanced the pleasures of coitus. According to the Dutch there were other uses of the clove, "too many to recount."[2]

The earliest evidence of the presence of the clove outside Maluku comes from a recent archaeological find dated at about 1700 B.C. in the

1

Mesopotamian site of Terqa in present-day Syria. Among the plant remains in the pantry room in a common household were some cloves. Since it is accepted that at this time the clove tree was found only in Maluku, the presence of cloves in an ordinary middle class home in Syria suggests the existence at a very early period of a specialized long-distance trade in this perishable commodity.[3] By the third century B.C. the spice was sufficiently known in China that the Han emperor could order his courtiers to have cloves in their mouths to sweeten their breaths whenever they addressed him.[4]

K'ang T'ai, one of the two envoys sent in the third century A.D. by the Wu government of southern China to Funan in modern-day southern Cambodia, reported that the clove came from the islands to the east.[5] Although a number of pre-fourteenth century Chinese sources mention areas which can perhaps be identified with Maluku, only one dated about 1350 actually refers to the fact that Chinese junks sailed annually to Maluku.[6] There is, however, no corroborating evidence that the Chinese sailed their junks so far east. It is far more likely that the large Chinese junks went directly to Manila, where the goods were transferred to smaller vessels and taken by local traders to their final destinations in the region. Writing in the mid-sixteenth century Miguel Lopez de Legazpi mentioned that, because many of the local Muslim traders from Brunei and Luzon carried Chinese goods, they were referred to as Chinese and their boats as Chinese junks. He further observed that the true Chinese junks were far too large to sail safely between the islands. It appears very likely, therefore, that the shallow-draft native boats manned by local inhabitants were used for the redistribution of Chinese goods as far as Maluku.[7]

Though the clove was being traded from a very early period, a significant change occurred in the late fourteenth century. It was then that the northeastern Javanese coastal towns, with their ruling Chinese, Arab, and Javanese elite, became the major nodes of a vibrant inter-archipelago trade network which linked the spice islands to the rest of the world. The prosperous Malay entrepôt of Melaka (c. 1400–1511) became the major collection and distribution port of the clove and other Southeast Asian spices and contributed greatly to the prosperity of Maluku.[8] Europe, which was rapidly becoming accustomed to a steady supply of this indispensable condiment and medicine, did not benefit from the new development. It continued to rely on Muslim traders who carried the spices by land from Bassorah on the Persian Gulf to Damascus or Aleppo in the Mediterranean. When this land route was disrupted by the Turks in the second half of the fifteenth century, the trade shifted to the Red Sea but remained in Muslim hands. The major links in this route were dominated by the Muslim kingdom of Melaka, the Muslim Gujarati traders of Cambay in northwest India, and the Muslim Mamelukes of Egypt. Although the Red Sea route was on a more direct line from Calicut in west coast India to the Mediterranean, spices continued to be dear because the cost of transfers and portages was high. Christian Europe's desire to remove its dependence on its religious enemies and to acquire cheaper spices became a major motivation in its search for a sea route to Asia.

Portugal was the leading European nation in this endeavor because of a systematic program of discovery begun under Prince Henry the Navigator in the early fifteenth century. A major breakthrough came with Bartholomeu Dias' rounding the tip of Africa in 1488, which was followed a decade later by Vasco da Gama's successful voyage to the west coast of India. Though the Portuguese had not yet reached the home of the fabled clove, nutmeg, and mace in Maluku, the cargo loaded in India of spices "together with the boughs and leaves of the same" aroused considerable excitement in Portugal.[9] To destroy the existing Muslim-dominated spice trade, the Portuguese admiral and later viceroy of India, Afonso de Albuquerque, conceived a plan to control the vital centers of the international route. It very nearly succeeded, with the Portuguese forces seizing Goa in west coast India in 1510, Melaka in 1511, and Hormuz in 1515. Only Aden at the mouth of the Red Sea resisted in 1513 and remained outside Portuguese control.[10]

After the conquest of Melaka, Albuquerque dispatched three ships to search for the spice islands. The arrival of the Portuguese ships in Maluku in late 1511 signaled the beginning of a long and troubled relationship between Europeans and Malukans which continued well into the twentieth century. While economic motivations were undeniably a major element in the conflicts which arose, there were other equally compelling social and cultural factors that contributed to misunderstandings. This book is a history of this interaction focusing on the cultural environments which shaped and influenced each group's relationships with the other. At the same time it aspires to make the story of the Malukans comprehensible in their own terms during a period of intense foreign intrusion in their society.

The Historical Perspective

Ethnographers and ethnohistorians have been aware for a number of years of the practical and philosophical problems of describing and chronicling activities of another culture. The growing realization of the intellectual and hence political dominance imposed by Western scholars in depicting other cultures has provoked discussion and experimentation in representation. James Clifford expressed the challenge facing ethnographers, but his words are equally relevant to many other fields of study: "In ethnography the current turn to rhetoric coincides with a period of political and epistemological reevaluation in which the constructed, imposed nature of representational authority has become unusually visible and contestable."[11] Clifford signaled a development in the humanities and the social sciences which involved questioning omniscient, authoritarian standpoints in the guise of objective, scientific observations.

For historians the shift from Leopold von Ranke's positivism in the nineteenth century to Hayden White's recent demonstration of the presence of rhetoric in the historian's choice of narrative styles represents an important reassessment of the discipline.[12] The Rankean interpretation of historicity based on written documents whose reliability was rigorously examined to determine the "facts" was considered by some to be too rigid, preventing insights into motivations of historical actors. A leading proponent of this position was R. G. Collingwood, who advocated the application of the historical imagination to enter into the minds of historical figures. The reconstruction of this imagination was nevertheless to be based on a vast knowledge of the historical circumstances acquired through the Rankean methodology. There was a belief in the historical truth which could be uncovered through these methods, and the objectivity of the trained historian was assumed.[13]

But the certainty of this type of history has gone the way of all certainties in the postmodern world. Historians are now more willing to admit that selectivity of sources, the lacunae in documents, the rearranging and structuring of the material, and the narrative form all contribute to a subjective and rhetorical history. Paul Ricoeur goes even further and argues that history is a "literary artifact" because it creates an internal system of meaningful symbols, and that it is a "representation of reality" because the events which it depicts claim to be those of the real world.[14] While some may lament the passing of certitude in history, history writing has become more provocative. Differing approaches applied to the same material have brought complementary as well as contradictory views of the past. Such differences should not be regarded as mindless relativism, but rather a multifaceted and fuller account of situations and occurrences in former times.

While historians have debated ideas of historical representation within their own societies, those attempting to write a history where two distinct cultures are involved face even greater difficulties. These ethnohistorians must confront the problems involved in attempting to create a "narrative," hence a conceptual framework, which will do justice to the differences in language, cognitive system, and conceptions of time, events, and significance. A major influence on these ethnohistorians has been the "new ethnographers,"[15] but they themselves do not agree on the best strategy to adopt. Clifford advocates a "visible and contested" position of the ethnographer, which allows the reader to view the knowledge of the other culture as "contingent, the problematic outcome of intersubjective dialogue, translation, and projection."[16] Like Hayden White, Clifford believes in the necessity for the ethnographer to abandon the position of omniscient authority and to be recognized simply as a subjective observer creating one view of the society observed. The ethnographic problem, according to Henry Sharp, then becomes one of interpreting between two cultures with different realities.[17] Such a demanding approach is developed further by Gewertz and Schieffelin, who contend that the aim is "to allow these alternative cultural viewpoints to be juxtaposed in a way that enables each to constitute a critique of the other; and second to allow the establishment of a broad ethno-historical perspective that encompasses them both."[18] These are indeed admirable goals but extremely difficult to attain. There is furthermore the niggling question raised by Robert Borofsky when speaking of a native perspective: which native and how many?[19]

In reconstructing the "cultural realities" of both the Europeans and the Malukans in this period, my focus has been primarily on the elite groups because of the nature of the evidence. Yet there is much to recommend Marshall Sahlins' view of the influence of this group in society in a period where one can speak of "heroic history." For both the European court chroniclers and Dutch East India Company scribes, as with the Malukan oral traditions, the subject is the heroic individual around whom the events are structured. Even today villagers remember the past in the context of exploits of specific rulers.[20] Moreover, in Malukan society the activities of the rulers and the leaders of the community, the *bobatos,* had an enormous impact on the actions of the people. It was, as Sahlins has described for Fiji, "a history of kings and battles, but only because it is a cultural order that, multiplying the action of the king by the system of society, gives him a disproportionate historical effect."[21] For Europeans, too, the accounts were written by and for the articulate elite classes. This was the case not only for the court chroniclers, but also for those missionaries and travelers who wrote accounts of their experiences abroad. Even the reports of trading companies were intended for the information and approval of leaders with direct links to the nation's ruling circle.[22]

As in the case of "heroic history," the Pacific Islands have provided an instructive source of comparison with Maluku. Historical linguists have suggested that it was from eastern Indonesia that the Austronesians continued their migration out into the Pacific Islands about 1500 B.C.[23] Eastern Indonesia remained outside the main international trade routes centered in the western half of the Malay-Indonesian archipelago, and it was only from about the fourteenth century that it began to be frequented regularly and more intensively by foreign traders. By the time that the first detailed accounts of Maluku were recorded in the early sixteenth century, Maluku was only just beginning to adapt its institutions to Islamic and European models. It was thus possible to detect various aspects of "indigenous" Malukan culture. Until the eighteenth and nineteenth centuries, Pacific Island societies, too, were relatively unaffected by foreign influence, except for the brief sojourn of traders, shipwrecked sailors, and the occasional European expedition. Indigenous customs and rituals in the Pacific Islands are therefore stronger and far better documented than was the case anywhere in Indonesia. Because of the ancient Austronesian links between the Pacific Islanders and the eastern Indonesians, one would expect to find certain customs and practices in common. This seems indeed to have been the case in this study of Maluku. The Pacific Island example has proved useful in explicating certain otherwise obscure Maluku customs and attitudes. It is my belief that historians would gain new insights into the evolution of Southeast Asian society by widening their scope of inquiry to include historical and cultural developments in the Pacific.

In this study I have attempted to reconstruct two separate cultural realities of the past, with their differing assumptions and attitudes, and to convey the significance of their interaction to a modern Western and Western-educated society. While I have been influenced by the ideas of the new ethnographers,[24] the historical materials often do not provide sufficient information about Malukan society to conduct a true dialogue between the two separate cultures. I was therefore forced to rely on European accounts, while undertaking field trips and conducting interviews with present-day Malukans for explanations of their own past. There is, fortunately, enough material on European society in the sixteenth, seventeenth, and eighteenth centuries to make possible a more confident reconstruction of the European world. Events in Maluku tended to highlight certain types of concerns, and it was the aim of explaining these concerns that guided my selection of themes. The book is nevertheless about the Malukans, and their story can be told adequately only by understanding the Europeans who interacted with them and were responsible for leaving almost the only contemporary reports of the Malukan past.

The book is divided into two major parts. "The Two Worlds" is a reconstruction of the cultural realities of the Europeans and the Malukans; and "The Encounter" is an examination of the interaction between the two worlds based on these cultural realities, but with the primary focus on the Malukan conception of the past and its significance. In Part 1 there are three chapters highlighting features of European and Malukan societies that help to explain their motivations and activities. Mindful of Borofsky's concern, in Chapter 1 on the Europeans I have discussed the Greek and Christian heritage regarding views of the East and then focused on the Portuguese, the Spaniards, and the Dutch in the sixteenth, seventeenth, and eighteenth centuries. When possible I have included comments on regional differences which may have played a part in the perceptions of a national group. Chapters 2 and 3 discuss the "Malukan" reality and the organization of the groups into the center and the periphery. Although I use the term "Maluku," the discussion focuses on north Maluku and principally on Ternate. "Maluku" in this period referred only to the clove-producing islands of north Maluku, the most powerful of which was Ternate. The importance of Ternate as the major clove-exporting port and therefore the home of foreign traders and military posts assured it of a well-documented past. Tidore was equally prominent, but the small and relatively short European presence on the island meant that fewer documents were written about Tidore. Ternate and Tidore formed a dualism and occupied the symbolic center of Maluku. As these two kingdoms expanded, the name Maluku came to be applied to all areas which acknowledged Ternate's or Tidore's dominance.

There is a historiographical problem in Part 1. The world of the Malukans in the sixteenth, seventeenth, and eighteenth centuries is reconstructed entirely from contemporary European sources because of the absence of any indigenous materials from that period. I have had to work with Portuguese, Spanish, and Dutch translations of Malukan traditions recorded by explorers, missionaries, traders, and officials. Understanding something of the world of the Europeans made it possible to interpret their descriptions in reconstructing the world of Maluku. While these do not have the authority of sources written or told in the native languages, I have relied upon them for several reasons. First of all, in the absence of any contemporary indigenous material I believe that European translations and reports of Malukan traditions from that period, no matter how faulty, can be useful if rigorous historical methods are applied. Second, some of the European commentators were genuinely interested in the customs and history of the area and wished to provide as accurate an account as possible. They were of course constrained by established Christian European conventions of depicting alien lands and peoples, as well as by professional and national considerations. Nevertheless, once these constraints are recognized the descriptions of Malukan society are useful. Third, oral traditions were still strong in Maluku and many of the stories collected by the Europeans would have been those regarded of particular importance by the local population. Fourth, these European written accounts of Malukan oral traditions acquire significance when placed in the context of occurrences as recorded in European reports of this period, and in turn help to elucidate otherwise obscure comments in European sources. Having said this, I am still very much aware that what constitutes "tradition" in the three hundred year study of Maluku would have been constantly redefined. It is my contention, however, that certain elements in Malukan society remained of great concern and continued to serve as the basis for perceptions, motivations, and actions.

The second part of the book, "The Encounter," is the record of the interaction between European and Malukan worlds employing both the European and Malukan time frames. A chronological sequence of events or a linear arrangement of time was the way in which the Europeans in this period recorded and interpreted their involvement with the Malukans. Mundane daily occurrences were legitimate items for the written record. The Malukans, on the other hand, were concerned with the significant past and structured events by two coexisting and overlapping conceptions of time. The first was an underlying cultural imperative, which one scholar has termed "the myth of the eternal return," another "cosmic time," and others "cyclical time."[25] It was a Malukan belief that there was a basic unity in the world of Maluku whose prosperity and well-being were assured by the maintenance of the "four pillars" and the dualisms. In the course of its history these basic determinants of Malukan stability would be undermined, leading to decline and disorder to be followed by a new cycle with the restoration of the "four pillars" and the dualisms. Operating within this overarching time frame is another determined by significant individuals, which Nancy McDowell has called "episodic time."[26] It focuses only on individuals who are attributed with a noteworthy contribution to the society. These "cultural heroes" tend generally to be associated with spiritual prowess and are mainly the leaders of the community. Sahlins' discussion of the heroic kings in Fijian and other Pacific Island societies would apply most appropriately to the situation in Maluku in the period under study.[27] Only certain significant individuals are worthy to be recorded, and they are given the responsibility of representing whole generations. Sultan Babullah of Ternate and Sultans Saifuddin and Nuku of Tidore are examples of these special individuals around whom meaningful episodes collect and are retained for the benefit of the whole society.

The chapters in the second part of the book interpret the interaction of Europeans and Malukans, employing their respective methods of organizing time and events, as well as conceptualizing their significance. There was never, however, a strict division between a European idea of linear time and a Malukan cyclical and episodic one. Rather, the Europeans in the beginning of the sixteenth century shared a belief in cycles in the recurrence of events in agricultural and religious rites, though their major concept of time was linear in orientation.[28] Similarly, while the Malukans conceived of their past as framed by an overarching idea of an eternal return within which events were organized around significant individuals, they became aware of the linear development of time because of Islam with its stress on genealogy as a basis for determining the legitimacy of religious teachers and sultans.

In describing the interaction between the Europeans and the Malukans, it is important to be aware of the differing bases upon which each side approached a particular problem. The headings and the analyses in each of these chapters reflect the juxtaposition of the two cultural perceptions of events. The linear time frame, "beginning" with the arrival of the European in the early sixteenth century and "ending" with the triumph of Nuku, is encompassed in a wider cyclical understanding of the past moving from a time of unity and harmony evident by the presence of the "four pillars" to one of disunity marked by their absence. The concluding chapter highlights important features of Malukan history and suggests some of their wider implications for the study of Southeast Asian history.

The Sources

Sources for the study of Maluku before the nineteenth century are almost exclusively European. They differ so markedly between nations and centuries, however, that it is essential to know something of these sources in order to evaluate their contents. The contrasting styles and concerns between, on the one hand, the Iberian court chroniclers and church missives of the sixteenth and early seventeenth centuries and, on the other, the Dutch trading company reports of the seventeenth and eighteenth centuries at times obscure the activities and aspirations of the Malukans. Only by recognizing how the particular European source constructs and constricts the Malukan past is it possible to begin the process of reconstructing an indigenous history of the area.

Portuguese reports on Asia written by officials, as well as accounts by those who had been to the East, were jealously guarded by the Portuguese Crown. King Manuel I (r. 1495–1521) decreed on 13 November 1504 that, on pain of death, complete secrecy had to be observed regarding the new discoveries. This ban appears to have been successful, for not a single book on the new information being collected on Asia by the Portuguese is known to have been published during the first fifty years of the sixteenth century. Even as late as 1565 all materials on Maluku held by private Portuguese individuals were required to be surrendered to the state.[29] The entire *Suma Oriental,* one of the earliest detailed descriptions of trade in the East written in Melaka and India between 1512 and 1515 by Tomé Pires, remained unpublished until 1944.[30] Parts of this work and that of Duarte Barbosa dating from 1517 were published only in 1550, but by the Venetian compiler Giovanni Battista Ramusio. Despite these restrictions the Crown could not prevent other non-Portuguese sources of information about Asia from reaching Europe. Magellan, one of the first Portuguese to reach Maluku in 1512 when still in the service of the Portuguese Crown, gained the patronage of the Spanish ruler to return to the East. He sailed westward from Spain believing in the view made popular by the fourteenth century *Imago Mundi* of Cardinal Pierre d'Ailly that the East could be reached sooner by traveling west from Europe. Though Magellan himself was killed in the Philippines, his crew successfully returned to Spain and became the first to circumnavigate the globe. Antonio Pigafetta, an Italian doctor on the expedition, kept a diary of the voyage which contained valuable information about routes and places and people that they had visited, including Maluku. The crew were also questioned by Maximilian Transylvania, who then reconstructed the journey in a book published in Valladolid in 1522.[31] King Manuel's periodic gloating announcements of Portuguese expansion and letters from foreigners in Portuguese service, especially the valuable report by the Dutchman Jan Huyghen van Linschoten, enabled Europe to piece together an alluring picture of the riches of Asia.[32] Most of the documents on the East remained inaccessible, however, enabling Portugal to retain its early advantage which had been won at such enormous costs.[33]

This glorious achievement of the Portuguese could not go unheralded, and two authors began almost simultaneously to record the story of Portuguese expansion. One was Fernão Lopes de Castanheda, whose opening volume, *História do descobrimento e conquista da India pelos portugueses,* was the first to appear in print in 1551. But he was forced to recall this volume and to revise it because it contained slanderous accusations of pecuniary misconduct in Asia of certain members of the leading families in Portugal. He also suffered from the rivalry of the official court chronicler, João de Barros, who may have played a part in the recall of this first volume. Although Castanheda lacked the court contacts and access to official documents which were available to Barros, he emphasized the importance of his firsthand observations knowing that Barros had never been to the East. He wrote: "He who writes histories must make the efforts I made and see the land that he is to write about, as I saw it, for so was it done by ancient and modern historians. . . . Very supernatural must be the talented man who will know how to write about things he never saw."[34]

Castanheda wrote his work in the early sixteenth century when the Portuguese were enjoying considerable success in establishing coastal strongholds stretching from Maluku to the east coast of Africa. He was especially proud of the Portuguese military achievements in Asia and his history is laudatory of Portuguese deeds in the East. He based his writings on his own experiences in Asia, from information he obtained by questioning captains and other officers of noble or gentry background (the *fidalgos*) who had served in the battles in the East, and from letters and memorials. Sometime during his ten years in India, he may have gone as far as Maluku. He returned to Portugal in 1538 and continued to collect material from those who had been to Asia. He worked on his history fully aware that Barros was himself undertaking a similar task with all the advantages of being designated the official court chronicler. Castanheda's lack of any official attachment to the government enabled him to express concern at some of the activities of Portuguese leaders in Asia and, moreover, provided him with a point of view somewhat different from Barros'. Unlike Barros he did not shy away from describing the bad along with the good deeds of the Portuguese because he was imbued with a confidence in the entire Portuguese endeavor in Asia.[35]

Castanheda's principal rival in writing the history of Portuguese expansion in the sixteenth century was João de Barros. Barros is described as an official historian *par excellence* who wrote under royal patronage "but voluntarily and out of conviction . . . not merely to record but to celebrate and justify."[36] The reigns of Manuel I and João III (r. 1521–1557) were a golden age in Portugal. Great national pride was fostered by the discoveries and the establishment of Portuguese posts in Asia, as well as by the literary achievements of the humanists. This background encouraged Barros to conceive of the official history of the Portuguese expansion in an epic framework. By 1520 he had a plan for the writing of this chronicle, but first he began to collect the material to add flesh to his projected epic. As treasurer and then factor in the India Office in Lisbon between 1523 and 1567, he had access to secret documents, including descriptions of Magellan's expeditions, the Latin version of Varthema's travels, and Galvão's *Treatise on Maluku*. In addition to official documents, he consulted the various missionary letters from Asia and obtained Persian, Arabic, Indian, and Chinese sources and had them translated for his use.[37] His acquaintance with certain principal figures involved in Portugal's expansion provided close personal detail to specific events. Armed with this vast array of materials, he employed an epic style influenced strongly by the Classical and Renaissance authors. He wrote in Portuguese as a spokesman of his country and of his age and hoped that his epic would compare favorably with the great writers of the Classical period.[38] However, during his lifetime he was noticed only because of the Italian translations of his first two *Decadas* by Ramusio in the 1554 edition of volume 1 of the popular *Delle Navigationi e Viaggi*. Barros managed to complete only three of his *Decadas,* his story ending in 1526. His fourth *Decada* was edited by Lavanha from notes and published posthumously. By the time of Barros' death, he had achieved a modest international reputation in the learned circles of Europe. His work was valued, and most European scholars who published on Asia in the remainder of the sixteenth and the seventeenth centuries consulted it with or without acknowledgment.[39]

Diogo do Couto was commanded by the king to continue the story of the Portuguese expansion where Barros had ended. Couto was not of fidalgo background but was educated at court as the page of the brother of King João III. He spent most of his life in India, first as a soldier (1559–1569), then as Master of the Arsenal (1571–1594), and finally as Keeper of the Records of Goa and official chronicler of the Portuguese in Asia (1594/1604–1616). He continued the history of the Portuguese overseas enterprise in nine *Decadas,* officially known as the fourth to the twelfth *Decadas,* which brought the story from 1526 up to 1599. Only parts of the eighth, ninth, eleventh, and twelfth *Decadas* have survived, and they are either incomplete or summaries rewritten by Couto himself in his old age.[40] Among the sources which Couto consulted were those of Castanheda, Barros, and Damião de Goes, the official chronicler of Portugal. He also had access to Gabriel Rebelo's work on Maluku and the official archives of Goa and the bishopric of Goa.[41] A distinct advantage he had over Barros was the time spent in Asia where he had been able to obtain eyewitness accounts of many of the events he was narrating. His descriptions of battles, cruises, and councils are detailed, even listing the names of most of those participating. He provided a lively portrayal of individuals, accusing many of the clerics of greed and meddling in state affairs. Couto is considered by modern scholars to have been remarkably blunt about Portuguese misdeeds, but he was not averse to flattering a friend or patron. In broad terms Couto accepted Barros' grand conception of the Portuguese role in the East. His style may have been less elegant than Barros', but his frankness added a dimension missing in Barros' careful and circumspect narrative.

The thirteenth and last *Decada* was written by Antonio Bocarro, appointed Chronicler and Keeper of the Records at Goa in 1631. Since he expected Couto's last volume to take the story to 1612, he began his work on events in 1612 and covered a five year period in his volume. There is, therefore, a conspicuous gap in the history of Portuguese expansion in the East in the years between 1600 and 1612. Bocarro, like his predecessors, had access to official documents, but he exhibited a greater caution in his writings due to his brush with the Inquisition. He indicated the difficulty he faced in relying on information "which in India is always directed by self-interest, hatreds, or affection." He succeeded nevertheless in compiling a detailed and extensive account of Portuguese activities in Asia along the general pattern of Barros and Couto.[42]

For a history of Maluku, Castanheda, Barros, and Couto are especially valuable because they provide the earliest systematic European accounts of the spice-producing islands in eastern Indonesia. Yet even a brief description of the background of these chroniclers and how they came to write their histories makes apparent the strictures within which they wrote and the structures which they imposed on their works, such as their desire to please patrons and friends, generally to avoid antagonizing powerful individuals, and to glorify the Portuguese enterprise in Asia. But there are other aspects of chronicle writing which imposed certain values onto the material itself. The specific task of the chronicle writing of Castanheda, Barros, Couto, and Bocarro was somewhat different from that of the official chroniclers of Portugal itself. They were commissioned (except for Castanheda, who was nevertheless inspired by a similar motivation) to record the glorious achievements of the Portuguese in Asia. Because they were dealing with areas and cultures which were unfamiliar to their Portuguese readers, these chroniclers provided a fuller description and identification of places, peoples, and flora and fauna than is normally included in a chronicle. A new form of historical writing, termed by one historian "the chronicle-narrative," thus evolved. There are frequent flashbacks and cross references to other areas of the world, encouraging comparisons with heroic achievements of the Classical Age. Portuguese heroes are compared to those of Homer or Virgil, and Asian cities are analyzed in terms of their likeness to European centers. Portuguese military prowess and technology are favorably compared with Asian weakness and primitiveness. In this chronicle-narrative there was also a tendency to compare one region of Asia with another, placing each explicitly or implicitly in a hierarchical scale of civilization. In such a scale, Southeast Asia tended to be placed below East Asian and Indian civilizations whose governments and material culture impressed the European.

Barros' *Decadas,* organized along the model of Livy, has an epic quality in which heroic events predominate. He contrives speeches for his heroes befitting their bravery and position. Throughout his narrative, he inserts ethnographic and geographic information about the new lands "discovered" by the Portuguese, but he never strays far from his primary concern of depicting Portuguese grandeur in the conquest of the East and of providing posterity with moral lessons from the past. Barros, along with the other chronicle-narrative writers, was to an extent confined by the annal form, which tempts the writer to maintain equal balance in the different sections, irrespective of the importance of the material. The need to moralize was another constraint which saw a disproportionate number of pages devoted to a minor event but with an important moral. There was the inclination, especially in Barros, to focus primarily on the noble or lofty, whether persons, words, or deeds.

Though Castanheda, Couto, and Bocarro were less ambitious in both language and style than Barros and tended to be less pretentious and personal, they too wrote very much in the chronicle-narrative style.[43]

In addition to the purely personal and stylistic aspects which affected these chroniclers' perceptions of Asia, there was a particular Portuguese set of cultural values which determined what was to be included and how it was to be described. One of these was the Portuguese expansion in the late fifteenth and early sixteenth centuries, which marked the apex of Portuguese nationhood. It created the fields of glory for the Portuguese warrior nobles, the *fidalguia,* and displayed the technological superiority of its culture and moral rectitude of its position to the rest of the world. The overseas expansion was a herculean achievement worthy of praise in the heroic epic mode. Luis Camoes' *Os Lusiadas,* "the Sons of Lusus" (Lusus being the mythical first settler of Portugal), was a paean to the Portuguese nation. It was written in the style of the *Aeneid* and contained a synthesis of all the elements of myth and reality in the Portuguese overseas enterprise:

> Over the Eastern Oceans cast your eyes,
> And see where islands numberless are spread:
> Tidore, Ternate view, mountains whence arise
> Flames undulating round the burning head:
> Trees of hot clove thou shall behold, likewise,
> With blood of Portugal e'en purchasèd;
> Here are the golden birds, who ne'er descend
> On earth, while living, but when life doth end.[44]

All chroniclers of the Portuguese achievement overseas were conditioned by this national passion. There was no question that the whole enterprise was worthy and Portuguese grand intentions pure and made even purer when contrasted with the evils which they overcame. Those like Castanheda who attempted to focus on the less savory activities of the Portuguese were compelled to reconsider their perception. Though the chroniclers included tales of corrupt and cruel Portuguese administrators, it is significant that many were set in Maluku. Both Barros and Castanheda stress that "evil and strife are endemic to Maluku, for the clove, though a creation of God, is actually an apple of discord and responsible for more afflictions than gold."[45] In keeping with the high moral tone of the chronicle-narratives, the evils of the Portuguese in Maluku were related to Maluku's position at the periphery of Portugal's world.

Because the subject was Portuguese achievements in the East, it was heroic exploits which were heralded within an epic mold. The principal Portuguese protagonists were supplied with speech befitting their elevated status, their deeds equaled those of mythic figures in the Classical past, and their vanquished foes were worthy opponents but inferior in valor and skill. The superiority of the Portuguese over the brown, the black, and the other white (East Asian) peoples supported the belief which equated skills, intelligence, and abilities along a color scale with black at the bottom and white at the top. The Portuguese victories over the other races were regarded as a consequence of their natural superiority. The chroniclers were part of a nationwide celebration of a glorious Portuguese epoch, and they were expected to recapture the mood of this period for the present and future "sons of Lusus." In the beginning of the seventeenth century, this self-confident image of Portuguese enterprise had been undermined by the forced union with Spain in 1580. But the glory of the early sixteenth century continued to motivate chronicle writers.

Two striking exceptions to the chroniclers' version of the history of Maluku are António Galvão's *História das Molucas* (A Treatise on Maluku) and Gabriel Rebelo's *Informação sobre as Malucas* (Information on Maluku). Galvão served as Governor and Captain of the Portuguese settlement and fortress in Ternate between 1536 and 1539. During this period he compiled information about the people and the land which became the basis of the original *Treatise* written between 1543 and 1545. It was never printed and was eventually deposited in the archives in Seville, where it was rediscovered and finally published in an English translation in 1970. The *Treatise* in some form appears to have been consulted by both Barros and Castanheda.[46] Rebelo arrived in Maluku soon after Galvão's departure and remained in the islands for thirteen years. In 1543 he is mentioned as a judicial clerk and judge for the Portuguese fortress. He was posted to India in 1554, returned to Maluku in 1566 as a factor, and remained until the murder of Sultan Hairun of Ternate in 1570. The first version or "Text 1" of the *Informação* was completed in 1561, the second or "Text 2" in 1569. Couto relied on this work and called it *Informação das couzas de Maluco, e dos costumes dos moradores delle* (Information on the Affairs of Maluku and the Customs of the Inhabitants Thereof).[47]

Both Galvão and Rebelo provided the substance for much of what was eventually written about Maluku by the principal chroniclers of the Portuguese in the East. But unlike the chroniclers who framed the events to suit their principal aim of glorifying the deeds of their countrymen, these two officials were less impressed with the glorious national endeavor and more critically aware of the impact of their countrymen on local society. Their long association and pragmatic relationship with the Malukans had fostered an appreciation of the differences of the two societies. Very much products of the contemporary European trend to learn about the newly discovered lands, they collected data on the fauna, flora, and local inhabitants and attempted to reconstruct the history of the Malukans and the Portuguese in Maluku based on the information which they gathered from both oral and written sources.

Both these works reflect sixteenth century European belief that both the real and the fabulous coexisted and that Christian Europe was the center and therefore morally superior to other parts of the inhabited world. They present their material within a dominant intellectual tradition which made it respectable to the intended readership. Carefully sited at crucial junctures in a description of Maluku are statements which would assure the Renaissance reader of its veracity. After presenting information about Malukan society which would find acceptance in any modern ethnology, Galvão then adds: "They are intriguers, treacherous, malicious, untruthful, and ungrateful: they have all the evils. . . . This is what Holy Scripture confirms for us, saying that the land along the sea will be fruitful and its people very malicious. . . . All who wrote on the inhabitants of islands take them to be among the worst of men; and they also affirm that where the trees do not become securely fastened and well-rooted in the ground, people will be unstable, not constant, neither good nor firm."[48] Within this conventional European manner of structuring information about the East, it is possible for a historian or anthropologist with some knowledge of Maluku to appreciate many of Galvão's and Rebelo's comments in light of what is presently known about that society.

Apart from the court chronicles and the valuable personal accounts by Galvão and Rebelo, additional information on the sixteenth and early seventeenth century history of Maluku can be found in missionary reports. The early years of Portuguese presence in Asia were dominated by the Observants, or Friars Minor, following the vows of poverty of St. Francis. These friars sent many informative dispatches to Europe, but much of the material on Asia remained relatively unknown to those outside these Mendicant orders until the twentieth century. With the establishment of the Society of Jesus in 1540, the Jesuits became involved in the missionary enterprise in Asia. King João III of Portugal founded the Jesuit College in Coimbra in 1542 to train missionaries for the field, and over a period of two centuries it sent out some 1,650 Jesuit missionaries to various parts of the world. Coimbra became the clearing-house for all Jesuit mission correspondence. Letters from the field were selected, edited, translated, published, and distributed throughout Europe. The Constitutions of the Society approved in 1558 reveal the method of selection and the aim of this highly elaborate process of information processing: "And about this letter-writing the superiors, and in particular the General and the Provincials, will take a special care. They will order things in such a way as to obtain that in every place they should know about the things that are being done in other places, which knowledge is a source of mutual consolation and edification in our Lord."[49]

The annual letters, which were compiled from mission reports and sent from Goa back to Europe, were composed with a dual aim of serving as edification to the brethren as well as a source of information on Asia. As a result the vast numbers of converts reported in the sixteenth and seventeenth centuries were intended primarily to edify rather than to provide an accurate statistical picture. Moreover, only those adults who were baptized were counted and not those who had died or had apostatized. These numbers were therefore often rounded off to figures in the tens of thousands and even the hundreds of thousands. Rivalry between differing religious orders also encouraged the inflating of numbers.[50] To satisfy the curiosity of fellow Jesuits and friends in Europe, these letters contained mundane information on geography, climate, peoples, customs, and religions. Loyola himself informed Goa in 1554 that "some leading figures. . . . [in Rome] want to know, for instance, how long are the days of summer and of winter; when summer begins; whether the shadows move towards the left or towards the right. Finally, if there are other things that may seem extraordinary, let them be noted, for instance, details about animals and plants that either are not known at all, or not of such a size, etc."[51] The desire for information on the East was strong in the middle of the sixteenth century, and the Jesuit letters fulfilled part of this need.

There are five types of Jesuit mission letters: separate sheets (*hijuelas*) which contain detailed information intended for the Superiors; letters to the Society in general; accounts for public distribution; letters to personal friends; and other relevant documents on the whole Jesuit enterprise. Depending on the type of letter, the tone and the contents could vary with the recipient in mind. In Asia itself the early missionaries sent their own reports from different stations onward to Europe, often leading to confusion because of contradictory information. Finally in 1581 it was decreed that only one "true" annual letter would be sent to Europe from India incorporating the various reports from the mission stations. These "true" annual letters became the official statement of the progress of the mission in Asia and were published first in Latin and then in the European vernaculars for distribution. Thus was the European perception of Asia in general, and Maluku in particular, as a mission field molded by the efficient Jesuit system of dissemination of letters. None of the other orders had a system of regular reporting and publishing of letters which was comparable to that of the Jesuits.[52]

The importance of Maluku to the entire Jesuit missionary effort in Asia in the sixteenth century is attested by the fact that in 1557 nine of the forty-five Jesuits in the Province of India, which encompassed an area stretching from Mozambique to Kyushu in southern Japan, were assigned to Maluku. Instrumental in convincing the Society of the great prospects of conversions in Maluku was Father Francis Xavier, who spent the period between July 1546 and June 1547 working among the people of northern Halmahera and the Portuguese and local inhabitants on the island of Ternate. His success, measured by the thousands of converts on Halmahera and the conversion of the royal women in the Ternate court, inspired the Jesuits to invest their limited resources in order to complete the task Xavier had begun, including the expected conversion of Sultan Hairun of Ternate. As a result of this attention to Maluku, the Jesuit letters from this area for the period 1545–1571 are numerous, if of uneven quality.

The most important of these Jesuit documents for Maluku have been published in an annotated collection of Jesuit letters in Hubert Jacobs SJ (ed.), *Documenta Malucensia*. There appear to have been no extant missionary letters from Maluku during the period of upheaval in Ternate from 1571 to 1578, and except for reprints of earlier reports, the Jesuits published nothing else about these islands for the remainder of the sixteenth century.[53] Selected documents from the Jesuit and other orders have been compiled and published in three important series. The first is António da Silva Rego's *Documentação para a história das missões do padroado português do Oriente. India;* the second is Artur Basílio de Sá, *Documentação para a história das missões do padroado português do Oriente. Insulíndia;* and the third is Josef Wicki (ed.), *Documenta Indica.* In these collections, especially that by Sá, the letters frequently encompass matters of wider interest than simply Church affairs.

Spanish documents form another source of information on Maluku. While they reflect similar attitudes and values expressed in the Portuguese material, they are less extensive because of an accident of history. When Christopher Columbus set out to reach the lands in the East on behalf of his Spanish sovereigns, he encountered instead a new world which came to monopolize the attention and the resources of the Spanish realm. Only after the needs and the problems of the Spanish colonies in the Americas were met and resolved was attention paid to the sole Spanish colony in Asia, the Philippines. Even then the Philippines were governed from the viceroyalty of Nueva España in Mexico. Matters dealing with Maluku were handled from Manila, making Maluku the colony of a colony of a colony. There are relatively few Spanish sources about Maluku in comparison to those in Portuguese and Dutch. Nevertheless, those that are available provide a sufficient basis for understanding Spanish perceptions and actions in the sixteenth and seventeenth centuries.

The first Spanish accounts of Maluku are mostly concerned with the early dispute with the Portuguese over jurisdiction of these islands.[54] There are, however, some important contemporary records of early

Spanish exploits in Maluku. In addition to the previously mentioned works by Antonio Pigafetta and Maximilian Transylvania,[55] another useful early sixteenth century report is by Andrés Urdaneta, who was in Maluku from 1528 to 1535. It was his unpublished account which formed the basis for Gonzalo Fernandez de Oviedo's section on Maluku contained in his *História general y natural de las Indias* published in 1548. Oviedo was named "Chronicler of the Indies" by the king of Spain in 1532, and his work is written in the epic style in the manner of his Portuguese contemporaries, Castanheda and Barros.[56] The second great Spanish chronicler of the Spanish realm and the Indies and a contemporary of Oviedo is Francisco López de Gómara. It was most likely Hernán Cortés who urged him to write his *História general de las Indias o "Hispania vitrix, "* which he began in 1540. He was given much of the information about the Americas from Cortés himself and from his own talks to explorers, conquistadors and others. His work also touches on Spanish exploits in Asia, but they are clearly secondary to the story of the Americas.[57]

The most extensive Spanish account of Maluku is Bartolomé Leonardo de Argensola's *Conquista de las islas Malucas*. When news reached Spain of the victory of the Spanish forces in Maluku in 1606 under the governor of the Philippines, Don Pedro de Acuña, Argensola was asked by the president of the Council of the Indies, the Count of Lemos, to write a celebration of this glorious victory. Argensola consented to undertake the task, and the Count then sent him all the papers and relevant accounts found in the archives of the council. In this regard the work is valuable not only for a detailed description of this important expedition, but also because it brings together information from the Spanish archives of the Indies which was not available elsewhere.

In addition to the official histories and the few eyewitness accounts, the only other Spanish sources on Maluku are the records of the various Church orders. The most valuable were the collections mentioned above, but there were individual works of value for the study of Maluku in this early period. Lorenzo Pérez, OFM, compiled a history of the Franciscans in Maluku and Celebes, entitled *Historia de las misiones de los Franciscanos en las islas Malucas y Célebes*. This work is useful because it is one of the few sources which covers the period in Malukan history from the ousting of the Portuguese from Ternate in 1575 until the return of the Spaniards to that important kingdom in 1606. There are a few other mission histories from the different orders which also include the work of Spanish missionaries in Maluku. One of the most comprehensive studies of the work of the Jesuits in Asia is Francisco Colín SJ and Pablo Pastells SJ, *Labor Evangélica: Ministerios apostólicos de los obreros de la Compañía de Jesús*. These volumes not only discuss the work of the Jesuits but also contain valuable accounts of the history and societies in the Philippines and Maluku.

Finally, there are various letters and reports of officials, commanders, and Church functionaries which are housed in the Arquivo General de Indias in Seville. Most of the material on Maluku are contained in papers collected under those of the Philippines and have been incorporated in the useful and comprehensive D. Pedro Torres y Lanza and Pablo Pastells SJ (eds.), *Catálogo de los documentos relativos a las Islas Filipinas existentes en el arquivo de Indias de Sevilla. Precedido de una história general de Filipinas.*

Contemporary sources for Maluku in the seventeenth and eighteenth centuries are mainly from the official records of the Dutch East India Company (VOC) housed in the General State Archives in The Hague. One notable exception is *Oud en Nieuw Oost Indiën* (Old and New East Indies), by François Valentijn, a Calvinist clergyman who served two terms under the VOC, mainly in Ambon in 1686–1694 and 1705–1713. In the original five volume work published in eight folio parts, the first three volumes are devoted almost exclusively to eastern Indonesia. Although he had never been to north Maluku, he relied on travel descriptions, VOC documents, and personal contacts to write his extensive account. One of his important sources of information was Governor Robertus Padtbrugge, who had been reassigned to Ambon from Ternate shortly before Valentijn's arrival on the island.[58] Valentijn was a product of the times, quick to make moral judgments based on traditional European views of Muslims and peoples inhabiting the periphery of the European world. Nevertheless, his detailed accounts of the traditions and history of foreign lands were part of a trend in the seventeenth century to document exotic societies. Unlike others, he considered himself to be among an elite group who spoke the language and lived among the people being described. By depicting these societies in the East in terms of earlier European civilizations, there was already a built-in assumption that the former were at a lesser stage of development than the contemporary European states. Within this structure which prefigured the superiority of the European center, Valentijn described the history and the customs of many of the groups in the Indonesian archipelago, including Maluku, as told to him by his informants and from his own analysis of written and oral documents.

Except for Valentijn's work, materials for the study of Maluku in this period originate almost entirely from the VOC archives. They have been described and analyzed in previous studies of the Malay-Indonesian archipelago,[59] but a few other comments should help to place the reports in perspective. Dutch perception of Maluku in this period was not shaped by a few dominant court chroniclers as in Portugal and Spain. Those who participated in the expansion regarded Dutch accomplishments with great pride, but the Establishment at home harbored the view that the Dutch Company overseas represented the antithesis of the ideals (if not the practice) of the Dutch nation. From the outset the profit motive informed the Company's every activity. Reports from local posts to Batavia, the nerve center of the Dutch Asian trading empire, contained accounts of trade items available for sale and purchase, prices of trade items, the state of the Company's post, as well as local custom, history, and politics. Personal interviews were conducted with specific individuals, both Asian and European, to obtain information. Company officials also continued a policy practiced at home of interviewing captains of vessels to gather information about the places they had been.

It is true that much of the reporting by VOC officials appeared matter-of-fact and was indeed believed by the writers to contain an accurate assessment of a local situation. Yet one could find oneself in the position of the Benedictine monks who accepted the description of a runaway horse from a Franciscan observer who had never laid eyes on the creature. Their endorsement of the description was based on the fact that the Franciscan recited the Benedictine's view of an ideal horse, rendering irrelevant the actual physiognomy of the horse in question.[60] Company reports in Asia often focused on miscreant behavior, partially because the Company did attract some of the dregs of European society and partially because of the tendency of the Dutch in the East to believe in the denigrating image of themselves held by their compatriots at home. It is no surprise, therefore, that the deeds of Company officials were often described as being dastardly, their motivations mean, and their punishments severe. Their perceptions of Malukans were also tempered by the old Christian European tradition that, the farther away one was situated from the "center," the less "civilized" and the more depraved and deprived one was. It was a case of shifting perceptual centers with Amsterdam at the very heart, Batavia at its periphery; Batavia at the center, Ternate at its periphery; and Ternate at the center and the various outposts in Maluku at its periphery. The deprivations suffered and the depravities committed by Company servants would have reinforced the view of their compatriots in Holland that these occurrences were in keeping with God's plans for those occupying the fringes of the civilized world centered in Europe.

To suggest what may have been the overriding concerns of the Malukans in the past is a risky business at best. Having to rely on European accounts, even those purported to be translations of Malukan letters and statements or renditions of Malukan traditions, makes it a doubly difficult task. A historian lacking access to extant contemporary indigenous documents but interested in reconstructing a local society's view of the past may either abandon the attempt altogether or else make the effort with an acute awareness of the problems involved. Because this reconstruction of the history of Maluku will be based primarily on contemporary European documents, it is important to examine the varying styles of the European recorders, ranging from the court chroniclers' epic-narratives to the lowly trading company clerks' humble official jottings. Such an analysis is useful because it allows one to delve beneath the stylistic and cultural overlays of European accounts to extract meaningful observations and comments about Malukan society. But it also assists the historian in interpreting the motives and the acts of the European in Maluku and other non-European worlds in these early centuries.

Ultimately, of course, everyone including a historian from that society is an outsider and will never have direct access to the thinking of the Malukans in an earlier age. All that he or she can do is offer a particular perspective in the study of the past. I shall argue that there is a specific Malukan way of organizing and interpreting their history. When events in the period under study are placed within this indigenous conceptual framework, the activities of both outsiders and locals acquire a specific significance which provides a distinctive interpretation of Maluku's past.

PART ONE

The Two Worlds

THIS SECTION INVESTIGATES the intellectual milieu from which the Europeans and Malukans arose and suggests which ideas may have come to affect their perception of the world and those outside it. For the Europeans the foundation of their views can be traced to the ancient Greek idea of the dichotomy between the *oikumene* (the world inhabited by the Greeks and those like them) and the sphere of the "barbarian." In Christian Europe this old division resurfaced in the debates regarding Creation and the peopling of the world. Those in God's image inhabited the "center," which meant Christian Europe; those who were less than human, the "monsters" (created by God to enable people to ponder the wonders of his work), occupied the regions at the "periphery," including the East. In addition to these general influences there were specific preoccupations of the Portuguese, the Spaniards, and the Dutch, stemming from their particular geographic and historic circumstances, which came to structure their perceptions of and interactions with Malukan society.

The foundation of Malukan ideas about the world can be found in the myths, tales, and fragments of the past still retained in the collective memory. These traditions indicate an indigenous belief in a mythic unity known as Maluku, which linked all the numerous islands with their many ethnolinguistic communities within it as one family. In keeping with this image, the relationship between the "center" and the "periphery" was characterized by all the mutual responsibilities, obligations, squabbles, and shifts of authority found in a human family. Even kinship terms were used in formal communication to identify the center (father or mother), periphery (children), and the relative statuses within the periphery (older to younger sibling). The world of Maluku, delineated and legitimized through myths, was a unique entity which served as a cultural map in the relationship of the individual communities within it and with those outside, including the Europeans.

CHAPTER ONE

The World of the European

WHEN THE PORTUGUESE first arrived in India in 1498 under Vasco da Gama, they came with well-established views of what they would find. Even when personal experience proved many of these views to be ill-founded, the Portuguese continued to harbor certain well-entrenched ideas and incorporated the new experiences into the dominant framework of structuring the Asian world. In this regard the Portuguese were no different from their European neighbors. Many of these views, despite the enormous advances made in the knowledge of the East, continued to survive up into the eighteenth century.

European Perceptions of the East

Early modern Western European perceptions of other peoples and cultures evolved over a long period beginning in ancient Greece. Like many other cultures, the Greeks had various ideas regarding the evolution of people and civilizations. One of these was the belief that cultural development evolved in stages from a primitive time in the remote past to the civilized present where people lived in cities. At the other extreme was the idea that the world operated in cycles and that the present was a degeneration from a former golden age. But it was the former view which triumphed in Europe, reflecting the self-confidence of a civilization that regarded itself superior to those with which it came into contact. It is not surprising that the idea of stages in the development of humankind found greatest favor in the fifteenth and sixteenth centuries which the Europeans ethnocentrically termed "The Age of Discovery."[1] This European conception of time and "progress" was in stark contrast to the Malukan idea of cyclical and episodic time. These two distinct modes of interpreting the past, present, and future constituted a fundamental issue in the relationships between the groups in this early modern period.

In the writings of the ancient Greeks there are statements about the effects of the environment on the character of the inhabitants. The most influential of the many ideas regarding this view is the doctrine of the four elements or four "roots" originally described in the fifth century B.C. With some revisions, including the addition of ether by Aristotle, the elements of earth, air, water, and fire became the basis of Greek science and medieval interpretations of nature. These elements had their counterparts in the human body in the "humors," and good health depended upon the maintenance of proper proportions of the humors. It was believed that the environment could affect the humors, and temperature was most often cited as the cause of the imbalance. Climate was therefore regarded as one of the prime reasons for instability in individuals and even in whole societies, with extremes in temperature disturbing the mind and soul. There were those who even saw a direct causal relationship between savagery in nature and savagery in humans. This view of the effect of the elements and humors on humans prevailed in certain fields of scientific thinking well into the eighteenth century.[2] European climatic descriptions of Maluku with its excessive heat, its monsoon rains, and its treacherous currents affected by seasonal winds were routinely listed alongside the volatility and untrustworthiness of the local people as further confirmation of the wisdom of the Greek sages.

A second influential theory on the relationship between peoples and the environment has been termed "astrological ethnology." Claudius Ptolemy's second century work, *Tetrabiblos,* is a good example of this position. His views arose from the general belief among the Greeks that the globe was divided into two uninhabited polar zones; two temperate zones, the northern and southern, with the northern one the location of the *oikumene;* and an equatorial zone believed to be incapable of sustaining life because of the heat.[3] Ptolemy divides the inhabited world into four quarters which are correlated with the four triangles in the zodiac. He proceeds to demonstrate how each quarter is subject to certain astrological influences thus affecting whole regions and peoples. In this way he explains the characteristics of certain peoples who inhabit specific parts of the then inhabited world.[4]

While these theories current in Greek and Roman times sought to explain the differences of various cultures and peoples in the known world, they also provided a general framework for understanding the unknown world. Since Homeric times there existed tales of fabulous races, animals, and plants living in lands and climes far beyond the borders of the Greek "civilized" world. The Greeks conceptualized their wonder and fear of the unknown through their belief in monstrous races, satyrs, centaurs, sirens and harpies. The various environmental and astrological theories domesticated these distant and unknown areas and made them less threatening to the ancient peoples. Although tales of unusual creatures and plants continued to be included in reports from the civilized center, they were always discussed within a reassuring and controlled intellectual framework.

One of the themes which came to characterize the reports of the monstrous races was their location in India. Herodotus was responsible for the Western conception of monsters in India, though he himself based his account on others. Then about the fourth century B.C. Ktesias from Knidos, who had been a royal physician in the court of the Persian king for seventeen years, published his *Persica* and *Indica* which continued the traditions of monsters and added a few others to the list.[5] India was said to be populated by pygmies who fought with the cranes; by the sciapodes or people with a single large foot with which they moved with great speed and shaded themselves from the heat of the sun; by the cynocephali who were men with dogs' heads who communicated by barking; by those without heads but with their faces between their shoulders; by people with eight fingers and toes whose hair was white until they reached the age of thirty and then turned black; by people with ears so large that they covered their arms to the elbows and their entire back; by giants, satyrs, martikhora (an animal with a man's face, the body of a lion, and the tail of a scorpion), unicorns, and griffins which guard the gold. In addition the cocks, goats, and sheep of India were said to be of an extraordinary size.[6]

Although Alexander the Great's incursions into India in 326–324 B.C. extended the geographic knowledge of the ancient world, the descriptions of the people encountered in the campaign continued the tradition of marvelous beings and gave rise in the Middle Ages to the Alexander cycle of romances. The new knowledge was not ignored, but conventions demanded the inclusion of established lore of the East. It was an exercise in reassurance to the public both of the account's authenticity as well as of the already determined place of these new/old cultures within a well-ordered universe. The Greek Megasthenes, who was sent by the heir to Alexander's Asian empire in 303 B.C. as an ambassador to the court of Chandragupta, founder of the great Mauryan dynasty in Pataliputra on the Ganges, described the social and political institutions and the customs of the people he had visited. He nevertheless continued to refer to the older tradition of "marvels" of India and even added some of his own. He described, for example, people whose heels were in front while the instep and toes were turned backwards. These people would later appear in literature as the antipodes or "opposite-footers." In addition there were wildmen who had no mouths and subsisted on the smells of roasted flesh and the aroma of fruit and flowers; people who lived a thousand years; others with no nostrils and with the upper part of their mouth protruding far over the lower lip; and those who had dog's ears and a single eye in the middle of their forehead. These fabulous creatures were not solely from the fertile imagination of Megasthenes himself, for he admitted that many of the stories of these unique beings were borrowed from the Indian epics.[7]

The Greek traditions of India and the unknown East persisted during Roman times, and Pliny's *Historia naturalis* (completed in A.D. 77) became one of the main sources for the medieval lore of monsters. He accepted all the stories of fabulous beings of previous writers and particularly those of Ktesias. But the more important influence on the medieval writers was Caius Julius Solinus, whose *Collectanea Rerum Memorabilium,* written in the third century A.D., was a collection of fabulous tales of creatures and plants of the East which was based principally on Pliny. This book became very popular and was consulted by medieval encyclopedists and chroniclers.[8] Relying on Solinus, Isidore wrote his chapter "De Portentis" in his encyclopedic work, the *Etymologiae,* in the sixth century. These were among the most important writers to have consolidated the ancient Greek tradition of monsters and marvels which continued to adorn travel accounts through the Middle Ages and the Renaissance.[9]

In the description of these monstrous races, not only are they unlike the humans living in the center of the world, but they are also characterized by features which are found wanting in the "measures of humans." Their diet is characterized by one major food which is viewed as "exotic." They are therefore referred as the Fish-Eaters, Root-Eaters, Elephant-Eaters, Dog-Milkers, and the like. They utter sounds unlike that of civilized humans in the center, or they bark like the dog-headed cynocephali. They live in caves, mountains, deserts, rivers, and woods, and not in cities. They wear clothing which is foreign to that worn by civilized humans, often dressing only with animal skins or going naked.[10] There was a strong belief in the troglodytes, who "have a language of their own which they speak in a whistle" and who were caught and used as servants "in many places in the East Indies."[11] These monstrous characteristics were applied by early European observers to the Malukans, who were sago-eaters, spoke with unfamiliar sounds, lived in huts in their jungle gardens, and wore only narrow barkcloth to cover their genitalia.

Although strange tales of the East persisted, the explanation for the existence of marvels varied to suit certain dominant theories of the world at the time. During the period of the ancient Greeks, the creation of these beings was a way of dealing with fear of the unknown. In the patristic period between the first and sixth centuries A.D., the wondrous tales of the East had to be reconciled with the authority of the Bible. The most authoritative and ingenious explanation for the monstrous races was given by St. Augustine, who suggested that God may have created these races so that humankind would not think that such a birth among them was a failure and an imperfection of God's work.[12] His arguments were accepted by all the writers of the Middle Ages, and Isidore reaffirmed this view in the *Etymologiae* by stating that monstrosities were not against nature. Nevertheless, the fear of the unnatural, the deformed, the less than human saw these monsters being placed at the fringes of the known world in the East, beyond the jurisdiction and responsibility of "true" humans.[13] The prevalence of these views colored the European perception of Asian societies and hindered any relationship of equality.

One of the most popular works in the Middle Ages, which reinforced a belief in such traditional tales, was *The Travels of Sir John Mandeville.* He claimed to be an English knight who had served the Sultan of Egypt and the Great Khan of Cathay during his travels between 1322 and 1356. By 1400 this work had been translated into every European language including Latin, and by 1500 the number of extant manuscripts was vast. It was so valued, especially as a repository of information about the East, that it was incorporated into a number of important compendia.[14] With the invention of the printing press in the mid-fifteenth century, Mandeville's *Travels* reached a wide audience since most of the printed copies were inexpensive paper editions and there existed a network of informal book borrowing among the general populace.[15]

So dominant were the traditions of the Classical and the Christian world on the medieval mind that mapmakers reflected the fascination with the fantastic. With a few notable exceptions, medieval maps were more works of art than of information and preferred to ignore new geographic knowledge rather than upset their schematic designs based on received wisdom. Mandeville's *Travels* was used as a source in the preparation of the Catalan Atlas in 1375, the Andrea Bianco map of 1434, and the "Behaim" globe of Nuremberg in 1492. These were the chief maps which many explorers of the Renaissance brought with them in the voyages to the East. It may not be pure coincidence that right up to the end of the sixteenth century there appears to have been a direct correlation between the major voyages of exploration and the frequency with which editions of Mandeville's *Travels* were issued. Columbus relied on it as one of his principal sources, and Mandeville's ideas of circumnavigation constituted one of the influences affecting Columbus's decision to sail westward to Cathay from Spain.[16] It appears that Columbus and other explorers were so familiar with the *Travels* that it contributed to their preconceptions and interpretations of the "discoveries."[17]

While it is difficult to determine precisely why the *Travels* achieved such great popularity, it is possible to see that it followed certain conventions which contributed to its success. The medieval and Renaissance assumption that all writing must have a serious moral intent was evident in this work. It stressed the medieval ideal in travel literature of combining pleasure with instruction, hence the inclusion of certain entertaining fabulous tales to stress a moral lesson. Moreover, the *Travels* relied on previous works for the marvels of the East, very much in keeping with the medieval convention of reworking "olde feeldes" for "newe corne" and the use of "olde bookes" for "newe science." Thus the stories of fabulous beings and a fantastic natural world, which would have been transmitted through the centuries in the works of Herodotus, Pliny, Solinus, and others, found their way into the *Travels* and helped to mold the medieval and Renaissance manner of perceiving the East.

When European explorers and missionaries appeared on the Asian scene and reported what they saw, they did so in a way dictated by conventions of the time. They interpreted things within a moral framework, or inserted tales from other works as their own experience in order to emphasize a moral stance. Interspered with prosaic accounts of daily life and labors of a new people were more lurid, fabulous tales of yore to satisfy the medieval and Renaissance demand for entertaining and oftentimes titillating descriptions of "monstrous" races. Later travelers, who actually were in places claimed to have been visited by Mandeville, used the *Travels* to provide more, and most likely entertaining, detail to their own accounts. The desire to satisfy the demand for "lust and lore" in travel literature dictated the manner in which the East was reported to the European medieval and Renaissance person.[18] Münster's popular *Cosmographia* was published in 1544 and was intended to supplant Mandeville's *Travels*. However, the latter work was so popular and deeply rooted in European perception of other cultures that Münster incorporated Mandeville's marvels and his publishers simply used Mandeville's woodcut illustrations.[19] The marvelous had become an essential feature in Europe's representation of the new societies encountered abroad and enabled it to deal emotionally and intellectually with the vast unknown being unfolded.[20]

Despite the popular perceptions of the East being the region of marvels, there were individuals who had long assimilated the information slowly seeping to the West since Alexander the Great's Indian campaign in the fourth century B.C. In the first century A.D. an anonymous Greek wrote the *Periplus of the Erythraen Sea*, which was a manual covering the Indian Ocean as well as the lands and coasts beyond. For the first time the Malay Peninsula is mentioned as the Islands of Chryse, while China is called the region of Thin and said to be located at the very end of the East. In the first half of the second century A.D. Ptolemy compiled a geographical treatise which was the most important work on geography until the account of Marco Polo. In dealing with the East he attributed his information to "those that had sailed from there and had spent a long time in traversing those parts." In common with other geographers of his day, Ptolemy believed that the lands in the East were joined ultimately to the east coast of Africa, making the Indian Ocean a major inland sea.[21]

A significant development was the reinterpretation of biblical ideas of geography which prepared the European mind psychologically for exploration of the East. In the thirteenth century Albertus Magnus argued that the long-held view of the equatorial belt being unpopulated might not be true.[22] On the basis of Aristotle's works Roger Bacon, a contemporary of Magnus, believed there was a short seaward passage to India going westward from Spain. The French churchman and geographer Cardinal Pierre d'Ailly went further than previous scholars by suggesting that there was an open Indian Ocean, that Africa was an island, and that the tropical zone was habitable. In his *Imago Mundi* he argued that only a seventh part of the globe was covered with water, which was a small stretch of sea running in a narrow band from pole to pole. He was convinced that there was only a short distance separating the west coast of Africa and the east coast of India, a view which supported the theory advanced by Roger Bacon in the previous century. In confirmation of this view he cited the presence of elephants in these two places.[23]

While the Catalan Atlas of 1375 relied upon the information brought back by travelers such as Marco Polo and Odoric de Pordenone, and while it provided the most complex geographical knowledge of the Middle Ages, it continued to incorporate aspects of popular mythical geography.[24] The recovery of the long-lost *Geography* of Ptolemy in the early years of the fifteenth century and its translation between 1406 and 1410 consolidated earlier ideas because of its tremendous popularity in the fifteenth and sixteenth centuries. However, opposing views of the geography of the world were becoming more widely disseminated and respectable as a result of the travel accounts of the Polo brothers and others. An indication of this development was Pope Pius II's *Historia Rerum Ubique Gestarum,* which was based largely on Ptolemy's work, though he argued for the circumnavigation of Africa and believed that the information on the East brought back by Marco Polo in the thirteenth century was reliable.[25]

There developed in the sixteenth and seventeenth centuries a move to "collect" manners and customs of exotic places. Instead of attempting to find new categories and descriptions for the cultures encountered in distant areas of the globe, the European "collectors" preferred to adhere to certain monstrous characteristics and to accept the formula established by Herodotus for the analysis of other cultures. They gathered material on marital customs, funeral and religious rites, dress, dwelling, and diet. Exotic practices which lacked an equivalence with the known civilized worlds of the past and present were implicitly regarded as barbaric or savage. Even when similarities were found, often newly described societies were compared with an earlier stage of European development and hence provided "documentary evidence" of the inferiority of these societies. It was this European manner of observing the East which often obscured indigenous customs and activities by substituting conventional interpretations for observed phenomena.[26]

The depiction of those in the East as physically and spiritually marginal remained a vital part of Christian European literature. Inhabitants of this region were regarded frequently as objects and part of the European collection of curious fauna and flora, or at best as producers of wondrous works and deeds.[27] New knowledge in general did not undermine this perception but was itself translated to conform to the traditional Wonders of the East. To a considerable extent this dominant structure of reporting the East prevented an understanding of and sympathy with these cultures because they were simply cast as counterimages.[28] From the outset of the meeting of East and West, the latter had prefigured a relationship of oppositions and confrontations all in accordance with God's Divine Plan.[29]

Only in the eighteenth century after the scientific and philosophical advances of the previous two hundred years did the educated populace begin to become more critical of traditional opinion and established authorities. The fabulous tales of the East still proved popular, but there was at least a school of thought which argued that the societies encountered on the opposite side of the world were not necessarily inferior to those of Christian Europe. Advancing such views was part of the general reorientation of eighteenth century thought toward religious relativism and questioning of the authority of the Church.[30] Although such ideas were present in Mandeville's *Travels* and influenced the thinking of ordinary people, the Church had been swift in its punishment of such heresy.[31] By the eighteenth century, however, the Church too was adjusting to its greater knowledge of the complex and sophisticated religious beliefs which it had encountered in Asia.

The Christian Mission in Asia

In the patristic period there was the theory of a flat earth with Jerusalem in the center and the terrestrial paradise located in the East. A typical Beatus map, named after the Spanish priest Beatus at the end of the eighth century, depicts the Twelve Apostles located in that part of the globe where he is said to have preached. At the top, which marks the

East, was a vignette of Adam, Eve, and the serpent. The terrestrial paradise with its four westward-flowing rivers remained a constant and important component of the *mappae-mundi* of the Middle Ages. So potent was this image that in 1498 after his third voyage to the New World Columbus wrote to the king and queen of Spain: "There are great indications of this being the terrestrial paradise, for its site coincides with the opinion of the holy and wise theologians St. Isidore, Bede, Strabus, the master of scholastic history, St. Ambrose and Scotus, all of whom agree that the earthly paradise is in the east."[32]

The location in the East of both the terrestrial paradise and the monsters does not seem to have troubled Columbus nor many of his contemporaries. For the Church, however, the association of Eden and the East offered a spiritual challenge to restore the fallen creatures to the Christian faith. The Church's mission was considerably enhanced by the widespread popularity of the Prester John legend. The story of a Christian king living in the East had long been a part of European oral tradition. In 1144 a bishop claimed to have met this Prester John who was said to be a Nestorian king of a country in the Far East, descended from Magian kings, and possessing fabulous wealth. Then came the famous forged Prester John letter which circulated in Europe around 1165, exciting the European Christian world fed by earlier stories of the East, travelers' tales, and the popular legends of Alexander the Great. It was addressed to Immanuel I, Emperor of Byzantium, and contained a number of passages which confirmed an already established legend:

I, Prester John, who reign supreme, surpass in virtue, riches and power all creatures under heaven. Seventy kings are our tributaries. . . . For gold, silver, precious stones, animals of every kind, and the number of our people, we believe there is not our equal under heaven. . . . Every month we are served in rotation by seven kings, sixty-two dukes, and 265 counts and marquises. . . . And if we have chosen to be called by a lower name and inferior rank, it springs from humility. If indeed you can number the stars of heaven and sands of the sea, then you may calculate the extent of our dominion and power.

The letter continues in a similar vein describing a country which appeared to the European audience for which the forgery was intended as the closest thing to paradise on earth—the Eden in the East of earlier Christian writers. The invention of the printing press and the advances made in woodcut and engraving techniques contributed further to the popularity of the legend.

Inspired by this letter a number of attempts were made to establish contact, and various figures from Odoric of Pordenone to Marco Polo claimed to have found Prester John's kingdom among certain Christian Turkish tribes in Central Asia. By the late fourteenth century

European courts believed that Prester John's kingdom lay in Ethiopia, identified as one of the "three Indias" within that ruler's vast domains. The Portuguese court sent an embassy to the court of the ruler of Ethiopia in 1487 and was aware that, though a Christian ruler, he was far less powerful and his lands much poorer than the twelfth century letter had claimed. This knowledge, however, did not destroy the European desire to preserve this hope of a powerful, good, and wealthy Christian ruler in the East. The quest for Prester John's kingdom—whether to benefit from its wealth, to acquire a powerful Christian ally against the Muslims, or to satisfy a need to believe in an ideal Christian ruler—became a readily identifiable goal which united the efforts of rulers, the Church, and ordinary people in the expansion eastward.[33]

As word of the discoveries of new lands in the Americas and contact with non-Christian peoples in Asia reached Europe, there was great excitement in the Church. Franciscans in particular spoke of the resurrection of the Primitive Church of the pre-Constantine era, and it was the dedication and the poverty of the early Church which became the yardstick for their missionizing activities in the new lands. A yearning for the simplicity and innocence of humans before the fall of Adam was fulfilled by the discovery of many "primitives" in the New World and certain areas of Asia. Expectations were raised of offsetting the losses to the Reformation by converting large numbers of these newly discovered souls.[34] For the Franciscans and other orders in the Church, these discoveries brought the challenge of adapting to new circumstances. The old missionizing experiences of the late Middle Ages were no longer considered to be appropriate in extending the faith. As a result of the Counter-Reformation in the first half of the sixteenth century, the Church had been revitalized and had viewed the discoveries as an opportunity to demonstrate to the peoples in the Americas and Asia that the Christian Church was something new and a worthy displacer of the older beliefs in these lands.[35]

In its mission the Church was assisted by rulers who were strongly influenced by the apostolic idea of Christian kingship so prominent in the Middle Ages. The image of a missionary-king or an apostle-king whose duty it was to spread the gospel among the heathen was to encourage the establishment of national missionary endeavors.[36] This development was a concomitant of the decline in the prestige of the papacy as a result of the Avignon experience, the Great Schism, and the intrigues of the Medicis.[37] Pope Calixtus III in 1456 granted the Padroado Real, or the royal patronage, to the Portuguese Crown. Through this Padroado the crown of Portugal was granted spiritual jurisdiction over an area which stretched from the island of Madeira, to the coast of Africa, on to India, and into the Far East. This precedent was reaffirmed in 1493 when Pope Alexander VI made it a duty of all

Catholic monarchs to provide missionaries in lands newly discovered or yet to be discovered. Spurred by this challenge the Spaniards sought and received their Patronato (or Patronazgo) Real from Pope Julius II in 1508.[38] It was these two Iberian nations, then, which led the way in the proselytizing of Asia and the Americas.

According to the royal patronage, the papacy entrusted the task of conversion of the heathens to the Portuguese and Spanish rulers. They were authorized to build cathedrals, churches, monasteries, convents and hermitages within their patronages; to present to the Holy See a list of candidates for all colonial archbishoprics, bishoprics, and abbeys, as well as for lower offices to the bishops concerned; and to administer ecclesiastical jurisdictions and revenues, and veto papal bulls and briefs not cleared properly through the respective Crown Chancery. In effect it meant that the Iberian monarchs had control over the transfer, promotion and removal of any cleric and could arbitrate in any dispute between themselves and between ecclesiastic and civil power. The nationally oriented mission eventually led to the exclusion of missionaries from other countries and the inevitable identification of missionary with the secular government. In Asia the Portuguese disputed Spanish claims to spiritual jurisdiction over Maluku and the Philippines. Eventually, however, they agreed to acknowledge Spain's rights to the Philippines in return for Spain's relinquishing all claims to Maluku.[39]

The strength and the resources of the Iberian governments in the sixteenth century enabled the rapid and successful spread of the religion in the Americas and Asia. In the seventeenth century the papacy began to regret having relinquished so much power over foreign missions to the Iberian rulers, and it attempted to reassert itself through the Congregatio de Propaganda Fide (the Congregation for Propagating the Faith) founded in 1622. It was powerless to prevent the continuation of the royal patronage, however, especially when the Iberian nations employed eminent canon and civil lawyers to defend their positions. In Spanish America and the Philippines, and in Portuguese Brazil, the Royal Patronage survived into the nineteenth century. In Asia, however, the Portuguese were challenged by the Propaganda Fide from 1622 and from the Missions Étrangères de Paris from 1658. The arrival of the Protestant missions in this century further weakened the earlier dominance of the Portuguese mission in Asia.[40]

To adapt to an entirely new situation, the method of propagation of the Christian faith between 1500 and 1800 differed in important ways from the previous thousand years. The catechism, which was intended to instruct young children born of Christian parents, was now applied to heathens to prepare them for Christian baptism. Serious moral issues arose regarding the use of force in conversion, the propriety of communion for newly baptized Christians, and the adaptation of the religion to certain indigenous practices. In the Americas, the Philippines, and eastern Indonesia, other races were kept under a white political and ecclesiastical tutelage on a greater scale than ever before, raising some opposition among missionaries who deplored this exploitation. The Catholic Church sought to respond to these developments by creating specialized training centers for missionaries. It was from one such center, the Jesuit College in Coimbra founded in the mid-sixteenth century, that many of the Jesuit missionaries were sent to India and eventually to Maluku. Within the areas under the Dutch East and West India Companies, the Calvinist clergy were assigned principally to serve the needs of the Europeans, though efforts were also made to convert the indigenous inhabitants. The civil officials of the Companies determined the territories where the clergy were to be sent, the language to be used in services, and the salaries that the clergy were to be paid. In this regard the Calvinist clergy were simply a small part of the much larger and more dominant concerns of a commercial organization.[41]

The European missionaries, like the conquistadors, traders, and officials, were a product of the times and influenced by well-ingrained belief in the "marvels" of the East. However, their views were modified by the parallel tradition of the terrestrial paradise also located in the East and by the revitalization of the Church after the events of the Reformation and Counter-Reformation. Their enthusiasm and attempts to justify their activities colored their portrayal of conversion and their success in propagating the faith. Since they were encouraged in their letters not merely to inform but to edify, at times accuracy was sacrificed for the more important Christian message. Such was the case in many of the missives sent to Europe by the Jesuit missionaries in Maluku in the sixteenth and early seventeenth centuries.

The National Enterprises

In addition to the general attitudes which European nations shared as part of their Classical and Christian cultural milieu, each individual nation had its own visions and concerns which affected its relationships with the East. By examining these features it is possible to detect the specific national logic which structured the reporting of Malukan events.

The arrival of the Portuguese in Maluku in 1511–1512 was the culmination of an ambitious program of exploration which had begun in the early fifteenth century. Portugal's overseas expansion became a great collective endeavor shaping the vision of its people and the attitudes which they adopted toward the new lands. A significant aspect of this overseas enterprise was Portugal's long-standing struggle with Islam. Between A.D. 711 and 718 the Moors crossed the Straits of Gibraltar and became the masters of Portugal until they were finally expelled at the end of the thirteenth century. The struggle resumed with the Portuguese invasion of North Africa in the beginning of the fifteenth century. Many of the Portuguese commanders who later served in Asia received their training in this Moroccan campaign where little quarter was given, prisoners were routinely slaughtered, and corpses were frequently mutilated.[42] The Portuguese transferred many of their attitudes and tactics from North Africa onto the Asian scene, and instinctively attributed any social, moral, and intellectual deficiencies among the Asian Muslims to the teachings of Islam.

Along with the contempt, suspicion, and cruelty exhibited by the Portuguese in Asia, there was a self-interested pragmatism which was also a product of their experience with the Moors. Throughout the wars, trade between the two parties was rarely interrupted. The brutality of battle mingled with commercial profit as each side engaged in the lucrative practice of ransoming prisoners. By the twelfth century this practice was well established, and the institution of the *alfaqueque*, or "broker of prisoners," was created. An ordinance of 1388 even regulated how prisoners seized on land and sea were to be divided among the king, the admiral, and those of the royal fleet.[43] The Portuguese in Maluku continued the tradition of engaging in trade with their Muslim enemies in the midst of war and ransoming prisoners, a practice common also among the Malukans.

In the ongoing struggle against the Moors, the existence of the Padroado Real in theory encouraged the cooperation of religious and secular authorities in promoting Christian conversion.[44] In 1545 King João III urged the rapid but peaceful conversion of both Muslim and heathen. The response was dramatic as reports began to arrive of mass conversions in the new lands. The leading figure in this process was Father Francis Xavier, whose reports from Maluku describe large-scale baptisms after only the most cursory of instructions in the faith and without the customary rites and trial period. Xavier justified his methods to his superiors by citing biblical authority that "He who believes and is baptized will be saved." After each baptism Xavier presented the new convert with a Christian name and a set of European clothes to mark the new life. Xavier's successful methods were imitated by fellow Jesuits who hoped to demonstrate the dynamism of Catholicism, which was expanding rapidly in areas outside Europe.[45]

Despite the desire for converts, the Jesuits were nevertheless restrained by ingrained prejudices fostered in the European view of peoples inhabiting the "periphery." A leading Jesuit figure stated bluntly in 1575 that no dark-skinned natives should be admitted to the

Society of Jesus since they were "naturally" inclined to wrongdoing and motivated by base instincts. For many, color came to be a convenient symbol to distinguish the center from the periphery, the human from the "monsters." The moral and intellectual decay was explained by the nature of Islam, the antithesis to Christianity.[46]

In addition to Portugal's experience with Islam, another distinguishing feature of the vast Portuguese national enterprise was the influence of the fidalguia, or nobility. The overseas expansion provided an opportunity to serve God and to attain glory on the battlefield, an important badge associated with fidalgo status. With the capture of the Moorish city of Ceuta in North Africa in 1415 and the transferral of the battleground to Moorish soil, the fidalguia prospered and thrust up a growing list of heroes for the national pantheon. The *Amadís de Gaula*, a romance where chivalry was supreme and ordinary soldiers behaved like supermen, served as the martial ideal for the Portuguese commanders. It is believed to have been recited among the Portuguese long before it was first published in 1508, and it is referred to directly in Galvão's *Treatise on Maluku* published in 1544.[47] A century after its publication, fifty new works on chivalry appeared in Spain and Portugal. In the second half of the sixteenth century, the popularity of this genre of works earned the denunciation of churchmen and moralists who attributed to them much of the delinquent behavior of the populace. But the older romances continued to be printed and circulated.[48] The royal courts and the noble households reveled in the romances, where the harsh realities of warfare and political intrigue were transformed into acts of chivalry. It is the same atmosphere which is conveyed in the chronicles dedicated to the deeds of these heroic sons of Lusus on distant shores.

The goals of the fidalguia in Asia were threefold: to pursue the war against Islam; to raise or resuscitate the standing of their family by achievement on the battlefield or outstanding service to the king in Asia; and to enrich themselves and assure the preservation of the status and lifestyle of their family. The fidalguia reported their activities with these goals in mind, transforming minor skirmishes with the local inhabitants into full-fledged battles, informal gatherings with native chiefs into royal audiences, the occasional Islamic teachers and their followers into hordes of Muslim fanatics, and mundane activities into an arena of confrontation where intentions and acts were constantly being assessed and honor upheld. The chroniclers were very much influenced by the concerns and the code of the fidalguia in framing the story of the Portuguese in Asia.

In short, Portuguese attitudes and activities in the fifteenth and sixteenth centuries were based on a general Christian European tradition and shaped by Portugal's major national enterprise: the overseas expansion. Within this all-encompassing endeavor the struggle with Islam and the glory of the fidalguia were dominant themes which informed Portuguese views of the new worlds encountered. Since the sources for the history of Maluku in the sixteenth century are principally those of the Portuguese, it is with this knowledge that their commentaries on Malukan society, politics, religion, wars, and racial characteristics should be read.

Much of what has been said of the Portuguese can be applied equally well to the Spaniards. They, like the Portuguese, were imbued with the fervor of their great national enterprise and motivated by their papal grant of the Patronato Real. They, too, had their *hidalguía* which produced some of the most infamous and ruthless conquistadors of that age, and their relationship with Islam was a prominent element in their nation's history. By 1492 Granada, the last major Muslim kingdom in Spain, had fallen in the great Reconquista, the Reconquest of lands taken by the Moors in days past. Spain, like Portugal, then extended the struggle against the Muslims to North Africa, but with much less conviction. The Castilians regarded the Reconquista as an opportunity for booty, but the campaign became overshadowed by the prospects of advancement and riches in the New World and Asia. With the Castilian pro-aristocratic mentality they implemented the idea of the Reconquista, which in practice meant the conquest, the seizure, and the exploitation of the land for the benefit of the conquistador. The domain thus created came under some nobleman who used it to gain glory and riches for his family. Over these personal benefices were superimposed a bureaucracy which attempted to apply laws, organize defense, and collect taxes for the Spanish realm.[49]

In the early sixteenth century the conquistador was supreme. He was usually from a poor noble family and saw that the possession of land and riches would improve his rank and social status. While the risk of death was always present, survival could mean improving one's material and social position in Spain.[50] Toward the end of the sixteenth century and in subsequent years, however, there was less reliance on the conquistadors since the overseas territories came to be administered by officials of the central government. Castile systematically produced trained personnel who were recruited to staff the various councils. In the overseas colonies a type of government evolved which sought to meld the experience of the titled nobility, the army commanders, and the various lower nobility with those of the new bureaucrats who were graduates *(licenciados)* of Castile.[51] The result was not always happy, and there arose in America and Asia a philosophical conflict between those who advocated the rule of the conquistador and those who defended the rule of law.

Great care was taken by the Spaniards to emphasize the legality of much of their action in dealing with societies in the Americas and Asia in order to allay criticism at home concerning the inconsistency of Spanish conquests with Christian ethics.[52] They justified their right to rule upon "prior discovery and just conquest," which were reinforced by the papal bulls of 1493 granting Spain the "islands and mainlands . . . towards the West and South . . . with all their rights, jurisdictions and appurtenances," except those with Christian princes. In accordance with the doctrine of universal papal dominion a jurist in the Council of Castile was ordered in 1510 to draw up a policy known as the *requerimento* calling on the people of the Americas (and later those in the Philippines and Maluku) to submit peacefully and receive the Christian faith. The long and complicated document was to be read aloud to the natives on all occasions before any military operations commenced.[53] When the Spaniards returned to Cebu in the Philippines in 1565, they made the native chiefs request pardon for their fathers and grandfathers for killing Magellan and attacking his crew some fifty years before. The intention was not to punish them for their deeds, but to make them swear to a renewal of the oath of allegiance first made under Magellan. In this way the legalistic Spaniards could justify the use of force in the establishment of their colony,[54] as indeed occurred in the conquest of Ternate and the wholesale exile of its government in 1606. The commander of the Philippine expedition, Miguel Lopez de Legazpi, was instructed to take formal possession of any lands in the name of the king "in the presence of a Notary and witnesses, and [to] have the legal document drawn for the occasion sent back along with all the other information."[55]

Spain's efforts to establish a permanent presence in Maluku had been a dismal failure. Its hopes had been raised by the arrival in Maluku of Magellan's crew in 1521 and their successful return to Spain. Although they brought with them only a small cargo of spices, it was enough to convince the court of the feasibility of sponsoring further voyages. A second expedition under García Jofre de Loaisa was sent in September 1525 but proved a disaster. A similar fate befell the third fleet under Alvaro de Saavedra in 1528, thus damping any further desire by the Spanish crown to become involved in costly ventures. It was the financial burden of Charles V's European wars, coupled with the abortive Spanish expeditions to the spice islands, which finally persuaded the Spanish ruler to sign the Saragossa Treaty of 1529 relinquishing his claim to Maluku for an agreed 500,000 cruzados from Portugal.[56] Nevertheless, the Spaniards made one final attempt in 1542 under Ruy López de Villalobos to establish a permanent presence in Maluku, but this too failed. The only real success in Asia for the Spaniards was the expedition under Legazpi in 1564 which resulted in the occupation of the Philippines. Almost total attention in Asia was devoted to the new colony, and Spain regained interest in Maluku affairs only after the union of the Spanish and Portuguese crowns in 1580. After that date Maluku became a remote outpost under Philippine administration and suffered from neglect by the Spanish authorities in Manila. Though the Spaniards maintained a formal presence in Maluku until 1663, toward the end they became ineffective and only survived at the pleasure of the Dutch governor.[57]

The Spanish nobility who came to lead the troops and to man the garrisons in Maluku were instilled with the same desire for glory and riches as their Portuguese counterparts. Their campaigns and their accounts of them, though of minor importance in the larger Spanish world, were nevertheless resonant with heroes and glorious deeds. The special situation of Maluku, where the Spaniards were always the weaker of the European powers present, fostered the conquistador mentality. The Spanish official who represented the crown was the military commander, and it was the concerns of the conquistador in a hostile land which determined Spanish activity in Maluku. Although the Spanish Church was a significant force in the Philippines, in Maluku its role was muted. The application of the system of the Patronato/Padroado Real left evangelization and the maintenance of the Church in Maluku in the hands of the Portuguese even after the union in 1580. For the Spaniards, therefore, Maluku was regarded simply as a place where glory and riches could be attained on the battlefield. For the Castilian nobility, especially, this was a goal well worth the stigma of being exiled to the farthest ends of the Spanish empire. It was these qualities of the Spaniards in Maluku which colored their version of local events.

Of all the Europeans it was the Dutch who had the longest and most durable impact on indigenous society in Maluku. Their expansion into Asia was part of a commercial and technological revolution which transformed the Low Countries from a colony of Spain to the leading European nation in the seventeenth century. From the late fourteenth century successful innovations in preserving herring and in the manufacture of large fishnets had laid the foundation for a major Dutch economic expansion. By the sixteenth century the new wealth enabled the Dutch to create a large merchant navy which dominated the Baltic trade, the carrying trade in Europe, and the much older river trade. This development was stimulated by the vast financial resources of the Calvinist merchants and industrialists from the Flemish cities who came with their capital and expertise to the north to escape Spanish persecution. It was they, with their long experience in the Portuguese and Spanish ventures, who initiated new commercial and trade opportunities between these nations and the northern Netherlands. The combination of capital and expertise also enabled the United Provinces of the

Netherlands to play a leading role in commerce and industry in the seventeenth century.[58]

The readiness of the Dutch to invest in Asia at the end of the sixteenth century was a natural outcome of the economic expansion of the Netherlands. Asia was well known because of the participation of Dutch seamen in the Portuguese and Spanish Asian fleets and because of the long experience in the financing and operation of the Portuguese-Asian trade by wealthy merchants, industrialists, and financiers from Bruges, Antwerp, Ghent, and Brussels.[59] The first ship flying the Dutch flag sailed to Asia in 1595, and it was followed by a number of others in subsequent years. Initially the profits of the fleets sponsored by certain Dutch coastal towns participating in this so-called *wilde vaarten* or "free navigation" amounted to no more than two or three months' earnings from the herring fisheries.[60] Nevertheless, the lure of the fabulous profits that could be made in the spice trade attracted competing groups which proved to be counterproductive. After much bargaining and compromising, the various local companies formed the United Chartered Dutch East India Company (VOC) in March 1602 and agreed to combine their resources and talents to promote Asian trade. The availability of vast reserves of capital was evident in the large initial investment of six million guilders in the newly formed Company.[61]

The VOC was the creation of the Dutch state but in many ways its very antithesis. The charter of the new Company granted it the privilege of exercising sovereign rights on behalf of the republic in its relations with Asian powers, but it came to encourage values which the new Dutch nation had come to reject. One such conflict was in the attitude toward the freedom of the seas. The Dutch nation prospered from its carrying trade, which cut across all possible divisions, as well as from its role in importing raw materials or semifinished items from one country and sending back finished products. It therefore employed its most brilliant advocate to argue the case for open seas. In March 1608, six years after the foundation of the Company, the States of Holland passed a secret resolution that they would never "in whole or in part, directly or indirectly, withdraw, surrender or renounce the freedom of the seas, everywhere and in all regions of the world."[62] To have succumbed to pressures of mercantilism would have been disastrous to the Dutch economy. But in Asia the Company almost from its inception rejected the policy of open seas and free trade because it operated at a severe disadvantage to the already well-entrenched Portuguese and Asian trade networks. The only real chance the Dutch had of displacing them was by instituting a closed sea policy. The *mare liberum* argued by Hugo de Groot on behalf of the Dutch nation and the 1608 secret resolution of the States of Holland were conveniently forgotten in Asia.

A second striking difference between the Company and the Dutch nation was in their self-perception and lifestyles. The United Provinces had selected a republican form of government and extolled the virtues of simplicity, thrift, cleanliness, and sobriety. It was not uncommon to find leading statesmen and military leaders exercising a conspicuous frugality, inspiring admiration from their compatriots and bemusement from foreign observers. In Asia, however, the governor-general, the Council of the Indies, plus all the major Company officials serving in posts throughout the Dutch Asian empire, were wont to exercise the rights and privileges of Asian potentates. In the Malay-Indonesian archipelago, kings and princes came to offer friendship or obeisance to the governor-general and the council, and were in turn regaled in a style which befitted the Company's status as an Asian power. The use of golden parasols (the sign of Malay-Indonesian royalty), carriages, and large retinues of slaves was commonplace among leading Company officials. The wealth from the Asian trade and the numerous opportunities for venality and other forms of corruption contributed to the rapid spread of wealth in Batavia. Married women in Batavia, whether Dutch, Eurasian, or Asian, were accustomed to appear in public with silks, satins, and jewels, and with a train of slaves.[63] Frugality in the East was a sign of poverty or stinginess, and the Company was quick to dispel any such judgments on the part of its Asian neighbors. Its leaders set a style and a standard of conduct which provided the norm for other Company officials in distant posts. A certain amount of corruption, greed, and debauchery was considered to be the natural concomitant of this brand of life. Everyone from the captain down to the lowest officer carried privately-owned commodities on Company ships, while ashore the governors, directors, and merchants of a post all participated in ventures also for their own personal gain. The most blatant abuses were punished, but most "illegal" activities by Company personnel were left unreported.[64]

Because the VOC had evolved into a counterimage, or in Calvinist parlance an "Anti-Christ," to God's elect in the Netherlands, the tendency among contemporaries of the period and modern historians has been to see the servants of the Company as standing in direct contrast to upright society at home. Batavia was referred to at the time as "an honorable prison" by those in Amsterdam and The Hague,[65] while an eminent twentieth century Dutch historian described the Company as "a good refuge for all libertines, bankrupts, failed students, cashiers, brokers, bailiffs, secret agents, and such-like rakes."[66] In the frequent conflicts between parents and adolescents in the seventeenth century, a radical solution was to banish the rebellious sons to the Company lands in the East Indies. A Leiden professor in 1678 referred to these lands as "a real sewer of a country into which flows all the garbage of Holland."[67] A recurrent criticism appearing in the missives written

by the Company directors in Amsterdam concerned the ignoble character of those who served in Asia.[68]

In condemning the activities of the VOC in Asia, Dutch historians
have been quick to emphasize the large non-Dutch element among its
employees: "From all the corners of Protestant Germany men eager for
adventure and gain came flocking; there were also Englishmen, and
especially Scotsmen, Frenchmen, Swiss, and Scandinavians. Flemings
and Brabanters were not lacking either."[69] In the Netherlands the presence of numerous foreigners was interpreted as a sign of the attractive-
ness of the country, a land of freedom and opportunities. Holland itself
was described as "a cosmopolitan center, the focal point of divergent
trends of thought and culture."[70] But the judgment on the foreign element in the Company in Asia is clearly negative. They remain outside
the official hierarchy and can penetrate the system only if they learn to
write Dutch. As good Dutch folk refused to immigrate to the East,
Dutch overseas communities became "an unfree society of hierarchi-
cally-bound officials, diluted here and there with dependent free
burghers, [a society which was] distressingly materialistic and gross."[71]

This judgment by Pieter Geyl, the leading Dutch historian of seventeenth century Netherlands, reflects the dominant attitude which the
Dutch have held toward the Company and its empire in Asia since the
formation of the VOC in 1602. Such a view is strongly colored by the
ingrained Dutch perception that their golden age in the seventeenth
century was created by God-fearing Dutch men and women who were
frugal, hardworking, innovative, sober, and counted among God's
elite. The state itself, created in a republican form and dominated by a
merchant oligarchy, thrived on the fruits of trade. Acquisition of goods
was an honorable goal with the resulting prosperity a demonstration of
God's favor to his chosen people. By contrast, in the Company lands
these very same virtues were transformed into vices. It mattered little
that there were individuals who by their honest toil sought to better
their station. Their very presence in these distant Company lands was
sufficient condemnation.

Nor were the Dutch unique in this attitude. An English East India
Company official writing from Bantam in the early seventeenth century
echoed a similar dichotomy between home and abroad:

Many [Englishmen] are invited out by golden rewards but none stay, indeed it
were madness to do so. At home men are famous for doing nothing; here they
are infamous for their honest endeavors. At home is respect and reward; abroad
disrespect and heartbreak. . . . At home is content; abroad nothing so much as
griefs, cares, and displeasure. At home is safety; abroad no security. And, in a
word, at home all things are as a man may wish and here nothing answerable to
merit.[72]

Being very much products of long-held classical and medieval views, the Europeans believed that "abroad" (that is, the periphery) could not be anything but the antithesis of everything that was good at "home" (that is, the center). This prevailing attitude strongly influenced European perception of Maluku, located in one of the remotest corners of the East Indies.

European Structuring of Maluku's History

The structuring of European knowledge of other cultures has a long and illustrious history. Dating from Greek and Roman times the distinction between the center and the periphery became not simply a geographical expression but also a moral and philosophical judgment. Those of the oikumene, the area inhabited by the Greeks and those like them, represented the center and true civilization. By this reasoning those inhabiting the periphery were by nature lacking in the proper measures of central/civilized human beings and hence were "barbarians." India's own traditions of strange and wondrous creatures contributed to Europe's belief that the East, at the very periphery of God's creation, harbored the monstrous races. Books appeared with illustrations of these fanciful beings. Even when European travelers visited the East, their accounts were peppered with references to the exotic habits and creatures that they allegedly encountered. Ironically, inclusion of such fables was a way of confirming to their European audience the veracity of their travels. Without mention of strange and fantastic tales, many would have doubted a traveler's claim to have been to the East. Moreover, there was a blurring of the division between personal observation and received knowledge, with fact and fantasy coexisting as reality. Another reason for the persistence of the belief in God's deformed creatures was the popularity of such accounts up to the eighteenth century. This tradition of identifying the periphery, with all its moral connotations and association with monstrous races, with the East did influence European attitudes and actions toward the indigenous population of Maluku in the sixteenth, seventeenth, and eighteenth centuries.

Another common European perception was the belief that good health among humans depended upon the proper proportion of the "humors" in the body. Extremes of heat or cold brought an imbalance of the humors, causing a disturbance in mind and soul which affected whole societies. The unrelenting heat of the tropics could thus be cited by Europeans for the "strange" and inexplicable behavior of the natives. Maluku was a place which gained a reputation for breeding a number of unsavory individuals, both European and native. While there is substance to the claim that many of the worst European elements were sent there as punishment, the catalog of misdeeds committed by European and native alike would have been easily explained in terms of Maluku's climatic conditions.

Missionaries in the field sent reports of wondrous events and monstrous creatures in praise of the miracles of God's creation. Their task of converting the heathen and edifying their brethren and Christian flock at home structured their observations and interpretations to convey moral and religious messages. The excitement of gaining new souls in the spirit of the early Church encouraged the missionary in the field to believe in mass conversions, miraculous events, and victorious encounters with local demons and satanic Muslim forces. In addition there were the individual national attitudes toward other religious ideas which colored missionary reports. Both the Portuguese and the Spaniards had a long history of conflict with Islam, first in their homeland and later in North Africa. Their encounter with Muslims in Maluku was thus viewed as a continuation of their ancient struggle. For the Dutch the Muslims were regarded as a threat to Calvinism, but not more so than Catholicism. The Dutch came to refer to the Muslim religious scholars, the *ulama, as papen,* or "popes," a derogatory term reserved for Catholic priests. Unlike the Iberians, the Dutch were mainly concerned with administering the spiritual needs of those already part of God's elect among the Dutch community overseas.

Despite the importance of spices to the European, Maluku was always regarded as a peripheral outpost and even a place of exile for the European soldier or administrator. What made the posting tolerable, at least to those from the lower nobility of Spain and Portugal, was the opportunity to demonstrate valor and thus be rewarded with title, land, and riches. For these individuals what occurred in Maluku was a matter of national pride and honor. The foes were dastardly and their armies vast, for it would not have done for the Iberian noblemen to have met unworthy enemies or even worse to have suffered ignominious defeat at the hands of unworthy opponents. The role of the individual nobleman in the glorious victories was praised and the battle accounts heroically constructed in missives sent back to the courts of Spain and Portugal. For the Dutchmen a Maluku posting offered the opportunity to enrich themselves, but it had to be done while satisfying their leaders in Batavia and Amsterdam that all was being done to maintain the monopoly in spices. More often than not the reports of Dutchmen from Maluku contained fabrications of activities undertaken to preserve these precious goods for the Dutch alone.

Contemporary sources for the study of the history of Maluku in the sixteenth, seventeenth, and eighteenth centuries are almost entirely European in origin. The information contained in these sources has been structured around both the Classical Graeco-Roman and the

Christian European views of the center and the periphery, as well as the national foibles and specific concerns of the Portuguese, the Spaniards, and the Dutch. Only by recognizing how the European information is intellectually organized is it then possible to extrapolate ideas and rescue nuggets of information in order to begin an interpretation of Maluku's history using an indigenous structure. The basis for such a structure, however, can only be determined by identifying the most significant concerns expressed in Malukan traditions.

CHAPTER TWO

The World of Maluku: The Center

THE LOCAL PERCEPTION of a unified world known as "Maluku" is a basic assumption which structures the history of the area in the early modern period. The Portuguese in the early sixteenth century recorded traditions emphasizing this unity, and nearly three hundred years later the Dutch suffered the consequences of ignoring such traditions. For the European the name "Maluku" itself was incomprehensible, let alone the perception of a unity involving such a vast and diverse area.[1] In the mid-sixteenth century Francis Xavier was told that the word *maluku* meant "the head of a bull." He interpreted it to mean that Ternate, whose raja was referred to in one tradition as the king of Maluku, was the head of a large empire.[2] The sixteenth century Portuguese chronicler Couto repeated Xavier's interpretation, stating that the word came from a local language (which he he did not name) and meant "the head of something large."[3] Drawing upon documents in the Spanish court archives, Argensola concurred with this interpretation.[4] The fact that all the Iberian chroniclers and observers appear to have agreed that "maluku" meant "a head" may be traced to Xavier's original definition. Only in later centuries was there an attempt to provide an Islamic explanation, even though the name predated the arrival of Islam in Maluku in the late fifteenth century. One local historian, for example, argues that maluku was derived from the Arabic *malik* (pl. *muluk*), meaning "king."[5]

The difficulty which the Europeans faced in obtaining a precise definition from the local inhabitants reflected the indigenous attitude toward the name.[6] For them it was not the literal meaning of Maluku which mattered but rather its symbolic representation of the unity of the many islands and ethnic groups in the area. Their identification with Maluku was clearly and precisely presented in different local traditions which described their link to a specific island community and to a wider Maluku world. These cultural perceptions served as a map to guide and

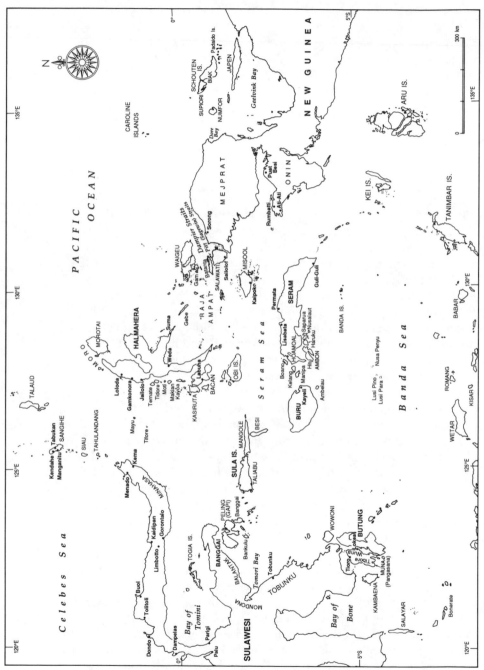

MAP 2. The Maluku world

legitimize political expansion, while offering an acceptable basis for common action without political coercion among many different cultures and peoples. In this regard Maluku was neither a political state nor a "stateless" society, a term used to refer to the ethnic solidarity of groups such as the Batak.[7] In Maluku, geographic isolation and the proliferation of ethnic groups and cultures ruled out the formation of any unities based on political force or a common ethnic identity. Instead, unity was forged through common commitment by these groups to legitimizing myths which established the physical and cosmic parameters of their world and the social orders within it. There were variations of the myths which reflected shifts in political power in the area, but the idea of a sacred unity of the group remained inviolate.

The Traditions of Unity

There are three basic myths representing traditions which address the notion of "unity" at three different levels of inclusiveness: that of an island, an area, and Maluku as a whole. Although there are no village-centered tales originating from the period under study, a recent anthropological work on a village in Tidore notes that the people place great significance on their historical origins and ritual traditions to maintain the village's unique identity and link it to the state. It argues that "establishing settlements, receiving titles, and otherwise becoming incorporated into the structure of the island" form an important part of village histories.[8] Such traditions would have existed in the past for the same reasons that they are maintained today.

The tales regarding the unity of Maluku were regarded as "true" in Mircea Eliade's sense that they speak of sacred occurrences which are the only "indubitable reality."[9] They were also "true" in the Malukan sense of the word. In Tidore there is a term *madihutu*, which can be glossed as "genuine" or "true." When it is used to qualify a word, it implies that the particular thing being qualified is original and hence genuine. The telling of a "true tale," such as narrating a group's history in a ritual context, is said to transform the relationship between the teller and the audience. The latter no longer exercises any questioning or skepticism but instead receives the narrator's words as "true." To "tell the history" is *fato*, meaning to "place into order, or give order," and is the same word from which the title of the traditional leader, the bobato ("that which gives order"), derives.[10] The telling of "true tales" or "history" appears to be linked to the conception of creation or the establishing of order out of a primeval chaos or confusion. These tales are thus told and received as "true" in the sense that they deal with the original/genuine stories of the beginnings of the group.

The earliest "true" tale describing the creation of a unified island community comes from François Valentijn's work entitled, *Oud en Nieuw Oost-Indiën* (Old and New East-Indies), published in Amsterdam in 1724–1726:

In the beginning the island [of Ternate] was undeveloped and only very lightly populated. The earliest settlement was Tobona, which was located on the top of the mountain and founded by a headman called Guna. One day as Guna went to the forests to tap the sugar palm to make toddy *(tuak)*, he came across a golden mortar and pestle. He brought it back to the village, and it soon became an object of great curiosity. So many people came to see this remarkable phenomenon that he could no longer cope. He therefore decided to give it to Momole Matiti, who was head of the village of Foramadiahi, halfway down the mountain. Once Momole Matiti accepted the unusual object, he too was besieged with visitors so that he in turn gave it to Cico, head of the coastal village of Sampalu. Although many came to Sampalu to view the golden mortar and pestle, Cico was able to deal with them admirably and was honored by all the other heads of the island. He was therefore asked to become the principal head with the title of *kolano,* or lord.[11]

The prominence given to the mortar and pestle in this Malukan myth may have an ancient significance. Peter Bellwood, a noted Pacific prehistorian, observed that stone pestles and mortars formed "one of the most enigmatic classes of prehistoric artefacts from New Guinea" and the basis for the so-called New Guinea-Bismark pestle and mortar complex.[12] They may have been sacred objects in a megalithic culture, traces of which were still evident in Nias and Bali in the early twentieth century. In these megalithic cultures a large monolith was placed upright, while before it was placed a flat horizontal stone. The male-female symbolism expressed in the arrangement of these megaliths was retained when Indian ideas penetrated Southeast Asia in the first millennium and a half of the Christian era. The upright stones became merged with the Hindu god Shiva and represented his phallus, the *lingam,* while the horizontal stones became the female counterpart, known as the *yoni.*[13] While the fertility symbolism of the mortar and pestle would have been apparent to the Malukans, it appears that they may also have noted the resemblance of the clove to mortar and pestle. On parts of the island of Makian, for example, the word *odai* is used for both the clove and the rice stamper.[14] The latter object, together with the base, resembles a larger version of a mortar and pestle. It is possible that the Malukans may have interpreted the golden mortar and pestle to mean the riches brought by the clove. The myth appears to be describing the process in which the demand for cloves encouraged the relocation of the principal settlement from the mountaintop to the coast.

In keeping with the symbolism of the myth, the headman is known as "Guna," a Malay word meaning "fortune." He was able to find the extraordinary and spiritually potent golden mortar and pestle precisely because he possessed the unique spiritual quality inherent in the idea of *guna*. The identification of individuals of "prowess," who possess that unique quality or "soul-stuff" to effect change, is well documented in Southeast Asian history. They possess such names as Hang Tuah ("Lord of Fortune") or Phumiphon ("Person of Merit") to indicate their special status.[15] In the Pacific the generally used term is *mana,* an ancient concept associated with the Austronesian-speaking peoples (the ancestors of the Malukans) to refer to those favored by the gods. Because many observers tend to focus on the effects rather than on the intrinsic nature of this quality, the term is often translated as "luck" or "success" or "fortune."[16] Guna can be seen as the Ternaten culture hero who discovers the golden mortar and pestle which transforms the island. The use of a Malay name would not have been unusual because of the prestige of the kingdom of Melaka in the fifteenth and early sixteenth centuries. Many distant courts, including those of Maluku, adopted some of the customs, dress, and language of the Malays in emulation of Melaka.[17]

This seventeenth century tale captures in essence the process by which the people on Ternate under their various heads *(momole)* became united under a kolano. Similar myths are found on the other major islands in north Maluku. In the early sixteenth century, for example, the Portuguese recorded a Tidore tradition recalling a time when the original settlement was sited on the mountain at Mareku. It then moved to the coast because of foreign traders coming in large numbers in search of the clove.[18] Mareku remained a sacred center to the Tidorese in later centuries because of its prestige as the source of Tidore's first rulers.

A second type of tradition deals with the unity of a specific area larger than the individual islands. The Dutch governor in Ternate, Robertus Padtbrugge, in his *Memorie van Overgave* (Outgoing Report) to his successor in 1682, mentioned the following epithets which were commonly known among the Malukans:

Loloda, Ngara ma-beno (Loloda, Wall of the Gate)
Jailolo, Jiko ma-kolano (Jailolo, Ruler of the Bay)
Tidore, Kië ma-kolano (Tidore, Ruler of the Mountain)
Ternate, Kolano ma-luku (Ternate, Ruler of Maluku)
Bacan, Kolano ma-dehe (Bacan, Ruler of the Far End)

The antiquity of these titles was not only evident in the inability of any local informant at the time to explain their meanings adequately, but also by the inclusion of Loloda. While a Raja Loloda still existed, his kingdom had disappeared long before the arrival of the Europeans. At first glance the meanings given appear to be based purely on geographical considerations. Loloda's title was popularly interpreted as "the beginning" since it was located in the north at the "beginning" of Maluku. With Loloda as the "gate" or "the beginning" in the north, Bacan was logically the "far end" or "exit" in the south. Both Jailolo's and Tidore's titles seemed to be mere recognition of the fact that Jailolo is located on a bay and Tidore has the largest and most prominent mountain in north Maluku. What was easiest to explain in the seventeenth century was the identification of Ternate with the epithet, "Ruler of Maluku" in acknowledgment of its preeminent position in Maluku.

If one were to examine these names more closely, however, one would be able to recognize in them a survival of another "true" tale now long forgotten but still retained in an incomplete form in these epithets. In creation myths there is often a description of a time when there was frequent intercourse among those inhabiting the three different spheres of life—the Upperworld, the Earth, and the Lowerworld. The Upperworld is depicted as being separated from the Earth by a wall. It is through the gate in the wall that access is gained. Loloda's title, "Wall of the Gate," is perhaps a reference to the gate dividing the Upperworld and the Earth within the world of Maluku. Similarly, in creation myths the gate to the nether regions is often referred to as the "farthest end," the "exit." Bacan was therefore regarded as the "exit," or the gateway to the Lowerworld. In this cosmological scheme, Loloda represents the Upperworld and Bacan the Lowerworld, hence forming an upper/lower dualism. In the middle is the Earth occupied by the remaining three kingdoms, with Jailolo being identified with the sea and Tidore the land, forming a bay/sea-mountain/land dualism. Ternate occupies the center linking both dualisms into a whole. Its epithet, "Ruler of Maluku," refers to its pivotal position in the universe known as "Maluku."

In the late seventeenth century the Dutch noted that, although the ruler of Tidore was the *Kië ma-kolano* (Lord of the Mountain), his more common title was *Kaicili'* (Lord) *Maluku,* a form of address which he shared with the ruler of Ternate. What the Dutch were observing was the operation of the Ternate/Tidore dualism, beyond doubt the most significant of the dualisms in Maluku in this period. Both were referred to as lords of Maluku and as lords of the mountain, each being seen as forming complementary halves of the society. The dualism was also expressed in the form of an East/West opposition which became evident in the expansion of these kingdoms. Ternate's fields of conquests were generally in the West, while Tidore's were in the East. The unity of the area of north Maluku could therefore be formulated in another way through reference to the four cardinal points: Jailolo (N), Bacan (S), Ternate (W), and Tidore (E).

A third tradition concerns a still larger unity embracing the wider world of Maluku. The earliest surviving version of this Maluku myth is in Portuguese and was recorded by Antonio Galvão between 1536 and 1539. He commented that the local inhabitants had no tradition of written chronicles or histories but preserved their past in "aphorisms, songs, and rhyming ballads, of which they are very fond." The tale, the inhabitants told Galvão, was true, as were all their "poetic fables." In this "true tale" the setting is the southernmost clove-producing island of Bacan:

Once long ago there were no kings and the people lived in kinship groups (Port., *parentela*) governed by elders. Since "no one was better than the other," dissension and wars arose, alliances made and broken, and people killed or captured and ransomed. In time some became more powerful than others, captains and governors were created, but there were still no kings. One day a prominent elder of the island, named Bikusagara, went sailing on a kora-kora [a local double-outrigger vessel]. He spied a clump of beautiful rattan growing near a precipice by the sea and sent his men ashore to cut some stalks. When they arrived at the spot, the rattan was nowhere to be seen, and so they returned to the kora-kora. Exasperated, Bikusagara himself went ashore and immediately located the clump of rattan. He ordered his men to cut down some of the stalks, but as soon as they started to hack into the rattan, blood gushed forth from the cuts. Startled by this strange phenomenon, Bikusagara jumped back and noticed nearby four *naga* [serpent] eggs hidden among the rocks. When he approached these eggs he heard a voice ordering him to take the eggs home with him because from them would emerge individuals of great distinction. Mindful of the command Bikusagara carefully placed the eggs in a *totombo* [a rattan box] and brought them home where they were guarded with great care. After some time the eggs brought forth three males and a female. When they grew up one of the men became the king of Bacan, the second the king of the Papuas, the third the king of Butung and Banggai, and the woman became the wife of the king of Loloda. From these original four descended all the kings of these islands, "and ever since they have paid great honor to Bikusagara and to the rocky precipice, and they consider them a very holy thing, consecrated to the gods."[19]

By Galvão's time Bacan, the Papuas, Butung-Banggai, and Loloda were politically insignificant, and yet the tale was still being recited because its message of unity continued to be meaningful to the group.

The theme of a person with unusual spiritual skills revealing the presence of the god in a material object is widespread in monsoon Asia. He or she becomes responsible for restoring the severed links between the Upperworld and the Earth. The special gift from the gods enables this rare individual to assume a position of importance in the community as a religious and later a secular leader.[20] Bikusagara's special quality is evident in his "revelation" of the sacred rattan. The image of the rattan, or in other Indonesian tales the bamboo, is usually associated with the spiritual forces of the land which provide the progenitors of a ruling dynasty.[21] The discovery of the naga eggs in the rocky precipice by the sea combines all the elements of the Underworld so prominent in this tale. The naga is an ancient mythic element found in India and Southeast Asia associated with snake spirits and centered around sacred sites. The rocks, too, form a familiar feature in Southeast Asian belief, for they are regarded as partial manifestations of the earth deity.[22] Through the recitation of these sacred elements, this tale was regarded as "true" and as legitimizing the boundaries of the Malukan world and the peoples who belonged to it. By the first half of the sixteenth century new political alignments and power centers were already coming into existence which no longer reflected the central importance of these areas. Yet the tale continued to be recounted precisely because it dealt with sacred activities creating exemplary models for the group within the wider Maluku world.

In all of the myths mentioned here, the clove, the mortar and pestle, the mountain and the sea, and the naga and the eggs form a male/female sexual or fertility metaphor for the unity of the world of Maluku. The ruler or kolano is characterized by his possession of "fortune," enabling him to control the golden mortar and pestle which is the symbol of the clove and the reproductive capacity of the community. Historical sources confirm this imagery of wealth resulting from the clove trade and of communities providing women for the ruler. In the opposite direction flow prestige items in the form of imported cloth, iron, and other goods, as well as titles and institutions. The maintenance of this male/female relationship thus becomes the guarantee of the continuing prosperity and well-being of the whole group.

What is equally significant about these myths is the creation of a cultural boundary defining those who belong to the "family" of Maluku. Though the myths describe unities at different levels, each is linked with the others to form the largest area of inclusiveness known as Maluku. There is no mention of a political unity, and the emphasis is clearly on the separate parts. At each level the sacred four, with occasionally an added fifth to represent the center, form the boundary of the group. In north Maluku in this period the survival of the "four pillars or kingdoms" was regarded as crucial to the spiritual well-being of the community. The number four signifies totality and perfection in Maluku and appears to have been a feature of the Austronesian-speaking peoples.[23] In southwest Sulawesi the significance of four is even applied to the explanation of its writing system to imbue it with greater significance.[24] The Papuan Raja Ampat islanders also symbolize whole-ness and perfection in the number four, although this may have been due to their historical links with north Maluku.[25]

Dualism features prominently in each of these myths, and even today one encounters use of dual (paired) words and phrases in ritual speech and song in Tidore.[26] The existence of dualisms in north Maluku accords with the presence in many eastern Indonesian cultures of systems of complementary dual classifications. These social and cos-mological dualisms consist of asymmetric relationships among ordered pairs, such that "wife-giver" may be seen as superior to "wife-taker," "elder" as superior to "younger," and so forth. It has been suggested that the dualistic perception of the world in this area may be due to the pervasive parallelisms found in many of the languages of eastern Indo-nesia.[27] In north Maluku during the period under study it was believed that the survival and prosperity of the society depended on the proper functioning of these dualisms.

The most significant dualism was that between Ternate and Tidore located at the epicenter of the world defined as Maluku. Both the sultans of Ternate and Tidore claimed the title "Lord of Maluku," with Tidore in the ritual role as wife-giver to Ternate.[28] They repre-sented opposing and complementary tendencies which were considered necessary for the survival and prosperity of the community. The Euro-peans were clearly puzzled by the relationship. Despite the sworn enmity between these two kingdoms, they continued to advise each other against any European activity which could threaten the other's well-being.[29] In the mid-sixteenth century the practice of intermarriage between the royal houses of Ternate and Tidore was so well established that Galvão assumed that "the king of Ternate has to marry a daughter of the king of Tidore."[30] Even in the midst of war, intercourse between the people of the two kingdoms continued. The dualism of Ternate and Tidore within the tradition of the "four" kingdoms was viewed as essential for the survival of the group. Sultan Saifuddin of Tidore (r. 1657–1687), well regarded as an expert on Malukan traditions, frequently reminded the Malukans and the Dutch that as long as the two pillars—Ternate and Tidore—remained, all was well with Maluku.

Creation of the Center

The origin myths identified a world whose center was justifiably located around the clove-producing islands of north Maluku, for it was the clove trade which assured this area's dominance. Until the arrival of Europeans, arrangements for the delivery of cloves were simple but sat-isfactory. Each village had its own area of clove trees, and each household regarded particular trees as its own. People would harvest their trees by breaking clove-bearing branches and then carrying them in baskets to waiting ships to be exchanged for foreign goods. The Portuguese brought an end to this system by insisting that only the more valuable *cravo de cabeça* ("head of the clove") and not the lower-quality *cravo de bastão* ("stalk of the clove") be purchased. Eager to maintain the lucrative market with the Portuguese, the local leaders agreed to institute this new method of gathering and preparing the clove in the early sixteenth century.[31]

The Portuguese demand for larger quantities and better quality cloves required greater planning and organization than previously. The clove heads had to be separated from the stalks, dried, and bagged in readiness for the regularly scheduled arrival of the Portuguese ships. The Portuguese also sought to assure a uniform system by requiring that all measuring devices for cloves be destroyed and only two maintained: one to be kept by the Portuguese, the other by the local ruler. Since the return route for the Portuguese went via Melaka to Goa and then on to Portugal, the timing of the monsoon winds was of particular importance. The Portuguese therefore demanded that the cloves be ready for loading within a fairly tight schedule. To meet these requirements, new Malukan officials were appointed or old positions assigned new duties in order to oversee the smooth functioning of the clove trade.

From the end of August to November, both Portuguese and Malukans would harvest the clove forests on the various islands. The eviction of the Portuguese from Ternate in 1575 had little impact on the spice trade since they continued to operate from their new base in Tidore. For the greater part of the sixteenth century the Portuguese accounted for about 75 percent or more of the spices brought to Europe, and the 1570s and 1580s marked a resurgence in the trade after a decade of declining sales.[32] With the withdrawal of the Portuguese from Ternate, many foreign groups which had been forbidden by the Portuguese to trade there returned and contributed to the resurgence of Ternate as an entrepôt. A Spanish document dated 1584 reported the vitality of Ternate where ordinarily some thousand Javanese, Sangleys (Chinese from the Philippines), and Acehnese came to trade. In response to increasing demand from foreign traders, the Ternatens were once again sailing to East Seram (a term used to indicate the eastern end and offshore islands of Seram, plus the Goram and Seram Laut archipelagoes) to sell their cloves to Javanese, Malay, and Turkish traders.[33]

Initially, international trade was comfortably incorporated into the traditional ritual exchange. Galvão described a long-established practice whereby products of the land were first delivered to the ruler via an official known as the *pinate* and then later consumed in a community feast.[34] Such ceremonies are well-known in anthropological literature and are interpreted as a symbolic exchange reaffirming the bonds between the people and their chiefs. The "raw" products offered by the people to the ruler represent an acknowledgment of the latter's rights to the first fruits of the land. The products are prepared or "cooked" literally and symbolically on behalf of the ruler, who thus domesticates or "socializes" the natural goods and people.[35] European desire to centralize the collection of spices simply added cloves to the list of "raw" products presented by the *ngofagamu*, or the "people of the land," to the ruler. The "cooked" exchange redistributed by the ruler was in the form of imported textiles, ceramics, iron implements and weapons.

By the middle of the seventeenth century, the intensity of international trade had contributed to a growing disparity in the exchange between the ruler and the people. There was a vastly increased wealth at court and a correspondingly greater poverty and dependence among the people. What exacerbated the situation was the introduction of the VOC's *extirpatie* ("eradication") policy for the destruction of all spice trees and the payment of compensation primarily to the ruler. With compensation rendered in cloth, iron, and other much desired foreign goods, the ruler obtained the means to create an economic and social gap between himself and his people.[36] The imbalance in turn led to a transformation of the exchange from a ritual one based on spiritual values to a purely economic one based on profit and power, favoring the ruler. The change was signaled by the disappearance or absorption of the indigenous post of pinate into a position with the foreign title of *syahbandar.* The office of syahbandar was instituted by the court to handle the thriving international trade in cloves in Maluku, and its status rose in direct proportion to the wealth flowing to the port.

A second important factor which contributed to the growing strength of the center was Islam. The ruler of Ternate was the first to embrace the new religion sometime in the last quarter of the fifteenth century. According to Ternaten traditions Java was the source and inspiration of the new religion in north Maluku. A Javanese trader named Hussein is credited with the introduction of the faith to Ternate, while a later Javanese priest from Giri is acknowledged as "the most important propagator of that religion in this region."[37] Nevertheless, Galvão noted sometime between 1536 and 1539 that Islam was confined principally to the ruler, his family, and those of his followers.[38] This situation had not changed radically since Pires's observations two decades earlier that, though the Malukan rulers were Muslim, three-fourths of the people remained unconverted.[39] Despite the apparent lack of success in the spread of Islam, the sources indicate a gradual acceptance of this creed among the people of north Maluku through the efforts of the court.

The ruler of Ternate in the early sixteenth century began the practice of appointing a brother or relative to the post of *kali,* or chief Islamic official of the kingdom. As Islam grew in importance, two new posts were created which bore the Islamic title *hukum.*[40] The hukum served as administrators and magistrates and became increasingly important as representatives of the center in its newly developing relationship to the periphery. These new Islamic posts remained outside the indigenous sociopolitical structure and came to offer their allegiance directly to the ruler. Islam also brought major economic benefits and prestige to the center since Muslim traders and scholars preferred to go to ports where they were assured a mosque for worship and the protection of a Muslim ruler.

European notions of the proper authority of kings were another factor contributing to the creation of a Maluku center. Because the Europeans assumed that the north Malukan rulers possessed privileges and powers similar to those of their royal counterparts in Europe, they sought to make all economic and political arrangements directly with them. If duties were to be paid, they were paid to the royal treasury; if arms were to be sold, they were sold to the ruler; if any private trading arrangements were made, they were done with the knowledge of the ruler. Letters were exchanged between the Malukan sultans and the kings of Europe, placing the former, at least on paper and in the eyes of the Europeans, within the exclusive category of royal beings as understood in Europe. Any formal political arrangements, such as treaties, could therefore be legitimized only by these rulers. As a consequence the Malukan sultans were treated with a dignity not shared by other local kolanos. Treaties became a useful vehicle for clever rulers to call legitimately upon the Europeans to accomplish political goals, such as maintaining order within their borders or suppressing "rebels." The frequency of "rebellions" in the sixteenth century was more an indication of a ruler's reliance on the European treaty than a phenomenon of increasing dissatisfaction among local communities. In the art of diplomacy, as in the art of war, the Malukans proved to be excellent students of the Europeans. By the last quarter of the sixteenth century, the Malukan rulers were becoming much more like the image which the Europeans projected of kings. Sultan Hairun of Ternate dressed like a Portuguese, spoke their language fluently, and governed his kingdom with an assurance bred of long familiarity and friendship with Portuguese officials. The Portuguese, and later the Dutch and the English, continued to deal almost exclusively with these sultans, assuring them unimpeded access to foreign goods and the ability to preserve the center's prestige.

As a result of the clove trade and Islam, as well as European perceptions of royal authority, the kingdoms of Ternate, Tidore, Jailolo, and Bacan came to be acknowledged as the "center" of an expanding Malukan world. In the process, however, there arose a steadily widening social and economic gap between the officials in the court and the people of the land.

The Court

Changes in authority within the court are best documented for Ternate because it was the major focus of European activity in this period. Galvão's comments about the Ternaten court were strongly influenced by Portuguese experience with Islam and by an older Christian European attitude toward that religion. Moreover, he was convinced that "the creed of the Muslim is well known to all of us."[41] In describing the position of sultan, he repeated a formula which was taken directly from his understanding of Muslim practice. The succession, he explained, went to the eldest male child born of the "noblest" legal wife, as long as he was without physical disabilities. "And among both noblemen and common people all is inherited by the eldest, at least if he is a male; for among the Moors [that is, Muslims] no woman is able to come into an inheritance."[42] Because Galvão regarded the rulers as Muslims first and Malukans second, he relied on his knowledge of Islam rather than on his direct observations to characterize Malukan kingship. Yet Galvão's own description of events in Maluku, as well as those of other contemporary European observers, depicted a kingship which had much more to do with indigenous ideas of leadership than with a formalized and idealized view of Islamic sultans.

In Galvão's description of Ternate's leaders, he used the title *kolano* for ruler. Kolano is not a native Malukan word but is probably a loanword from Javanese. In the Panji tales (Panji is the East Javanese version of Arjuna, "the ideal noble prince, invincible in battle and irresistible in love") a prominent figure is Klono (Klana), who is described as a king from overseas.[43] Since it was from East Java that the impetus came which transformed cloves from a rare spice obtained through occasional exchange to a major international commodity traded in major centers, it appears likely that the Malukan title kolano originated from the popular Javanese Panji personage Klono (Klana), who is depicted as the worthy foreign royal adversary of the Javanese rulers.

Galvão also spoke of kolanos as leaders of individual domains and occupying the highest rung of the social hierarchy. With Islam the position of sultan arose from the kolano group, and as kolano the sultan had direct allegiance only from his own domain as its traditional leader. Some of the other kolanos received the official title of *sangaji,* which comes from the Javanese *sang,* an honorific reserved for heroes, demigods, kings, and other dignitaries, and *aji,* meaning "king." As sangajis they acknowledged their political subservience to the sultan, but as kolanos they retained equal social status. The bobatos were heads of sociopolitical units or *soas* aggregated into residential sections within the sultan's or the sangajis' domains. Politically, at the very highest rung was the sultan as religious and political leader of the kingdom, followed by the sangajis and other kolanos who governed their own traditional domains, then the bobatos as heads of soas within these lands.

In 1523 a Portuguese long resident in Maluku described the kings, meaning the sultans, as being rulers in name only. He observed that, while the people paid them reverence, they would only perform services when it suited them. As a result these "kings" had little income, no more than any other "noble" person.[44] These comments reflect a common misinterpretation of the sultan's position in society. The Portuguese could only judge the institution of kingship in terms of their own, and they found it difficult to distinguish between the role of the sultan as a political head of the land and his role as leader of his own domain. He was shown the respect given to all those who occupied the social status as kolano, but direct allegiance and services came from his own particular territorial jurisdiction. There would have been little to distinguish a sultan from the other kolanos, except on the occasions when he was acting as a political leader for the whole kingdom and thus provided by the other kolanos with the authority to act as the highest political voice in the land.

Other early observers of Malukan kingship were Antonio Serrão, Antonio Pigafetta, and Maximilian Transylvania. Serrão's reports were based on his experiences as the first European to reach Ternate in 1512 and as a trusted advisor of the ruler. Pigafetta was a member of Magellan's expedition and recorded what he saw in Maluku in 1521, while Transylvania wrote his account after interviewing the survivors of this epic journey. Like other travel accounts by their contemporaries, the reports consisted of a combination of personal experience and received wisdom regarding the East.[45] All three agreed that the individual who occupied the position of sultan was one who had to demonstrate his ability to assume such a responsibility. One of the qualities admired and encouraged in a sultan was physical prowess. In wartime it was customary to see the ruler at the front of his men.[46] The Sultan Jailolo was admired for being "very powerful" and a great fighter in his youth, while the Sultan Tidore was similarly praised for being "well built."[47]

Spiritual potency, another attribute desired in a ruler, was measured in terms of oratorical ability and the gift of prognostication. Serrão reported that Sultan Abu Lais of Ternate was considered to be a living oracle by his people. The arrival of the Portuguese was seen as the fulfillment of his prophecy that from a distant part of the globe would come men of iron who would become inhabitants of his land and use their power to extend "the dominion and glory of Maluku."[48] Pigafetta made an identical claim for the Sultan Tidore, reputed to be an excellent astrologer who had predicted the coming of the Spaniards. The sultan told Pigafetta of a dream some time before which foretold the arrival in his land of ships from remote parts. Seeking further assurance, he had consulted the moon and had seen the ships, which were indeed those of the Spaniards.[49] In Maluku, dreams were regarded as the means by which spirits and the gods communicated with human beings, and to be chosen as the mouthpiece for the dreams was a revered position. This was a belief well known in Indonesian and Pacific Island societies,[50] and one which was shared by sixteenth century Europeans.[51]

The gift of oratory was another sign of spiritual power in north Maluku's basically oral society. Galvão observed that those in the islands "have no chronicles nor [written] history and they keep no archives. As far as I understood from them, they commit their past to memory by way of aphorisms [motes], songs [cantigas], and rhyming ballads [trovas], of which they are very fond. They make good ones which are handed down from one to another like the Hebrews used to do."[52] Although the Perso-Arabic script had been introduced with the adoption of Islam in the late fifteenth century, its use was still very limited by the beginning of the sixteenth century. When the Sultan Tidore sent an envoy to deliver an oral message to the Portuguese, he asked that credit be given to his words "because they are not accustomed to writing." The casises,[53] or Islamic religious teachers, wrote on planks which were painted over as soon as the lessons were completed. If the need arose, palm leaves and paper imported from India were used for writing, using pens made of ferns and ink from China.[54] Both formal and informal communication, however, continued to be conducted principally through oral means.

The Sultan Tidore was admired as one who possessed "a royal presence and eloquence." The pairing of attributes in that single phrase reflected the high esteem with which the spoken word was regarded. Oratorical ability was an especially useful asset in a society where government was conducted through consultation and consensus in open assembly. But the value of the orator transcended mundane considerations for greater spiritual concerns. In many societies in eastern Indonesia today in ceremonies involving oration, important words are said to generate "heat" and considered powerful and dangerous. Thus those who are able to "take the voice" are regarded with great respect.[55] The same attitude toward those blessed with the gift of controlling words for the benefit of the society may have been the reason for Malukans citing oratory as one of the most important attributes of a ruler.

Until the first half of the sixteenth century, the dominant practice of personal achievement as the basis for a ruler's status was evident despite the Islamic emphasis on primogeniture in inheritance and succession. An examination of the Portuguese sources reveals a pattern in which a kolano was appointed sultan according to Islamic law, but actual power was wielded by a powerful relative who was called a "regent" by the Portuguese.[56] By adhering to primogeniture and providing the sultan with the full regalia and outward symbols of kingship, the Ternatens were able to satisfy both the Muslims at court and the powerful Portuguese officials resident in Ternate. Ternaten sensibilities and proprieties were also preserved by the appointment of a "regent," continuing the usual local inheritance pattern of leadership which went to the most capable individual in the ruler's large extended family. In the first half of the sixteenth century the indigenous political pattern was maintained, although it was beginning to be modified by Islamic practice.

Islam provided the newest and perhaps the most important basis of royal authority in Maluku. It offered an effective spiritual counter to the local gods and a new rationale for the ruler's superiority. To add to his spiritual armory a newly Islamicized ruler could use the title of sultan, along with the awe-inspiring Persian-derived epithet "The Shadow of Allah on the Earth" *(zill Allah fi'l-alam)* or even the Sufi appellation "The Perfect Man" *(al-Insan al Kamil)*. Moreover, he was acknowledged as leader of the new Islamic officialdom and acted as religious teacher to his people.[57] Islam's emphasis on patrilineality and primogeniture forestalled any challenges to the existing leadership since it confirmed as heir the eldest son of the reigning leader, provided that he had no physical or mental handicaps and was born of a woman legally married by the laws of Islam.[58] The Islamic royal model came increasingly to challenge the indigenous one, in which achievement and a certain degree of ascription associated with founding families were paramount.

The economic advantage of embracing Islam would have been obvious to any Malukan ruler. Rich and powerful Muslim kingdoms in the western half of the archipelago, India, and the Middle East promised to be a source of trade goods and even military support to a newly Islamicized kingdom. Signs of wealth from this international trade were clearly visible when Magellan's crew reached north Maluku in 1521. They noted that, when Sultan Tidore came to visit the Spaniards in their ship, he was in a boat "seated under a silk awning which sheltered him on all sides. In front of him was one of his sons with the royal scepter, two persons with gold jars to pour water on his hands, and two others with gilded caskets filled with their betel."[59] At another time his arrival was heralded by the playing of gongs.[60] Imported Chinese silk, gold ornaments, and copper gongs were now a common part of the ruler's possessions.

The unique status of the rulers was reinforced by a number of privileged practices. The Sultan Tidore explained to the Spaniards that it was not customary for rulers to leave their island, though he had made an exception for the Spaniards. On the rare occasion when this happened, he asked the neighboring sultans, including his enemies, to give him a fishing line, a drum *(tifa)*, and a few other symbolic objects. In this way he could depart without fear because he was being given an assurance that his sovereignty, his lands and waters, and all therein would be safeguarded. Every household had to provide him with one or two daughters, and he rewarded faithful followers with titles, weapons, houses, villages, and towns.[61] Only the sultan's brothers and sisters were allowed to use the title of *kaicili* (for men) and *naicili* (for women) when in his presence.

The royal *baileu,* which was a type of reception hall located at the front of the ruler's residence, was square, taller than the average, and covered with spires. On all sides were low verandas or galleries for those who served him. It was covered with various carpets and cotton and silk patterned cloths called *patola.* The baileu of the ordinary person, which served as a place of relaxation and to greet guests, stood on legs like a bed and was narrow and long with a veranda. The floors were made of bamboo, and the four-sided roof was thatched with palm leaves. In the ruler's baileu only his "ministers" and their sons were allowed entry. It was here that the king greeted and entertained exalted visitors. In the sitting arrangement in the royal baileu, the most honored guest sat closest to the ruler, then his brothers, the sangajis, and finally the "ministers" according to rank. These "ministers" were those who served the ruler within his own domain and had only restricted authority in the domains of the sangajis or provincial lords.[62]

The rulers and the sangajis lived mostly by the seashore or along a river in houses constructed on four poles with a ladder which could be withdrawn at night. A large entrance, like an oversize window, opened out onto a small, low, one-storied house with two rooms and a reception hall in the middle. The floor was made of bamboo and fastened with rattans; the roofs were two-, three- or four-sided and thatched with the leaves or the dark-brown hairlike fiber of the sugar palm. It was surrounded by a bamboo hedge with parapets. For furnishings there were beds with legs, which were introduced from India, with covers, carpets, and leather cushions. Though Galvão contemptuously referred to these houses as resembling birdcages, they were far grander than those of the ordinary people and therefore fulfilled the need to demonstrate the distinction between the groups. The commoners built their houses on the ground with earthen floors and split bamboo walls, and they slept on mats on the floor. Furnishings would have been of local origin or of an inferior quality of imported goods.[63]

The utensils and clothing of the ruler were distinctive as well. He used imported gold cups, porcelain pitchers, finger bowls, copper jugs, and small vessels of porcelain and bronze. The commoners, on the other hand, used banana or palm leaves for plates; for cups they used leaves wrapped around to form a cone and attached by a sliver of wood. To further emphasize the ruler's special status, a yellow patterned bark-cloth was tied to his cups. Yellow was reserved exclusively for royalty, and the act of wrapping, binding, or containment was associated with the sacred.[64] This Malukan practice may have originated in a distant Austronesian past, for similar attitudes were found in the Pacific. In Polynesia yellow barkcloth (tapa) was used in religious and other cere-monies for status enhancement, and in Hawaii only the chiefs were allowed to wear a yellow tapa loincloth. The association of tapa with the gods may have arisen because the bark was taken from certain trees regarded as sacred. In addition the act of wrapping the sacred cloth around an individual or image of the gods represented the act of bind-ing the object with all the sacred powers and presence of the gods. The ritual significance of barkcloth is explicit in Fiji, where it is hung at the rear or sacred end of the temple to serve as "the path of the god" when the deity descends to enter the priest.[65]

The resplendent dress of the ruler further reflected his superior status. On special occasions he wore a fine gold-embroidered silk or cot-ton outer garment with an open short waistcoat and gold buttons. For a covering on his head he had a round cap with gold-leaf adornments or a headdress, consisting of a cloth from fine Bengal muslin or other equally valuable fabrics, wound around the head and known by the Malay term destar. When he went out umbrellas of Chinese silk were held over him. The jewelry also befitted his status: many objects were made of gold, a metal of great rarity and of a natural yellow, or royal, color.[66] More important than the material value attached to these rare objects was the association of jewelry with amulets and gold with royalty, thus symboli-cally representing the ruler's potent spiritual protection over the whole society.[67]

The exalted position of the king was emphasized at his installation ceremony. The prominent men in the domain came to offer the sembah-yang, which is an obeisance performed by placing the palms of the hands together and raising them to the forehead in a gesture of great respect. They then kissed his feet and ended with another sembahyang. The ruler was brought to the mosque in a procession headed by a red and white pennant wound around a bamboo staff about 3 meters ("thirty palms") long and accompanied by sword-bearing men. Music was pro-vided by an ensemble consisting of Javanese bronze gongs hung on wooden poles, small drums (tifa), an oboe-like instrument (serunai), flutes, and others. During the course of these ceremonies, the alifuru, the interior inhabitants of Halmahera, performed the ritual dance

called the *lego-lego* at the gates of the ruler's residence. The ceremony
ended with the conducting of the king back to his residence.[68]

Echoing an earlier observation made by a compatriot in 1523,
Galvão remarked that the kolano had hardly any income "because the
country produces nothing but cloves, which is exchanged for all types of
merchandise and cloths from India."[69] In this instance, as in others
interspersed in his account of Maluku, Galvão understandably interpreted what he saw or what he was told in accordance with his own cultural perception. The lack of substantial amounts of local currency
caused Galvão to conclude that the ruler had little income. Yet it was the
principal exchange in cloves which was the key to Maluku's prosperity
and influence in the region. In addition to cloth from India and elsewhere, cloves were exchanged for weapons. The Malukans had Javanese krisses, or daggers, two-handed swords, lances, surcoats, coats of
mail, cuirasses, habergeons, shields, bucklers, helmets, bombards, and
muskets, which they imported from Melaka, Java, and Banda. They
also obtained saltpeter and gunpowder from the Spaniards, and most
probably from other Indonesian areas such as Java. Crucial to the success of this exchange were the Halmahera alifuru and the *ngofangares*,
subjects who were regarded as having a special relationship with the
ruler. The Sultans Ternate and Tidore accumulated properties in areas
away from their residence and often on the coast of Halmahera, lands
which were poor and "neither worked, nor turned, nor harrowed for
lack of iron and of animals." These fields were tilled by the alifuru and
ngofangares, who provided the rulers' sago bread, meat, palm wine,
fish, areca, betel, and all other needs including spoons, firewood, and
water.[70] But most importantly they were responsible for harvesting the
clove in the ruler's lands, thus enabling the kings to obtain the foreign
goods necessary to attract and retain a large following.

The transformation of the ruler's position and his new pretensions
reinforced by sumptuary laws may have elicited the observation in later
years that these rulers were "foreign and not well loved."[71] But in fact
the Portuguese appear to have been repeating a Malukan traditional
formula which emphasized the ruler's unique position. The idea of a
"stranger-king" who stands both outside and within society is prominent in Malukan myths, and the use of a foreign title *kolano* reinforces
that perception. The myth of the establishment of Ternate's royal family
gives the founder the Malay name of Guna ("Fortune"), indicating that
he possessed special qualities and that he may have been foreign. In the
Bikusagara tale from Bacan, the kings of Maluku are provided with a
similar foreign and unique origin from the naga eggs. Later traditions
incorporate Islam into the tale of the establishment of kingship within
north Maluku, but the emphasis is still on the foreign "heavenly" origin of royalty.[72]

Though these myths collected by the Europeans do not provide sufficient detail to establish a systematic analysis of the relationships between the stranger-kings and the indigenous societies, the evidence points to a common theme found in traditions of both the Indo-Europeans and Austronesian-speakers. It is of the stranger-king from the sea (foreign origin) who marries the daughter of the local lord and thereby gains access to the land. The original mythical/historical union of the stranger-king from the sea with the daughter of the lord of the land is symbolically reenacted in each subsequent reign to reaffirm the two complementary forces which assure the fertility and well-being of the community. This process is described by Dumézil for Indo-European societies in terms of the opposing forces of *celeritas* and *gravitas*. The former is regarded as the active force, youthful, disorderly, magical, violent and associated with the conquering prince; the latter is the passive force, venerable, orderly, priestly, peaceful, and associated with the productive capacities of the established people. Through the merging of both comes sovereign power which balances these two forces and makes possible the proper functioning of government.[73]

In Maluku a similar process was described by the Portuguese who arrived in the area in the beginning of the sixteenth century. The practice of the king having a woman from each of the villages was interpreted by the Portuguese as part of a Muslim ruler's practice of establishing a harem. For Malukans, however, it was the sacred reenactment of the vital union between the first foreign king and their ancestor, reaffirming the ruler's continuing access to the fruits of the land. The reenactment of the original exchange occurred annually with the people bringing produce to the sultan in the form of spices, sago bread, meat, wine, fish, areca, betel, utensils, firewood, water, labor, and women. In return the ruler reciprocated by redistributing imported prestige items, such as cloth, iron, and porcelain. The exchange was not simply one of goods but of spiritual values and was understood in much the same way as that between the Sultan Tidore and his subjects, the Papuans of the Raja Ampat islands. The Papuans brought the objects of their *rak,* or head-hunting expeditions, and other products of the sea to the sultan, who in turn reciprocated with such items as titles, clothes, and insignia, which were seen as impregnated with the spiritual powers of the ruler.

Women played an important role in the maintenance and preservation of the ruler's special status. Wherever he went he was accompanied by a retinue of women, a select few carrying his sword and his betel service, others contributing to his aura simply by their presence. Among them were hunchbacked women and female dwarfs whose inclusion in the retinue was to harness the spiritual powers believed inherent in these "god-favored" creatures for the benefit of the ruler.[74] He only married women of other royal families, thus limiting the circle of marriage partners and preserving his exclusive position in society. But perhaps of greater significance was the practice of receiving women from the families of the bobatos. It was probably to this practice which Pigafetta referred when he claimed that "every" household provided the kolano with one or two daughters.[75] The Dutch in 1599 also commented that the ruler had wives in every village, so that "he was at home wherever he went."[76] Judicious marriages provided blood ties with leading families throughout the kingdom, ties which were crucial to his ability to govern.

Women from kolano families were regarded as the guardians of rank and eschewed marriage with any but those of equal or higher status. Anyone guilty of transgressing this social rule was punished with death and loss of property. A bride price had to be paid to the parents to underscore the value of women as status markers in society. But for Galvão the custom was seen purely as an economic proposition. He remarked that the more daughters a man had the richer he became, and "for the noblemen [the kolanos] they represent a treasure." When the "queen," or the principal wife of the ruler, and other women of high rank went out, they were carried on the backs of other women. As befitted their position, their feet were not permitted to touch the ground. Men preceded them out of sight to shout and warn all men to remove themselves from the roads which were to be traversed by the high-status women.

The maintenance of the purity and hence the sacredness of these women was linked to the belief that power was concentrated among those most closely associated with the gods, the ultimate source of power. In Pacific Island societies the purity, or sacredness/power, of a ruling house could be enhanced by the refocusing of dispersed sacred "blood" through marriage between siblings, a practice noted also in southwest Sulawesi traditions. For Maluku, however, there was a proscription against such marriages. Shelly Errington offers one likely explanation for this apparent contradiction between theory and practice by arguing that in eastern Indonesia the ideal was to concentrate power, though the reality was to disperse it in order to assure exchange (of women and goods) and the preservation of life.[77] Maintenance of this "flow of life" was clearly paramount since there were clear prohibitions in Maluku against incest. Male relatives of a royal woman, even a father and brother, did not enter her home once she was married. This social restriction also applied to foster sisters, a custom which underscored the equality of milk and blood relationships in Malukan society.

Only a male child born of a marriage between a ruler and woman of kolano background could become the legal heir to the throne, a practice which helped to regularize succession. When the ruler's wife gave birth to a child, she was honored with special celebrations for seven days. All those of rank came to pay respects to the mother and offer congratulations to the father. If it was a male child, the "noblewomen" (that is, females of kolano status) brought water in bamboo containers to wash the baby and a piece of firewood to prepare his meal. If the child was female, then the "noblemen" brought the firewood and the women the water. A male child was provided with noblewomen as his wet nurses, each suckling the child for one or two weeks.[78] In this way the position of the heir to the throne was strengthened by his relationship to his kolano "milk-mothers," a relationship which in Maluku and certain other Indonesian societies was regarded spiritually and emotionally as being as strong as that between child and mother.[79]

The daughters of these kolano families were taught reading, writing, carving, drawing, embroidery on the loom, spinning cotton on the wheel, and weaving small narrow fabrics probably on waistlooms.[80] The weaving of cloth seems to have been the preserve of female kolanos, a practice which may be linked to the days when barkcloth was still the main dress material and item of gift exchange. Among Polynesian societies where barkcloth was still widely used in the late eighteenth and early nineteenth centuries, the wives and daughters of chiefs took pride in the manufacture of superior cloth, striving to excel in the elegance of the pattern and the brilliance of the colors they brought to barkcloth pieces. It was felt to be demeaning if anyone of lower status were to finish a cloth better than they.[81] Like their counterparts in Pacific Island societies, the Malukan women were skilled in these tasks because barkcloth was still being made. When increasing numbers of textiles began entering Maluku, these women applied old techniques to the new cloth and continued to embroider or sew their own local material onto the imported pieces to enhance their beauty.

Because of the special position of women, the wife-giver was accorded a high ritual status in Malukan society. In the early sixteenth century it was possible to establish the "ranking" of various groups and individuals through the exchange of women. Galvão described the practice of the rulers giving their daughters and sisters to sangajis as brides and mentioned that he himself was offered the Sultan Ternate's daughter in marriage.[82] The rulers regarded the Portuguese governor as belonging to the local ruling elite, though of lower status. Tidore had the highest ritual status based on wifegiving, though Ternate was regarded as most powerful politically and militarily. Two Ternate rulers in the early sixteenth century, Sultan Abu Lais (d. 1522) and Sultan Hairun (r. 1535–1570), were married to daughters of the Sultan Tidore, and rulers of Ternate continued to receive wives from Tidore for the remainder of the century.

In addition to the sultan, the sangajis formed another element in Maluku's political structure. The sangaji title appears to have been given to the most important kolanos who acknowledged the sultan's authority. Galvão noted that there was little difference in practical authority between the rulers and the sangajis, and "in their districts and domains [the sangajis] are obeyed, feared, and venerated like the rajas [that is, the sultans]."[83] If the sultan were to visit a sangaji, the latter had to provide him with everything he required and a sister or relative to entertain him. But this gesture was reciprocated by the sultan when the sangaji returned the visit.[84] The position of the sultan was created to be politically a *primus inter pares* to serve the interests of the kolano class, but the holder of that office could also descend in political status to a sangaji.[85] In government the sangajis administered civil and criminal justice on behalf of the sultan and with the latter's insignia, but they continued to maintain their local boundaries and "landmarks" to assert their own spiritual and territorial claims to the land.[86] What Galvão described as "landmarks" were probably spiritual markers associated with the local soil deity.[87]

The most important "ministers" *(mandarins)* mentioned by Galvão were the *kolano magugu*. The title was translated as "he who holds the king and the kingdom in his hand" and was likened to a major-domo. But this position of kolano magugu was more than just that of the chief royal steward, for Galvão also described him as someone who was the tutor of the ruler and more feared and obeyed than the ruler himself. Unlike *kolano*, which was a Javanese term, *magugu* was a Ternaten word constructed from the prefix *ma-* and the rootword *gugu*, meaning to grasp a handful (such as earth) in one's hand.[88] The significance of this definition becomes apparent only by comparing an identical office among the Papuans in the Raja Ampat Islands. These islands had initially acknowledged the overlordship of Bacan and later of Tidore, and in the process the leaders had adopted the customs, the religion, the titles, and even the style of dress of their overlords. In addition to the title of kolano, or *kalana* in the Raja Ampat islands, they had also adopted the office of kolano magugu, which became generally known in north Maluku as *jogugu* (Ternaten)/*jojau* (Tidorese), from the words *jou*, meaning lord, and *gugu*. *Jogugu*, or in this case the Tidorese *jojau*, was rendered in the Raja Ampat languages as *rejao, jaja*, or *jajau*. Among the Papuan islanders of the Raja Ampat, the term rejao/jaja/jajau meant "lord of the land" and was used to distinguish it from *raja* (an Indianized Malay term equivalent to kolano), a title associated with the sea.[89] The strength of the northern Malukan cultural expansion is demonstrated by the existence to this day in Buru of the title *mat gugul*, from *mate*, a local title for a leader, and *gugul* from the Ternaten *gugu*. Buru was one of the islands which acknowledged Ternate's superior position, and in the past the title mat gugul was created to serve as the Sultan Ternate's representative.[90]

Another "mandarin" mentioned by Galvão was the *pinate*. His principal task was the supervision of the food levies from the different settlements and the preparation of major banquets. In this task he was assisted by a number of *kalaudi,* who were officials in the various settlements entrusted with its implementation. Although Galvão saw the pinate simply in the role of superintendent of the royal household, another contemporary Portuguese observer realized that his position was far more august and spoke of him as a person of great eminence.[91] The pinate had the delicate and important task of regulating the exchange of goods and women between the ruler and the principal families in the kingdom, thereby reinforcing reciprocal arrangements essential for the proper functioning of society.[92] He held a crucial mediating role between the sultan and the other local leaders, and he was ultimately responsible for the well-being of the whole community. The voluntary nature of this exchange and its efficacy were suited to a political arrangement in which there were multiple centers under independent heads, all of whom acknowledged the sultan as a primus inter pares.

Next in importance among Ternate's officials were the two Islamic posts of *hukum,* which were "bought" and held by those of the kolano class. These hukums were administrators and magistrates who heard and adjudicated disputes. Despite their Islamic titles they functioned more as part of the indigenous decision-making process than as Muslim officials applying Islamic laws. They conducted judicial inquiries "by reason and custom," and when confronted by serious cases they summoned the elders who met and made the final decisions in the central meetinghouse or baileu.[93] In the sixteenth century attempts were made by the sultans to manipulate Islam for their own purposes by selling these offices to supporters from their own class. In Islamic lands the position of hukum was one of great prestige held by Islamic scholars, but the Ternaten hukums who were appointed by the sultan apparently lacked this knowledge as was apparent by their reliance on local *adat* or, in Galvão's words, "reason and custom."

Finally, there was a deliberative body consisting of twenty aged councillors or elders. Before the commencement of deliberations by the council, the members ceremonially partook of a communal narcotic drink.[94] Once formalities were over, the council debated major issues and through consensus made decisions which had considerable authority in the community. So highly respected were the elders that an embassy always consisted of these honored patriarchs. Age was acknowledged as a crucial determinant of wisdom, and no young man could be admitted to the role of councillor no matter what his rank or status. The importance of the elders lay also in their role as ritual authority. To this day in the more isolated settlements in Tidore, the young will always defer to the elders in the reciting of their true tales or history for fear of supernatural reprisals.[95] Nevertheless, changes were already evident in the composition of the council which increasingly tended to include members of the sultan's retinue and those kolanos of whom he approved.

These elders were chosen from the bobatos, who were heads of the soa, the sociopolitical units which comprised each village.[96] The bobatos' links to the land are nowhere more clearly captured than in a ceremony still practiced in Tidore where items of the regalia are referred to as "bobato."[97] This description accords with a general phenomenon in all of monsoon Asia where the deity of the soil is made immanent among humans in an object which becomes part of the regalia. During the ceremony the leader of the group is identified with the deity and becomes the medium through which the powers of the deity flow to guarantee the fertility and hence prosperity of the community.[98] The identification of both the leader of the soa and the regalia as "bobato" would be in accordance with this conceptual framework of Southeast Asian indigenous beliefs and explains the ritual alliance of the bobatos with the jogugu as principal lord of the land.

Another dignitary mentioned by Galvão was the çaboia, who was used as an envoy in important missions. There is no other mention of this functionary in the remainder of Galvão's work, though the editor located a Spanish reference from this period which mentions a saboya, the king's teacher.[99] Both descriptions fit the position of sowohi kië, meaning literally the "guardian of the mountain/land/kingdom." It was not equivalent to the position of jogugu, the lord of the land, but appears to have been the religious functionary with closest links to the jogugu. He was entrusted with the harnessing of spiritual powers for the benefit of the whole society. In the late nineteenth century a Dutch official observed that he was in charge of the regalia of the kingdom,[100] a highly appropriate function which clearly demonstrated his links to the forces of the land.

There is no similar detailed study of the sociopolitical structure of Tidore, Jailolo, or Bacan for this period. As first described by the Dutch in 1662, Tidore's structure appears to have been similar to that of Ternate. The sultan was basically the head of a clan whose influence did not extend far beyond the boundaries of the royal settlement. The other villages on the island were linked in a loose alliance to the center, but the sultan had little real power to enforce his will on these villages or on other territories which formed part of Tidore's realm. The next important official was the jojau, the Tidore version of the Ternaten jogugu, and in the mid-seventeenth century he was the sangaji of the royal settlement of Mareku. The second leading figure was the kapita laut, who was the sangaji of the settlement of Tahula. There were two hukums, but like those in Ternate they were more political than religious functionaries. By the second half of the seventeenth century, Islam was becoming more prominent in the islands, and one of the hukums came to be replaced by a proper Muslim religious official. The strength of the Islamic element in the Tidore government caused a temporary split in 1662 into two royal houses with succession alternating between them.[101]

Despite the similarity in offices, there were certain differences in the development of the governments in Ternate and Tidore. The court in Ternate had to contend with the presence in the kingdom of the Fala Raha, or the "Four Houses" of the Tomagola, Tomaitu, Marsaoli, and Limatahu, who were said to predate royalty and represented the principal families in the land.[102] They were associated with the forces of the land, which in practice meant the bobatos, and were regarded as the champions of the indigenous community against external forces represented by the sea and the stranger king. Valentijn referred to them as "the flower and the most esteemed among the people." Their favored position in society as the "great electors" highlighted their strength in relation to the ruler.[103] Although these families benefited from the greatly increased revenues from the clove trade, a far greater proportion of the wealth was flowing to the court. In time it enabled the ruler to use his influence to "encourage" these families to demonstrate their loyalty by conquering foreign lands. This led to the establishment from the late fifteenth to the seventeenth centuries of Ternaten colonies by members of these families in the Sula Islands, the so-called Ambon Quarter in south Maluku, and in north Sulawesi. From these outposts cadet branches of the Fala Raha, in cooperation with their original households in Ternate, were a constant irritant and occasionally a serious threat to the court.

In Tidore there is no mention of powerful families like the Fala Raha. Perhaps the relatively smaller proportion of revenue coming to Tidore from international trade made it more difficult for such families to prosper and challenge the court. There arose, however, two royal houses competing for the right to govern the kingdom: the elder and more prestigious at Mareku and the other at Soa Sio, which remained the center of Tidore for most of this period. Another instructive difference between Ternate and Tidore was the role of the kapita laut. Although Galvão does not mention this title by name, in Ternate this position of commander of the fleets arose as a result of the dynamic expansion of that kingdom into new lands. In Tidore, on the other hand, the title was associated with territorial leaders, perhaps reflecting the fact that Tidore's expansion was not characterized by numerous wars as was the case with Ternate. A third notable difference was the far greater prominence given in Tidore to the office of sowohi kië than in Ternate. His task was to ensure the performance of the proper rituals for the maintenance of the welfare of the kingdom. As the most spiritually potent figure in the land, he was entrusted with the care of the state regalia. The ordinary sowohi responded to appeals by the people for differing needs, ranging from help in securing the love of an individual to interceding with the gods for rain. But it was in the courts that the sowohi kië's function was especially valued. One of the groups, the Tosofu Lamo of the Soa Rumtaha, was traditionally entrusted with the making of iron, an occupation of great prestige because of the sacred nature of forging. Only the sowohi kië was sufficiently imbued with sacral powers to be able to place the spiritually potent crown on the ruler's head or to maintain the royal cemetery. In times of war he summoned the spiritual forces to assist the ruler in combat.[104]

As Islam grew in importance in both Ternate and Tidore, the sowohi kiës would have surrendered many of their functions to the rising new religion. The later creation of an *imam sowohi,* combining two spiritual offices, was a reflection of the attempt by the Malukans to preserve the powers of both instead of having to choose one or the other. With the decline of the jogugu's indigenous function and the arrogation of his authority by those closely tied to the ruler, the position of sowohi kië lost its significance to Ternatens. Tidore, however, has continued to retain a sowohi kië until the present day. The strength of this institution in Tidore may be explained by the fact that the epithets for the four north Malukan kingdoms first recorded by Padtbrugge in the late seventeenth century clearly associate Tidore with the "land." The sowohi kië's presence would therefore have been considered essential to Tidore's ritual role in Maluku.

The Ngofagamu: "The People of the Land"

In discussing the common people, Galvão focused on customs which he found to be "curious." He was critical of the manner in which Malukans raised serious matters in a seemingly casual fashion. At the end of a social visit, the Malukans would take leave and, as an afterthought, introduce an issue which had always been the aim of the visit. For the Malukans this way of addressing a delicate matter allowed both parties to save face if nothing were to be done. The Malukans saw the wisdom of indirectness just as, conversely, many Westerners admired directness. Galvão also noted that, "when [the Malukans] have to do some important work, for example, to besiege towns, to move temples, royal palaces, and other similar things, all of them assemble and they divide themselves into shifts for months, weeks, or days."[105] What Galvão was referring to was the practice of summoning the populace to work on specific projects of benefit to the leaders, as well as to the whole community. The description fits the practice known in Malay areas as *kerahan,* or corvée labor, and was part of a general concept of mutual assistance, which characterized the cooperative nature of local life in the archipelago. It applied not only to major community projects but also to daily living involving the erecting of houses, the harvesting of crops, or the collecting of forest products. Even the labor given to the leaders was reciprocated in terms of payment in kind, currency, and future protection and patronage. The mutual assistance aspect continued to undergird these relationships.

Another custom which attracted Galvão's attention was the Malukan manner of conducting business. He observed that "it is the women who negotiate, do business, buy and sell."[106] The role of women in the marketplace is well documented in Southeast Asia, and the women to this day continue to be prominent in business. In Maluku in Galvão's time this particular role of women was enforced by the fact that sago, in the form of baked and dried rectangular pieces of bread, was a major item of exchange. Since the making of flour from the sago palm demanded strenuous physical labor over long stretches of time away from home, men were usually assigned this task. However, the baking of the sago flour into bread pieces, the drying process, and the sale of the finished product were the preserve of women.

In commenting on business practices, Galvão explained that when any decision is made "all members of the family have to give their advice and opinion, and if only one says 'no,' even if he is only six or seven years old, they cannot do it."[107] Though Galvão believed it to be the case only in business matters, the custom was followed in every area of life throughout Maluku and in the archipelago. It is a concept practiced at the family and state level and known in Malay as *musyawarah*, which is decision making through consultation. Among the ngofagamu serious affairs affecting the family required consultation not only among the living but also among the ancestors. Crucial decisions were therefore made at the graves of ancestors or at sites regarded to be the abode of guardian spirits of the group. Galvão mentions that in the past idols were made "to revere their ancestors in wood or stone with faces of humans, dogs, cats and other animals which they favored."[108] It was these ancestors, both human and nonhuman, who were regarded as an extension of the living human community and a vital part of the musyawarah process.

In mourning, the members of the affected household honored the deceased by locking themselves in their homes for eight to ten days to avoid contact with others. Firewood, water, and everything necessary to run the household were arranged by others. The mourning dress was of barkcloth with black trimmings. At the death of a prominent person everything was done in a way which indicated that the world had been turned upside down and order transformed into chaos. Daily routine was reversed and customary practice ignored in order to demonstrate the calamity which had befallen the community. The men wore their headgear wrapped around their chin like women and sailed their ships stern forward. The women, too, showed their despair by carrying their loads not on their shoulders or backs as normal but under their arms. The people shaved their heads and eyebrows and wore rattan rings on their feet, arms, and legs. In the woods and valleys and other solitary places they played the nose flute.[109] The Malukan manner of mourning great leaders in the sixteenth century is found in Pacific Island societies in the nineteenth as well, indicating perhaps yet again the survival of a feature of their shared Austronesian heritage.

Another of Galvão's observations about the people of the land was their dependence on the sea. He claimed that only the alifuru and the ngofangare traveled by land. As a result there were only a few paths and it was difficult to find anyone outside the two groups who knew how to go by land from one place to another. They did "all their traveling, fighting, trading, and merrymaking" by sea. Their kora-koras were propelled by both paddles and sails, and they were considered by the Portuguese to be very swift and impossible to overtake. Despite the Malukans' familiarity with the sea, they were not open-sea voyagers. They kept close to the land, following every bay, rock, and cove, and avoided even crossing from one cape to another. This caution may have been well placed since the boats which the Malukans used were not made for the strong winds and large waves of open-sea sailing. Both the Portuguese and later the Dutch commented on the frequency with which the Malukan boats, with double outriggers and a platform in the middle, broke apart in rough weather.[110] Nevertheless, the Malukans were able to travel considerable distances by exercising extreme caution, hugging the coastlines when possible and quickly beaching at the first sign of storm. Other boats more seaworthy than the kora-kora enabled the Malukans to undertake long sea journeys to their distant territories.

Observations of the lifestyle of the Malukans are scattered throughout the rest of Galvão's account, with much greater attention given to the kolanos than the ngofagamu. But to describe the status of the kolanos, he was forced to make comparisons with the common people. From these comparisons and the sections on trees and plants, he provided sufficient material to reconstruct something of the material lives of the people. His botanical description is not free from error since he sometimes attributed uses or properties to the wrong tree or plant. On the whole, however, it was a remarkable display of collection and recording which was more characteristic of observers in subsequent centuries. In listing the variety of trees and their uses, he would not have known that, in addition to their practical value, the trees served a symbolic function to Malukans. By planting trees on ancestral lands and enjoying the fruits thereof, the people asserted their rights to the land and commemorated their founding ancestors.[111]

Of all the trees mentioned, the sago palm (*Metroxylon rumphii*, Mart.) was perhaps the most useful. From its trunk was made a flour which was the staple food in Maluku. Sago trees were plentiful, and it has been variously estimated that a full-sized tree could supply sago flour for an ordinary family for a month or more. The men usually spent several weeks at a time in the sago swamps to do the physically demanding task of felling the trees, gouging out the trunk to break up the fiber into fine pieces, sieving the prepared fiber with water, collecting the sago flour residue, and then packing it into large containers made from sago leaves. Part of the prepared sago was brought home, and the rest was stored at the site for future use. Since sago swamps abounded in Maluku and the trees grew quickly, the people were assured of a steady supply of this staple. The other parts of the sago tree were valuable as well. Its leaves were harvested, folded in the middle over some poles, sewn along the side, and then tied to the rafters for roofing. The leaves could also be shaped into a tablecloth, plates, and drinking cups. From the spine of its leaves were constructed the walls of houses.

The sugar palm (*Arenga pinnata*, Merr.) was another tree of great practical value. In addition to a drink which it provided from its flower-buds, the liquid could be cooked into a tasty brown palm sugar. Its black, stiff netlike fiber was used as roofing for mosques, royal residences, and tombs because it did not decay easily. The nipa palm (*Nipa fruticans*, Wurmb.) provided bread and drink, thatching for roofs, and material for baskets and mats. A fourth type of palm, the areca (*Areca catechu*, Linn.), was said to produce an even better flour and bread than the sago or nipa palms. Its nut was popularly chewed with the leaf from the pepper vine (*Piper betle*, Linn.), inducing an intoxicating effect. From its straight, hard stems were made spears and spearheads. The banana tree (*Musa sapientum*, Linn.) was greatly favored for its fruit which could be eaten raw, roasted, or boiled; for its buds which when boiled could be eaten or applied to heal wounds; and for its broad, long leaves which uncut could be used as an umbrella and which cut could serve as plates or as a tablecloth. Almost as versatile was the coconut tree (*Cocos nucifera*, Linn.), of which there were the tall and the dwarf varieties. From the flesh of the coconut was made oil, and from the liquid a fermented drink. There were other types of fruit trees, such as mangos (various varieties of *Mangifera*, Burm.), durians (*Durio zibethinus*, Linn.), Indian almond or ketapang (*Terminalia catappa*, Linn.), langsat (*Lansium domesticum*, Jack), citrus fruits, breadfruit or chempedak (*Artocarpus champeden*, Spreng.), jackfruit or nangka (*Artocarpus inte-*

gra, Merr.), and watermelons which Galvão introduced from Mindanao.

From one unidentified tree the people fashioned their small circular shields, which they called *salawaku,* and from the bark of another they made medicines. The *baru* tree *(Hibiscus tiliaceus)* produced a sort of cotton called *panha,* which they used to caulk their ships and to make matches. The resin of another tree, the *fitako (Calophyllum inophyllum),* was applied to joinings and used as soap, while the *mariela* tree (a *Machilus* tree of the Lauraceae family) served mainly to provide planks for boats and floors. From a type of areca tree called *pua* and from the "beech/poplar" tree (Port. *faia*) they obtained their masts, crossjacks, yardarms, and planks for rudders. The leaves of the pandanus tree *(Pandanus,* Linn.) provided the material for baskets, while the resins of other trees produced pitch, poisons, antidotes to poisons, and soothing oils.

But of all the trees in Maluku, it was the clove tree which proved most valuable. The fruit was used both as a medicine as well as a condiment, and Pires claimed in 1515 that only within the last ten years had the clove become a major item of trade.[112] The increased Portuguese demand for cloves had resulted in greater control over the trade by the rulers. The common people were therefore organized to gather cloves for the ruler, and the benefits from the trade were going via the ruler to the people in the form of jewels, gold, copper gongs, ivory, porcelain, silk, and cotton cloth, which they stored in earthenware jars and buried secretly in the mountains.[113] Galvão offers one of the earliest descriptions of the local method used in harvesting the cloves. With a basket known as the *saloi* on their backs, the pickers climbed the trees, broke off the ends of the branches bearing the cloves, and then placed them in the baskets. Long poles were used to get to branches out of reach. When the baskets were filled, they were lowered by means of a rope to another person waiting on the ground. The cloves were then set out to dry on mats in the sun or placed on a bamboo rack and smoked.[114] Another method, which is mentioned by the Dutchman Jan Huygen van Linschoten in the late sixteenth century, involved passing a rope through the branches and then shaking off the cloves.[115]

Other useful plants found in Maluku were the many varieties of bamboo and rattan. The large bamboo stalks were usually cut in sections to serve as containers to carry and store water and to cook food in an open fire. Lengths were also cut in order to serve as planking for the floors of houses. The thorny jungle vine called the rattan was equally valuable when stripped and twisted to make cables and ropes for binding. Certain plants in Maluku could be fashioned into spears, swords, knives, and daggers, while thick spiky bushes served as defensive hedges around settlements. Various other herbs and leaves were valued for their healing properties or as condiments, while berries were used in the making of glue. A seaplant resembling algae seems to have been the source of thread to make their fishing nets.

Among the domesticated animals listed by Galvão were the dog, cat, pig, sheep (brought by Europeans), and goat. In addition there were rats, wild pigs, civet cats, crocodiles, monkeys, *kusu* (a marsupial resembling a ferret and related to the kangaroo), pigeons, ring-doves, parrots known as *nuri* and *kakatua,* plus many other types of birds. The nuri and the kakatua were prized as pets and often sought by foreign traders. In later years the rulers of Maluku tended to send these birds as gifts to the Europeans. Galvão did not talk about the bird of paradise because it was found mainly in the islands to the east of Ternate. They were highly desired for their beautiful feathers and were sent as tribute from the eastern islands to the north Malukan rulers, who sold them at great profit to foreign traders. Since it was the feathers and not the live bird which were valued, these unique creatures were traded with their feathers intact and without their legs. As a result for some time there circulated the view among the Portuguese and other Europeans that the bird of paradise flew continuously and only stopped when it died. Some local traders called it the "bird of the gods" *(manuk dewata),* and the name became generally used among Europeans.[116] Linschoten appears to have been the first to present a slightly different interpretation of the name, calling it in Latin *Avis paradiseus,* or "bird of paradise."[117]

In north Maluku food was principally obtained from the sea and from the various plants and animals. There appears to have been only minimal sowing and planting of cereals using two different cultivation techniques. The first was by the slash and burn method, in which land was burned off and the ashes allowed to provide the nutrients for the crop. Shallow holes were made with pointed sticks, and into each were placed two or three grains. The holes were then covered with dirt using the feet or hands. Once planted there was nothing left to be done but wait for the plants to grow and be harvested. This type of agriculture required vast amounts of land because the nutrients were depleted after perhaps two or three years. The depleted land then had to be left to regenerate over a number of years. This method was used by the ali-furus and the ngofangares (the personal servants of the kolano) who worked the kolanos' lands in the interior of Halmahera. The second type of cultivation involved the use of the plow and draft animals for the planting of small quantities of rice and some other grain (perhaps millet). It would have been a method more conducive to the broad plain stretching some 7 to 10 kilometers from Jailolo to Sahu in northwest Halmahera than to the smaller volcanic islands of Ternate and Tidore.[118] The people also grew broad beans, lentils, sesame, beans, long

pepper, Indian corn, yams, and peas. What they could not grow themselves, they obtained from the market, which was located at a different
place each day of the week.

The main diet of the Malukans consisted of fish and sago cooked
in different ways. Fish was found in great abundance in the warm
waters of these islands, and sago was readily available in the swampy
areas, especially in Halmahera. The prepared sago flour could be made
into a type of porridge, which was then eaten with fingers or simply
slurped up, it could be mixed with a fish soup and peppers, or it could
be baked into a hard bread and then dried for storage to be eaten when
needed. A variety of vegetables and fruits supplemented this basic diet.
Oil, vinegar, water, and local wine *(arak)* were stored in lengths of bamboo and used whenever required for a meal. Salt was obtained by gathering driftwood on the coast, drying the wood, and then setting it on
fire. As it burned, saltwater was thrown on it carefully so the fire would
not be extinguished. Once the wood was totally consumed by the fire,
there remained a paste consisting of the ashes and the salt from the
ocean water. This paste was dissolved and placed in pots to boil; the
product was then distilled and filtered through cloths. Once it curdled,
it was placed in a loaf-shaped receptacle to produce a somewhat firm,
not very white, but definitely saltlike substance. The people ate with
their fingers, using plates of sago or banana leaves, and drank from
cups made of the same leaves fastened together with a sliver of wood to
form a receptacle. There were containers made of porcelain, copper,
and bronze, but these were not for everyday use.[119]

The people's manner of dress on formal occasions was characterized by Galvão as being in the "Malay style." This meant a length of
cloth *(sarung)* worn around the waist and extending down to the knees or
as far as the ankles, depending on the number of folds around the waist,
and a short blouse *(baju)* with sleeves down to the elbow or wrist. A
piece of cloth was then wound two or three times around the waist with
the back end hanging down to the thighs and the front end reaching to
the ground. The people were especially fond of colored fabrics. For
everyday use they wore a cloth made with a hole in the middle and the
ends tied together in two knots under the arms. This was probably a
barkcloth, since it was still being made and worn at this time, and it was
described as "a scapular." Most barkcloth made for clothing had one
opening and was tied in the fashion described. For protection from the
sun, straw hats were worn.[120]

The houses of the ngofagamu differed from those of the kolanos
and the sangajis. While the houses of the latter were on poles, those of
the common people were on the ground with earthen floors and split
bamboo walls. The roofs were thatched with sago leaves or with bam-

boo. For beds they used a mat on the floor or placed on top of a slightly raised wooden platform *(balai-balai)* where they slept with a piece of cloth wrapped around them.[121]

Though Galvão's picture of the people of the land in Maluku in the sixteenth century is sketchy, it does suggest a self-sufficient society obtaining its food and daily living requirements from the surrounding lands and seas. He further observed that the clove trade presented a greater opportunity for the ruler and his officials at court than the ordinary individual to acquire wealth in the form of prestige goods. This differentiation became the basis for a developing status distinction between the kolanos and ngofagamu which was already becoming evident during Galvão's time.

When the Dutch first appeared in Maluku in May 1599, their observations did not differ markedly from Galvão's. From their initial brief encounter with the Malukans, they concluded somewhat hastily that the island produced only goats and a few chickens and not much fish. But they later contradicted themselves when describing a vibrant market dominated by women traders buying and selling salted and fresh fish, chickens, bananas, sugarcane, fresh ginger, and other goods. As in the time of Galvão there were many fruit trees, including the banana, the coconut palm, and the citrus. But what naturally impressed the Dutch because it was the reason for their presence in Maluku was the vast forests of clove trees. The Dutch commented that the Malukans used no money but dealt in cloves "for which they could get anything they required." Sago was still the staple diet, but its value as a medium of exchange was being replaced by cloves. In short, Maluku was described as self-sufficient in food with freshwater wells and a thriving international commerce based on the clove trade, the benefits of which were already visible in the widespread popularity of imported crimson and purple cloth.[122] But the Dutch in 1599 caught only a glimpse of the changes resulting from the clove trade. Already in train were developments which were to affect the people's lifestyle, their social and political organizations, and the relationship between the center and periphery.

Toward an Indigenous Structuring of Maluku's History

Indigenous concerns expressed in the origin myths offer a way of structuring Malukan events and analyzing their significance. One of these concerns was the creating of binding relationships across vast areas and among various cultural communities. The myths provided the legitimation of a "familial" relationship which was depicted as one based on a common sacred origin. The four or five members of the family, located

at the four cardinal points and the center, represented a totality incorporating all groups contained within these "four corners" of the Malukan
world. The acknowledgment of a family of Maluku established the geographic and spiritual boundaries of interaction inside and outside this
group. Despite the presence within this world of people from numerous
ethnic groups with different languages and customs, they had come to
accept the validity of the origin myths and thus acknowledged their
place within this cultural unity.[123] The attitudes adopted and the actions
taken were influenced by the knowledge of who constituted a part of this
"family" as depicted in the myths.

Another important concern was the maintenance of the "four pillars," which symbolized wholeness and perfection. In the myths different sets of four were named, but each set represented the symbol of
unity within a specific circumscribed world. The preservation of the
belief in the four was an overriding preoccupation among Maluku's
leaders, even when this did not accord with the political situation. What
mattered was the adherence to the idea of four because it was "real" in
both Eliade's and the Malukan sense of being there at the beginning of
creation, hence original and genuine.

Crucial to the survival of the four pillars was the continuing health
of the dualism between Ternate and Tidore. This dualism was a third
significant concern arising from the myths and was regarded as essential
in undergirding the four pillars to assure the harmony and prosperity of
the world of Maluku. The political and economic changes which accompanied the arrival and consolidation of Islam and the Europeans in the
sixteenth, seventeenth, and eighteenth centuries assured the location of
the center of the Malukan world in the clove-producing islands in the
north and the dominance of Ternate and Tidore at its core. By the late
sixteenth century the courts of Ternate and Tidore had decided to emu-
late the other Muslim kingdoms in the archipelago in style of dress, language, and government. Although a new political hierarchy and other
innovations emerged in these kingdoms, they were channeled and
assimilated into older cultural constructs. As Ternate and Tidore
expanded, they tended generally to follow the boundaries established by
the myths; as new political realities emerged, they were reinterpreted in
terms of the maintenance of the four pillars and the dualism at the center. Malukan events flowed through the channels of a well-conceived
structure which helped to determine their significance to the local
inhabitants. The oscillation of power between the ruler and his officials
in the court and the bobatos in the villages, between Ternate and Tidore
at the center, and between these two kingdoms and the territories identified as their periphery, introduced a dynamism in the affairs of
Maluku and provided a shape to its history.

CHAPTER THREE

The World of Maluku: The Periphery

AS A RESULT OF THE RAPID expansion of the clove trade at the end of the fifteenth and early sixteenth centuries, Ternate and Tidore came to be acknowledged as the center of Maluku. The other communities, bounded by Banggai-Butung in the west, the Papuas in the east, Loloda in the north, and Bacan in the south, were identified by the Bikusagara creation myth as belonging to the family of Maluku and became the periphery. The relationship between center and periphery was formulated in familial terms in keeping with the myths. The "family" of Maluku consisted of the "father/mother," represented by Ternate and Tidore, and their children in the periphery. Conflicts between the center and the periphery were therefore described as family squabbles and reconciliations. The dualism between Ternate and Tidore remained a feature at the center: as Ternate expanded northward and westward, Tidore went southward and eastward. The myths thus provided a legitimation for the creation of a center as well as a blueprint for its expansion to the periphery. The conscious detail to the re-creation of the center in the periphery through transferral of ideology, titulature, and dress was part of this process.

Very little was known about the Malukan periphery until it was described with some detail by François Valentijn, a Calvinist preacher who served in Ambon and Batavia in the late seventeenth century, and by the Dutch East India Company officials in the seventeenth and early eighteenth centuries. Dutch reports were written by officials who had usually served in an area for more than a year. They relied for their information on their own experiences and observations, on other Europeans, and on interviews with local inhabitants. Because they were serving a trading company, these officials were instructed to provide social and political information on indigenous affairs only insofar as it contributed to a greater understanding of the economic process. The detail is therefore of an inconsistent quality, and many features of geography or native institutions are left incomplete or unmentioned. More-over, despite the appearance of sober, matter-of-fact reporting, com-ments on social mores and religious beliefs tend to reflect the general European perception of groups in the periphery. Asia to the Dutch of the seventeenth and eighteenth centuries was no longer perceived as a world of wondrous beings, but the basic Western European attitude of the centrality and hence superiority of Christian European civilization continued to prevail. The Company's demand for exactitude, which arose from its economic preoccupations, led to reports containing ques-tionable statistics on population numbers. The Dutch did not reveal their survey methods (if there were in fact any), and many of the statis-tics are almost impossible to verify. They are used in this chapter simply to provide a rough relative comparison among the groups described. Since these early reports present the first historical glimpses of many of these societies in Maluku, they have been culled to reveal as much as they can of Maluku's periphery.

This chapter also highlights the concerns and the perceptions of the peripheral groups based on their comments and actions recorded by Dutchmen. Much of this interpretation is a result of a study of recent ethnographic material to elucidate information provided by early Dutch accounts. The difficulties which the Dutch expedition experienced in Tidore's periphery resulted in detailed reports on local communities, something which is sadly missing in the discussion of Ternate's periph-ery. In the description of both Ternate's and Tidore's periphery, the life of the people is sketchy at best, and even detail about the principal polit-ical officials is often missing. The nature of the evidence does not allow a direct comparison between the center and the periphery, but it does reveal the manner in which the links were maintained in order to pre-serve the idea of the unity of the Malukan world.

Ternate and Its Periphery

Ternate's territories included a large number of cultures scattered throughout the eastern Indonesian area. Some of these places had ac-knowledged Ternate's overlordship before the arrival of the Europeans, while others had become incorporated into Ternate's sphere of influence in the sixteenth century. In Ternate the early expansion was led by the Fala Raha, consisting of the Tomagola, Tomaitu, Marsaoli, and Lima-tahu families. In the late fifteenth century the Tomaitu family led an expedition to the Sula Islands and brought them into Ternate's sphere of influence. For this deed the Tomaitus were created *salahakans* or gov-ernors of Sula and established a permanent Ternaten presence on the island of Sula Besi. Sometime in the late seventeenth century the

Tomaitu family was temporarily displaced by the Tomagola but later recovered its appanage. In the early sixteenth century the Tomagola family extended Ternate's influence to Buru. Under Samarau the Buru branch of the Tomagola family became a dominant force in what the Dutch called the Ambon Quarter, which included the islands of Buru, Ambelau, Manipa, Kelang, Boano, Seram, Seram Laut, Nusalaut, Honimoa (on Saparua), Oma (on Haruku), and Ambon.[1] The Ambon Quarter continued to acknowledge the nominal overlordship of Ternate through the Tomagolas, though by the late seventeenth century the governorship had been transferred from the Tomagola family to the VOC.[2] Neither the Marsaoli nor the Limatahu families created appanages in the periphery, perhaps because they were already exercising great influence in the center. So important were the Marsaolis that the Portuguese equated the term *marsaoli* with "nobleman."[3] By the seventeenth century the Marsaolis frequently filled the position of jogugu, and the *kimalaha* Marsaoli came to be synonymous with one of the most prominent officials in the kingdom. Next in importance to the Marsaolis may have been the Limatahus,[4] though the sources from this period are relatively silent on their activities.

The Sulas and Ambon Quarter were the only areas given in appanage to powerful Ternaten families. In the other territories the Ternaten ruler acknowledged the authority of the local lords over their own lands in the establishing of center/periphery relationships. One of the major political windfalls for Ternate arose from the Bungaya treaty of 1667, which was signed after the defeat of the Makassar kingdom of Goa at the hands of the Dutch East India Company. In this treaty Ternate was rewarded for its participation as an ally of the Dutch by being given lands seized from Goa.[5] These included the islands to the north of Sulawesi up to Mindanao; the settlements in north Sulawesi, including the Tomini Bay area from Gorontalo and Limbotto as far west as Kaili and Palu; the Obi islands near Bacan; the Sula Islands; Banggai, Tobunku, [Butung is inadvertently omitted], Tibore, and Salayar, the westernmost lands under Ternate; and Batochina (that is, the northern half of Halmahera).[6]

Of these areas Ternate's hold on the islands and settlements of north Sulawesi was most precarious. According to local tradition, in the mid-sixteenth century Sultan Hairun sent his son Babullah to north Sulawesi where he succeeded in making the various settlements mindful of Ternate as the center. Later in that century the Spaniards from Manila seized the northern Sulawesi islands, while Goa extended its sway over north Sulawesi itself. The rulers of Tabukan and Manganitu on Sangihe Island came to acknowledge the dominance of Ternate in 1662, while Menado, Tahulandang, and Kendahe, which had never been part of Ternate, were presented as its vassals by the 1667 Bungaya treaty. Ternate's continuing difficulties with the northern Sulawesi area were in stark contrast with its generally favorable relations with the other members of its periphery. The location of north Sulawesi at the crossroads of major competitors in the region—the Bugis-Makassar kingdoms, the Spaniards, and the Ternatens—contributed to the problem. Another reason may have been the exclusion of north Sulawesi and the islands to its immediate north from the family of Maluku as depicted in the Bikusagara myth. This myth was cited as a factor in Butung's continued adherence to its relationship with Ternate and could have been equally significant in north Sulawesi's rejection of Ternate's position as the center. As a good ally of the Company, Ternate went through the motions of an overlord but left it to the Dutch to maintain control. In time the Company simply formalized existing practice in north Sulawesi by becoming its legitimate overlord.

Obi became part of Ternate's periphery in 1667 as a result of the Bungaya treaty, despite the fact that it belonged to the kingdom of Bacan. According to traditions collected by Valentijn, Obi claimed to have had its own rulers in the beginning of the fourteenth century who were no less important than those of the four major Malukan kingdoms. Although it never achieved the status of the four, its royal family regularly intermarried with Ternate's. At some unknown date Obi fell under the control of Bacan. Bacan's severe loss of population, already noted in the sixteenth century, may have led to the transferral of Obi's population to Bacan. By the mid-seventeenth century Obi, Obilatu, Tappa, Large Tawali, and Little Tawali were all uninhabited, though the islands had vast sago forests and the surrounding seas were full of fish.

In addition to the lands settled by the Tomagola and Tomaitu families and those awarded by the Bungaya treaty, Ternate's periphery included the important Banggai Islands. These islands are mentioned in a Chinese text dating from 1304, which suggests that Banggai was part of an old established international trade network and may account for its prominence in the Bikusagara myth.[7] According to a 1682 report by the Dutch governor of Ternate, R. Padtbrugge, the Banggai kingdom consisted of the islands of Banggai, Peling (or Gapi), Labobo, a hundred little islands, and a part of southeast Sulawesi known as Balantak and Mondona. These latter two areas produced a surplus of rice and sago, while the southernmost island named Sago was the point of departure for kora-koras going to Tobunku to obtain sago and water. These islands were as a group strategically placed to benefit from the trade routes moving in all four directions, and the island of Banggai served as their central place. In the past it was the kingdom's ability to attract this trade which had enabled it to dominate surrounding lands and be remembered in Malukan traditions as worthy of being a recipient of one of the four sacred naga eggs. The inhabitants were found concentrated on a few islands: Banggai had the largest population, with smaller groups found on Peling, Bangkulu, Labobo, and the southeast coast of Sulawesi from Tomini Bay at Balantak to the Bay of Tobunku. The rest of the more than a hundred islands, many of which were larger than Ternate and Tidore, were uninhabited. In 1679 the whole of the Banggai kingdom had an estimated ten thousand men, most of whom were non-Muslims.[8]

A 1706 report by the Dutch governor of Ternate, Pieter Rooselaar, contains revised and additional information about Banggai. He states that there were twenty-three Banggai islands but only two were inhabited, one of which was the island of Banggai where the ruler had his residence. There were four settlements on the island, each under a sangaji with a total population of 1,450. The ruler himself had only 150 men, and he was dependent upon the approval of the sangajis before acting on any important matter. Peling was the largest island in the group with twenty-three settlements consisting largely of a non-Muslim population. Those from the island of Banggai often came to Peling to obtain slaves.[9] In 1710 another Dutch governor at Ternate added that Banggai's strength came mainly from the island of Banggai and from Mondona, which together had some four thousand able-bodied men. He also noted the existence of a large population in the settlements surrounding Mondona, but this area frequently changed hands since it was a territory under dispute with Tobunku.[10]

During the latter half of the seventeenth century Banggai was caught between two of the strongest powers in eastern Indonesia: Goa (and, after 1667, Bone) and Ternate. After the final capitulation of Goa in 1669, Banggai came under the undisputed control of Ternate. The power of Bone came to fill the vacuum left by Goa, however, and the Banggai area continued to be influenced by a Sulawesi power. Bugis and Makassar traders came frequently to Banggai's shores and were a source of support for rival factions within the kingdom. For Ternate, then, the benefits of tribute in the form of services and sago were often outweighed by the problems associated with clashing factions and the involvement of the Bugis and Makassar people in these quarrels. Yet perhaps because of the prestige associated with Banggai's direct link with one of the four mythical naga eggs, Banggai remained very much part of the Malukan world. It continued to send missions to Ternate rather than to the closer and more powerful southwest Sulawesi kingdoms.

On the southwest border of Mondona was Tobunku, another state in Ternate's periphery in southeast Sulawesi. It was located south of a deep bay called Tomori, and dotted around the bay were other settlements which had once been under the ruler of Banggai but had been seized from time to time by Tobunku. In 1679 Padtbrugge found

Tobunku a well-populated land, with twenty-four villages located north
and twenty-seven villages south of the royal settlement. Each of these
villages had between 100 and 500 people. From the northern border to
the royal center at Tobunku, the Dutch expedition saw nothing but villages and planted fields. There were also numerous Bajaus, or seafaring
people, many of whom lived wholly or part of the time on shore in settlements along the coast and on a hill overlooking the royal town. They
had once been boat people, but many now planted crops and followed
the lifestyle of their Tobunku neighbors. The country was exceptionally
fruitful. In addition to the herds of water buffalo, goats, and pigs which
the people tended, there were numerous wild boar in the jungles. The
people also grew rice, beans, groundnuts, maize, and many other tree
and root crops. Foreign traders who desired to buy any of the crops had
to pay in goods in advance, even when the plants were not yet fully
grown.[11] A 1706 report lists seven settlements in total around the bay
with some 5500 men. South of the bay where the residence of the ruler
was located there was a total population of 8,000 to 9,000 men, of whom
6,000 belonged to the ruler's settlement.[12]

Tobunku's location gave it easy access to the Bugis, Makassar,
and Tomini markets. From the inner bay it was only a day's journey
overland to the Bay of Bone or to Tomini Bay. From here it was a short
trip to Mamuju in Mandar, then down the west coast of Sulawesi to
Makassar. As one of the secondary trade centers in eastern Indonesia,
Tobunku earned the reputation among the Dutch as a "smuggler's
dream," and even Bugis traders from Melaka frequented its ports.[13] At
Tobunku slaves, spices, tortoiseshell, wax, tobacco, and many other
products from the east could be found at lower prices than those offered
by the Dutch. At a time when the VOC was desperately short of tortoiseshell, Tobunku had good supplies from the Togia and the Banggai
islands.[14] In addition, Tobunku possessed vast quantities of accessible
iron ore, which the inhabitants dug up and smelted into weapons or
tools on demand. Tobunku swords, knives, and axes were highly
prized, especially among the Papuan islanders and the interior tribes of
Halmahera and Seram. There were groups which refused to trade their
goods for anything but iron implements. In quality, however, the iron
ore from Tobunku was judged by the renowned seventeenth century
naturalist G. E. Rumphius to be inferior to that found around nearby
Lake Matano in Luwu, where "swords were better and one worth more
than six of Tobunku's." People living around this lake were so skilled in
the working of iron that Rumphius regarded the final product to be as
good as steel.[15] Attempts by Tobunku to control the iron trade led to
intermittent conflicts with Luwu over control of the Lake Matano area.

Though Tobunku was considered to be part of Ternate's periphery, its relationship with the center was often strained and from 1689 it

refused to acknowledge Ternate's position. The Sultan Ternate admitted that he was unable to persuade Tobunku to comply with his wishes without the Company's help, and he was afraid to undertake any action against it for fear of failing and losing face with the other territories in the periphery.[16] The belief that Tobunku could successfully repel any Ternaten attack was well founded in the late seventeenth and early eighteenth centuries. Tobunku had a large number of men and boats, and within its waters it was a formidable foe. Moreover, Bone was eager to preserve Tobunku's independence from the Dutch and Ternate in order to safeguard a dependable source of spices and slaves. Unlike its neighbors Banggai and Butung, Tobunku continued to exercise flexibility in its policies in order to balance the demands from Ternate and the Bugis kingdom of Bone.

Butung, another of the kingdoms in the west which belonged to Ternate's periphery, presented a unique problem. Its status in Maluku was high since it shared with Banggai the prestige of having kings who could trace descent to one of the four mythical naga eggs. But like Banggai and Tobunku it was very much influenced by the proximity of the powerful Bugis and Makassar kingdoms. In the first half of the seventeenth century it was under constant threat from Goa and was finally conquered in 1626.[17] With the defeat of Goa by the Dutch East India Company and the signing of the Bungaya treaty in 1667, Butung became once again a part of Ternate's periphery. Hostilities between Ternate and the Company in 1679–1681 altered the situation once again. Butung claimed that its appeals for help from Ternate had gone unheeded, therefore demonstrating that Ternate was no longer able to afford protection to its "child." In time Butung reestablished its links with Ternate, invoking the familial alliance depicted in the origin myths to acquire a valuable ally against the danger posed by the Bugis-Makassar states of southwest Sulawesi.

Next to Butung is the island of Muna, called Pangasana in Ternaten, which was divided into the kingdoms of Tibore and Wuna. Both Tibore in the western half and Wuna in the eastern half originally had their own sovereign lords and came to acknowledge Ternate's overlordship as a result of Babullah's campaigns in the last quarter of the sixteenth century. When a princess of Wuna married a king of Butung, she brought Wuna into Butung as part of her personal lands. The chaos caused by the war between Ternate and the VOC in 1679–1681 forced both Tibore and Wuna to seek "protection" from the Sultan Butung, rather than from their more distant overlord.[18]

The westernmost territory in Ternate's periphery was Salayar, which Ternaten traditions claim was another of the lands seized by Babullah. It later became a vassal of Goa and then was once again placed under Ternate by the Dutch East India Company in 1669. The people of Salayar were reluctant to accept the overlordship of Ternate for fear of incurring the displeasure of its powerful nearby Bugis and Makassar kingdoms. The situation was resolved to the satisfaction of all parties in 1683, when a treaty signed between Ternate and the Company gave the VOC post in Makassar the authority to govern Salayar "on behalf of the Sultan Ternate."[19]

Among the most valuable of Ternate's subjects were the Sula islanders who lived on the three principal islands of Sula Besi, Taliabu, and Mangole. The western half of Mangole was called Sapelula, while the eastern half was divided into two with the northern part referred to as Waitina and the southern part Mangole. By 1679 there were only two villages on the entire island of Mangole, both in the Mangole district. One of them contained the seven or eight families who had abandoned Sapelula and joined those from Mangole. The other village was composed of people from Waitina. According to the Sula people, in the past and even during the time of the Spaniards and Portuguese (that is, the sixteenth century), the islands were very populous. Due to the continual raids by the Papuans, but especially by the Gamrange ("The Three Settlements," consisting of the southeastern Halmaheran settlements of Maba, Patani, and Weda, but often in practice also including the nearby island of Gebe), the people had abandoned Sapelula and Waitina. Sula Besi and Taliabu were also nearly deserted. Most of these Papuan raids were directed at Banggai, but on their return voyages they usually stopped and raided the Sula Islands, especially Taliabu, as well as the Obi Islands south of Bacan. By 1682 the situation had changed and the people had begun to return to Sula Besi. In that year it had ten villages, in 1706 nine, and in 1710 thirteen. In 1706 there were 3,205 fighting men on the island, but no figures for the other two years. Taliabu had eight settlements and a population of 532 fighting men, while Mangole had three settlements with 205 men.

Unlike the other Ternate periphery areas in the west, the Sula Islands were governed directly by representatives of the Sultan Ternate. He was represented in these islands by a salahakan from the Tomaitu family, who resided at Ipa on Sula Besi with a large following of Ternatens, and had direct control over both the islands of Sula Besi and Mangole. The island of Taliabu was under another of the Sultan Ternate's representatives, the kalaudi, who lived on this island with his own coterie of Ternaten followers. Taliabu was said to have been once under the Banggai kingdom, "when the latter was in its full might and power . . . laying down the law to all its neighbors, who were then very weak."[20] Sapelula, Mangole and Waitina were also said to have been at one time under Bacan, while Sula Besi was under another power (though the people could not recall much about this). There were frequent movements of population between the Sula Islands and Ternate, making the former much more like Makian and Halmahera whose proximity to the center resulted in close interaction between their peoples.

Although the Sula Islands are visible on a clear day from Obi, Buru, or Banggai, the Sula people told the following story to indicate how they were "discovered" by the Ternatens. One day a Ternaten official went to Obi to cut sago with some Tidorese. At Obi he went fishing and saw a hawk with a fish in its beak flying westward. He realized then that there was land further west. When he returned home, he told his king about this observation and then went with a boat with his men and found the Sula Islands. This official, who was called Kimalaha Taloki Besi, was thus attributed with having made the islands part of Ternate's periphery. He was then rewarded by being appointed the first salahakan of Sula.[21] In this Sula version of the relationship with Ternate, what is stressed is the "discovery" of the islands by Ternate and the origins of the institution of the salahakan. The establishment of the link is not a generalized vague past event but is associated with a specific individual remembered in folk memory. For the Sula Islanders, their having been "located" physically and symbolically within the Malukan world was an event worthy of perpetuation in local lore.

Sula was an area considered by the Dutch to be the "bread and spice basket" not only for Ternate but for the whole of eastern Indonesia. Those from Ambon went regularly to obtain rice and sago from the islands.[22] Sula Besi was the most prosperous of the Sulas with various types of wood which were excellent for shipbuilding. It was a fertile island, growing maize, cassava and other root plants, cloves, and a good supply of rice. The principal product of both Taliabu and Mangole was sago baked into hard biscuits, which comprised one of the products sent regularly as tribute to the Sultan Ternate. Slaves from the non-Muslim interior of Taliabu were another greatly valued contribution of the islands to Ternate.[23]

On Halmahera, Ternate's periphery was located in the northern half of the island as well as on the western coast of the southern peninsula. The most important settlements were at Jailolo, Sahu, and Gamkonora.[24] As the position of the jogugu in Ternate came increasingly under the control of the sultan, the latter came to use his influence to appoint a jogugu from one of the three northwest Halmaheran settlements in order to assure their continuing allegiance. The destruction of the Jailolo kingdom by the Portuguese in 1551 led to its eventual incorporation into Ternate. Its ruler lost the right to be called sultan and was instead referred to as "sangaji," as befitted Jailolo's new subordinate status. Nevertheless, for ceremonial purposes Jailolo retained its honored place as one of the four pillars of Maluku. After its defeat Jailolo rapidly declined, and by 1686 it was described as "a village" with not

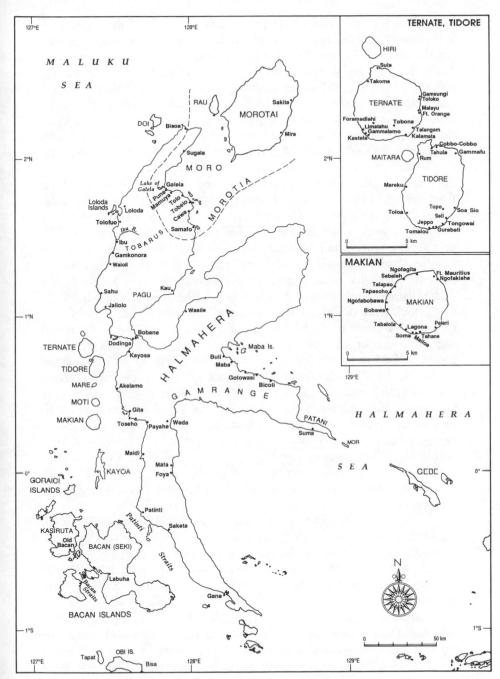

MAP 3. North Maluku

more than four or five original Jailolo folk. The rest of the population were from Morotia in northeast Halmahera who had settled there during the reign of Sultan Muzaffar (1606–1627) to escape the marauding Maba and Patani people. The four sangajis in Jailolo retained the names of their four Moro home villages of Mamuya, Samafo, Cawa, and Tolo. These villages, the hope of the Portuguese missionaries in the sixteenth century, were now ironically transplanted into the very kingdom which had once been the bane of their existence. In 1662 there were an estimated hundred fighting men in Jailolo, but by 1686 only fifty remained of a once proud and powerful kingdom.

Sahu to the north of Jailolo consisted of three settlements. The first was the Muslim village of Saroa where the sangaji, the jogugu, the hukum, and the lesser heads lived. In 1662 there were only thirty men in Saroa because one kora-kora, which normally carried between fifty and seventy men, had been captured by the Tidorese. By 1686 the number had increased to 120, including those of Chinese *mestizo* descent. The Muslim sangaji at Saroa governed the area, including the non-Muslim populations of the other two settlements of Talai and Palisua, which were described as possessing "the most pleasant and fertile agricultural lands in all Maluku." The Muslims at Saroa purchased sago and rice or bartered with those of Talai and Palisua for these goods. Talai was located on a hill a half-hour's walk to the northeast of Saroa, and in 1686 it had eleven households. About six or seven families lived in each longhouse, making the Dutch estimate of a total of seventy-two fighting men somewhat low. Palisua, which had three hundred men able to bear arms, was another half hour further in the same direction and consisted of two beautiful villages about a quarter hour from each other called Gamouro and Gamsongi. Three times a week a market was held in Palisua, attended by those in Sahu. Sahu itself had an abundance of sago, which formed a major part of its trade with the outside world.[25]

The communities known collectively as Gamkonora lay about six hours of rowing to the north of Sahu, with the main settlement located a half hour from the coast on the banks of a stream. This formerly powerful kingdom consisted of the settlements of Gamkonora, Ibu, Waioli, Galela, and interior Tobelo. With its fertile lands and a total fighting force estimated at more than a thousand, Gamkonora was one of the most important areas in Ternate's periphery. The settlement of Gamkonora had an estimated four hundred men in 1662, but by 1686 the number had declined to about a hundred, sixty of whom were Muslim and the rest Tobaru and other interior tribesmen. Obtaining sufficient food for this large population was a serious problem. The people told the Dutch that once there was a large sago forest which had supplied their needs, but it had been destroyed by a volcanic eruption. Even with the dispersal of its population during the Ternaten-Dutch hostilities in 1679–1681, Gamkonora was unable to provide enough sago to feed those left behind. Waioli was situated on a little hill about one and a half hours south of Gamkonora. The people here had mainly gardens for their own subsistence, and they could muster about thirty fighting men. Ibu, with forty warriors, was about one and a half hours north of Gamkonora and built near a freshwater river whose origin was in a mountain in Tobaru country.

About three hours of rowing north of Gamkonora was Tolofuo, a settlement located on the banks of a river. The fourteen Muslim inhabitants were once the personal subjects of Sultan Amsterdam (r. 1675–1690), but after the 1679–1681 war they were led by a sangaji. Upriver lived about three hundred Tobarus who usually came to the river's mouth to fish. It was the presence of these Tobaru warriors which made Tolofuo of importance to Ternate. The interior Tobarus had such fearsome reputations that they were said to have the power to make themselves invisible in order to vanquish their enemies.

Loloda was another area acknowledging Ternate's central status. It was a kingdom of sufficient stature in the past to have been remembered in myths as having its lord marry the only female born of the four sacred naga eggs. Yet at the time that Galvão recorded this tradition, Loloda was a small inconsequential village left with only the memory of its illustrious past. Although it had been under Ternate for a long time, the ruler still retained the title of raja and in 1662 could summon some two hundred men, half of whom were Galelas living in the interior. In 1686 the Dutch described Loloda as a dirty village located on the banks of a saltwater river full of crocodiles. The Raja Loloda was poor and had no slaves, and his mother (a close relation to Kaicili Alam, last prince of the Jailolo royal line) did all the housework for him, including cooking and getting firewood from the jungle. If he wanted food, he himself had to go fishing or cut down a sago tree to make flour. Loloda consisted of a Muslim village, where the raja and his mother lived, and five alifuru villages located in the interior about forty-five minutes away. Loloda itself had about sixteen fighting men, while the alifuru villages had approximately ten households each with a total of about sixty able-bodied men. Like Jailolo, Loloda retained a special place in Maluku ceremonies because of its link with the naga eggs. Its right to use a kingly title was respected, despite its greatly straitened circumstances.

From Loloda the shortest way to the east coast of Halmahera was not by going around the island but by going east through the mountains and then onto rafts down the river to the east coast. About two and a half kilometers south of the river's mouth was Galela, whose inhabitants lived in two villages close to each other on the shores of an inland lake.

There were abundant sago, coconut, and other palm trees which supplied their food and materials for daily living. The people also grew rice, obtained fish from the lake, and hunted wild pigs in the forests. With their substantial food surplus, they were able to supply Ternate's needs as well as carry on a profitable trade. The Galelas were led by a hukum who was accountable to the Sangaji Gamkonora, who in turn represented the interests of Sultan Ternate. In the late seventeenth century, there were an estimated three hundred able-bodied men in Galela.

South of Galela on the northeast coast of Halmahera were the seaward settlements of Tobelo (Tobelotai), where the Muslims and the alifuru lived together. The sangaji and the lesser officials had their homes on a hilltop, while the rest of the population lived on the lower inclines to the north and west. The people were mostly engaged in making sago bread because of the abundance of sago forests. Every three or four months they would go to the seashore to catch fish and gather oysters which they smoked and brought back with them upriver. The landward settlements of Tobelo (Tobelotia) were located inland on the shores of a freshwater lake and consisted of eight villages. The Tobelos had a reputation among their neighbors for being "evil and murderous," and only those from Gamkonora dared to visit them. Nevertheless, they were regarded as an industrious people, an assessment which seemed to be borne out by the presence of large amounts of silver and gold ornaments in the community. Some wore three, four, and even five silver and gold bracelets at a time. The Dutch claimed that Sultan Amsterdam offered silver and gold to the Tobelos to entice their six hundred warriors to fight alongside the Ternatens in the 1679–1681 war against the VOC.

Off the northeast coast of Halmahera is the large island of Morotai, which in the sixteenth century had four settlements governed by sangajis. At the order of Ternate's Sultan Muzaffar the people were moved in the early seventeenth century to Dodinga, a settlement located at a strategic pass on the west coast of Halmahera across from Ternate. Morotai had large numbers of sago trees and an abundance of fish. Sometime in the seventeenth century Ternate and Tidore came to a pragmatic arrangement giving each equal access to the resources on the island.

Further south along the northeast coast was Kau, which appeared to be a poor area. The Dutch remarked that there were only a few boats capable of carrying ten to twelve rowers, and not even the sangaji possessed one. Sago from Kau could be obtained only in exchange for cloth, but the sago was usually poorly baked and improperly dried. Before a trader could go overland through the pass from Bobane to Dodinga, the sago would have turned green or yellow and soft. The Dutch estimated that there were about 140 Muslim and 60 alifuru men capable of bearing arms. About one and half hours by river to the west was another alifuru village called Tololiku with some thirty-five men. About 3 kilometers upstream from Kau was Pagu. Sometime in the past the Sangaji Kau had presented the settlement to Sultan Amsterdam and his wife to honor their visit. Though the sangaji claimed that Pagu had been given solely to the sultan's wife and only for the period of her lifetime, the people of Pagu asserted that they had been given to the sultans of Ternate in perpetuity and therefore needed no longer serve the Sangaji Kau. The Dutch believed that the people of Pagu would side with the VOC even against the Sultan Ternate. Two hours upriver from Pagu on the northern stream was the settlement of Mondole, which could field some 130 fighting men and whose inhabitants were considered by their neighbors to be "wild, shy, and fearsome."

From the mouth of the Kau River it was a day's row to a small beach at Bobane, which was the starting point of a half-hour journey through a pass in the mountains to Dodinga on the west coast. In Bobane the inhabitants made exceptionally fine clay pots which one Dutch governor in the late seventeenth century considered to be even finer than the ones made at the more well-known pottery production site on the island of Mare off the south coast of Tidore. Dodinga was not suited for agriculture since the crops expired in the dry weather and rotted in the rainy season. The inhabitants were not native to the area but were forcibly brought there from Morotai in the early seventeenth century. There were only about forty fighting men in Dodinga, but its importance lay in being the endpoint of an important pass used both by Ternate and Tidore to maintain links with their territories on the east coast of Halmahera. In 1686 there were two forts at Dodinga to protect the inhabitants and those using the pass: one was maintained by the Company and the other by Ternate. The Tidorese had two other longer passes further south, one going between Weda and Toseho, the other between Weda and Gita. The settlement of Toseho was a constant source of friction between Ternate and Tidore, as both claimed the area. In 1642 it was taken by the Dutch and given to Tidore, but a later agreement provided each the right to a particular section of the valuable sago forests in Toseho.

Ternate's territories in the southern peninsula of Halmahera consisted of Saketa and Gane. Saketa had large sago lands and two hundred fighting men from the alifuru settlements of Foya, Mafa, and Fedoa. Gane was the name of an island in the Patinti Straits, as well as the land on the opposite shore. In the late seventeenth century it was inhabited by alifuru because many of its original inhabitants had been deported to repopulate Moti and Makian after the Spanish conquest of 1606. Gane was noted for its abundance of sago and pinang trees, but its importance lay in its location on the route taken by Maba and Patani raiders. Victims of raids to Tobunku, Banggai, and Sula were sold in the market at Gane, thus assuring Gane of a healthy source of revenue. Both Gane and Saketa acknowledged the authority of the Sangaji Kayoa who lived in Makian.

The island of Makian was Ternate's most important territory in the periphery. It was described in the early sixteenth century as the most populous island with the largest clove harvest and the only safe harbor in north Maluku.[26] The large population on Makian was possible because the inhabitants made use of every available plot of land. Even in the seventeenth century there is reference to the land being cleared right to the summit of the mountain. Makian's importance in Maluku is suggested by the fact that in 1518 one of the earliest letters sent from Maluku to the king of Portugal was from "the king of Makian," named Lebai Hussain.[27] Although this is the only reference to an independent ruler in Makian, it would not be inconsistent with sources depicting an island with all the ingredients for a successful kingdom in Maluku. In some of the traditions Makian is mentioned among the first four kingdoms in Maluku, along with Ternate, Tidore, and Moti. According to these stories, the royal line from Moti eventually moved to Jailolo, while that of Makian went to Bacan to form the later but better known four kingdoms of Ternate, Tidore, Jailolo, and Bacan. By about 1520 Makian was divided between Ternate and Tidore, and a few years later Tidore was forced to give up any claims to that island. In 1606, after the Spanish conquest of Ternate, the entire island of Makian was given to Tidore. Two years later the Dutch assisted the Ternatens in reconquering Makian, and from 1648 Ternate's claim to the island was supported by the Dutch.[28]

Throughout Makian's history its active volcanoes have played havoc with the island's settlements. Many of its inhabitants have been forced to settle temporarily, and some permanently, on other islands. While some have abandoned the island, others seeking a new home have replaced the emigrants. One notable new group which came in 1662 was the entire population of the island of Kayoa.[29] Disease, natural calamities, and political oppression were all reasons given for resettlement. Despite these frequent dislocations, the group maintained its identity and links to its original homeland. The principal settlements on Makian in 1662 were: Ngofakiaha with 400 men and Ngofagita with 170 (both governed by sangajis, thus indicating their importance); Talapao, Sabaleh, Tapasoho, Bobawa, Ngofabobawa, and Lagona with a total of 349 men (all under kimalahas); those from Kayoa and elsewhere in the Goraici islands with 160. The inhabitants of Soma and Tahane had gone to live at Ngofakiaha, and together they had 260 men. The reason for the small number was Tahane's loss of an entire kora-kora with many of its young men against the Spaniards. A few other villages were said to have another fifty men, making a total on the whole island of Makian of 1,389 men. According to Dutch reports this number was well down from the period of eleven to twelve years previously. The reasons given for the decline were deaths resulting from epidemics and from an expedition against "rebels" in the Ambon region which had cost many Makian lives.[30]

The bond which held many of the settlements in the periphery together was the shared perception of belonging to a Maluku family sanctified in myth. The settlements of north Sulawesi and the islands to the north never participated in this shared sentiment and lacked any reason for maintaining their allegiance to Ternate. They were "returned" to Ternate by the VOC in the 1667 Bungaya treaty because of Dutch desire to have "neat archipelagoes" controlled by rulers friendly to the Dutch. The absence of any greater reason for loyalty made these areas far more volatile in their relations with Ternate than those which saw themselves as belonging to one family as defined by the myths.

The potential for challenges to Ternate's central status from the periphery was high. Some were themselves formerly substantial kingdoms in their own right and had played at one time an important regional role. Banggai, Butung, and Jailolo were examples of such kingdoms. Others, such as the Sula Islands, Buru, and the Hoamoal peninsula in western Seram, had become prominent in Ternate's affairs after being colonized by the Tomagola and Tomaitu families of the Fala Raha. With links to influential families in Ternate, these areas operated as independent entities with pretensions to becoming the new center. Some of the settlements which were located between the two powerful centers of Ternate on the one hand, and the southwest Sulawesi kingdoms of Goa or Bone on the other, used the rivalry as a leverage to their advantage. The communities in north and southeast Sulawesi, notably Tobunku, prospered in this position. Then there were the numerically large and resource-rich areas of Makian and Gamkonora, whose proximity to Ternate and access to the same sources of power made them natural competitors for dominance as a center.

Ternate had a special relationship with the alifuru of Halmahera, but especially with the Tobaru people. Through the reaffirmation of a common myth, the exchange of women and goods, and in some cases through the establishment of a permanent Ternaten governor and enclave in the territories, Ternate managed to retain the allegiance of the alifuru. The demands which Ternate made on them were the traditional indigenous ones of acknowledgment of the overlord's right to the first fruits of the land and to people for purposes of war and exchange. Both these acts of submission were regarded as essential to enable Ternate to perform its role as the guardian of the spiritual and material well-being of the whole kingdom. The relationship would have been strengthened by the common adherence among the Tobelo, Galela,

Loloda, and Tobaru people to the local concept of *madutu,* which acknowledges the universal existence of hierarchy whereby the superior partner "owns" and "commands" the inferior and the latter perceives itself as "belonging to" the former.[31]

Although the alifuru were under a Muslim sangaji or some other official based in a Muslim village on the coast, in reality the sangaji had only symbolic status as a representative of the sultan. Except for the seaward Tobelo settlements, where the Muslims and the alifuru lived among each other in one settlement (though probably in separate quarters as is the case today), the two communities were culturally and physically separate. Rather than submit to a Muslim sangaji, the alifuru preferred to give their allegiance directly to the Sultan Ternate. They genuinely believed in his special powers, which were made even more imposing by the myths surrounding his being. Nowhere was this more demonstrably evident than among the Tobarus. Their fierce loyalty to the person of the Sultan Ternate made them a major factor in the ruler's ability to withstand challenges to his authority. In the war between Ternate and the VOC, only the Tobarus remained faithful to Sultan Amsterdam up to the very point of his capture. As the Europeans quickly learned, the Tobarus earned their reputation as fierce and ruthless jungle fighters. Not even Portuguese, Spanish, or Dutch settlements on Ternate were beyond reach of these warriors, who were sent in shifts to undermine the confidence of the enemy in their homegrounds. They were greatly feared and deterred any contemplated hostile acts against the Ternate ruler.

Despite the distinction between center and periphery, they were conceived as one. Politically, the periphery came to adopt Ternaten titles as soon as it acknowledged Ternate as the center. Although these specific Dutch reports do not discuss the titles, other contemporary documents from Ternate indicate the use of the titles jogugu, sangaji, kimalaha, and kapita laut in the periphery. Even Magindanao, which was not included in the myths as part of the Malukan world, borrowed these Ternaten titles in the seventeenth century to demonstrate its acknowledgment of Ternate's central status.[32] Socially, there was frequent intermarriage between members of the royal family in Ternate with those in the periphery. But nowhere was the integration within the periphery, and between the periphery and the center, so clearly demonstrated as in the economic sphere. Each area in the periphery created its own local trade relationships, which were linked to those in other areas in the periphery, and eventually to Ternate as the hub of a regional economic network. Ternate's domination of the clove trade was the key to its ability to maintain a major role in the economy of the region and thereby affirm its claim to being the center.

Tidore and Its Periphery

The Gamrange, consisting of Maba, Patani, and Weda in southeast Halmahera, as well as the Papuan islands of the Raja Ampat, were the most important territories belonging to Tidore's periphery and were regarded as "the true breadbaskets of the Tidore kings."[33] However, it was not food that these areas provided but a rich tribute of ambergris, tortoiseshell, birds of paradise, slaves, and spices. As the Europeans, but especially the Dutch, made the trade in these items more difficult, Tidore began to rely more and more on its outlying Papuan and Halmahera subjects to find other outlets for these valuable products. It was Tidore's ability to obtain these tribute goods and to sell them in these far-off settlements free from European interference which helped to preserve Tidore's independence till well into the eighteenth century.

In 1702 a Dutch expedition was sent to Patani for the first time to observe the area at close hand and obtain information about the Gamrange. The island of Gebe off the Patani coast was not part of the Gamrange, but it always maintained close links with it. Gebe was called one of the Tidore ruler's "treasure houses" because, according to those in Patani, a lot of ambergris was found there.[34] The island itself was infertile and the coastline forbidding, and yet since the sixteenth century the Portuguese sources often listed Gebe as one of the four rajas of the Papuas. In 1703 the Sangaji Gebe was the collector of tribute for the Sultan Tidore in the Papuan islands, indicating that Gebe was still a place of importance to Tidore in the beginning of the eighteenth century.[35] When the Dutch conducted their own investigation, they found that a major reason for its prominence was the ability of its seamen to attract traders to Gebe's ports and make that island an entrepôt for local goods. Gebe was not the site for ambergris, as the Dutch had been told earlier, but it could obtain ambergris because of its role as a central marketplace for the region. In 1702 the Patani folk discouraged the Dutch from making the journey to Gebe to prevent them from discovering the truth about that island.[36] A Dutch description of 1706 mentions three settlements on the northern side of the island, with half the population Muslim and the other half followers of a local belief. In total there were some four to five hundred fighting men on Gebe.[37]

Patani was described as stony and hilly with very little flat land. Fortunately, off the coast of Patani was a small island called Mor with fertile soil where the people had their gardens.[38] There were numerous cliffs at the Hook of Patani and no good anchorage. Officially no one could come to Patani to trade without the consent of the Sultan Tidore, and to arrive without a letter from the ruler was to court danger. Whenever a boat appeared in the harbor, hundreds of Patanese would rush to the beach with bows and arrows. They were considered by the Dutch to be "the greatest pirates and rogues known in these eastern quarters." In 1706 there were a sangaji and seven gimalahas (the Tidore equivalent of the Ternaten kimalaha, one of the terms used for a village head) governing a population of which only half was Muslim. In the whole of Patani there were an estimated twelve hundred men capable of bearing arms.[39]

Maba's two principal settlements were on an island of the same name located about 400 meters from the southeast Halmahera mainland and at Bicoli. They were both governed by sangajis, while the rest of the villages were under gimalahas. Maba had access to good freshwater springs, rivers, and anchorage, and had a total of 2,000 to 2,400 able-bodied men. The first Dutch expedition to Maba was marked by open hostility. Maba had thrived on the spice trade, and it resented the arrival of the joint Dutch-Tidore expedition in 1702 to destroy the spice trees. When the Dutch approached the village accompanied by the Sultan Tidore's representatives, they were chased away. Though the visitors were recognized, these Maba folk cursed the Patanese for bringing the Dutch to their settlements, and they showed scant regard for the Tidorese. When after repeated conferences the Tidore envoy in exasperation asked whether they no longer wished to obey the Sultan Tidore and to return once again to a situation without a king, their reply was to make an obscene gesture by striking their genitalia, screaming, and shooting off a volley of arrows. The inhabitants resented the fact that they were required to point out all of their clove and nutmeg trees to the expedition, which planned to destroy "the flower of clove gardens [which had been in existence] since the time of the Spaniards."[40]

Weda's lands in the beginning of the eighteenth century extended as far to the northwest as the overland route at Bobane, and from its settlements some eight hundred to a thousand fighting men could be assembled. The prominent people in Weda were Muslims, but the greatest part of the population were believers in the local religion. Nevertheless, the Weda folk appeared to be more Islamic than the other groups on southeast Halmahera, though the occasions when Islam was invoked raised suspicion that the people had found religion an ideal pretext to oppose Dutch wishes. When the Dutch requested some fifty men for the spice eradication campaign to be assembled the following day, the Weda folk asked for a postponement since that particular day was the Islamic Sabbath. They also claimed that they did not have any tortoiseshell because, being Muslims, their religion forbade the catching of tortoises. They explained to the Dutch that on certain occasions they went to the Papuan islands to get tortoiseshell to trade for cloth with the Tidorese, who were found at Weda in large numbers throughout the year.

In 1705 the Dutch outfitted an expedition to the Raja Ampat and

obtained the first detailed description of the Papuan islands. On Salawati were two settlements located on opposite sides of a large river
which ran through the island. All the houses were on high piles, and
most were perched over the river. A fair way inland the river was fenced
like a maze so that the Dutch had to turn left, then right, and then pro-
ceed straight ahead until they reached the Raja Salawati's residence far
upriver. A letter from the Sultan Tidore was delivered by his envoy to
the jojau since the Raja Salawati had gone to the island of Numfor. The
jojau received the letter and brought it up to his head with both hands in
a sign of great respect for the Sultan Tidore. The letter was then handed
back to the envoy who read it in Tidorese to the assembled chiefs, which
included by chance the raja and kapita laut of the island of Misool.
When the letter ended, all those present uttered an "Amin," the
response normally made at the end of a Muslim prayer. Since their
incorporation into Tidore's periphery, the Papuans associated Tidore
with Islam, and so they accorded the Sultan Tidore's words and physical letter with the same veneration reserved for the word of Allah in the
Holy Koran.

The Raja Salawati had gone to Numfor to buy tobacco, mats
(kajang), and other necessities. He returned before the Dutch expedition
had departed, and so he requested that the Sultan Tidore's letter be
read again with the Dutch present, but this time at his house. When this
was done, the raja replied with an "Amin." In response to the Dutch
request that he prepare a boat for them, he answered that they were not
to ask but to command. All that he possessed, even his own life,
belonged to the Sultan Tidore and the VOC. The women then came
and performed a ritual dance, which one Dutchman described as "that
miserable dance which lasted from shortly after midday until the evening." The Tidore envoy remained on the kora-kora with the Raja
Salawati and his close followers because, he explained, if he did not do
this the people would not offer the Raja Salawati their obedience.[41] As a
representative of the Sultan Tidore, the envoy was considered to be
imbued with the sacred royal presence which the Papuan leaders could
absorb via the ruler's proxy.

On the southeastern and southwestern part of Salawati were
numerous islands and reefs. Salawati itself was "reasonably populous,"
with most of the people living an itinerant existence in the interior and
the mountains in small temporary hamlets. Those who lived on the
coast, especially the chiefs to whom the interior people paid allegiance,
were Muslims though not knowledgeable about Islam. All claimed to be
the subjects of Tidore. The raja and the kapita laut both lived in the
same settlement located on the southeastern side of the island on the
banks of a river. They earned their living mainly from slaves (especially
from New Guinea), sago, tortoiseshell, ambergris, and spices, which

they sold to the traders from Tidore but especially to those from Keffing.[42]

The Dutch went from Salawati to Waigeu, home of the second of the four rulers of the Raja Ampat islands. Waigeu, with a length of about fifty-five kilometers, was the largest of the Papuan islands and was full of bays. The Dutch entered the bay on the southeast side of the island where the Raja Waigeu had his residence. Warjo was located on the eastern hook and Umpain, consisting of four villages, on the western side of the island. The Dutch expedition of 1705–1706 went first to Waigamerok, the kapita laut's settlement, close to Lake Waigeu. The next morning the Raja Waigeu arrived from his own settlement at Kabilolo. They both received the letter from the Sultan Tidore with great respect as in Salawati, and they all concluded the reading of the sultan's letter with an "Amin." The Dutch noted that at Salawati, Waigeu, and the islands in the Sagewin Straits between Salawati and Batanta, the Papuans did not utter a single word except through one of the Tidore envoys. Their reticence may have been caused by the fact that three months before the arrival of the Dutch, the Sangaji Patani and the Sangaji Maba, who were ordinarily the intermediaries between Tidore and the Raja Ampat, had come to the settlement of Muka on Waigeu and had taken away its chief.

From Waigamerok the expedition paddled into the inland lake and after about an hour entered a large river flowing between high sheer cliffs. This led them into another lake "as wide as the distance between Ternate and Halmahera." From the beginning of the lake to its furthest point, where the Raja Waigeu had his residence, measured about 11 kilometers. There were rugged cliffs along the lake and a piece of flat land jutting out into the water. Near the Raja Waigeu's settlement, which consisted of about fifteen houses, were a reasonably large island and a few smaller ones. The Dutch were told by the raja that there were no spice trees on Waigeu and that whatever spices they had were obtained by trade with those from the Gamrange. No one exchanged more than about eight whole nuts from the nutmeg tree at one time since they were used only for medicinal purposes. The people did not use spices as condiments and ate mainly sago and smoked fish. In exchange for these spices/medicines, the local people gave *kokojas* (mats?) or *kabilangs* (a type of knife). When some of the Waigeu leaders arrived in the raja's settlement, they gave similar responses to Dutch questions about the presence of spices on the island. In Waigeu the raja, the kapita laut, and the jojau had a total of only fifty-six fighting men, although those who had gone to Misool on a boat were not counted among them. On Waigeu, as on Salawati, Batanta, and Gam, there were large rivers, and the main sources of food were freshwater fish, sago, a few fruits, and tubers.

The Dutch expedition did not visit the island of Misool where the remaining two rajas of the Raja Ampat lived. However, the Dutch had compiled sufficient information about Misool for Governor Pieter Rooselaar to make his report in 1706. He described Misool as being about 64 kilometers in circumference and consisting mainly of islands and reefs. It was divided between the kingdoms of Misool and Waigama, "both tributaries, or better, subjects of the king of Tidore." On the east side was the kingdom of Misool, located at the furthest inland point of a bay. Right next to the raja's settlement was that of the kapita laut. Both these chiefs were supreme in their own settlements, which had a total of three thousand fighting men. The vast majority of the people retained their local beliefs and lived inland in the mountains and recognized the leadership of the Muslims, who lived in houses on stilts on the coast. The settlement of the Raja Waigama was located in the northwest part of the island, not far from the westernmost point of land, although in 1706 he was living in the south of the island. The inhabitants of Waigama, like those of Misool, were divided into subjects of the raja and those of the kapita laut and had a total fighting force of five or six hundred men. The island produced almost nothing but a few fruit trees, and the people's main staple was sago. The most important trade of the island was slaves, which they obtained through raiding and from the market in Salawati. Another trade item of less importance was birds of paradise which they sold to those from East Seram. A great advantage which Misool possessed was its good water and reasonable anchorage.

The Papuan islanders were described as of "medium" height, black, with kinky hair which they grew long. Both men and women went about naked except for a cover over their genitalia. They wore strings of objects, such as corals and pieces of pipe, around their necks and arms as decorations. According to the Dutch they were "simple and artless, but cruel, rapacious, and murderous." Their weapons were the bow and arrow, the shield and sword, and the spear. They frequented the coastlines with their small but fast rowboats and were very good seamen. No one could sail into these waters with safety if not accompanied by a Tidorese. The Dutch believed that they worshiped all manner of land and sea plants, as well as idols of humans, beasts, and fish which they themselves made and to whom they presented offerings. Each household was said to have its own special deities. The heads of the coastal villages were mostly descendants of settlers who had come from Tidore and East Seram. In contrast to the true natives of the region, they had long straight hair and dressed like the Tidorese. Outwardly they were Muslims, but in the ritual dance they momentarily abandoned their attachment to Islam and demonstrated a strong empathy for local beliefs. It was even said that they paid greater heed to the local deities than to the Muslim god, though they were careful to mask this preference in the presence of the Tidorese.[43]

These eighteenth century Dutch observers were the first Europeans to describe in some detail the inhabitants of the Gamrange and the Papuan islands. While they understood that the Papuan islands and the Gamrange acknowledged the leadership of Tidore, they could not have known how intricate and old their relationship actually was. A historical reconstruction based on linguistic evidence provides a time frame between 15,000 and 10,000 years ago when the first Papuan-speakers settled in the eastern Indonesian islands. The language spoken in Halmahera and Morotai, which are classified as belonging to the West Papuan Phylum, are said to have stemmed from this period. It is suggested that around 3000 B.C. there was a second expansion by another Papuan group who spoke a Trans New Guinea Phylum language and settled on the north coast of New Guinea. They migrated west of New Guinea to areas which were already inhabited by Austronesian-speakers, and also came to replace the earlier West Papuan languages in Timor, Alor, and Pantar. Other evidence indicates, however, that the Austronesian-speakers may have arrived somewhat later, perhaps about 2500 B.C., after the second Papuan migration.[44] At an unspecified but more recent date, there were further movements of Papuan populations from the Biak areas of the Schouten and Padaido Islands to east Halmahera and the Raja Ampat Islands. According to one tradition, this was the time of the Biak culture hero Gurabesi who came to serve the Sultan Tidore against Ternate.[45] Some Tidore court documents state that Gurabesi appeared during the reign of Sultan Mansur, the tenth ruler of Tidore, who ruled sometime in the second half of the fifteenth century.[46] However, another court source indicates that the events occurred under Mansur's successor, Sultan Jamaluddin (r. 1495?–1572?).[47]

In Maluku the Austronesian-speakers came into contact with the numerous and well-established Papuan-speaking communities,[48] leading to the mutual borrowing of words and concepts and the blurring of distinctions at the very edges. Today in north Maluku the people of Ternate, Tidore, half of Makian, and northern Halmahera speak Papuan languages; the other half of Makian, Bacan, and most of south Halmahera except for pockets in the southwest speak an Austronesian language. Despite possessing different languages, the two cultures have become so intermingled over the centuries through social and economic interaction that they share a number of common elements. The closeness of the ties between the Papuan groups and the other Malukan peoples is evident in Malukan traditions. The Gamrange in southeast Halmahera comprises Austronesian-speaking communities who in the past were accorded special esteem by the Papuan islanders. When the

Austronesian-speaking Papuans of Biak arrived in these islands, they found an earlier Papuan group known as the Sawai, who had first settled in the Gamrange and later in the Papuan islands. The Papuans therefore came to regard the Sawai as the original settlers and possessing greater prestige than the latecomers.[49] It enabled the Gamrange to play a leadership role in the affairs of the Raja Ampat. Their sangajis were delegated the responsibility of collecting tribute for the Tidore ruler, and they were often at the head of Papuan fleets which the Sultan Tidore summoned against his enemies. So valued was this position of head of the Papuans that in 1728 the Sangaji Patani petitioned the Sultan Tidore to be reinstated as the administrator or tribute-collector of the Papuan islands.[50]

The Sultan Tidore's relationship with the Gamrange and the Papuans of the Raja Ampat is explained in another tradition from the Tidore court. Before the arrival of Islam, Ternate and Tidore were constantly at war with one another. The ruler of Tidore, Sultan Mansur, thus summoned the Sangaji Patani Sahmardan to ask him whether there was any man in his village or in neighboring areas who was brave, strong, and able to assist him against the Ternatens. Sahmardan promised to seek such a person, and so he traveled through the islands and reached Waigeu. At a place called Kabu he met the Kapita Waigeu named Gurabesi. When Gurabesi was informed of the search and the prospects of the individual receiving from the Tidore ruler special clothes to mark the occasion of his new official position, he asked permission to hold the clothes for a few moments. He took the clothes, kissed them, and raised them above his head as a sign of respect for the Sultan Tidore. Gurabesi then summoned his men and traveled to the Tidore court where they were greeted by the ruler and hosted to a feast in their honor. Gurabesi offered his services to the ruler and was rewarded with a suit of clothes. In battle Gurabesi distinguished himself and was given the ruler's daughter, Boki Taebah, for his wife. They later returned to Waigeu to live.

After ten years had passed, the ruler of Tidore began to wonder what had become of his child. At the time he was dissatisfied with the small size of his kingdom and the few subjects which he possessed. These two factors encouraged him to undertake an expedition to the east. He went to Patani, Gebe, and the Raja Ampat Islands. At Waigeu he again met Gurabesi and they, along with the Sangaji Patani and the large following which the ruler had gathered at each place, went to the New Guinea mainland. Wherever the ruler stopped, he selected individuals to be his officials with titles of sangaji, gimalaha, and so forth. On the return trip the expedition again stopped at Waigeu, where the ruler made his four male grandchildren the rulers of Waigeu, Salawati, Waigama, and Misool. Another version of this expedition says the kapitas of the southeast Halmahera settlements of Buli, Maba, Bicoli, and Patani were raised by the Tidore ruler to become the rulers of the four Raja Ampat kingdoms.[51] A third version speaks of a conflict among four brothers which led to their being separated. The youngest settled in Waigama but eventually left and went to Seram. "Until he returns," so goes the tale, "the unity remains broken because four was the number of the kings who ruled these [Raja Ampat] islands."[52] All the lands which the ruler visited became his vassals. The Sangaji Patani Sahmardan was officially made the *utusan*, or the ruler's representative, in Tidore's periphery. The entire expedition was said to have taken seven months and seventy-seven days.[53]

The tale explains the prominent position held by the Sangaji Patani in the affairs of the Raja Ampat Islands and the Gamrange. Among the kings of the Raja Ampat the position of Waigeu seems to be highlighted because of the role of the Biak culture hero, Gurabesi. Misool, on the other hand, appears to have had closer relations with Bacan. In the early seventeenth century it had even agreed to sell products exclusively to Bacan. Bacan's links with the Raja Ampat may even have predated those of Tidore, which would be in keeping with the Bikusagara origin myth emphasizing Bacan's antiquity. In 1569 the Papuan rulers of the Raja Ampat paid a friendly visit to Bacan, and intermarriages between the royal families were not uncommon.[54]

Another interesting feature of the tale is the mention of the distribution of official clothing and titles to the various areas visited by the ruler of Tidore. This is a process suggested in the contemporary European sources, and it seems to have been attractive to the Papuan leaders. An explanation of this phenomenon is suggested by F. C. Kamma, who described the Papuans' desire to absorb the spiritual powers associated with any object which had had contact with the Tidore ruler.[55] In the eighteenth century during the annual and sometimes semiannual tribute-gathering expeditions to the Papuan islands, no representative from the Tidore court could forgo the formal physical transfer of the letter from the Tidore ruler to the Papuan lords. The document itself was believed to be as potent as the words contained in it, and an important aspect of the ceremony was the physical contact with the letter to obtain the Sultan Tidore's mana. The Tidore sultan's envoy was also regarded as a repository of the sacred royal presence. The Raja Salawati insisted that the sultan's envoy remain on board the boat with him to assure that his subjects continued to give him allegiance. The Raja Salawati, through physical propinquity to the sultan's proxy, was believed to be absorbing the ruler's mana. The process was similar to the practice of Papuans bringing tribute to Tidore and crawling on all fours on the court floor to "sweep up" any spiritual traces of the ruler's sacred being. On the return of the tribute mission, equated with the rak or head-hunting expedition, an important part of the Papuan homecoming ceremony was the sharing of the booty. The people gathered and solemnly touched the hands of the leaders of the tribute mission in order to share in the sacred power of the Sultan Tidore while it was still "hot."[56] What the ceremony celebrated was the acquisition of spiritual powers, either through association with the sultan or through the taking of heads, for the well-being of the community.

In speaking of the Papuan areas, the Dutch reports of the early eighteenth century made a clear distinction between the coastal population, many of whom seem to have been Tidorese or East Seram descendants who were Muslim, and the interior Papuan groups who retained belief in their own gods. There were nevertheless local Papuans who had embraced Islam as part of the total acceptance of the world of their lord, the Sultan Tidore. The chiefs were given the principal titles of raja, kolano, jojau, and kapita laut or their local variations. They in turn appointed subordinates in their community to receive other "foreign" titles such as sangaji, gimalaha, and sowohi. The titles were believed to be imbued with the sacred force of the Tidore ruler which could shield those who held it. As a result it became a practice to transfer titles to the various clans (keret) to assure them of permanent spiritual protection. The importance of the titles is indicated by the general view among the Papuan islanders that the main purpose of the tribute missions to Tidore was to receive titles.[57] In dress, too, the newly found status was emphasized. While the rest of the population usually wore loincloths, the newly "Tidorized" leaders wore shirts and other items of clothing associated with Tidore.

The adoption of foreign titles did not indicate a shift to a more centralized hierarchical structure, but rather a way of distinguishing the major chiefs of a particular island or the most important leaders within one community. On Salawati, for example, the raja and the jojau lived in the same settlement but were of equal status. When the Dutch conducted their business with the jojau in the absence of the raja, the latter on his return insisted on being treated in the same manner. On Misool, the raja and the kapita laut lived in separate settlements and had equal powers in their respective communities. There is little indication in the Papuan islands of a central court with officials, despite the adoption of the Tidorese court ranking system and the presence of the *Kalana Fat*, or "Four Kolanos," which mirrored the four sultans in north Maluku.

In addition to being the source of new titles, dress, and religion for the Papuan islanders, Tidore was the chief supplier of foreign goods. Because the Papuans associated these objects with the ruler of Tidore, they believed that possession of such spiritually imbued items would guarantee material wealth, health, and happiness.[58] The coastal communities were the principal beneficiaries of the link with Tidore. By gaining access to iron implements, weapons and cloth from Tidore, items of great value to the interior Papuan groups, the coastal lords were able to exercise considerable influence over the interior Papuans. In ritual matters the coastal inhabitants differed little from their interior brethren. They regarded their links to the local deities as essential and continued to perform the customary ceremonies, despite having embraced Islam. For the Papuans, as in many other Indonesian and Pacific Island societies, life consisted of interlocking worlds of relationships, all of which had to be carefully nurtured.

Dutch description of the Muslim Papuans of the early eighteenth century resembles in many details the Portuguese account of the Muslims in the north Malukan states in the early sixteenth century. Islam in north Maluku then was very much a coastal phenomenon and confined to the circles of the rulers or chiefs. Even among the Muslims there was a strong belief in local spirits and little adherence to religious food taboos. They were the dominant group though numerically inferior to the believers in local gods. Although the Islamization of the Papuan islanders took place some two centuries after the introduction of Islam to north Maluku, the process was very similar. Islam was brought first to the leading members of the community and only later spread to the rest of the populace. This would accord with what is known to have happened in the rest of the Malay-Indonesian archipelago. The Papuan case is especially instructive because it provides an explanation for the merging of political and spiritual motivations for conversion, which was very much in keeping with local perceptions of the proper functioning of relationships in Maluku. To enter into a beneficial relationship with an overlord required a total commitment to his world, which was demonstrated in the "transformation" of the subject in name, dress, and spiritual belief.

Papuan traditions contributed to the establishment and maintenance of links with Tidore. According to Biak stories the west, the land of the souls, was regarded as the origin of power and wealth. The Papuan islanders therefore found little difficulty in accepting as appropriate that their overlord should come from a western area known as Tidore. Another Biak belief was that the center of mythical power was the source of the flood in the Lowerworld. Combining these two traditions, the Papuans created a myth in which the source was located in Tidore, while another explained that in times of crisis, the source of eternal bliss moved from the south (or from "below" in local directional terminology) to Tidore.[59] In thirty-five of seventy-five Biak myths collected by a Dutch missionary-anthropologist in the early twentieth century, a prominent theme was ceremonial valuables. In addition to the "older" treasures, such as shell wristbands, canoes, and utensils, there were also "newer" items of porcelain, beads, bronze gongs, and especially cotton lengths, which were so esteemed that they were counted as units of value or *chelopen*. Since the manufacture of these items was a mystery to the Papuans, these objects became associated with their source.[60] Tidore was the major source of these items and thus acquired prestige in the eyes of the Papuans. Tidore's location in the west and its possession of ceremonial objects were comprehensible to the Papuans as signs revealing a center of power and wealth. As in the societies in north Maluku, the Papuans sought explanation of present realities within an established cultural framework.

The special relationship between Tidore and its periphery was prefigured in two myths, one from north Maluku and the other from the Papuans from the Raja Ampat islands. In the Bikusagara myth, one of the elders of Bacan discovered four naga eggs from which issued four individuals who came to establish the royal houses of Bacan, Butung-Banggai, Loloda, and the Papuas. A close familial link between the Papuan areas and north Maluku was thus affirmed by this creation myth. Among the Papuans there was another myth about a hero or *mambri* named Gurabesi who went on a voyage to the west to Tidore, married the sultan's daughter, and became a subject of Tidore. It was from this Gurabesi that the four rajas from the Raja Ampat kingdoms of Salawati, Waigeu, Misool, and Waigama were descended. Thus in these two myths, plus other traditions among the Papuans stressing the special position of Tidore, both Tidore and the Papuans would have found cultural explanations for their special ties.

The Gamrange and the Papuan islanders proved to be among Tidore's most important subjects in the periphery. They had a large number of able-bodied men whose expertise on the sea and fierceness in battle were well documented. The swift Papuan boats, which proved highly effective in open-sea sailing, went as far as the northern coast of New Guinea and to north Sulawesi, trading and raiding in all of these areas. The Papuan islanders were also valuable in establishing Tidore's links with areas further east. Those from Raja Ampat moved easily between the islands and the lands of their ancestors in Biak in north New Guinea, thereby preparing the way for Tidore's expansion into the New Guinea mainland. The Raja Misool had a special relationship with the people in Onin on the southwest coast of New Guinea, while those of East Seram had their own reciprocal arrangements with different Papuan groups on the mainland. Through trade friendships established among groups in Halmahera, the Raja Ampat Islands, the coast of New Guinea, and East Seram, a thriving economic network existed in Tidore's periphery. When the Dutch applied stringent measures to control Tidore's trade, the Tidorese used the passes at Toseho and Gita to Weda in southeast Halmahera to bring their products to the Gamrange, the Raja Ampat Islands, and eventually to Keffing, which in the eighteenth century became a thriving redistribution center for eastern goods. As Dutch restrictions began to increase in the second half of the seventeenth and the eighteenth centuries, the periphery became crucial to the survival of the center.

Center/Periphery Relations

The Christian European tradition of the center and the periphery representing moral and spiritual polarities was in sharp contrast to the Malukan idea of complementarity and unity in center/periphery relations. Within Maluku the dominant sociopolitical imagery was of the four pillars or kingdoms which upheld the Malukan world and helped to define its extent. Within this circumscribed world lived societies which expressed relationships with each other in familial terms in accordance with the creation myths. The conceptualizing of a world as a family with each group responding to the other on the basis of either father/ mother to child, or older child to younger child, emphasized an ideal which encouraged mutual respect and proper protocol in accordance with one's status. As in a family unit, the situations within the group could change. With the death (demise) of a parent (dominant state) and the assumption of this role by the child (dependent state), a new familial relationship would result but based on the same principles as previously. Crucial to the success of the relationship between center and periphery in Maluku was a mutual acknowledgment of the superior power and resources of one area over the other. Nevertheless, the relationship was intended to be of mutual benefit, and there was continual assessment by both sides to assure that such an arrangement was maintained. This placed considerable pressure on the center to demonstrate its superiority in the face of ongoing demands and challenges from the periphery. Shifts of allegiance were a barometer of change in the center and the periphery and were regarded as a natural state of affairs. For the Malukans, therefore, the center and periphery did adjust to political realities, but the crucial element defining this relationship remained unchanged: they belonged to a single family inhabiting the world of Maluku.

One consequence of the fluidity of center/periphery relations was the emphasis on the human community rather than on geographic location as a basis of identity. There was frequent dislocation in Maluku due to the harsh physical environment, natural disasters, wars, and epidemics. The presence of many different groups on one island became commonplace. Nevertheless, each group retained its separate identity in its new location by preserving the name of its original homeland. Padtbrugge observed in 1679 after his long expedition visiting the various areas of Maluku that, "because of the uncertainty of a permanent residence, the people gave their name to the land, and not the land to the people."[61] For example, the Butung inhabitants of Kaloncucu retained their special identity by giving their new settlement in Ternate the name of their original village. A similar practice was followed by those forcibly removed from their homeland and resettled on other islands in Maluku. The frequent movement of populations, and the presence of different transplanted groups within a single community, helped to reaffirm the notion of plurality within a larger Malukan family as depicted in the origin myths.

Also noteworthy was the ritual division of the Maluku world into a Ternate sphere, generally to the north and west, and a Tidore sphere to the south and east. The consistency of the north-west and south-east division was also maintained on the larger islands of Halmahera and Seram. A tale from Tidore's periphery "explains" it by saying that Ternate went by sea while Tidore went by land.[62] This is a cultural explanation which is based on a general acknowledgment of the complementary relationship between Ternate and Tidore. In the list of titles of the four kingdoms collected by Padtbrugge in 1682, Tidore's ruler is called "Lord of the Mountain" while Ternate's was provided with the epithet "Lord of Maluku," whose precise meaning remains a matter of speculation. Marriage arrangements between Ternate and Tidore suggest that Tidore was the superior ritual partner and therefore most likely associated with the land, or the indigenous element. Ternate's greater involvement with foreign groups or the overseas element, as well as its ritual dualism with Tidore, would have made it logically the "Lord of the Sea" as the complementary half to Tidore. It would have been comprehensible to Malukans accustomed to overseas influence coming almost exclusively from the north and the west.

The association of Ternate with the sea and the directions north and west, and Tidore with the land and the directions south and east, appears to have support in historical linguistic evidence. The proto-Austronesian term for north was *laSud "toward the sea," and for south *Daya "toward the interior," while west was *qabaRat "northwest monsoon" and *qaCimur "southeast monsoon." Though later the Sanskrit term utara was used for north, and the local Malay word selatan or "straits" for south, the original meanings of the proto-Austronesian terms were not discarded in many areas.[63] In Maluku too this older Austronesian directional pattern may have been retained to form the basis for the ritual association of Ternate with the sea and the directions north/northwest and Tidore with the land and the directions south/southeast.

Another feature of Maluku's center/periphery arrangement was the importance of the origin myth of the four naga eggs in determining the Maluku family. In 1667 certain lands were seized from the Makassar kingdom of Goa and given to Ternate. These were Salayar, the various settlements in north Sulawesi, and the Sangihe-Talaud islands. Although Ternaten sources say that under Sultan Hairun (r. 1535–1570) and Sultan Babullah (r. 1570–1583) these areas had come to acknowledge Ternate's suzerainty, they were never regarded as being a true part of Maluku in the same way as Butung or Banggai. By the late seventeenth century these areas had broken away from Ternate and asked to become vassals of the Dutch Company. To the Dutch the inability of Ternate to enforce its authority in this region was an indication of the weakness and lack of resolve of the Ternaten leadership. Yet Ternate at the same time was able to maintain its control over other distant areas with little difficulty. The difference lay in what was regarded as the proper sphere of Ternate activity as defined by Malukan traditions. In the origin myths delineating the larger boundaries of Maluku, the areas of Salayar, north Sulawesi, and Sangihe-Talaud were never perceived as being part of this world. On the other hand, areas of southeast Sulawesi and the islands off the coast were definitely regarded as belonging to Maluku. The element of compulsion was never as effective in maintaining links between the center and periphery as was the belief in the shared myth of origin. Even in the late seventeenth century a king of Butung proudly boasted of his origin from one of the four sacred naga eggs.

What appears to have been a crucial factor in the maintenance of center/periphery ties—one which more adequately explains the relationship than the hierarchical power implications of the frequently used opposition "lord/vassal"—was the recognition by both that they belonged to a large family sacrally conceived and that cooperating as family members would be of mutual benefit. The nature of the exchange of products and services for prestige goods and spiritual blessings was in no way regarded as an unequal and oppressive arrangement. An excellent example was seen in the Papuan tribute missions to the Tidore court. During the prostration ceremony, which was expected of all those who came in the presence of the ruler, the Papuans believed it to be an ideal opportunity to "sweep up" the ruler's mana still clinging to the floor and surroundings. Unlike the European perception of the periphery as being remote and foreign to the center in its physical, moral, and intellectual aspects, the Malukan periphery was viewed in every way as a necessary complement to the center which together assured the unity and prosperity of their total world.

PART TWO

THE ENCOUNTER

THE STORY OF MALUKU in the early modern period involves the encounter of the European and Malukan worlds. They represent two distinct ideological standpoints within which national and ethnic microcosms with more localized and specific concerns proliferated. These latter concerns predominated in relationships within the overarching world to which they belonged. But in relationships between their world and others beyond it, the identification and concerns of the separate parts were subsumed to those of the greater entity. Both the Europeans and the Malukans in these centuries had well-established notions of the "Other," notions which often led to mistrust, misconception, and eventually conflict. This was particularly evident in the sixteenth century when neither the Portuguese, the Spaniards, nor the Malukans transformed their basic conceptual framework but instead found ways to explain and hence domesticate the other within the context of their own particular worldview.

By the seventeenth and eighteenth centuries, both the Dutch and the Malukans had benefited from the experiences of the previous century and were far more knowledgeable of each other. Nevertheless, both continued to adhere to the basic assumptions which defined and gave meaning to their world. What made the encounter in the seventeenth and eighteenth centuries more serious than that of the sixteenth was the fact that the Dutch were far better equipped technologically than their Iberian rivals to assert their dominance in Maluku. To continue to pursue their concerns the Malukans were forced to adapt to new rules imposed by the Dutch. But this they did admirably and succeeded in maintaining the unity of their world.

CHAPTER FOUR

The Meeting of the Two Worlds in the Sixteenth Century

WHEN THE EUROPEANS and the Malukans first met in the early sixteenth century, they both reacted in a way conditioned by their particular views of the world. The Europeans, though exposed to recent experiences in India, were still inclined to suspect the "humanity" of the East. Though enlightened enough to question the more exaggerated claims of monstrous races, they nevertheless retained attitudes of moral superiority to a society inhabiting the very periphery of the "civilized" European world. For the Malukans the Europeans, like other groups flocking to the region to obtain spices, were strangers who did not belong to the exclusive Malukan family depicted in the myths. As outsiders, the Europeans could never hope to enjoy the privileges reserved for the group. These two differing perceptions of the other almost immediately placed the two worlds on a confrontational footing. Exacerbating this state of affairs was the character of the European personnel sent to Maluku, which in every way simply confirmed the European view that the periphery naturally attracted those less than civilized.

European Initiative and Christianity

In 1511 a Portuguese fleet under the command of Afonso de Albuquerque conquered the prosperous and powerful Malay kingdom of Melaka. The conquest had major repercussions throughout the region, but especially in the spice-producing islands of Maluku. Melaka had not only been the major center for the collection and redistribution of clove, nutmeg, and mace, but also Maluku's principal source of prestige goods for the pretensions of the kolanos and sangajis, as well as useful items for daily use of the common folk. The dismay at the loss of this market prompted Ternate and Tidore to seek out the new conquerors with the hope of reestablishing former trade arrangements in Melaka. Before

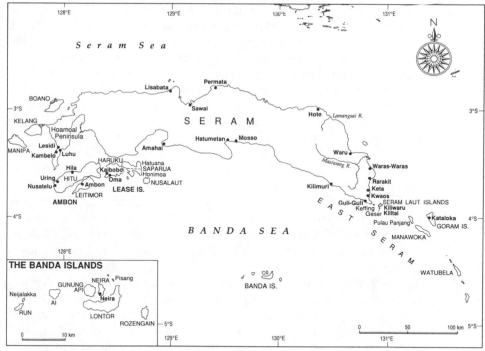

MAP 4. Central and South Maluku

they were able to send a mission to Melaka, however, three Portuguese ships under the general command of Antonio de Abreu were sent by Albuquerque to search for the spice islands. Since the Malays and Javanese were the chief traders in spices, they were employed as pilots to guide the Portuguese expedition which left Melaka sometime between November 1511 and January 1512.[1]

The ships went via Gresik in Java and then eastward to Buru, Ambon, and Seram. At Guli-Guli in eastern Seram, Francisco Serrão ordered his ship to be burnt because it had become too old and unseaworthy. From Guli-Guli the expedition continued southward to Banda where Serrão bought a junk and loaded it with cloves, nutmeg, and mace. On the return journey from Banda in early 1512, the fleet was struck by a storm, and Serrão's junk was sunk on the shoals of Lusi Para. Only Serrão and six or seven others survived, and they were brought by some local fishermen to the settlement of Ambon (though some say to Nusatelu, in present-day Asilulu). Their presence was reported to Sultan Abu Lais of Ternate,[2] who was already familiar with Portuguese exploits through information brought by traders and a Muslim teacher returning from the pilgrimage in Mecca. Eager to befriend this powerful nation and to gain its alliance, Abu Lais sent his brother Kaicili Vaidua, an important casis in the kingdom, to serve as his personal envoy to the shipwrecked Portuguese. Vaidua succeeded in persuading Serrão and his men to return with him to Ternate on a junk in 1512.[3] In a vessel owned by another nation and without fanfare, the Portuguese ended their long search for the holy grail: the homeland of the clove, nutmeg, and mace, the so-called holy trinity of spices.

For the Ternatens Serrão's arrival was immediately interpreted as confirmation of Sultan Abu Lais' special powers. He was acknowledged as a living oracle by his people, and the arrival of the Portuguese was regarded as a fulfillment of his prophecy that from a distant part of the globe would come men of iron who would become inhabitants in his territory and extend "the dominion and glory of Maluku."[4] The sultan therefore welcomed Serrão to his kingdom and promised to deliver cloves to the Portuguese on the condition that when Serrão returned to Portugal he would persuade the king, Dom Manuel, to build a fortress on Ternate "and in no other place."[5] In his letter Abu Lais entrusted Dom Manuel with "his land and all in it" and asked for arms for their defense.[6] Motivated by the prophecy, Abu Lais sent two of Serrão's crew members back to Melaka to request "more Portuguese men, arms, and a factory for the clove trade." To the Portuguese captain of Melaka he explained: "I have heard that the king of Portugal helps all those kings who are one with him, thus enhancing their kingdoms. . . . I want to say to you that in this land of Maluku there is trade in cloves, nutmeg, and mace, and this kingdom is yours to command. Sir, I have heard of the king of Cochin who received the mercies shown him by the king of Portugal." Abu Lais was referring to the ruler of Cochin on the west coast of India, whose arrangements for the delivery of pepper to the Portuguese had brought him wealth and power. With visions of a similar lucrative agreement which would substantiate the prophecy, he requested from Melaka a *dachin* with the seal of the king of Portugal on it. The dachin was a measure of Chinese origin used widely in the archipelago by traders. Since the traders refused to use the Ternaten ruler's dachin, he hoped that an official Portuguese one would reassure the traders and again attract them to his port.[7]

Not to be outdone, Tidore seized upon the arrival in Maluku of the two remaining ships of Magellan's expedition in November 1521 to seek a similar arrangement with the Spanish. Sultan Mansur of Tidore, in keeping with his royal status, was able to regale the Spaniards with his own dream which foretold the arrival of ships from a distant land. Being "an excellent astrologer," the ruler had consulted the moon and had seen the ships, which had been those of the Spaniards.[8] The latter for their part regarded their friendship with Tidore as a natural alliance to counter their archenemy's favored position in Ternate. When the Portuguese learned of the arrival of the Spaniards in Maluku, they were determined to exclude their rivals.[9] Antonio de Brito was chosen to take some three hundred men to build a fortress and establish a factory in Ternate. The first stone was laid on the day of St. John the Baptist in 1522, and so when the fortress was completed on 15 February 1523 it was named São João Bautista after the saint. It encompassed an area 26 by 27 fathoms square, had walls a fathom high, and possessed a tower with two levels rising to a height of 5 fathoms.[10] The Portuguese attempted to allay the Ternatens' fear at the size of the fort by explaining that it was intended, as was already foreseen in the prophecy, to enable the Sultan Ternate "to become the greatest lord of all the isles, have many islands and lands under his dominion, and be the greatest servant of His Highness."[11]

The building of the Portuguese fort created more than simply a physical barrier between the Ternatens and the Portuguese. It reinforced well-entrenched prejudices on both sides. The walls enclosed a separate European world in which the Portuguese could safely maintain their dress, food, and customs unbesmirched by contact with "uncivilized" society. For the Malukans there must have been a corresponding feeling of relief in viewing the outsiders confined within a specific place which served as a continual reminder of their alienness in the Malukan world. The fort thus became an imposing and unnatural implantation on the landscape and came to symbolize the vast cultural gap which separated the Malukans and the Portuguese.

Sultan Abu Lais died a few months before Brito's arrival from Melaka in February 1522, perhaps poisoned by jealous Muslim traders who feared that he intended to favor the Portuguese. He was succeeded by his seven year old son, Kaicili Abu Hayat (r. 1522–1529, "Boheyat" in some sources), though actual authority was exercised by Kaicili Darwis, a brother of Abu Lais.[12] The Islamic prescription of primogeniture in succession precluded a brother ascending the throne, but it did not prevent his assuming real power as would have been expected in pre-Islamic times. One of Darwis' chief rivals to the throne was the queen mother, widow of Abu Lais, who was favored by the late ruler to succeed him, but she too was excluded because of Islam's succession laws.[13]

In the Malukan kingdoms the strongest of the legitimate contenders, which included both the male and female members of the royal line, was expected to succeed. The queen, like Darwis, was theoretically disadvantaged because of yet another Islamic prohibition against women inheriting the throne, but this formal prescription did not prevent her from attempting to gain control of the kingdom with the help of her father, Sultan Mansur of Tidore. Darwis was able to persuade Brito to provide military assistance against the queen and Tidore and to offer as bounty a piece of Indian cloth for each Tidore head or prisoner delivered. The bounty had the desired effect, and the Portuguese claimed that "six hundred" heads were presented for payment. Although the Tidore forces succeeded in repulsing three attacks, the combined Portuguese-Ternaten contingents finally succeeded in seizing the sultan's settlement of Mareku and destroying it in late 1524. Just prior to its destruction, Sultan Mansur died and was succeeded on the Tidore throne by his young son, Amiruddin, who was placed under the "regency" of Kaicili Rade. In Tidore, too, Islamic laws of succession were formally observed while customary practice assured that the strongest contender would exercise power in the kingdom.

In November 1526 some Spanish members of the ill-fated expedition under the command of García Jofre de Loaisa landed in Samafo in Halmahera. From a former slave they learned that the royal settlement on Tidore had been burnt down because it had offered shelter to the Spaniards under Magellan. The Spanish chronicler Oviedo depicts the Spaniards as being so moved by the account that they immediately dispatched a letter to both the rulers of Tidore and Jailolo. It explained that, since these two kingdoms had suffered because of their friendship with the Spaniards, the latter had now returned to help them "with ships, men, artillery, munitions, and all the rest to be used both against the Portuguese and whatever nation or people who were their enemies on land and sea."[14] Both kingdoms responded by immediately sending envoys to reestablish their vassal relationship with Spain, even though Tidore's ruler was an exile from his old capital at Mareku which remained a wilderness after its destruction by the Ternatens and the Portuguese.[15] Despite the Spaniards' brave words, they were too enfeebled by their long journey to fulfill the hopes of those in Jailolo and Tidore. In the end the Spaniards were forced to leave the area, exposing their two local allies to even greater danger from their enemies than before. Subsequent Spanish expeditions to Maluku under the command of Alvaro de Saavedra in 1528 and Ruy López de Villalobos in 1543 again raised hopes of a counterbalance to Ternate's alliance with the Portuguese, but both ventures failed. After 1565 the Spaniards turned away from Maluku and devoted their full attention to the establishment of a Spanish colony in the Philippines under Miguel López de Legazpi.[16]

Darwis' friendship with Brito had helped both the Ternatens and the Portuguese to pursue their respective goals with a fair degree of success. The situation between these two allies changed dramatically, however, with the arrival in 1527 of the new Portuguese Captain Dom Jorge de Menese. He distrusted Darwis' intimacy with the Portuguese and treated the Malukans with utter contempt. In one characteristic incident he accused Kaicili Vaidua, the uncle of the king and an important casis, of killing a pig owned by a Chinese subject of the Portuguese.

Vaidua was arrested and subsequently released because of appeals for clemency from Darwis. As he was leaving the fort, a Portuguese sergeant acting on the orders of Menese smeared bacon fat on the face and mouth of this important Muslim dignitary, gravely offending him and other Muslims to whom pork is considered to be ritually unclean. Although the Ternatens refrained from undertaking any immediate retaliatory measure, Vaidua himself proceeded to visit a number of islands seeking vengeance for the insult to him, the nation, and the Islamic religion.[17]

On another occasion when the supply ship from Melaka did not arrive, Menese ordered his men to "forage" around Ternate. The soldiers took this to mean license to seize whatever they needed without payment. At Tobona the Portuguese were attacked by the local inhabitants, and in the ensuing fight some of the Portuguese were killed and wounded. When Menese learned of the affair, he demanded that Darwis deliver the sangaji to the Portuguese. Darwis, believing that the sangaji would be held for a few days and then released, complied. However, Menese ordered that the sangaji's hands be cut off, his arms tied behind his back, and two fierce dogs set loose on him. Despite being unable to defend himself, the sangaji retreated into the ocean pursued by the dogs, then seized each of them in turn by his teeth and drowned them, and later himself.[18]

Menese's catalog of atrocities continued with the seizure and hanging of the most important dignitaries in Ternate: the kapita laut, the hukum, and Darwis himself. It was alleged that they had called upon the other Malukan kingdoms, including the four Papuan Raja Ampat kingdoms of Waigeu, Misool, Waigama, and Gebe,[19] to oust the Portuguese from the region. There was no real proof of the allegation, but then it mattered little since Menese's low opinion of the Ternatens had made any justification superfluous. Fearing that Menese would continue his destruction of Ternate, the queen mother, who was described at the time as "the person with most authority in the kingdom,"[20] led her people away from the royal settlement of Malayu to the safety of Toloko.[21]

There was an uneasy standoff between Menese and the queen until the death of Sultan Abu Hayat in 1529 in the Portuguese fortress, where he had been held hostage since the beginning of his reign. His successor and brother Dayalo (r. 1529–1533, 1536) was also brought to the fort by Menese, much to the anger of the Ternatens. The queen demanded her son's release, but when Menese refused she imposed a strict ban on all food supplies to the Portuguese. The siege ended only because Menese was forcefully replaced as captain by Gonçalo Pereira in November 1530. Any goodwill created by this action was, however, totally dissipated when news reached Maluku that the previous Captain

Menese had not been punished in Goa as expected but was allowed to return to Portugal. From that time on the Malukans made it clear that they "no longer expected to receive justice from the Portuguese."[22]

When the queen met the new Captain Pereira, she recited a long litany of Menese's misdeeds. "This," the queen lamented, "is our reward for allowing the Portuguese in our land."[23] Despite her disillusionment with the Portuguese, the queen realized that only by appeasing them would she obtain Dayalo's release. She therefore agreed to Pereira's condition that she accept Kaicili Leliato as "regent," though she continued to exercise effective power in the kingdom. Pereira proved no different from his predecessors. He humiliated the sultan by sending an armed guard to accompany him to the mosque during the Muslim fasting month of Ramadan; he physically attacked his own hand-picked Ternaten regent; and he spoke harshly to the queen and the bobatos.[24] The queen thus took matters into her own hands and arranged the escape of her son Sultan Dayalo, his brother, and others held hostage in the fort. The attempt was aborted when Pereira stumbled onto the rescue party and was killed while raising the alarm.

The failure to free the hostages forced the queen to take a step which came to prove the Malukans' most effective weapon against the Portuguese: the siege. Although the Portuguese were secure behind the walls of their fortress, they were dependent on the Malukans for their food supply. The queen obtained the cooperation of the rulers of Bacan, Tidore, and the Papuan islands to enforce the blockade and to kill any Portuguese found outside the fort. Only after the removal of Pereira and his replacement by the new Captain Vicente de Fonseca in 1531, a person held in high esteem by the queen, was the siege lifted. Once Fonseca was established in his position, however, he too conducted himself as all previous Portuguese captains had done. According to one version, he refused to release the sultan because he was persuaded by the *casados* (Portuguese men married to local women) who feared that without the king as hostage their lives would be in danger.[25] So once again the queen moved the Ternaten capital, this time to Limatahu, and resorted to another siege of the Portuguese fort. The siege proved to be much more effective than previously because all neighboring kings actively enforced the royal edict. The Portuguese, desperately short of food and with no aid from Melaka, finally succumbed and agreed to release Sultan Dayalo. Peace was restored, and food flowed once more to the fort.[26]

The Ternaten regent at the time of Fonseca was Pati Sarangi, a kolano "with considerable authority among the chiefs and officials and the people." Apparently hoping to assume control of the throne himself, he convinced Fonseca that when the sultan began ruling on his own account Fonseca would not enjoy the freedom he had had in previous

reigns. Fonseca and Sarangi together plotted the assassination of Dayalo but were thwarted by the queen mother. Realizing the danger that
both she and Dayalo faced, she arranged for their secret departure first
to a village a few kilometers from Malayu and then finally to the greater
security of Tidore, where the queen's brother Sultan Amiruddin
reigned. The refusal of Amiruddin to surrender Dayalo to the Portuguese led to an attack on Tidore. The combined Malukan forces were
routed, and Dayalo was forced to flee to Jailolo.[27] The situation was
then "normalized" in the Portuguese fashion by Fonseca. He raised
Dayalo's younger brother Tabarija (r. 1523–1535) to be the new sultan
and reconfirmed Sarangi's position as regent. Tabarija thus came to be
known among the Malukans as "Vicente da Fonseca and Pati Sarangi's
king."[28]

The removal of Fonseca and the arrival of Tristão de Ataide as
captain in October 1533 once again followed a familiar pattern.
Ataide's arbitrary and cruel behavior was no longer a surprise to the
Malukans; indeed, it was a leitmotif identifying Portuguese captains.
No restraint was exercised on those Portuguese who oppressed the local
population by seizing whatever they wanted and "making wives and
daughters serve them like slaves."[29] Because Bacan refused to obey
Ataide's requests for the delivery of spices, he attacked the royal settlement and burned it to the ground. He then ordered the royal tombs to
be destroyed and the bones of the kings disinterred in order to hold
them for ransom.[30] When Ternaten forces attacked the newly Christian-
ized settlement at Mamuya in northeast Halmahera and killed its
sangaji, Ataide deposed Tabarija and sent him, his mother the Naicili
Boki Raja, and her husband Pati Sarangi to Goa to be tried by the Portuguese governor-general.[31] Tabarija's half-brother Hairun (r. 1535–
1545, 1546–1570) was now placed on the Ternate throne. Ataide's
actions aroused fear and resentment among the Ternaten population,
and the Portuguese became witness to a spectacle of "women, children,
and servants abandoning their homes . . . and the common people cry-
ing out upon seeing the flight of their leaders." Even greater panic
ensued when the keeper of the regalia, the Ourobachela, was killed by
the Portuguese at the gates of the fortress.[32]

In keeping with the chivalric code of all fidalgo captains, Ataide
needed his military campaign. This he found in Jailolo, a kingdom
which had courted the Spanish and had openly defied the Portuguese by
harboring their enemies. Ever since 1521 when Magellan's crew first
reached Maluku, Jailolo had maintained a friendship with the Spaniards which had never waned. During the ill-fated Spanish expeditions
of Loaisa, Saavedra, and Villalobos, the Sultan Jailolo always welcomed the Spaniards into his kingdom, offering hospitality and protection against the Portuguese. In a letter dated 1 March 1532 to

Charles V of Spain, Sultan Zainal Abidin Syah listed his services to the Spaniards and requested assistance as a vassal. He explained that in previous Spanish expeditions his father Sultan Yusuf had offered his land to the ruler of Spain but had received no reply. He thus repeated this request and hoped for assistance in the future.[33] Though it is not known whether there was any response to this letter, it was an attempt, like those in the past, to seek the support of a European power which could serve as a balance to the Portuguese in Ternate.

The Spaniards gave the people of Jailolo guns and taught them how to use them so that their musketeers became the "most feared in these parts."[34] The strength of the Jailolo fortress and its well-placed artillery was probably a result of the assistance in the art of defensive fortifications introduced by the Spaniards. The local inhabitants in the past had not been interested in laying sieges, a practice which they acquired from the European.[35] In Ternate the siege consisted simply of refusing to continue to supply food to the fortress and killing those caught outside. Siege techniques did not arise until Europeans helped Malukans to build strong fortifications. Ataide accused the Spaniards in Jailolo, who were survivors of Saavedra's abortive expedition, of encouraging that kingdom not only to provide refuge to the enemies of the Portuguese but also to extend its protection to four or five settlements in Halmahera formerly under the Portuguese.[36] With these "just" causes, Ataide ordered the attack on Jailolo and forced it to surrender after a long siege. The young and sickly sultan was taken to the Portuguese fortress in Ternate where it is believed he was poisoned by Ataide with the complicity of Katarabumi, the "regent" of Jailolo. The latter was known to have won Ataide's favor by showering him with extravagant gifts, including golden umbrellas and large quantities of cloves.[37] With the deposing of the young ruler, Katarabumi assumed the title of Sultan Jailolo in 1534 and ruled on behalf of the king of Portugal as "the first king to be given vassalage by royal grant."[38]

Ataide's success against Jailolo encouraged Mamuya and Tolo, two powerful settlements from Moro in northeast Halmahera, to approach Ataide with the idea of converting to Christianity and thereby gaining Portuguese assistance against their Muslim neighbors. Moro, a highly valued area because of its abundance of rice, sago, meat, and fruits, was divided into Morotia, or "Land Moro," on the northeast coast, and Morotai or "Sea Moro," consisting of the islands of Rau and Morotai. A Ternaten attack on Mamuya provided the impetus for conversion. The Sangaji Mamuya escaped and sought the help of Gonçalo Veloso, a Portuguese casado married to the sister of the Sultan Ternate and with long experience in Maluku. Veloso advised him to seek Portuguese protection by becoming Christian, explaining further that only by converting would he be assured "protection for his soul and his state."[39]

The Sangaji Mamuya and the Sangaji Tolo were baptized and given the names Dom João of Mamuya and Dom Tristão de Ataide of Tolo. When they returned home they wore their gifts of "Christian dress" and were accompanied by a secular priest, Simon Vaz, who laid the foundations of Christianity in northeast Halmahera.[40]

In Maluku the Muslim/Christian encounter was clouded by a number of issues. First of all, the Christian Europeans arrived in the area bearing a long tradition of antagonism toward Islam. The Portuguese national experience of a Muslim occupation of their homeland, followed by a long and bloody North African campaign, had conditioned them to expect a continuation of the struggle in Maluku. Moreover, within Maluku itself commitment to one religion by a particular group assured the acceptance of another religion by a rival community. This was especially pronounced in Halmahera where settlements which opposed Ternate and Jailolo preferred Christianity to the religion of their hated enemy. Therefore, from the very outset the religious encounter in Maluku was one of confrontation in which political loyalties very often determined religious preference.

To protect the newly converted communities, Ataide established a redoubt in Mamuya and manned it with well-armed Portuguese soldiers. When the sangajis of Sugala and Cawa, two other settlements in Moro, saw the way in which those of Mamuya and Tolo were being treated, they too went to the Portuguese fortress in Ternate and became Christian. In these new Christian communities, the Portuguese missionaries urged the destruction of spirit temples or their reconstruction for Christian service. Two new churches were built where the new converts were baptized. Confident of support from Ataide, the Christian communities refused to send food and other goods to Ternate, rejecting its dominant position in their relationship. While the Portuguese were preoccupied with Ternate, Jailolo launched an attack on the Christian settlements on Moro causing the death or defection of many of the Christian converts.[41] Mamuya managed initially to repel the Jailolo forces, but the sangaji agreed to surrender to prevent the invaders from burning the rice fields and palm groves, which would have meant considerable hardship, even starvation, for his people. With the fall of Mamuya, the other Christian communities in northeast Halmahera soon surrendered. The Franciscan friars therefore abandoned Moro as a mission field until the coming of the Jesuit Father Francis Xavier in 1546.[42]

The alacrity with which Ataide pursued both his chivalric and religious aims in Maluku aroused great animosity among the Malukan kingdoms. They again united "the entire land from the Papuas to Java" to destroy all Portuguese presence in the area.[43] The Ternatens openly proclaimed the exiled Dayalo as their sultan, while Ataide chose a half-brother called Hairun as sultan to keep as a "guest" in the fort. Ataide's action contributed further to a total disenchantment with the Portuguese, and the Ternaten leaders now vowed to "destroy all the spice and fruit trees on the islands so the Portuguese would never again return."[44] The war lasted fourteen months, with the Portuguese for the greater part confined to the fort by a siege. When the new captain Antonio Galvão arrived in 1536 with the annual fleet from Melaka, he was greeted by an "island depopulated, the town burnt, and everything destroyed." The starving defenders of the fortress marched out to meet him with a cross singing the Te Deum Laudamus. Galvão took immediate control and very early on in his captaincy conducted his obligatory military campaign against the Malukans. In a decisive battle in Tidore in December, the long exiled Ternaten Sultan Dayalo was killed and the town (with the exception of the mosque which Galvão kept as his headquarters) burned down. Galvão claimed that Dayalo's death was not mentioned among the Malukans "since he was the first king of Maluku to die by the sword, and they considered this a great dishonor and disgrace because in those countries custom does not permit them to wound a king, still less to kill him."[45]

Galvão came to Maluku with a vision of implanting a successful Portuguese colony amidst friendly native Christian kingdoms. He arranged for a number of poor, homeless Portuguese settlers to accompany him to Maluku, lending them the money and other necessary items for the journey.[46] He ringed the town and the Portuguese settlement with walls, moats, and bulwarks and introduced the practice of providing each house with a garden, a well to fight fires, and a storehouse for food. To encourage more trade, he had one of the sea channels widened and enforced the use of Portuguese currency in everyday transactions. He condemned the Portuguese private trade in cloves and now required that all cloves be sold to him as the factor of the king of Portugal.[47] From the perspective of the Malukans, however, Galvão's measures would have been viewed with some alarm. The presence of larger numbers of Portuguese indicated a greater commitment to the area and a higher probability of conflicts. Even more threatening would have been the new fortifications, which extended still further the intrusive world of the European. The sense of alienation was reinforced by Galvão's introduction of Portuguese currency, new Portuguese settlers, and Jesuit missionaries into Maluku.

But it was Galvão's success in gaining Christian converts in Ternate which most disturbed the Malukans. The first cousin of the Sultan Jailolo became Christian and took the name of Antonio de Sá; he was soon followed by the conversion of Kolano Sabia, "one of the principal members of the court and the household of the king of Ternate." Hairun was so upset at this conversion that he came to the fortress and demanded Sabia's return. Galvão came out, sword in hand, and informed Hairun that he would not refuse anyone baptism and would make as many Christians as he could. Despite protests by the Ternatens, Sabia was baptized with the name of Manuel Galvão in honor of his patron and godfather. Antonio Galvão celebrated the event with a feast and arranged for a house to be built in the fortress for him and his household and to meet all their needs from his own purse.[48]

After these conversions Hairun complained to Galvão that as soon as his subjects converted, they became disobedient and he found it difficult to find any to do "necessary service" for him. Galvão, however, refused to take any steps which would interfere in "matters of conscience."[49] Many followed Sabia's example, even though the Muslim casises persuaded the Sultan Ternate to issue a decree that any prominent individual converting to Christianity would lose all of his property and income.[50] The most spectacular of Galvão's successes was the conversion of an Arab Muslim casis, an alleged descendant of the Prophet Muhammad, whose decision led many others to turn to Christianity.[51] It is said that Hairun himself was so moved by this particular conversion that he was on the verge of accepting Christianity. But Galvão's departure from Ternate in 1539 removed the principal pressure on Hairun to embrace the new faith.[52]

Because of Hairun's professed interest in Christianity, Galvão decided to allow him to leave the fort. Hairun became the first ruler of Ternate since the completion of the fortress in 1523 to live among his own people. On his release he began the process of restoring his authority by establishing his court in the royal settlement, visiting the most important villages in Ternate, Makian, and Moti, and continuing the well-established precedent of obtaining as his principal wife the daughter of Tidore's sultan.[53] Hairun followed the custom of relying on women as a means of establishing close links to the most important families in his kingdom. Having been incarcerated for a time, he had to regain support through marriage. This practice was commonplace in Maluku, but it still incurred the criticism of Portuguese observers. One Jesuit father remarked that Hairun's refusal to accept Chrisitianity was due to his "carnal vices."[54]

These measures were intended to strengthen Hairun against the real possibility of the return from Goa in India of his half-brother and predecessor, Tabarija. While in exile Tabarija had been befriended by Jordão de Freitas, who was instrumental in Tabarija's decision to become a Christian. When Freitas was made captain of Maluku in 1544, he sailed together with Tabarija, now known by his Christian name of Dom Manuel, to Melaka. His plan was to depose Hairun and reinstall Tabarija as ruler in Ternate as the first step in the conversion of that kingdom and the whole of Maluku. But when Tabarija and Freitas arrived in Melaka, they learned that Sultan Hairun was regarded among the Ternatens as "powerful, good, and calm." Freitas, foreseeing difficulty in reestablishing Tabarija on the throne, decided to leave Tabarija in Melaka and sailed alone to Ternate in November 1544.

On arrival Freitas announced to the Ternatens that their former ruler was now on his way home to resume power in his kingdom. Sultan Hairun and the Kapita Laut Samarau were then placed in chains to be exiled to Goa. Freitas wrote that it was his hope "with the arrival of the Christian king [Tabarija] the fire of the Holy Spirit would be fully rekindled." He summoned the elders and the most prominent Muslims and casises to the gate of the fortress to reassure them over Hairun's arrest and news of Tabarija's conversion. He explained that no one would be forced to become Christian, contrary to the rumors being spread, and that both Tabarija's mother and father (Naicili Boki Raja and Pati Sarangi) had remained true to the Muslim faith. Having heard Freitas' assurances, they agreed on the Koran to remain faithful to the Portuguese.[55] Freitas' plans were for the conversion of Maluku by making peace with the Spaniards, driving out the native rulers, and ruling Maluku without a king. In a letter to the king of Portugal he claimed that "a half dozen caturs [a light rowing vessel] manned by Indian canarins[56] from Goa and a caravel with eighty men and the help of the garrison [in Ternate] would be sufficient to achieve the plan in two or three years or a bit longer." Freitas was convinced that the whole island of Ternate was on the verge of accepting Christianity.[57] His hopes were dashed by the sudden and mysterious death of Tabarija in Melaka on 30 June 1545, some say poisoned on Hairun's orders. In a last will and testament written at his deathbed in Melaka and executed on 20 October 1545, Tabarija bequeathed to the ruler of Portugal his entire kingdom, which he claimed included Ternate, Moti, Makian, Kayoa, and Moro.[58]

Although there was now no longer any reason for Hairun to be sent to Goa, he insisted on going and arrived there in February 1546. The Portuguese governor in Goa received him with great honor and explained that the decision to bring Hairun to Goa was made to avoid any serious confrontation with Tabarija. Now that Tabarija was dead, the governor saw no objections to investing Hairun once again as Sultan Ternate. He also issued a warrant (alvará) affirming Hairun's right to the throne and replacing Freitas with Bernaldim de Sousa as captain in Maluku. Sousa carried out his instructions by assuming the captaincy in 1547 and sending Freitas back to Goa to defend his actions. Hairun arrived back in Ternate in November 1546 in triumph. He was wearing Portuguese clothes, and when he reached the gate of the Portuguese fortress "he showed deference to the Portuguese coat of arms over the entrance by touching the stone doorpost under it with his hand and then bringing his hand to his mouth and head." Reinstalled as Sultan Ternate, the Portuguese sources say that Hairun established a harem of a hundred wives and numerous concubines who were supplied by his leading chiefs.[59]

At the time that Hairun was reinstated as sultan, the Jesuit Francis Xavier arrived in Ternate. During the six months he spent in Ternate and Moro between July 1546 and January 1547, he was responsible for the first "mass" conversions in the area. Both Xavier and the other Jesuits quickly realized that it was the ritual of the Church, with its various ceremonies, candlelight, and music, and not the doctrine, which appealed to the local inhabitants.[60] The local Christians had great respect for the cross, the church, the saints, and the name of Jesus, all of which were believed to have power in themselves and could be used individually for specific purposes. Those in Tolo were said to believe in the efficacy of holy water because of certain "miracles" which resulted from its use. They drank it against all types of illnesses and as an antidote to poison. In Bacan, too, after its conversion in 1557, the people when sick would drink holy water or throw it into their mouths, believing that "by virtue of it, God would give them health." The use of oil lamps in the churches seems to have attracted the attention of the people. Once during a drought in Sakita in Morotai the chief went to the church to plead for rain. He beat his breast, and then lifted a porcelain bowl of oil heavenwards, while imploring God to send rain. He then proclaimed throughout the land that, if the people wanted rain, they had to bring all the oil they could find to the church as offering. The people of Bacan were also accustomed to bringing offerings of oil to the church.[61] The use of oil in the performance of libations to the spirits, and in lamps in Christian churches, may have convinced the people of its spiritual potency.

The confession was another ritual which was adopted with great enthusiasm by the local Christians. An old man explained to the Jesuits that, as soon as he confessed and "flung out his sins," he would become healthy in body. Others saw it as the only way in which one could go to the next world. Since even for non-Christians the belief in a form of afterlife was strong, the confession was regarded as a proven Christian method of attaining this end. A Christian son of a chief came to fetch a Jesuit father to administer the confession to his non-Christian mother on her deathbed saying, "How would she be able to accompany me to the next world if she had not been confessed?" In Bacan the first thing people did when they were ill was to call upon the Jesuit fathers to confess them, read the gospel, or pray to God for mercy. They then brought gifts to the church, especially oil for the lamps, and thus, said the Jesuits, "demonstrate their religious devotion to the Creator."[62] The Bacan Christians believed that Christianity was effective against the *suanggi,* one of the most feared evil spirits, which could assume human shape and drink the blood of humans. They believed that the Portuguese were unaffected by the suanggi because they had been Christian a long time. They, on the other hand, were inexperienced in the matters dealing with God and were still vulnerable to them.[63]

Although the Christian ritual and ceremony were regarded by the local converts as the essence of the new religion, they were also encouraged to learn about the doctrine through methods introduced by Xavier. He combined the native love of music with Catholic ritual to create a pleasant and effective way of conveying the Christian message. Xavier had already experienced the enthusiasm with which the inhabitants in India learned the doctrine set to music and their readiness to attend Mass when it was sung.[64] The children were subjects of attention because they were considered the most effective vehicle in spreading the Word to the elders and in assuring the preservation of the faith. Missionaries in the Americas had shown the effectiveness of these methods, and Xavier was to demonstrate their success once again in Asia.[65]

While at Melaka awaiting favorable winds to sail to Maluku, Xavier had decided to translate many of the sacraments into Malay since he was told that Malay was "generally known in these parts." Proceeding "with a great amount of labor" he set into Malay the Creed, the Declaration of the Articles, the General Confession, the Lord's Prayer, the Hail Mary, the Hail Holy Queen, and the Commandments.[66] He held classes daily for both adults and children, and the results were quickly apparent. In the open squares in Ternate and in the homes, the women and children at all times of the day sang the Creed, Our Father, Hail Mary, the Confession (Confiteor) and other prayers, the Commandments, and the Works of Mercy. According to Xavier, this program was so successful that in the fields and at sea the people sang these instead of their own secular songs. In addition he composed long explanations of the Creed in rhymed Portuguese for the children of the casados. One of the other practices he introduced was to arrange to have a man go every night with a small bell to the squares "as has been the custom in Paris, where he urges all to pray for the souls in purgatory and for those who are living in mortal sin and refuse to be converted."[67]

Xavier applied these methods first in Ternate and then in Moro. He went to Mamuya and, with the help of Jesuit companions, he explained the faith to the people in Malay. The main centers of Christian conversion in Halmahera were Tolo, Sakita, and Cawa, but substantial numbers also became Christian in Rau and Morotai. Outside Halmahera the island of Bacan was another Jesuit success. The ruler and some six or seven sangajis were converted by the Jesuit Antonio Vaz in July 1557. In the next two and a half months he went with the newly converted Bacan king, Dom Manuel, to the various islands in his kingdom, baptizing men, women, and children, including a large number of prominent people and relatives of the king. He then went to Ambon and Seram and made the chiefs Christian because "in these parts once the chief of a place becomes Christian there is no difficulty with the others."[68]

When the king of Banggai sent his son to Ternate sometime in 1564 to examine both Christianity and Islam, Sultan Hairun tried to sway the Banggai ruler toward Islam by arranging a marriage between his son and the daughter of the king of Banggai. It was, however, the king of Bacan who persuaded him to become Christian.[69] In Tidore the seventeen year old sultan was said to be favorably impressed with Christianity, and by 1564 two of his brothers and six other important individuals were baptized.[70] In Ternate itself Xavier was responsible for the conversion of Naicili Boki Raja, Pati Sarangi, and Kolano Sabia. The Sangaji Gamkonora and the first cousin of the Sultan Jailolo were two other leading figures who became Christians at this time.[71] It was from Ternate that a Jesuit father was sent in 1563 to convert the king of Menado and the king of Siau at their request. At Menado, whose inhabitants were "the most feared and courageous in battle in this land," the king and fifteen hundred of his subjects became Christian. The Jesuit father put a cross on the beach for them and gave both the king of Menado and the king of Siau the royal flag.[72]

The success of the Jesuit mission was due to the efficient use of very limited resources. Although at any one time there were no more than three missionaries in Moro, the Jesuits claimed that some twenty thousand people had become Christian by the middle of the sixteenth century.[73] The foundations of the mission in Moro had been successfully laid by a secular priest, Brother Simon Vaz. With Xavier's arrival the Jesuits took charge of mission activities throughout Maluku. There was usually a superior with one or two others in Ternate to administer to the Portuguese community on the island and to the local converts, many of whom were leading members of the nobility or royalty from different Malukan kingdoms now residing in the fortress. Of the other missionaries, some were sent to Bacan, some to Moro, and the rest to Ambon. Since there were never more than nine Jesuits at any one time in Maluku, there were very few actually working in the field.[74]

A Jesuit father was placed in the most important center, where there was a mission house and a church. He usually had charge of some eight places and would visit each one, spending an average of eight days at a place. He baptized the infants, married those who wished it, catechized the people, gave extreme unction, provided Christian burials for families which requested it, and confessed those who knew the Malay language. The Jesuits did not offer confession often because there were insufficient numbers of fathers who knew local languages. While Malay could be used on some of the major islands where contact with traders was frequent, in more isolated areas such as in Moro, the *lingua franca* was Ternaten or Tidorese. While many knew some words of Malay, their knowledge did not extend to the vocabulary required in a confession. At the three major centers of Tolo, Sakita, and Rau, they celebrated Mass in the churches, but in the other areas they met the converts in makeshift shelters.[75]

The conversion of Moro to Christianity in the first half of the sixteenth century created an effective Halmahera ally for the Portuguese. But these Christian settlements were always under the threat of attack by the Muslim kingdoms, especially Jailolo under Katarabumi, who was regarded as "the most powerful in the whole [Malukan] archipelago."[76] The very success of Jailolo earned the suspicion of the Portuguese and the envy of Ternate. When the Portuguese decided to attack Jailolo, Ternate rejected the latter's request for assistance and instead sided with the Portuguese. But even with this unlikely alliance the task appeared formidable. The Jailolo fortress was considered by many to be impregnable. It was described by the Portuguese as having an outer wall made of earth and stone upon which stood a stockade with two bulwarks. The stockade walls were high with stakes facing both inward and outward so that "not even a cat could pass through." The castle within the walls had two other bulwarks and another high wall. These walls were defended by one hundred guns, eighteen metal cannons, an iron mortar, and many other pieces from Java, and it was stockpiled with enough supplies to withstand a long siege. The defenders were also buoyed by the knowledge that their Tobaru allies were masters of the surrounding jungles. Their reputation as jungle fighters was so fearsome that people believed they had the ability to make themselves invisible.[77] When the fortress capitulated after a three-month siege in the beginning of 1551, it was not due to any successful military assault but to the fact that the Portuguese were able to capture the fort's source of water. The Jailolo ruler was then forced to relinquish his title of sultan and become once again a sangaji under Ternate and a vassal of the king of Portugal.[78]

Once the surrender was accepted, the doors of the fortress were flung open, exposing the defenders to widespread looting which lasted for several days. According to the Portuguese chronicler Couto, Katarabumi refused to witness the destruction of Jailolo. He donned a dark brown velvet cloth, given to him by Captain Ataide when he was first proclaimed sultan, and retired to the jungle to embark on a life as a hermit. His son, Kaicili Gujarati, was left to govern as the sangaji of Jailolo, and soon thereafter Jailolo acknowledged its subservience to Ternate.[79] After its defeat Jailolo quickly lost population and its political influence in Maluku. Nevertheless, the memory of this powerful and dynamic kingdom persisted into the following centuries, and Ternate continued to recognize Jailolo's separate identity in ceremonies requiring the four Malukan kingdoms. The ritual retention of Jailolo as an entity enabled the tradition of the "four" kingdoms to survive and helped to reassure the Malukans of the unity and harmony of their world.

The incorporation of Jailolo strengthened Hairun's position in Ternate. His flirtation with Christianity and his bold defiance of Jordão de Freitas had gained him admiration among the Portuguese. At the same time he had been careful to nurture traditional links with the bobatos through royal visits and marriages. As in previous reigns, however, the initial amity between the Ternaten ruler and the Portuguese captain quickly turned to enmity. Captain Duarte de Sá, who arrived in November 1555, began to behave in a now all too familiar arbitrary manner associated with all Portuguese captains. He appropriated the annual Makian clove harvest destined for the Ternaten sultan and ordered the seizure of Hairun, his brother, and his mother to guarantee the loyalty of the Ternatens. When pleas from the Ternate Council for their release were ignored, the council turned to the Sultan Tidore for help. Faced with the prospects of fighting both Ternate and Tidore, Sá sought Jailolo's assistance by promising Sangaji Gujarati that he would restore to him the title of sultan and remove all Jailolo's obligations to the Portuguese. So attractive was this offer that Gujarati accepted and in so doing temporarily regained the title of Sultan Jailolo. Despite the presence of local troops fighting alongside the Portuguese, the combined Ternate-Tidore forces proved superior both on land and sea. It was not the Malukan forces, however, but complaints against Sá laid by the Portuguese inhabitants in Ternate which eventually led to his removal and imprisonment and the release of the hostages.

Once restored to power Hairun resumed his goal of consolidating and extending the kingdom by recovering lost lands and sending his son Babullah to the coastal settlements of north Sulawesi to bring them under Ternate.[80] When François Valentijn began collecting oral and written material about Maluku sometime in the latter half of the seventeenth century, he felt justified in concluding that "[Hairun] was indeed a wise ruler, a brave warrior, extraordinarily correct in the exercise of law and justice, but most of all greatly devoted to his religion and a strong defender of the Islamic faith."[81] Hairun's reputation as a "strong defender of the Islamic faith" came after his disillusionment with the Portuguese. While he may not have seriously considered conversion, he was interested in Christianity and even contemplated sending Babullah to the Jesuit College of St. Paul's in Goa. However, his treatment at the hands of Duarte de Sá changed his attitude toward the Portuguese. His growing opposition to the Portuguese led to his assassination on 28 February 1570 on the orders of the new Portuguese Captain Diogo Lopes de Mezquita.[82] With Hairun's death ended a period when European initiative and Christianity had severely tested the Malukan views of rightful succession, political behavior, and religion. After 1570 the Malukans reasserted themselves and sought to reverse the trends which threatened their world.

Malukan Initiative and Islam

The accession of Hairun's son and successor, Babullah (r. 1570–1583), marked a change in the relationship between the Malukans and the Portuguese. The initiative now passed to the Malukans, and it was Islam which provided them with the means to regain control of their own affairs. Babullah, once regarded as a potential convert to Christianity, vowed to revenge the death of his father by removing all Portuguese and other Christians from the archipelago. In this goal he was supported by the Muslim leaders who saw in him the true defender of the faith who would restore Islam to its rightful prominence in Maluku. As the newly proclaimed ruler of Ternate, Babullah sent his uncle Kalasineo to lead a fleet of boats commanded by relatives to the Ambon Quarter. The fleet arrived first in Buru, described as "an island of Muslims which has always obeyed the king of Ternate and has always had many people and numerous large and powerful kora-koras."[83] From Buru they went to Lesidi and Kambelo in the Hoamoal peninsula and to Hitu in Ambon, gathering more men and boats. Even with these reinforcements, the Ternatens were unable to dislodge the Portuguese from their fort in Ambon.[84]

Babullah fared better closer to home. The Ternatens seized four Portuguese sampans from the Christian inhabitants of Moro loaded with food for the Portuguese fortress. An expedition was then sent to attack Moro, beginning in Galela and moving down the east coast of northern Halmahera killing all Portuguese, mestizos, and native Christians they encountered.[85] But the Ternaten force met considerable resistance, especially at Tolo, the largest and strongest of the Moro Christian settlements. At Morotai the settlements were destroyed, though the people continued to fight from their refuge in the jungle. Christian Bacan was invaded and defeated in 1571, and the king and his subjects forced to apostatize. By the end of 1573 the Jesuits acknowledged that almost their entire mission in north Maluku and Ambon had been destroyed.[86]

In 1570 Babullah laid siege to the Portuguese fortress in Ternate, which was apparently not rigidly enforced. Before Bacan's defeat in 1571, it had continued to send supplies to the fort. There was intermittent aid arriving from Moro and from Tidore, and the defenders were free to leave the fortress at various times to obtain supplies. What eventually spelled the doom of the fortress was the inability of the Portuguese in Goa and Melaka to send a sufficiently strong fleet to raise the siege. Three years in succession the annual ship from Melaka failed to arrive because it had left too late to catch the right monsoon winds to Maluku. During the long siege only four Portuguese ships managed to reach Ternate, and none made any long-term difference to the situation.[87] The siege had a dispiriting effect on the defenders, while the plague and illness took a severe toll on the Portuguese and native Christian inhabitants living in the fortress. In the last year of the siege only about four hundred people remained, some five hundred having died mainly from illness due to malnutrition.[88]

Portuguese morale was extremely low in 1575 when the Ternatens learned that a Portuguese ship from Melaka was at Mayu, an island located between Menado and Ternate. Fearing that the ship would bring reinforcements which could end the siege, Babullah ordered an attack on the fortress. When that failed, he sent his brother Kaicili Tolo as an envoy to the Portuguese to inform them that all the Malukans were united against them and there was no possibility of help arriving from the outside. Under these circumstances the Portuguese were urged to accept Babullah's generous offer to supply the Portuguese with boats to go to Ambon. Thus on St. Stephen's day, 26 December 1575, the fortress surrendered, and three days later the supply ship from Melaka arrived.[89] Babullah allowed the ship to land, buy cloves as was customary, and take the remaining Portuguese off the island to Ambon or Melaka. He then sent a letter to the king of Portugal in which he asked that justice be done to those responsible for the death of his father. In the meantime, he explained, he would maintain the fortress for the king of Portugal by manning it with a Portuguese captain, a factor, and twelve soldiers retained in Ternate for that express purpose. This small garrison eventually departed and Babullah came to reclaim the fortress. The old Portuguese fort now became the new site for the royal residence until retaken by the Spaniards in 1606.[90]

Most of the Portuguese and native Christians expelled from Ternate resettled in Ambon, although some of the Portuguese married to local women remained behind. Later when Tidore opened its lands to the Portuguese, they moved there permanently. Tidore's decision to court the Portuguese was made with the hope of attracting the clove trade away from Ternate and obtaining Portuguese support against Ternate. Despite the unity shown in the siege of the fortress, once the Portuguese were defeated Tidore resumed its hostility to Ternate in accordance with their dualism. Babullah raided the coastal settlements on Tidore and forced the inhabitants to seek safety in the interior hills. The

arrival of a hundred Portuguese to build a fortress near the royal settlement provided Tidore's ruler and court with a much needed ally to
counter Babullah's increasing dominance in the area.[91]

In 1576 Babullah sent Rubohongi of the Tomagola family to
Hoamoal, Buru, Manipa, Ambelau, Kelang, and Boano to bring these
areas under closer Ternaten protection. Babullah's choice of Rubohongi
to lead the expedition was a deliberate one since it was his father, Samarau, that Babullah blamed for "allowing everything there to decline."[92]
In 1580 Babullah gathered his kora-koras to join Cappalaya with his
Sula boats. The joint fleets sailed to north Sulawesi, Tobunku, and
Tioro and brought these places under Ternate's protection. They conquered Wolio in Butung and then went to Salayar, where they signed a
treaty with the ruler of the Makassar kingdom of Goa. As a result of this
campaign, Babullah became known as the "Lord of Seventy-Two
Islands."[93]

In these wars the Islamic element was particularly evident. The
Jesuits were convinced that large numbers of casises were arriving in
Maluku from Mecca, Aceh, and Malaya, "bringing great edicts (bullas)
and privileges" for the Muslims. Turks were also reported to be making
their way from Sumatra, to Borneo, and on to Ternate.[94] These casises
were believed to be urging the people to fight to the death in a holy war
since martyrdom assured direct access to syurga, the Muslim heaven.
The Portuguese commented on the marked change in the attitude of the
local inhabitants in warfare. In the past the death of a leader usually
resulted in the withdrawal from battle. Now, however, the people continued to fight regardless of the fate of their leaders.[95] The situation had
changed since the early years of the sixteenth century when the Portuguese commented critically on the lack of understanding of Islam
among the local inhabitants. At the time this factor was attributed to the
absence of religious teachers. By the end of the century, the Jesuits were
remarking on the large numbers of Islamic teachers coming to Maluku
and inciting holy war against all Christians. The Jesuits estimated in
1594 that of the formerly "forty thousand" Christians in Maluku,[96]
only a thousand were left in Ambon, a hundred in Labuha in Bacan,
and some thirty to forty casados in Tidore. The rest of the area had
become Muslim.[97] The only Christian success in this later period was
Labuha on the island of Bacan. Its sangaji had requested and received
Portuguese aid against the Bacan ruler, and in gratitude he had become
a Christian in March 1582. His mother and some four hundred of his
followers then followed suit, making Labuha the only Christian settlement on the island of Bacan. Nevertheless, the fear of attack had forced
them to live in small communities of four, five, or six houses at a distance of about 10 kilometers apart and well hidden in the jungles.[98]

That this hostility was not aimed at all Christians is apparent in the warm welcome accorded Francis Drake on his visit to Ternate on 3–9 November 1579. Drake described the initial meeting when three large kora-koras approached "in each whereof, were certaine of the greatest personages that were about him [the sultan], attired all of them in white Lawne, or cloth of Calecut, having over their heads, from one end of the Canow to the other, a covering of thinne and fine mats, borne up by a frame made of reedes, under which every man sate in order according to his dignity; the hoary heads of many of them, set forth the greater reverence due to their persons, and manifestly shewed, that the king used the advice of a grave and prudent Counsell, in his affaires."[99] Then came Babullah himself accompanied by six "grave and ancient fathers." He was "of a tall stature, very corpulent and well set together, of a very princely and gratious countenance," and no one dared to speak to him except on their knees and would not rise unless given permission to do so.

When Drake's envoys paid Babullah a return visit, they were conducted to the *baileu,* or reception hall, located in the Portuguese fortress. The baileu was square, open on all sides, and covered with cloth of various colors. On one side was the "chair of state" with a large, rich canopy of arras cloth. On the ground before him for "some 10 or 12 pases compasse" was laid the same rich arras tapestry. Standing outside the baileu were four elderly men dressed in red "attired on their heads not much unlike the Turkes" [that is, with turbans]. The Ternatens called them "Romans" or "strangers" and said that they served as "lidgiers [agents] there to keepe continuall traffique." In addition there were two Turks and an Italian who also were lidgiers for their nation. When Babullah appeared he was dressed from the waist down with a rich cloth of gold, "shooes of cordivant [leather], died red," a headdress "wreathed in diverse rings of plated gold," and a large gold chain around his neck. On his left hand he had diamond, emerald, ruby, and turquoise rings, and on the right hand a ring with many diamonds. The fan used by his page was "richly embroidered and beset with Saphires." Drake's final comment was that in the last four years Babullah had expanded his kingdom and was now "Lord of an hundred Ilands thereabout."[100]

An interesting revelation in Drake's description was the great stature and wealth of the sultan. The baileu was covered with "cloth" of diverse colors, including Indian cloth and French arras tapestry. The sultan himself was bedecked with jewels and gold cloth which demonstrated a ruler of far greater wealth than his predecessors earlier in the century. Even the ceremonies surrounding him were obviously intended to emphasize the social gap between him and his subjects. Nevertheless, an ongoing aspect of Malukan government which appears to have been retained was the presence of elders among the chief councillors. Since the earliest accounts the important place of the elders in Malukan society was stressed, and in this meeting with Drake in 1579 they were still there among Babullah's most highly respected advisors.

The presence of the four elderly "Romans," the two Turks, and the Italian as trade agents indicates a thriving international trade in the port of Ternate. The so-called "Romans," or in Malay "Rumi," was a general term used in the archipelago to refer to Muslims from the Middle East. They were there to oversee a "continuall traffique" in Ternate, which would account for the wealth which Babullah displayed on his person and the rich collection of cloths in the baileu. Portuguese sources state that there was a growing number of Muslims, both traders and religious teachers, who were in Ternate during Babullah's reign, and Drake's account seems to confirm this.

The increased source of revenue which was now Babullah's to command enabled him to pursue his political ambitions with the assurance of support from an extensive kinship network. In addition, Babullah was able to extend his influence outside his kin group and pursue warfare beyond Ternate's shores through judicious redistribution of prestigious exotic goods, especially cloth and iron. Once these lands had acknowledged Ternate's leadership, Babullah consolidated the relationship in the traditional manner through the exchange of women. Drake's statement that Babullah was "Lord of a Hundred Islands" was repeated by Valentijn who called him "Lord of Seventy-Two Islands." What both accounts were emphasizing was the vast extent of Babullah's conquest, a feat made possible by the wealth and guns from international trade.

Babullah made certain that Ternate continued to remain the most attractive entrepôt in the region. After the conquests of Tobunku, Banggai, Butung, and the surrounding islands, Babullah required all settlements "where Ternaten orders to the king of Butung are implemented" to buy and sell only at Butung.[101] Through a network of secondary trading centers ultimately linked to Ternate, a flow of tribute was established strengthening the center as never before. As the Spaniards acknowledged in 1584 in a report analyzing Ternate's strength, Ternate had only two thousand fighting men but a thousand Javanese, Chinese, and Acehnese traders.[102] Furthermore, areas as distant as the states of "Matheo" (that is, north Sulawesi), Honimoa (in Saparua) in the south, and Butung in the west were sending annual and sometimes semiannual tribute to Ternate.[103]

With the delivery of tributary goods, Ternate became unquestionably the most prosperous trading center in eastern Indonesia and attracted foreign traders from all parts of the archipelago. By the time of his death in 1583, Babullah had become less dependent upon his internal, kin-based sources of authority. He now possessed the wealth to attract and retain followers outside his extended circle of kin, though his own family members continued to remain his strongest supporters. Shortly before his death Babullah extracted a promise from his brother, Kaicili Tulo, to support as his successor Babullah's favorite son Said rather than Mandar, a son born of a higher-status mother. To seal this agreement Tulo was made kapita laut and hukum and "given many other honors," including the marriage of his daughter to Said. With this powerful patron, Said became ruler of Ternate with the title Sultan Said al-din Berkat Syah (r. 1584–1606).[104]

At the accession of the new ruler, the Portuguese and the Spaniards, whose countries were united in 1580, saw their opportunity to conquer Ternate with the help of Tidore. In 1584 a small Spanish force under Pedro Sarmiento seized the island of Moti, beat off a counterattack from Ternate, and handed over the island to the Sultan Tidore.[105] Then in February 1585 a squadron of four hundred men from Manila arrived in Maluku to begin the task of retaking the old Portuguese fortress on Ternate. It was, however, a far weaker force than that which had set off from Manila because it had lost most of its war supplies in a storm off the coast of Bacan. Moreover, the fort in Ternate had been strengthened by Babullah, who had built walls around the Portuguese settlement and had added bulwarks and towers defended by captured Portuguese guns. In the ensuing battle the Spaniards had to contend with some twenty Turkish gunners who "used a lot of bombs, grenades, and other instruments of fire." Thirty Javanese junks in port were mobilized and messengers dispatched to the sangajis in surrounding areas to organize their men to come to Ternate's defense. Although the Spaniards were assisted by men from Tidore, Bacan, and the north Sulawesi islands, they were unable to capture the fort. The Spanish commander assessed the situation and decided that any further action would countermand his original instructions, and so he ordered the squadron to return to Manila.[106]

Ternate's success increased the prestige of Islam at the expense of Christianity in the area. The Jesuit Father Antonio Marta noted that there was greater unity among the Muslims than previously and that opposition to the Christians came not only from the primary Islamic centers on Tidore, Ternate, and Hoamoal, but now also from Banda and Seram. In the attacks on Portuguese settlements in Ambon and elsewhere, Marta was convinced that the local people were being encouraged by "false prophets, Arabs and Persians, all ministers and priests of Muhammad to spread this religion." He further claimed that all the Muslims in these parts had joined together under the banner of Islam, and to maintain their resolve they had chosen the Bandanese as their leaders and "sworn to kill everyone until the Portuguese were totally removed." In the previous year the Bandanese and Ternatens from Hoamoal had come with a large number of kora-koras to besiege Ambon. Though the siege was eventually lifted, they threatened to return the following year, having left "fifty of their most important leaders in Ambon as hostages as a reminder of the vow which they had made." Marta called it the "greatest war that has ever occurred in these parts." It included every Muslim summoned by his chief and made to swear solemn oaths to fight for the faith or die in the effort and be rewarded in heaven. In Banda, Ambon, Ternate, and Tidore there was no shortage of chiefs with the authority to encourage the Muslims to advance the cause and honor of Islam.[107]

Sultan Said's hopes of permanently removing the Portuguese and Spaniards from Maluku received a considerable boost with the arrival of the Dutch in Ternate in 1599. So impressed was he with the Dutch demonstration of their firepower that he sought their friendship by giving them permission to "collect cloves, spices, precious stones, and pearls which are found in [his lands] as a result of the trade of the Japanese, Cambodian, and Chinese ships."[108] He boasted to the Dutch that he no longer feared the Portuguese and that his warfleets had conquered Moti and a large part of Halmahera belonging to Tidore. His warfleet consisted of about thirty kora-koras built on the island of Mayu, some with four and others with six metal guns, and each with forty to sixty rowers. Hanging from a certain tall building was a bell without a clapper which, the sultan explained, was struck in emergencies to summon his people with their weapons. For just such an occasion the sultan had stocked numerous metal guns and stone missiles in the royal settlement for distribution to his men.[109]

The Dutch were told that Sultan Said himself participated in battle and was known to be very courageous. He was described as "a short, square man of about thirty-six years of age, of a cheerful nature, very eager for knowledge, familiar with them [the Dutch], but always distant with his subjects who showed him great respect and authority."[110] In his presence the "captains," all of whom were distinguished elderly gentlemen, and the bobatos performed the traditional gesture of respect and obeisance by pressing the palms of their hands together and raising them above their heads. It was reported that the sultan had more than forty wives, at least one in each settlement, so that "wherever he went he was at home."[111] When the Dutch were preparing to leave, Said gave them a box of earth to be offered either to the queen of England or to Prince Maurits of the Netherlands to symbolize his desire to have either as Ternate's lord.[112]

Sultan Said appears to have benefited from the policies first initiated by Babullah to oust the Portuguese from the islands and open the Ternaten ports to other foreigners. The return of Japanese, Cambodian, and Chinese traders attested to Ternate's success in reestablishing links to the lucrative Asian trade. Despite the newly found wealth and apparent power of the sultan, features of traditional kingship were still prominent. His prowess on the battlefield was recognized, and he still relied on the elders as members of his council. Equally revealing was the Dutch comment that the ruler had wives in every settlement. As in Galvão's description in the early part of the century, the Ternaten king continued to reaffirm links through marriage with the bobato families throughout his kingdom. In this way "wherever he went he was at home," and as family he could rely on them for trade and war when summoned by the royal drum.

In February 1605 the Dutch returned to Maluku, but this time as employees of the Dutch East India Company which had been formed three years earlier. They seized the Portuguese fort in Ambon and allowed only the missionaries to remain behind. But in May they, too, were forced to board a ship and leave Ambon. A Spanish friar claimed that they were set adrift "without a pilot nor any sails and with little or no food and other necessities" but eventually reached Cebu and Manila. From Ambon the Dutch fleet sailed in May to Ternate, where they joined Sultan Said in an attack on the Portuguese and their Tidore allies. Just prior to their arrival, an English ship had preceded them in Tidore and brought news of the Dutch victory in Ambon. The English captain had then sold the Portuguese gunpowder and various provisions in exchange for cloves, but he refused to engage in any hostilities with the Dutch because in Europe England was at peace with the Netherlands. Despite this prior warning and unexpected assistance, the Portuguese were no match for the fleet of nine Dutch ships and their Ternaten allies. The Portuguese surrendered and were allowed to leave for Manila with boats supplied by the Dutch and one by the Sultan Tidore.[113]

When the English country trader Henry Middleton arrived in the Ternate court in July 1605, he brought a letter from King James urging Sultan Said to allow the English to establish a post in Maluku. Said was clearly less convinced of the value of a friendship with the English as with the Dutch. In reply to King James, he explained that the English had never helped Ternate against the Portuguese and had done little since Francis Drake's visit in 1579. At that time the reigning Sultan Babullah had given Drake a ring for Queen Elizabeth "in commemoration of their alliance," but the English had sent no help. He had therefore written to the Dutch Prince Maurits, promising that he would sell the fruits of his land exclusively to the Dutch, his "friends and liberators," whose guns he now eagerly awaited.[114] Sultan Said was confidently maneuvering among the Europeans and exhibited an aplomb in his relationship, secure in the knowledge that there were many foreign groups now eagerly competing to obtain the cloves. But Said, like

Babullah before him, was equally aware of the dangers of the trade which had been so painfully demonstrated in Ternate's relationship with the Portuguese. Profits of the clove trade were therefore not simply or even primarily being used for luxury items, but also for the purchase of guns. This policy was a prudent one because the Portuguese threat had now become a Spanish-Portuguese one, and Manila was far closer to Maluku than the Portuguese centers in Melaka or Goa.

According to Argensola, the Spanish chronicler of the Spanish conquest of Ternate, some time in the morning of mid-March 1606 there was an eclipse of the moon. The Ternatens interpreted this omen to mean that a calamity would befall their ruler or some other important person or even the whole community. They vowed to organize an elaborate procession of thanksgiving if no calamity occurred. Then on 26 March a large Spanish expedition arrived in Ternate under the command of the governor-general of the Philippines, Don Pedro de Acuña. The fleet consisted of thirty-six Spanish and Portuguese vessels carrying 1,423 Spaniards, 344 Tagalogs and Pampangans, 679 men from other Philippine groups and "other nations," and 649 rowers, a total of 3,095 men. This large army overwhelmed the Ternatens, and the fortress fell to the invaders. Sultan Said fled first to Jailolo and eventually to Sahu, accompanied only by the Sangaji Ngofakiaha of Makian, the ruler's kinsmen, the queen, and a few other women. All resistance ended two days later with the capture of the Ternaten outpost at Takome. Said was assured safe conduct by the Spaniards, and so he returned to Ternate. Upon his arrival he was greeted by the Spanish commander and the Sultan Tidore. The two sultans solemnly exchanged gifts and addressed each other in respectful terms. Said then signed a treaty of capitulation surrendering all the fortresses throughout his dominion and all the settlements in Moro, including the islands of Morotai and Rau. On 10 April 1606 the Spaniards planted flags in various areas and took possession of Ternate "in the name of His Majesty [the king of Spain]."[115]

The Spaniards began the process of repossessing and reffirming their political and spiritual dominance over the landscape. They retook the old Portuguese fortress near Gammalamo and garrisoned it with their troops. They restored the church of São Paulo and returned it to the Jesuits to allow the resumption of their missionizing activities. The principal mosque in Ternate was converted by the Jesuits and renamed the Convent of San Francisco; the home of the sultan's sister became San Augustin; and the house of a rich nobleman became Santo Domingo. Sultan Said of Ternate and his sangajis were forced to swear not to hinder nor prevent any Muslim or "heathen" from becoming Christian.[116] In the articles of capitulation signed in November 1606, the Ternatens agreed to return all former slaves of the Portuguese and

Spaniards who had become Muslim and to forbid any Christian slaves from becoming Muslim even if they requested it.[117]

In a traditional dualist gesture, Tidore seized upon Ternate's weakness to gain an advantage. The Sultan Tidore "informed" the Spanish Commander Acuña that eight settlements on Makian which had formerly belonged to him had been seized by Ternate. They were Sabaleh, Talapao, Talaosa (Tapasoho?), Ngofabobawa, Bobawa, Tabalola, Lagona, and Mogoa (?). These were therefore returned to Tidore and made to resume their tribute payments. To prevent future dispute, Acuña also placed the remaining nine settlements on Makian under Tidore: Guitamo (?), Ngofagita, Ngofakiaha, Powate (?), Peleri, Samsuma (?), Tahane, Mailoa, and Soma. However, the tribute from these nine places was to be divided between Ternate and Tidore.[118]

For his loyalty to the Spaniards and wounds suffered in assisting in the siege, Sultan Alauddin of Bacan was rewarded with the nearby islands of Kayoa, Adoba, and Bailoro, as well as the Seram settlements of Lisabata, Balomata (?), and others (unnamed). In a letter dated 2 May 1606 to the king of Spain confirming these donations of land, Acuña informed the king that he had instructed Juan de Esquivel, commander of the Spanish forces remaining behind in Ternate, and all subsequent commanders, to offer whatever assistance needed by the Sultan Bacan "to reduce, subject, and bring to obedience the aforementioned places, and to punish those who are disobedient and those who help them."[119] In gratitude for these favors, Sultan Alauddin wrote to Felipe III of Spain, dated 26 April 1606, explaining the position of his kingdom. He reported that, when he was only a child of about seven some thirty years before, Babullah attacked Bacan and seized him, his father the sultan, and various others, and forced Bacan to acknowledge Ternate's overlordship. Alauddin remained in Ternate for three years and then returned to Bacan. During the time of Captain Azambuja on Tidore (head of the fortress called Los Reis Magos between 1578 and 1586), the Portuguese had assisted him against Ternate, and therefore he had remained faithful to them.[120] Finally, to the Sangaji Labuha on Bacan, who was described as "a great Christian and vassal of Your Majesty," Acuña gave the island of Gane as an appanage.[121]

The rulers of Ternate, Tidore, Bacan, and Siau, plus all their sangajis and various others of kaicili status, all swore their vassalage to the king of Spain. They promised not to admit the Dutch to their lands and to give all the cloves to His Majesty and his vassals. Acuña believed that only a strong leader with the respect of the people would be able to organize the gathering, storing, and sale of the cloves. He regarded the Sultan Tidore as the ideal person for the task and even suggested that he become ruler of Ternate. Given the nature of the relationship between

Ternate and Tidore, that suggestion was never implemented. Acuña suspected that the Ternatens were waiting until the return of the Dutch before attacking the Spaniards. He therefore decided to remove the entire Ternate government to Manila and to have Sultan Said appoint governors to be responsible for the affairs in his kingdom. The two who were chosen as governors were two "peace-loving and well-intentioned" brothers, Kaicili Suki and Kacili Kafati. Juan de Esquivel was placed in charge of a force of six hundred to defend Ternate, while a captain and another fifty soldiers were sent to man a new fort built on Tidore. In May 1606 Sultan Said, his eldest son, and twenty-four sangajis and kaicilis were made to board the galley *Patrona* under Captain Villagrá, which took them away to a life of exile in Manila.[122]

The job of pacification did not end with the departure of the *Patrona*. The two Ternaten governors seized the first opportunity to flee to the hills of Sahu, attracting to them a large number of Ternatens who had earlier taken refuge in Jailolo and Sahu. A combined Spanish and Tidore force was sent to Halmahera to complete the subjugation of Ternate's territories. Despite opposition they seized Gamkonora, Bisoa, Mamuya, and Galela. The inhabitants of the Christian settlements of Tolo, Cawa, and Samafo sent ambassadors to greet the expedition with music and signs of peace in the form of "flowering banana stems and white and green cloves." They blamed Sultan Said for their defection from the faith and promised to return to Christianity.[123] Outside Halmahera, Mira in Morotai and the island of Mayu were subdued by the forces of the Sultan Tidore. Esquivel sent an ambassador to the heads of north Sulawesi with gifts of "European clothes . . . (which is currency there)." He announced their freedom from the tyranny of Ternate and offered them Spain's protection.[124] In reply the rulers of Buol and Tolitoli sent a letter to Esquivel seeking arms, gunpowder, and bullets against Makassar raiders. The queen of Kaidipan welcomed the ambassador and explained that "for many years she had wanted to have the king of Castille [Spain] as her Lord . . . and she had always been at war with the king of Ternate."[125]

In late 1606 all resistance to the Spaniards ended, and the Ternaten leaders signed an agreement of capitulation with the Spaniards on 27 November 1606. In it they agreed to (1) recognize the king of Spain as their lord; (2) not purchase any item of war without Spanish approval on pain of death and loss of goods; (3) offer the Spaniards one-third of the tribute normally given to the Sultan Ternate, leaving the remaining two-thirds for the sultan's governors; (4) heed the orders of Spain; (5) not trade or admit anyone except the Spaniards, Portuguese, and their friends; (6) not give aid to any native rebelling against Spain; (7) return all gold, silver, jewels, and religious items on the island; (8) return all former slaves of the Portuguese and the Spaniards who had become

Muslim; (9) not force any Christians to become Muslims; (10) not allow any Christian [slaves] to become Muslim even if they so desired but to return them to their owners; (11) free any natives captured from the Philippines; (12) allow the settling in Ternate of any person from whatever island or nation, with the approval of the [Spanish] governor (who will assign him a place), and not do him or his possessions any harm; (13) not make war or cause any damage to other natives and foreigners; (14) not trade or speak to the Dutch on pain of death and confiscation of goods; and (15) announce these points in their own language throughout the provinces so that the governors [that is, sangajis] could come and sign the document.[126]

For the Spaniards it was a glorious victory and another sign of God's great plan for those inhabiting the periphery. In the words of Argensola: "Thus was Maluku reduced and returned to our ministers and preachers, and the Evangelical Voice once again heard in the furthest ends of the earth."[127] But for the Ternatens the capitulation marked the nadir of Ternate's fortunes and the end of the period when its rulers had seized the initiative and made Ternate one of the most powerful nations in the archipelago.

Consequences of the Encounter

Because the Europeans and the Malukans were shaped by their own particular cultural worlds, their motivations and perception of events differed. The Portuguese and Spanish accounts of the sixteenth and early seventeenth centuries portray the interaction of the Europeans and Malukans very much in accordance with established conventions of the time. The Portuguese captains in Maluku treated the Malukans in a manner which was believed to be fitting to their moral status as the less than human creatures which God had relegated to the edges of the world. With very little provocation the Portuguese engaged in punitive expeditions against the Malukans. They cited religion or Portuguese honor as motivations but in fact saw little need for justification. They were of the fidalguia where defense of the realm and religion was an unquestioned creed. Justification, moreover, was reserved for those who shared similar laws and values, who were of the same world. Even Galvão, though professing to have conducted himself with more decorum than the others, regarded the Malukans in the mold created by the long Classical and Christian European tradition of those living outside the "civilized" world. He, even more than his predecessors, sought to transform the Malukan world by assaulting it with settlers, armies, and Christian missionaries.

In cataloging the activities of the Portuguese captains, the chroniclers of the great Portuguese overseas enterprise admitted to excesses. But this was explained by the fact that they were men exiled to the furthest edges of the earth and were living in a physical environment which produced such extreme behavior. Even before the establishment of a permanent Portuguese presence in Maluku, some of the men delegated to go and build a factory and fort in Ternate deserted rather than serve in this remote land.[128] The well-established association of the periphery with moral turpitude in the European mind was further reinforced by the Portuguese policy of sending the dregs of colonial society to an exile-cum-penal colony in Maluku.[129]

The ultimate judgment on these Portuguese colonial officials was based not on their actions against the natives, but on the impact they had on the glorious national overseas venture. Maluku had proved to be less than successful as a Christian Portuguese outpost in an Islamic world located in the periphery. This failure, then, could only be attributed to the captains who were overzealous in the performance of their duties. If the chroniclers, or more importantly their royal patrons, had seen these accounts as defiling the image of the great endeavor, they would have acted to expunge incriminating details from the record. The failure to do so with regard to the deeds of the Portuguese captains in Maluku has led modern scholars to praise the chroniclers' willingness to include even unflattering portrayals of individuals. When judged by the standards of the time, however, such heinous activities would not have been regarded as unusual in the periphery and did not therefore attract undue comment from the chroniclers.

The monotonous regularity with which certain sixteenth century events occur in the Portuguese chronicles reveals a pattern which appears to have more to do with the Portuguese than with the Malukans. It begins with the arrival of the Portuguese captain who initially establishes amicable relations with the sultan. The latter's death brings his son, a minor, to the throne under a "regency." The regent cooperates with the Portuguese and arranges to have the young ruler incarcerated in the fort. In the process of exercising royal power, the regent runs afoul of his people and the captain and is deposed or killed. The captain, meanwhile, is accused by the Malukans of insensitive and cruel behavior, and he is eventually removed by the arrival of a new captain. Good relations are reestablished, and a new regent is appointed who meets the approval of the new captain. The regent seeks to control the kingdom, and so forth, and a new cycle begins. Within this structure the chroniclers focus on activities that, like the medieval and Renaissance ideal in travel literature (which to an extent these chronicles were to their royal patrons), combine entertaining tales and moral instruction.[130]

Nevertheless, sufficient detail is provided to detect another story lurking in the interstices of the Portuguese structure. Despite Islam's prescription of primogeniture in inheritance, this did not appear to have radically altered the true manner of succession to the paramount position in the land. The formally chosen ruler was indeed the son born of a legal wife of the deceased king in accordance with Islam. Actual power, however, was exercised by any one of the royal family considered most capable, which involved acquiring the support of the bobatos. Prior linkages through marriage and gift-giving were a considerable advantage to a contender, and once he or she was in power these links were reinforced and expanded. When the Portuguese returned to Ternate in force in 1522, a young boy was the formal Islamic ruler but Kaicili Darwis held actual power. The Portuguese interpreted the situation through their own experiences and called Darwis a "regent," but he was in fact the acknowledged head of the community. Although Islam had been introduced in the last quarter of the previous century, it had not yet made great inroads outside the court. It appears that pre-Islamic concepts of leadership, based on both spiritual and physical prowess, were still dominant in 1522. Islamic ideas, therefore, did not prevent women from being accepted as heads of the society. After the death of Darwis at the hands of the Portuguese, the queen mother became the next acknowledged leader of Ternate and guided her people through a number of crises with the Portuguese.

Another example of the encounter producing two levels of interpretation is in the accounts of the wars. The Portuguese and Spanish chroniclers frequently characterize these wars as a "united Malukan (including the Papuans)" effort against the Europeans. From their experiences in the area, the Europeans came to accept the local perception of a group of nations which belonged to the idea of Maluku. Moreover, for the chroniclers a major alliance of kingdoms bound together by Islam produced a far more worthy opponent and thus a far more glorious victory for their fidalgos/hidalgos. Yet throughout these accounts of the wars, the chroniclers mention local rulers siding with the Europeans against the other Malukan kingdoms. This apparent contradiction is resolved by shifting the focus from European to Malukan concerns. The concept of a "family" of Maluku groups identified in specific origin myths formed the fundamental premise which governed their relationships with each other and with those outside the family. There were, however, other cultural imperatives, such as personal blood ties and dualisms, which took precedence over the bonds of the larger and hence looser Malukan family. For example, it was generally accepted that the dualism between Ternate and Tidore was crucial to the well-being of the world of Maluku. As a result it was necessary that both these kingdoms behave in a manner appropriate to their apposite and complementary roles, including being on opposing sides in a war. The significance of this dualism was never fully understood by the Europeans, who saw it as a purely political rivalry such as that found in Europe. They were therefore puzzled by the "feigned" battles between these two kingdoms, the frequent intercourse of their peoples, and the occasions when they appeared to act in concert against the Europeans. What they failed to appreciate was the consistency of the actions of both Ternate and Tidore from the standpoint of their active dualism.

The confrontation between Christianity and Islam was another result of the encounter which was perceived differently by the Europeans and the Malukans. The latter regarded the adoption of one or the other religion as a commitment to either Christian or Muslim sociopolitical institutions and economic networks. On the spiritual level, however, the people saw both religions as offering alternative but not necessarily conflicting ways of dealing with life. The efficacy of Muslim Sufi practices was now being compared with the powers said to inhere in the Christian holy water, the cross, the Bible, the confession, the oil, and the like. It is no surprise that both Christian and Islamic teachers sought to destroy each other's symbols whenever political circumstances allowed. But for the people Christianity and Islam were both useful because of their different sources of spiritual power. It was not uncommon to find local Muslims using both Christian and Muslim objects as talismans. The Portuguese and Spanish portrayal of a *religious* struggle between Islam and Christianity had a different meaning in Malukan society. For the latter the adoption of Islam or Christianity was not only a commitment to a particular overlord and style of governance, but also an opportunity to embrace a whole set of new spirits and powers to enhance their quality of life.

Portuguese accounts of communities "lost" to Christianity, then "saved," and then "lost" again suggest a fluidity in the religious situation in the sixteenth century. It is important to realize, however, that much of this "fluidity" was due to Jesuit perception of events. Both Islam and Christianity exhibited a flexibility in adapting to the Malukan situation. They did not interfere with widely held practices, such as the possession of many wives, or with deeply ingrained belief in spirit worship. For the ordinary Malukan the possession of wives established the necessary blood links with groups to ensure both personal safety and material benefits in trade. For the sultan the most effective bond in assuring allegiance to the center was that established through marriage with women from other kolano and bobato families. The retention of local sacred sites for Islamic or Christian places of worship, the addition of religious prayers and songs to the older spiritual incantations, and the adoption of new names alongside the old were accomplished by the people with little disruption to their way of life. The Malukans easily accommodated aspects of both new belief systems. They moved easily from Islam to Christianity and back again because their fundamental attitudes had not in any way been altered. This accommodation was unchallenged since both the Christian and Muslim missionaries lacked sufficient numbers to maintain a strict adherence to religious teachings. Despite claims by the Christian missionaries of "mass" conversions, what appears to have happened was a conversion of a kolano or sangaji, whose people then followed his lead as was expected in their relationship. The perceived "fluidity" of the religious situation in Maluku was in fact more an indication of political, rather than religious, turmoil in the sixteenth century. Moreover, the Jesuit obsession with numbers of Christian converts, in response to the need for reassurance in the Church and Jesuit communities in Europe of the spiritual health of the mission in Asia, encouraged reports of "mass" conversion.

Concerned with the race against Islam, and conscious of being bearers of Christianity through the royal patronage, the Portuguese and Spanish commentators transformed isolated cases of local raids into wars between "Muslims" and "Christians"; armed local opposition to Portuguese or Spanish demands into Muslim "holy wars" against the *kafir* ("unbeliever"); a local leader's curiosity about Christian practices into an impending conversion of great importance for Christianity; discontented local casises into sinister false prophets seeking to unite all Muslims against the Christians. Portuguese and Spanish captains wishing to please their great Christian monarchs and to assure their own salvation wrote with great regularity of impending conversions of Muslim rulers and their kingdoms. In reality, neither Islam nor Christianity up to the middle of the sixteenth century had sufficient strength within Maluku to have made any successful appeal on the basis of religion alone.

Perhaps the most significant feature of the history of the area in the sixteenth century is the transformation of the nature of government and authority among local kingdoms. But this vital record of Malukan history is visible only in the margins and spaces of the detailed account of the glorious deeds of the Iberian fidalgos/hidalgos. There appears to have been a definite break in the exercise of kingship with the accession of Sultan Babullah in 1570. The expulsion of the Portuguese from Ternate removed a source of instability in the political situation and enabled more foreign traders to enter the ports. With the traders came Muslim teachers who resumed the process of Islamization of the countryside which had been halted with the arrival of the Portuguese and the Jesuit missionaries. The restored links with the rest of the Islamic world through trade helped fill the royal coffers, while the growing presence of Islamic officials and teachers at the court enhanced the ruler's prestige.

A sign of the renewed Islamic influence in society was the greater responsibilities given to the hukums. Before 1570 these Islamic judicial officials had been under the control of the sultan but were unable to exercise much authority. In reaching decisions they were forced to defer to local customs and traditions and to use the Council of Elders as the court of last resort. During Babullah's conquests abroad, these hukums followed in his wake and helped to consolidate his rule by bringing Islam to those who had not yet embraced the new faith. Some were appointed to remain in the pacified areas and given the title of hukum to represent both the spiritual as well as the political interests of the sultan. The two principal hukums remained in the center but became transformed into major offices exercising far greater influence in Ternate than the jogugu. Although they retained their Islamic title, they were only incidentally associated with an Islamic judicial function. They became better known for their political roles as important executors of the will of the sultan and a major prop to his authority.

The undermining of the traditional sources of authority was apparent in the demise of the position of pinate, an office which reinforced the symbolic role of the jogugu as lord of the land. By the late sixteenth century the position of pinate disappeared and was replaced by an official known by the foreign title syahbandar.[131] Syahbandar was a Persian title which had come to Ternate via the Javanese or the Malays. He was in charge of international trade in the port, overseeing the needs of the traders and expediting the exchange of cloves for imported goods. The pinate's displacement by the syahbandar in Ternaten society mirrored a significant shift in the balance of power between the jogugu, whose authority stemmed symbolically from the land, and the sultan. The latter was becoming less dependent on the material and spiritual resources of the land, symbolized by the formalized annual reciprocity rituals with the outlying settlements, and more reliant on the sea and international trade. The increased stature of the syahbandar, who was often a foreign merchant appointed by the sultan because of his knowledge of both local and foreign languages and his international trading expertise, reflected the sultan's new wealth and authority.

The growing paramountcy of the sultan was further evident in the creation of a new position with yet another foreign title, kapita laut. Although the precise origins of the title are unknown, its function as leader of the fleet was not new. In 1530 a Ternate hukum was arrested by the Portuguese and referred to as the *almirante do mar* (admiral of the sea), a term which the Portuguese felt appropriate for an individual who was in charge of the fleets. But the actual title "kapita laut" was not used, and the head of the fleet was called by the Portuguese *ouvidor geral* (chief magistrate), the equivalent term for hukum. In this case it was the hukum who served as the head of the fleet; on other occasions it would have been a prominent official or even a bobato who was honored with the task.[132] The permanent post of kapita laut may have arisen as a result of Babullah's successful campaigns throughout Maluku, which required a more systematic and centralized operation than previously. His title, like many others introduced in Ternate in the sixteenth century, had an alien origin emphasizing the association with a foreign overseas lord (that is, the sultan), rather than with an indigenous "lord of the land" (the jogugu). The kapita laut, like the hukum and the syahbandar, arose outside the indigenous system as a creation of the sultan.

By the establishment of these new posts, the sultan was able to construct a whole new authority structure which bypassed the jogugu in his role as "lord of the land." The dominance of the sultan, symbolically representing the "outside" and the "sea," over the jogugu/pinate representing the "inside" and the "land," became assured once the powerholders associated with the land were replaced by those associated with the sea. The Council of Elders, however, retained their stature in society, but some of them were hand-picked by the sultan and therefore more susceptible to his intervention. By the beginning of the seventeenth century even the position of jogugu had been compromised by the sultan, who appointed one of his brothers to that formerly august and revered office. The "lord of the land," too, had finally succumbed, and the sultan was now preeminent in the kingdom.

The exile to Manila of Sultan Said of Ternate and his chief ministers in 1606 destroyed temporarily the strengthening of the ruler in Ternate. The sangajis and the bobatos were again thrust together to govern without much interference from the sultan. There was a reversion to an earlier situation of each settlement governing its own area with little direction from the center. But this situation did not last long. Soon the Ternatens were looking to the Dutch for protection as they had once turned to the Portuguese a century earlier. Argensola could have been describing the Ternatens when he wrote of the Ambonese: "The natives of the land favor the Dutch as their liberators from the Portuguese yoke. They are well liked there and wherever they trade because they have demonstrated that they would not interfere in their [the local inhabitants'] religion nor propagate theirs except to those who wish to receive it. They cause no discomfort nor injury to anyone."[133] Such may have been the hopes of the native populations on first contact with the Dutch, but subsequent years would show how sadly misplaced they were.

The only other Malukan kingdom which was able to challenge Ternate by the end of the sixteenth century was Tidore. It had survived the combined assaults of the Portuguese and their Ternaten allies in the first three-quarters of the century, and it had prospered as a result of the establishment of the Portuguese on the island after Babullah expelled them from Ternate in 1575. Despite various invasions by Babullah, Tidore survived and regained its position of power by the end of the century. Like Ternate it absorbed a number of areas which had been left without overlords by the demise of Jailolo and the weakness of Bacan due to its chronic lack of people. In 1603 the Spanish listed the following . territories as vassals of Ternate: Moro, Mayu, north Sulawesi (known as Matheo), Tahulandang and islands between Matheo and Siau, the northern half of Sangihe called Macampo, Buru, Veranula (Hoamoal), and three of the seven Banda Islands. This same report described Tidore as having "many subject islands which assist in times of need" with more people and fleets than the Sultan Ternate.[134] The perception of a unified world of Maluku persisted, but it was one that was becoming increasingly dominated by Ternate and Tidore.

CHAPTER FIVE

European Rivalry and
Malukan Dualism

THE SEVENTEENTH CENTURY introduced a new European rivalry onto the Malukan scene: that between the Spaniards and the Dutch. Early in the previous century the Spaniards had made a feeble attempt to establish a presence in the spice islands but had been thwarted at every turn by the more powerful Portuguese. More pressing needs in Europe eventually persuaded the Spanish monarch Charles V to relinquish his claims to the islands in 1529 for a payment of 350,000 cruzados. Only after the union of the Portuguese and Spanish crowns in 1580, followed by the Spanish defeat of Ternate in 1606, did a new era of Spanish involvement begin. But despite the hope for greater things in Maluku, where "the Evangelical Voice [was] once again heard in the furthest ends of the earth,"[1] the Spaniards had to contend with their rebellious subjects, the Dutch, who were still fighting their war of independence. The Dutch East India Company directors had given specific instructions to their servants overseas that their principal task was the maximizing of profit for their shareholders. Since it took approximately two years for a message to be sent from Amsterdam and a reply to be received back from Bantam and Batavia, the officials in Asia could exercise considerable independence of judgment in the implementation of central directives. Despite precise policy objectives from Amsterdam, the Dutch leaders in Asia encouraged military action against the Spaniards because they regarded profit and political motives to be inseparable.

While the Spaniards and the Dutch were preoccupied with their struggles, the Ternatens and Tidorese continued their ongoing dualistic contest for advantage over the other. Both the Europeans and the Malukans sought allies with one another to achieve their respective goals, though their alliances were never more than fragile accommodations because of the radically differing perceptions of the "enemy." For the Europeans it was a struggle between two powers for economic and political supremacy in Maluku and in Europe. It was indeed a rivalry which sought to achieve nothing short of a total victory over the other. For the Malukans it was not the elimination of the other which was contemplated, but the necessity of struggle or conflict itself. The continuing opposition of Ternate and Tidore was an integral part of the dualism in Maluku and was considered crucial for the welfare of their world. It was not simply an enactment of an ancient ritual, but very much a "particular mode of perception and action."[2] The problems inherent in the Spanish-Tidore versus the Dutch-Ternate alliances stemmed from the widely divergent perceptions and intentions of a European rivalry and a Malukan dualism. It was the interplay of these two conceptions which came to dominate the story of Maluku in the first three-quarters of the seventeenth century.

The European Rivalry

The Spanish victory over Ternate in 1606 by the forces of Don Pedro de Acuña marked the start of the first and only period of Spanish influence in the affairs of Maluku. Some six hundred Spanish and Filipino troops were established in the old Portuguese fort (known as Kastela by the local inhabitants) in Ternate, while another fifty remained in Tidore.[3] The signing of the capitulations ended formal hostilities, and Ternate was forced to acknowledge Spanish overlordship. From the outset, however, Spanish presence in the area was challenged by the Dutch. The first Dutch ship arrived in Indonesian waters in 1595, but it was not till the formation of the Dutch East India Company (VOC) in 1602 that the Dutch became a force in the region. The Company was assigned the monopoly of all the trade east of the Cape of Good Hope and west of the Straits of Magellan, while its charter granted it the privilege of exercising sovereign rights on behalf of the Dutch republic in its relations with Asian powers. Although the Company received a special subsidy to pursue the war against the Spaniards and Portuguese in the East, it was instructed not to put war before trade. It was to be a business concern above all, not a vehicle for the creation of empire. However, distance and local exigencies allowed Company officials in the East to pursue their own interests. When the Dutch seized the Portuguese fortress in Ambon in 1605, they were reported to have torn down the Catholic churches, destroyed the crosses, desecrated the holy images, and stolen the bells.[4] In the eyes of these company servants, the struggle against Spain took precedence over profit in the early years of the seventeenth century.

The Ternatens became the natural allies of the Dutch. When a Ternaten envoy came to visit Admiral Cornelis Matelieff on 29 March

1607, he was welcomed and given assurances that the Dutch would send a force to help the Ternatens remove the Spaniards from their land. Matelieff proffered this assistance on the condition that at least two thousand Ternatens participate in the campaign. The Dutch assembled a formidable fleet of six ships and two yachts carrying 530 Dutchmen and 50 Ambonese which arrived before Ternate on 13 May 1607. The Ternatens, under the young Sultan Muzaffar, his brother, and the Sultan Jailolo—all between the ages of twelve and fourteen—were able to raise only a couple of hundred men.[5] Unwilling to undertake action against a well-entrenched enemy without sufficient Ternaten support, Matelieff decided instead to establish a new Dutch presence on Ternate alongside the Spaniards.

Confident of Dutch naval superiority, Matelieff elected to build a fortress on the coast of Malayu, rather than on the mountain slopes of Maukonora. Maukonora was about half an hour from the Spanish (formerly Portuguese) main fortress near Gammalamo and was ideally situated on a hill. It was rejected as a site, however, because its water supply could be easily cut off by besiegers and there was no place to beach and shelter Ternaten boats bringing supplies. Furthermore, any movement of ships would be observable from Tidore. These strategic considerations were met by the site of Malayu, and so it was here that the Dutch built their fortress.[6] Within a short time they also established Fort Nassau on the northern side of Moti and Fort Willemstadt at Takome on the northwest coast of Ternate. On 23 November 1609 the Dutch defeated the Spanish-Portuguese garrison stationed in Bacan and forced the latter kingdom to relinquish both Gane and Kayoa, which had been seized from Ternate and given by Don Pedro de Acuña to Bacan as a reward for its services to the Spanish crown. The Dutch strengthened the captured Portuguese fortress and renamed it Fort Barneveldt. In two years the Dutch built eleven fortifications and manned them with a total of about five hundred Europeans. They were Malayu, Toloko, Takome, and Kalamata on Ternate; Tapasoho, Ngofakiaha, and Tabalola on Makian; Fort Nassau on Moti; Fort Barneveldt on Bacan; and one fortress each in Jailolo and Tidore.[7]

Once the Ternatens were convinced that the Dutch were planning to remain in the islands, they returned from Halmahera and began to rebuild their settlements around the Dutch forts. They abandoned the old royal capital at Gammalamo, which was controlled by the Spaniards, and built an entirely new royal town at Malayu. Some one thousand Moti islanders returned from Gane in southwest Halmahera to settle around Nassau, while three hundred Ternaten families came to build their homes near Willemstadt.[8] The inhabitants of Kayoa elected to settle in Tabalola on Makian where the Dutch had earlier built another fort.[9] For the Ternatens and their former allies, the recent fear-

ful memory of their ruler and all of the most important men in the kingdom being seized and exiled to a distant foreign land was a powerful
incentive to settle under the protective guns of the Dutch.

At first the Spanish showed every sign of countering Dutch moves.
On 20 June 1608 they joined forces with Tidore to seize Jailolo in a
dawn raid, destroying its "very opulent mosque." They then pursued
their advantage by forcing many from Jailolo, Sahu, and Gamkonora to
flee to the interior. These initial successes, however, could not be sustained because the Spaniards' chief ally, the ruler of Tidore, refused to
commit more of his manpower for fear of the arrival of a Dutch fleet.[10]
Nevertheless, the Spaniards remained a threat because of the relative
proximity of Manila whence came periodic supplies and reinforcements
for the Maluku garrison. In 1611 the governor-general of the Philippines, Don Juan de Silva, hoped to effect a reconciliation with the
Ternatens by leading a fleet to Ternate with the exiled Sultan Said, his
son and heir, and a number of important exiled Ternaten officials on
board. But Silva's promises and generous gifts made little impact on the
Ternatens, who remained wary of the Spaniards. After two months had
gone by without reaching the desired result, Silva ordered an attack on
Sahu and Jailolo which were less heavily defended than Ternate. The
two areas eventually capitulated, but even before the Spaniards raised
their sails to return to Manila, the combined Dutch-Ternaten forces had
routed the Spaniards. Thus ended the first attempt by Sultan Said to
return as ruler of Ternate.[11]

The Spaniards and the Dutch, aided by their Malukan allies, con-
tinued their seesaw struggle in the early decades of the century. The
Dutch seized the Tidore royal settlement at Mareku and deprived the
Spaniards and the Tidorese of the many fruit trees and fish supplies
which came from this port. Then in 1614 two other Spanish fortresses
on Tidore were taken by the Dutch with the aid of their Ternaten allies.
Siau and Tahulandang to the north of Sulawesi were next to fall to the
Dutch, while Sangihe avoided their fate by seeking Dutch protection.
Unable to fathom the dualism between Ternate and Tidore, the Dutch
suspected their Ternaten ally because it continued to maintain good
relations with Tidore.[12] The Spaniards in this same period led a number of expeditions against Ternate's periphery at Sula, Jailolo, and elsewhere, causing destruction wherever they went. They continued to
retain their strategic fortifications in the southern part of Ternate and
on the opposite shore of Tidore, and they were quick to respond to any
attempts by the Dutch to secure posts in the area. With assistance from
their Tidore allies, continuing access to supplies from Makassar, and
the occasional expedition from Manila, the Spaniards were successful in
maintaining themselves in Maluku.[13]

In 1623 the new Spanish governor of Maluku, Don Pedro de

Heredia, brought "letters of reference" from the exiled Sultan Said to Sultan Muzaffar (r. 1606–1627) and the queen mother of Ternate. The letters spoke of the good treatment and respect accorded him by the Spaniards in keeping with his status as ruler. Heredia also brought with him an oil painting of the exiled sultan done in Manila, which was hung in the court for all to honor. Upon receiving the letters and the portraits, the Ternate court expressed their satisfaction at the good treatment of their exiled lord and asked that the Spaniards meet their representatives to sign a treaty of friendship. Heredia complied, and in the subsequent meeting the Ternatens agreed to a peace with the Spaniards. They promised not to wage war on the Spaniards on land or on sea and not to aid the Dutch in their battles against the Spaniards. In return Heredia promised to seek Said's release on his next mission to Manila. For some unexplained reason, the supply convoy which arrived in Ternate in 1624 did not bring Sultan Said as had been arranged. This was interpreted by the Ternatens as a rejection of the agreement, and so they resumed hostilities against the Spaniards.[14]

The story of the rivalry between the Spaniards and the Dutch was marked by the occasional skirmish with the assistance of their respective Malukan allies. These minor conflicts usually ended with a Dutch victory because of their naval superiority and led to a subsequent jockeying for advantage in the location of forts. It was obvious that the Dutch could operate with almost total impunity in these waters, whereas the Spaniards were in essence "confined" to Maluku and dependent upon the supply ships from Manila. They were still free to obtain goods and to sell cloves through their allies in Tidore or in Makassar, but the Spanish garrison quickly realized that their activities were of little interest to Manila. As the Spanish challenge diminished, the Dutch looked more kindly on the Spaniards as companions in a difficult land. They exchanged good wishes during religious holidays and on other special occasions and even met socially. One of the consequences of the neglect of Maluku by the Manila authorities was the arbitrary powers wielded by the local Spanish governor. The maltreatment of the soldiers and the all too frequent nonpayment of wages, resulting from delayed arrivals of the supply convoys from Manila and mismanagement of funds by the local officials, led to desertions to the Dutch or to local communities. Intermarriage between Spanish deserters and local women in time produced a mestizo group which played an important commercial and cultural role mediating between the European and the Malukan communities. This group continued to maintain its influence even after the departure of the Spaniards from Maluku.

In 1662 the Spanish authorities in Manila decided to abandon the Maluku garrison and to bring back the soldiers because of the threat to Manila posed by Koxinga.[15] The actual withdrawal was in 1663, but the dismantling of the fortifications did not occur until the second half of 1666. Don Francisco de Atienza Ybañez, captain-general of the royal fleet sent to oversee the operation, left a report in which he spoke of the demolishing of the forts San Felipe, San Cristoval, Santiago, San Agustin, San Juan, San Lorenzo, San Pedro, Don Xil, and San Francisco Kalamata, as well as Nuestra Señora del Rosario (the former Portuguese fortress), the major fortification in southern Ternate and the home of the Spanish government in Maluku. The royal magazine, the powderhouse, the settlements, churches, convents, and all other edifices were put to the torch or pulled down in execution of his orders. He also made known to the Dutch authorities at Malayu that, although the Spaniards had withdrawn from Maluku, "the king our lord retained dominion and overlordship over it."[16] Thus ended the Iberian adventure in Maluku which had lasted more than 150 years, from the arrival of the Portuguese in the area in 1511 to the final departure of the Spaniards in 1666. The earlier departure of the English from Ambon in 1623 left the Dutch the sole surviving European nation in Maluku.

The campaigns between the Dutch and the Spaniards involving their local allies Ternate and Tidore had left few areas unaffected. In March 1619 the English Captain John Saris was told by some powerful nobles in Bacan that their land was being destroyed by the war with the Spaniards. Any area which had links with either Ternate and Tidore had suffered the consequences of that alliance, and both these kingdoms in turn had paid the penalty for siding with one or the other European power. In a letter dated 6 May 1612 the Sultan Tidore wrote to his counterpart in Ternate expressing the view that the only hope for an end to the conflict in Maluku was to effect a reconciliation between the Spaniards and the Dutch. His perceptive conclusion was that "for us to make peace without the Spaniards and the Dutch would mean that it would not last long."[17] In the accounts it is obvious that both the Dutch and the Spaniards regarded the local allies as simply auxiliaries in any campaign, and the latter's wishes were always subordinated to those of the European. The many war expeditions and the destruction wrought on the villages and the people were on a scale hitherto unknown in Maluku. No one was immune in the struggle being conducted by Europeans in Malukan waters, and movements of people reflected the principal concern in these times, which was to seek shelter and protection under a powerful lord. Except for the rulers of Ternate and Tidore, whose goodwill was still essential in maintaining the fine balance between the Spaniards and the Dutch, all other Malukan rulers were at the mercy of the struggle. Lands and rulers were destroyed if regarded as a threat to the balance, and in time only Ternate and Tidore remained as viable entities able to deal with the growing strength of the Europeans in the area.

The Ternate Half of the Malukan Dualism

For Ternate and Tidore the presence of the Europeans meant powerful new allies who could be useful in their own contest. One of the expressions of this dualism was the competition for people and territory, and neither allowed an opportunity to slip by without attempting to demonstrate superiority by seizing the other's property. The Ternatens took advantage of the protective presence of the Dutch to extend their control over neighboring lands.[18] In 1618 the Dutch were told by traders and a Ternaten official that a prince from Tidore was going with a fleet of kora-koras to seize the Ternaten areas of Kambelo, Lesidi, and Erang on the Hoamoal peninsula of Seram. Tidore boasted that Kambelo had been in contact for two years and that many of the leaders from Luhu, Lesidi, Erang and other places under Ternate in the Ambon Quarter wanted to reject the Sultan Ternate and accept the overlordship of the Sultan Tidore. It was said that these areas had met in council and, with the exception of the Kapitan Hitu who subsequently left the meeting, agreed no longer to accept the direction of Ternate's representatives from the Tomagola family, Kimalaha Sabadin and Kimalaha Hidayat.[19]

Such an act of rejection reflected badly on Ternate, and the sultan immediately blamed his representatives for this humiliation which Tidore had been quick to exploit. The Tomagola family had been given Luhu and the surrounding areas of Hoamoal, or "Small Seram" (Klein Ceram), as the Dutch called it, as an appanage in the early sixteenth century. The sultan now attempted to recall the Tomagolas on the pretext that there were no longer members of that house on Ternate to whom he could turn. He claimed that their wise counsel was necessary more than ever before because "our enemies are still strong [and] . . . all my council are composed solely of young men."[20] This plea was couched in terms which were readily comprehensible to Malukans and designed to arouse a sense of duty in the minds of the Tomagola family, one of the most influential of the Fala Raha in the kingdom. The reference to the council "composed solely of young men" may have been referring to the actual state of affairs or may have been a metaphor for the absence of the wisdom of the elders, including the venerable houses of the Fala Raha.

Despite the appeal, the Tomagolas in Hoamoal had reason to consider what they would lose in returning to Ternate. Their lands were covered with forests of clove and nutmeg trees and sufficiently distant from Ternate to allow them great freedom in governing and in participating in the clandestine trade in spices. By dealing directly with traders from the west, especially from Makassar, the Tomagolas avoided paying taxes to the Ternate sultan and submitting to the low fixed prices for spices set by the Portuguese, Spanish, and Dutch. Instead, they could ask for the best prices in the much desired cloth, iron, and other products brought by various archipelago traders, particularly the Malays, Javanese, Bugis, and Makassarese. With these goods the Tomagolas were able to attract more followers both in the immediate areas as well as in the surrounding regions. The Ternate ruler had viewed their growing power base with some concern, but far more threatening was the prospect of the area choosing to become part of Tidore. The loss of a prosperous territory and valuable human resources to his archrival was more than the Sultan Ternate could bear. A similar fear prompted him to request in 1625 that another "governor," the Kimalaha Besi from the Tomaitu family, return to Ternate from the Sula Islands which had been given to the family as an appanage sometime in the sixteenth century.[21] To further strengthen his position in the center, Sultan Muzaffar sought to assure the loyalty of Gamkonora and Makian, both areas of rich resources and large populations. Thus in 1632 the Sangaji Gamkonora was made the jogugu and the Sangaji Ngofakiaha in Makian the kapita laut of Ternate.[22]

Muzaffar's well-laid plans came to naught because of Dutch paranoia. Believing that Muzaffar was involved in a plot with the Spaniards, the Dutch forced the Ternatens to depose him. The Ternatens, however, refused to be influenced by the Dutch or the powerful lobbies in the periphery in the choice of their next ruler. Only the *soa sio,* the "Nine Soas" based in the royal settlement of Malayu, participated in the selection of Hamzah (r. 1627–1648), brother of Babullah, as sultan in June 1627. Neither the Dutch governor nor the powerful sangajis of Makian, Gamkonora, and Sahu were consulted. The soa sio were ostensibly swayed by the argument that, if they did not elect Hamzah, he would return to Manila and encourage another Spanish fleet to come and seize Ternate. The fear of the return of the Spaniards was a real one among Ternatens since they felt that the Dutch had demonstrated little commitment to Ternate, despite the presence of their forts. Insofar as the other contenders were concerned, Kapita Laut Ali was regarded as too harsh and uncontrollable, the jogugu too old, and the king's son too young. A young king would have had to rule with the advice of both the kapita laut and the jogugu, two officials who had demonstrated considerable independence from the ruler in the past. Moreover, the jogugu was still regarded as the leader of the bobatos—the authorities associated with the forces of the land and therefore a potential challenge to the sultan. To assure Dutch support for the soa sio's choice of the mild-mannered Hamzah as sultan, he was sent to the fort on the day of his election to declare his loyalty to the Dutch East India Company.[23]

Hamzah had been among those taken in 1606 by the Spaniards to Manila, where he remained until February or March 1627. During his

lengthy exile he had become a Christian and had taken the baptismal
name of Don Pedro de Acuña to honor the governor-general who had
led the Spanish conquest of Ternate. He had also married in a church
and was said to have been "Hispanized." These developments convinced the Spaniards that Hamzah would be favorably disposed to
them, and so they agreed to allow him to return under certain conditions. He was to remain a Christian, seek to convert his people, and
acknowledge the overlordship of the king of Spain. Hamzah's intimate
ties with the Spaniards continued throughout his reign, and he conducted almost daily correspondence with the Spanish government at
Gammalamo. Despite misgivings about Hamzah's links with the Spaniards, the Ternatens regarded him as the best choice. He was said to be
"gentle and discreet," descended from a prominent family, and possessed of sufficient influence to restrain some of the principal leaders in
the kingdom.[24]

Once in power Hamzah began the process of strengthening the
center by forcibly transferring his subjects to Ternate from the periphery. In 1621 the people of Maitara, an island between Tidore and Ternate, were brought to Malayu to prevent their being controlled by the
much closer Tidore court. Another thirty people were seized from the
Obi Islands in 1625, though they were subjects of the Sultan Bacan. In
two separate expeditions in 1627 and 1628, Hamzah seized some eighteen hundred men, women, and children from the Christian settlements
in Moro and resettled them at Malayu. The people of Loloda were also
ordered to move to Jailolo "to make that place more secure for them
[the Ternatens]."[25]

Along with the physical relocation of people to the center, Hamzah sought to undermine possible challenges by the kapita laut and the
jogugu, who were sangajis of Makian and Gamkonora respectively, two
areas which in terms of resources could challenge Ternate as a center.
The jogugu's advanced age made him far less of a threat than Kapita
Laut Ali, who was ambitious and popular among the people. To remove
this danger, Hamzah sent Ali as his representative to the troubled areas
in Ternate's territories "to implement in a proper fashion my law and
justice in Maluku as if I myself were present."[26] Many of the most
prominent leaders in Ternate pleaded with him to remain, for they
feared that if he, "the pillar of the kingdom," left he would never
return.

Of the twenty-seven kora-koras in his fleet, twelve of them were
manned by the inhabitants of Makian, thus removing a sizable proportion of Makian's manpower. He arrived in the Ambon Quarter with fifteen hundred men and replaced the recalcitrant Tomagola head at
Hoamoal with one more responsive to Ternate's wishes. From Ambon
he sailed westward to Tobunku and forced the ruler there to reaffirm his

allegiance to the Sultan Ternate. In Butung he fell ill and died, some say poisoned by the vengeful Sultan Goa who resented Ali's success in weaning Tobunku from his control. With Ali's death the people of Makian lost their one source of support in the Ternate court, and they began to complain to the Dutch of the "burdens and evil deeds" committed against them by Sultan Hamzah. They accused him of preventing them from harvesting their cloves and of demanding that a hundred Makian children be sent to him to perform domestic service while being held hostage to assure the good behavior of the people.[27]

The rapid and systematic consolidation of personal power through the relocation of population and the removal of challengers disturbed those responsible for putting Hamzah on the throne. Ternaten leaders began openly criticizing Hamzah's "bad" government, accusing him of acting without consultation in undertaking unpopular measures against Loloda, Gamkonora, Sahu, Jailolo, and Makian. Unwilling to tolerate his arrogation of power, they sought to overturn their choice and replace him with one of his children. In a gathering in the baileu, the council confronted Hamzah and warned him that they had the power to elect him and, if necessary, to demote him to an ordinary kaicili (royal offspring). Hamzah refused to be intimidated and instead employed his personal bodyguard, the *kolano ngofangare,* to strip the three most important council members of their offices and dignities. With their removal the other members of the council were sufficiently cowed to allow Hamzah to have his own way. By 1636 Hamzah felt confident enough to remove both the Sangaji Ngofakiaha in Makian and the Sangaji Gamkonora and to replace them with those who had met his approval. These newly appointed sangajis were then bound to Hamzah through marriage and "other friendships."[28]

Having reaffirmed his dominant position in the center, Sultan Hamzah turned his attention to Tidore and to the periphery. He masterminded the return of the Tidore prince Kaicili Gorontalo, who had been living in Ternate under his protection, to become the new Sultan Tidore (r. 1634–1652) on 30 April 1634.[29] When the soa sio in the royal settlement of Mareku continued to pay allegiance to the old sultan, Kaicili Garolamo, Hamzah arranged for his removal with the assistance of the Spaniards on Tidore, with whom Hamzah continued to retain good relations.[30] With the new ruler indebted to Hamzah, the latter was able to devote his attention to the periphery with little interference from Tidore.

One area which continued to pose a major problem to the center in the early decades of the seventeenth century was Hoamoal. Despite the removal of the ˙former Ternaten governor of Luhu, the Tomagola Kaicili Leliato, his replacement Kaicili Luhu proved to be equally intractable and dismissive of any direction from the center. Nearly a century of uninterrupted independent rule in Hoamoal by the Toma-gola family had made them unaccustomed to the type of direct demands now being made by Hamzah. Unlike other Ternaten rulers, Hamzah had spent more than twenty years in Manila where he had been exposed to Spanish ideas of the proper authority and power of rulers. Once he was made sultan, Hamzah attempted to put these notions into practice, which meant a rejection of government by consensus and consultation and a greater reliance on direct involvement in subject territories. Hamzah's new style of authority caused great resentment and led to a change in the character of Ternate's government in subsequent years.

Hamzah decided to send a punitive expedition against the defiant Tomagolas in Hoamoal to serve as an example to others, but in the end he was forced to seek help from the Dutch. It was therefore the Dutch whose reputation was enhanced by the whole incident. On 17 June 1643 the Hoamoal leader Kaicili Luhu, his mother, sister, and stepbrother were punished, not by Hamzah, but by the Dutch. In a public execu-tion which was intended to make the strongest impression on the local inhabitants, the "rebels" were beheaded by the Dutch in the square in front of Fort Victoria's main portal in Ambon. Hamzah's decision to rely on force rather than on mediation had the desired outcome, but at the expense of becoming gradually indebted to the Dutch. It was a development which may have weakened Hamzah's influence in his own government, for the Ternate Council forced him to agree to allow another Tomagola, the Kimalaha Majira, to govern the area.[31]

For the remainder of the year and well into 1644 Hamzah was relentless in removing all opposition in the Ambon Quarter, including the entire Hitu coast in Ambon. Those subdued were then forced to send tribute to Ternate worth 73,000 guilders, of which 56,875 was to go directly to Hamzah himself, in cloths, gongs, gold ornaments, small guns, and a few cannon.[32] The use of force and the levying of a "fine," rather than the more traditional methods of marriage, gifts, and persua-sion, were resented by the thirty Hitu settlements. They thus turned to the ruler of Goa in Makassar to ask him to become their patron and pro-tector. When Hamzah learned of this, he launched another attack on Hitu with the assistance of the Dutch. He then requested that the Dutch "govern all groups in my name," show no mercy, and uproot "the fam-ily of the Tomagolas and all other Ternatens who cause trouble or dis-turbance in my lands."[33] Hamzah had created a strong precedent of Dutch involvement in the governing of Ternate's territories, a legacy which came to haunt later rulers.

During this period Ternate's attention and resources were devoted mainly to Hoamoal and Hitu. When the salahakan of the Sula Islands, a member of a cadet branch of the Tomaitu house which had settled in Sula Besi, neglected to send the annual gifts to Ternate, Hamzah prudently avoided taking any action while the people of Hitu and Hoamoal remained in revolt. The island of Sula Besi was capable of dispatching from its eleven settlements some forty-three kora-koras, each of which normally carried between fifty to seventy men. Since the practice in the Sula Islands was similar to that in Hitu, where half to two-thirds of the men were kept at home to protect the women and children, the number of fighting men in Sula Besi could be conservatively estimated at about 4,300. In 1644 the other two Sula Islands of Taliabu and Mangole were capable of outfitting yet another sixty kora-koras. The force available on Sula Besi alone was larger than any that Hamzah could assemble for Ternate from his surrounding lands at the time.[34] Moreover, the swift Sula boats were well known and greatly feared in Malukan waters, and in the past they formed the greater part of the Ternaten fleets. During Sultan Babullah's conquests in the west in the late sixteenth century, it was the Sula boats under the command of Cappalaya which had been one of the chief reasons for his success.

In north Sulawesi the populous district of Gorontalo refused to acknowledge Hamzah's demand for tribute. Though Ternate could only assemble sufficient manpower for ten to twelve kora-koras, an expedition was nevertheless sent in December 1647. The rather pathetic fleet failed to impress the Gorontalo people and accomplished nothing. Hamzah was again forced to rely upon the Dutch, who sent two well-armed yachts in support of Ternate's small fleet. A major factor in the ability of Hamzah to command respect from the Gorontalo people on this occasion was the inclusion of the Sula fleet. By then the troubles between Hamzah and Sula had been resolved, and the former was able to appeal for assistance from the Tomaitu family in Sula Besi. Only in the smaller areas of Ternate's periphery was Hamzah's use of force effective. In 1643 Ternate's kora-koras went as far as the southern rim of the Banda Sea to the islands of Kisar and Romang, seizing some two thousand prisoners and a large amount of booty including much gold-, silver- and copperware.[35]

When Sultan Hamzah died in May 1648, he bequeathed to his successors a new model for center/periphery relations. He had been nurtured in the ways of the Spaniards in Manila during his twenty-year exile, and he was obviously convinced that, like the Spanish governor-general of the Philippines, a ruler should exercise direct control over all of his territories. It was rumored that, although he had become a Christian in Manila, he would claim to be either a Christian or a Muslim whenever it suited him.[36] It was this background which saw Hamzah from the beginning of his reign rely less on the traditional means of alliance and more on the use of force to maintain control over his territories. He was quick to call upon the Dutch to use their superior firepower to reinforce his position against what he regarded as "rebellious" subjects. But these so-called "rebels" were simply those in areas which had traditionally been under the leadership of old Ternaten families who had governed the areas as appanages and had continued to recognize the Sultan Ternate as their lord. Hamzah, however, saw their independence as a defiance of his own rule, and he therefore employed force in the first instance with predictable results. In addition to creating strains in the center/periphery relationship, Hamzah established a precedent of appealing to the Dutch in times of difficulty and even of allowing them to govern on his behalf in distant territories. The Dutch were willing to lend assistance, but as many local potentates soon discovered, the Dutch never offered anything without compensation. It was this compensation that the Dutch later sought to collect from future rulers which came to threaten the unity known as Maluku.

Hamzah's eldest son became the new ruler of Ternate and was installed on 19 June 1648 as Sultan Mandar Syah (r. 1648–1675). The choice was not a popular one among either the heads or the people of Ternate. It was said that his character was bad and that he lacked that special quality of authority which a Dutch source translated as *geluk,* a term meaning "luck or fortune."[37] Company officials, on the other hand, described Mandar as good-natured and accustomed to the company of Dutchmen. Moreover, they were confident that he would be a good friend since he had the Dutch to thank for having been chosen above his two other brothers.[38] Blatant Dutch interference in Ternate's affairs had become commonplace under Hamzah, and so they saw nothing amiss in supporting a candidate who would be beholden to them for his royal position.

From the outset Sultan Mandar Syah's authority in his kingdom was precarious and dependent more on the goodwill of the Dutch than on his own leaders and people. As long as the interests of Ternate and the Company converged, their relations remained excellent. One of their shared aims was the maintenance of orderly government in peripheral territories. Sultan Mandar wanted peace and prosperity in his lands because they were the traditional measure of a good and successful ruler. But the powerful Ternaten families opposed any punitive measures against the periphery. The leaders of these territories were members of cadet branches of the Fala Raha, which had created the appanages in outlying areas in the sixteenth century. The main Ternate branches of the Fala Raha were understandably reluctant to act against family members and resented the continuing arrogation of power by the sultans with the support of the Dutch.

Hoamoal and Hitu, under the Tomagolas, were two perennial trouble spots in Ternate's periphery. Sultan Hamzah had finally decided to ask the VOC to govern this area in his name, and after his death Sultan Mandar was persuaded by the Dutch to continue the arrangement.[39] Dutch interest in Hoamoal and Hitu was spurred by fears of the growing involvement of Makassar traders in the spice trade. The Makassar kingdom of Goa had developed into a major eastern entrepôt as a result of two migrant communities that had been displaced from their homelands by Europeans. After the conquest of Melaka in 1511, many Malays fled to Makassar bringing with them their trading skills and international connections. Provided with special quarters in the city and made exempt from arbitrary interference from local authorities, the Malay community thrived and quickly formed the heart of a burgeoning international trade based in Makassar.[40]

The Bandanese were the other foreign migrant group which contributed to Makassar's rise. In the early sixteenth century they were well known in Melaka as the principal carriers of spices from the east. They not only collected nutmeg and mace from their forests, but they also sent boats to north Maluku to bring the cloves south for the final journey to Melaka. When the Dutch arrived in these waters, they quickly recognized the Bandanese as a major threat to their aim of monopolizing the collection and sale of spices. They therefore attacked Banda to destroy or remove the entire population. Some of the Bandanese saved themselves by escaping by boat to nearby lands, while others went to East Seram. These resettled Bandanese became a major factor in the importance of Keffing in international trade in the seventeenth and eighteenth centuries. From East Seram the Bandanese were invited by the ruler of Goa to settle in Makassar. Those who accepted the offer arrived with valuable information, expertise, and commercial connections, which enabled Goa to maintain its position as the foremost trading nation in eastern Indonesia until its defeat by the Dutch in the Makassar War of 1666–1669. Many of the so-called "Makassarese" traders operating in the archipelago were in fact Malays or Bandanese. Goa's newly found trading wealth enabled it to extend its influence into areas formerly under Ternate's influence. By 1636 Goa had replaced Ternate as overlord in Butung, Banggai, the Sula Islands, Tobunku, Menado, and Buru. Both Ternate and the VOC therefore had a common interest in wishing to see the demise of Goa.

The close cooperation between Sultan Mandar and the Dutch East India Company aroused resentment within Ternate. On 2 August 1650 the Fala Raha and the bobatos in Ternate declared their opposition to Mandar and their election of his youngest brother, Kaicili Manilha, whom Company officials described as "not altogether in control of his senses," as the new Ternaten ruler. The reason for their choice of Kaicili Manilha appears to have been motivated by the desire to have a ruler who would be responsive to the wishes of the leaders of the community. Another much more capable brother, Kaicili Kalamata, regarded as an able prince and "learned in Islamic law," was rejected for fear that the position of ruler would be further strengthened. Those who worked to remove Mandar from power were Kaicili Said and Hukum Laulata of the Tomagola family, Kimalaha Terbile of the Tomaitu family, and Jogugu Kaicili Musa and Kimalaha Marsaoli of the Marsaoli family—hence three of the most prominent of the Fala Raha. These families together proved too powerful for Mandar, and he was forced to seek safety with the Dutch in Fort Orange accompanied only by his wives, children, three sangajis and a hundred others.[41] To safeguard their choice of Mandar as sultan, the Company sent a fleet under de Vlaming which arrived in Ternate in 1651. With the assistance of Kalamata, who wavered in support between one group and the other, the Dutch forced Manilha from the Ternate throne. But the fighting continued in Jailolo where Kaicili Said held out for a while until forced to move to Sula in 1652. He was finally captured and killed in Seram in July 1655. Laulata fought on briefly, but he too was eventually seized and put to death. From the Tomaitu appanage in Sula Besi, Terbile led the opposition to Mandar but was later captured and sentenced to death by the Dutch in 1653. The island of Taliabu remained defiant and faithful to the Tomaitu family.

Kalamata survived the fighting, having sided in the end with the Dutch and Sultan Mandar. His irrepressible royal ambitions, however, led him to join forces with Jailolo and Bacan in another effort to depose Mandar. As on the previous occasion, Mandar fled to the safety of the Dutch fortress. The Dutch were by this time disillusioned with him, and de Vlaming let the Ternatens know that the Dutch would support anyone on Ternate's throne as long as he remained loyal to the Dutch. Kalamata refused to tolerate the presence of Mandar in the fortress, and the ensuing deadlock created ill-feeling between the Ternatens and the Dutch which led to another round of fighting. De Vlaming defeated Kalamata and, for want of another suitable candidate, reinstalled Mandar as Sultan Ternate on 26 June 1655. Kalamata fled first to Buru, then to the Sula Islands, to Bacan, and again back to Sula. His places of refuge became less secure once the Sula Islands in 1656 and Buru in 1657 submitted to Mandar and the Dutch. Unable to find safety in Maluku, Kalamata decided to go to the one kingdom which continued to welcome all those seeking refuge from the Company: the kingdom of Goa in Makassar.[42]

With Dutch Company help Sultan Mandar was able to reclaim his kingdom. He asked the Dutch to govern Hoamoal and Hitu on his behalf, and he provided them with a local Ternaten assistant since they admitted being "not totally familiar with local customs and laws."[43] In the western periphery Tobunku, a kingdom which had acknowledged its allegiance to Ternate in the past as long as the links were loose and distant, was forced to accept a Ternate sangaji. Butung, too, was drawn closer to the center by being required to have its choice of ruler approved by and invested in Ternate. Only in north Sulawesi did Sultan Mandar face difficulties in enforcing his will. The association of this area with Ternate had begun during the reign of Sultan Hairun and had been strengthened under Sultan Babullah. But Ternate's hold was always tenuous, and in the early seventeenth century these north Sulawesi settlements came under Goa's domination. After Goa's defeat by the VOC in 1667, the former was forced to relinquish to Ternate "the islands of Salayar and Pangasana (Muna); the whole east coast of Sulawesi from Menado to Pangasana; the islands of Banggai and Gapi and the coasts which belong to them; the lands between Mandar and Menado: the lands of Langaji, Kaidipan, Buol, Tolitoli, Dompelas, Balaisang, Silensa, and Kaili, which in the past had belonged to the Ternate crown."[44] Nevertheless, these settlements rejected Ternate's claims to the area by arguing that the VOC was now the true overlord by right of conquest. Company directives, however, discouraged acquisition of territory because of costs and the policy of relying on local rulers to promote its interests. It therefore rejected all attempts by north Sulawesi to become part of its territories and even persuaded Gorontalo and Limbotto to forgo plans to prevent the Ternatens from trading there.[45] Company concerns, rather than any desire to satisfy the Ternaten ruler, determined the fate of north Sulawesi.

In other Ternate territories Sultan Mandar built upon a practice introduced by his predecessor to appoint important officials who would be loyal to the sultan and not to one of the Fala Raha. The sangajis of Makian and Gamkonora were given important posts in the kingdom in recognition of the strength and strategic value of these two areas. According to a Dutch report of 1662, the Ternaten ruler could call upon about 2,630 fighting men on northwest Halmahera; on Makian the settlement of Ngofakiaha on the northern side of the island had 400 men, Ngofagita a half mile further west 170, and the combined villages of Sabaleh, Talapao, Tapasoho, Bobawa, Ngofabobawa, and Lagona 345.[46] By contrast, there was a dearth of manpower available to Sultan Mandar in Ternate itself because of widespread disaffection with his rule. His principal support came from the soa sio in the royal settlement of Malayu, but his unpopularity had led to a steady loss of population. On one particular occasion he had insufficient men to outfit four korakoras, which required at most a total crew of about three hundred. To avoid the humiliation of undertaking a journey without adequate numbers of kora-koras befitting his status, he was forced to bring rowers from the Sula Islands, a practice which he continued throughout his reign.

The limited human resources available to the center were a matter of concern to all Malukan rulers because wars and natural disasters took a heavy toll in Maluku. In 1664, for example, an estimated three-fourths of Maluku's inhabitants had died from various wars.[47] The decline in population was also due to the practice of each village outfitting its own kora-koras. In one case the settlement of Tahane on Makian lost just one kora-kora in battle against the Spaniards, but because it had a crew of seventy young men this had serious demographic consequences for the community. To increase the numbers of his subjects, which was a measure of a ruler's power and prestige, Sultan Mandar pursued a policy instituted by his father Hamzah of moving communities from the periphery to the center. The dislocation caused by the succession troubles and the wars had made such movements of population possible. The people of Mayu and Tifore were brought to Malayu in 1653, while those of Moti living under their three sangajis in Makian (where they had fled a few years before) arrived between 1656 and 1662. Trouble from the Ternaten settlements of Takome and Sula in 1656 led to the transfer of the people to the royal town of Malayu. The village of Sula itself had been created earlier from rowers brought from the Sula Islands to serve the Sultan Ternate. In 1662 the inhabitants from Siko and the other Goraici islands joined the population in Malayu, and in 1670 the villagers of Kaloncucu in Butung were forcibly transferred to Ternate.[48]

Sultan Mandar's efforts to rebuild his power base were supported by the Dutch East India Company for its own self-interest. It was painfully aware that, despite its attempts to control the spice trade, large quantities of spices from Maluku were reaching the market in Europe and depressing profits. The Company was ready to embark on a new spice policy, and it needed Ternaten cooperation for its implementation. It proposed that all clove trees in the Ternaten kingdom be destroyed so that none of the ruler's subjects in the periphery would be able to exchange cloves to gain wealth and thereby challenge his position. It mattered little whether Sultan Mandar was persuaded by this line of reasoning, for he owed his position on the throne to the Company. Thus on 31 July 1652 he signed a treaty with the Company which inaugurated the spice eradication (extirpatie) policy.

The most important provision of the new policy was the ruler's agreement to fell and destroy all clove trees on Ternate and in the Ambon Quarter. In compensation for the loss of revenue from these trees, the Dutch promised to make an annual "payment for acknowledged service" (recognitie penningen) of 12,000 rijksdaalders to the sultan, 500 rijksdaalders to Kaicili Kalamata (who at the time had not yet rebelled against Mandar), and a total sum of 1,500 rijksdaalders to be divided among the bobatos. Although the treaty had specified a precise allocation of the compensation between the sultan and the bobatos, the Dutch usually delivered the entire amount to the sultan with the understanding that he would then supply the bobatos with their allotted share. In practice, however, the sultans used the compensation as a way of gaining support by withholding payment from recalcitrant bobatos. Even without this discretionary power, the sultan had a far higher proportion of the compensation than the rest of the bobatos.

Before the treaty the bobatos were able to use the proceeds from the sale of cloves from their trees and those of their village for their own needs. The ruler enjoyed income from his own clove trees and differed from other kolanos only in benefiting from customs collected in the royal ports. The effect of the Dutch eradication policy was to eliminate the bobatos' principal source of revenue and make them financially dependent on the sultan, who was given the task of alloting Dutch compensation in the form of Indian cloth, iron implements, weapons, and other goods. Since these were highly desired items in many areas in the eastern islands, the ability of the Sultan Ternate to control their redistribution gave him considerable influence in both the center and the periphery. The wide disparity in the sharing of wealth from the clove trade concentrated power in the hands of the ruler. The bobatos became dependent upon the sultan's largesse in order to maintain influence with their own people. They now either maneuvered to gain the sultan's favor to assure a share of the limited allotment of the compensation or else sought to maintain their own source of revenue by circumventing the spice policy. The treaty thus produced tensions and forced the sultan and the bobatos to a position of confrontation over the reallocation of a fixed income. The established process of governing through consensus and consultation became jeopardized by the new Dutch policy.

By the third quarter of the seventeenth century the various developments in Ternate had brought a significant shift in influence in the court. The office of sultan had become far more powerful than ever before because Islam had provided the rationale for its elevated status, and the clove trade and the Europeans had furnished the means to make it effective. With the introduction of the Dutch eradication policy in the mid-seventeenth century, the sultan had further consolidated his position at the expense of all other officials and bobatos in the land. Although the jogugu remained a prominent official in Ternate, there had been an erosion of his links to the bobatos as lords of the land. The loss of the jogugu's traditional support in Ternate's villages was evident in the frequency with which that position was now being filled by a non-Ternaten, principally from Gamkonora or one of the major settlements in northwest Halmahera. The post of kapita laut, literally "captain of the seas," had emerged in response to the increased foreign involvement in the spice trade and had come to challenge the jogugu's position as second in the land. The two hukums and the Council of State remained important institutions in Ternate from the mid-sixteenth century, but by the mid-seventeenth century the council had been revised to accord with new political realities. Previously, it had consisted of twenty elders, plus royal officials and three or four royal appointees, presumably all from Ternate itself. By the mid-seventeenth century, representatives of Makian, Jailolo, Gamkonora, and Ternate had become permanent members, symbolizing the four cardinal points of the kingdom. They were consulted on every important issue facing the government, and they were the first to cast their votes. The borders of the center had been expanded to include areas in close proximity and with resources equal if not superior to those of Ternate. In response to the changes which had occurred in the area, Ternate had come to acknowledge that its future direction and well-being lay with the maintenance of the four pillars which now formed the new Ternate center.

The Tidore Half of the Malukan Dualism

Unlike Ternate, Tidore was not well known to the Europeans. Only after 1575 was a permanent Portuguese post established on the island. Although the Spaniards occupied the Portuguese fort in Tidore in 1606, built a few others, and remained on the island until 1666, their main headquarters in Maluku was at Gammalamo in southern Ternate. The Dutch had a temporary garrison in Mareku, but it was not until the departure of the Spaniards that they maintained a regular establishment on Tidore. European activity in Tidore was insignificant compared to that in Ternate, and no detailed account about Tidore was ever written by any of the European groups. The VOC sources are the most substantial, but only a partial reconstruction of Tidore's past in the seventeenth and eighteenth centuries is possible because of the intermittent nature of reports which came from the occasional mission to the Tidore court and from the small Dutch garrison in Tidore.

The presence of the Portuguese in Tidore in the last quarter of the sixteenth and early seventeenth centuries served as a deterrent to Ternaten incursions, but it also brought difficulties. Being heirs to European traditions of the East, which included an inherent distrust of Islam, the Portuguese viewed every Malukan act with suspicion. They claimed, for example, that Sultan Gapi Baguna, who was ruling Tidore at the end of the sixteenth century, had asked a Christian tailor to come and measure him for a shirt and then forced him to become a Muslim.[49] Minor conflicts arose from such misunderstandings, but mutual needs forced the two parties to reach a modus vivendi. Even with the assistance of the Portuguese, however, Tidore was unable to prevent Ternate from expanding at its expense. It lost to Ternate its lands at Semola, Tofungo, and Payahe on Halmahera, which were described by the Portuguese as Tidore's three most important suppliers of sago and other food "without which these people [in the royal settlement in Tidore] and all the other places of this island of Tidore, vassals of the king, would suffer such great oppression and lack of food as can be imagined."[50] Only after the Spanish conquest of Ternate in 1606 was Tidore able to regain some of the areas previously lost and be given some of Ternate's territories by the conquering Spaniards.[51]

The new powerful alliance between the Spaniards and Tidore was quickly matched by the even more formidable combination of the Dutch and the Ternatens, placing the former clearly on the defensive. Superior Dutch naval forces enabled Ternate once again to expand at the expense of Tidore. The rich sago lands of Payahe in Halmahera changed hands several times before it and Toseho, with its equally valuable sago forests, were finally taken by Ternate in 1649. With the loss of these and other sago lands in the sixteenth century, Tidore turned to other areas for its supplies. Bacan's large sago swamp and good fishing grounds made it a natural target for Tidore, which was being ousted from its traditional food supplies on Halmahera's west coast. Tidore also turned to new sago supplies in the Gamrange, consisting of Maba, Patani, and Weda in southeast Halmahera, and in the Raja Ampat islands. Distance from the center and a difficult environment due to unpredictable wind patterns and dangerous currents made these two areas inaccessible to strangers, especially to marauding Ternatens and their Dutch allies. As greater restrictions were imposed on the Malukan rulers by the Company, Tidore came to transfer many of its trade activities to these areas. Thus began a new chapter of a close and often troubled relationship between Tidore, on the one hand, and the Gamrange and the Papuans on the other.

On Tidore the Spaniards, like the Portuguese before them on Ternate, sought to force compliance from the people by keeping an important member of the royal family in "protective custody" in the fort. They were convinced that the presence of Islamic teachers in Tidore could only mean that they were planning to overthrow the Christians. Sultan Saifuddin (r. 1657–1689) finally decided to approach the Dutch to seek help in removing the Spaniards from his kingdom. The timing of his appeal was significant, for by 1662 there were rumors of a possible Spanish withdrawal from the islands. More important, the appeal came at a time when Saifuddin needed support against a challenge from two of the most influential officials in his government. Saifuddin allegedly uncovered a Spanish plot involving the jojau who, like his counterpart the jogugu in Ternate, was a well-respected individual with strong links to the bobatos. The jojau was said to have been offered 2,000 reals by the Spaniards in order to overthrow Saifuddin. In the end it was the jojau who was seized, forcing 150 of his followers to seek safety in a

Spanish fort in Mareku. Another "plot" was uncovered involving the kapita laut. He was observed winding hair aound a bamboo lance *(sago-sago)* near Saifuddin's residence and was arrested for practicing witch-craft with the complicity of the jojau. Saifuddin had both of these offi-cials killed, which led to another exodus of followers but this time to the safety of Ternate.[52] In these actions against the jojau and the kapita laut, Saifuddin pursued policies similar to those which had made the Ternaten rulers dominant over the bobatos. Once all challenges to his position were removed early in his reign, he adopted a more concilia-tory policy in subsequent years with far less disruption to traditional institutions than occurred in Ternate.

The course of the dualistic contest between Tidore and Ternate was altered with Saifuddin's decision to reject the Spaniards and turn to the Dutch. Since only one European nation remained on the scene, both Malukan kingdoms had to vie for its favor to gain an advantage over the other. In 1667 Saifuddin reaffirmed the 1657 treaty with the Dutch East India Company, which included the spice eradication policy. Saifuddin was also willing to accept the provision allowing a Dutchman to become a member of Tidore's council, as long as it was made clear to Malukans that Tidore was now the equal of Ternate in the eyes of the Dutch.[53] Having become a "trade-friend" of the Dutch, Saifuddin demanded treatment which was no different from that given to Sultan Mandar. So insistent was he on this point that the Malukans referred to him as "Tossa" and Mandar as "Rossa" to indicate that they were both "from the same ball of wool."[54] Saifuddin understood the workings of the Ternate court and the Dutch since he had spent time in exile in Ter-nate before returning to become ruler. In 1661 he had even been given the title of kapita laut of Ternate. His familiarity with the Dutch and their relationship with Ternate enabled him to recreate a similar situa-tion in Tidore.

Unlike Sultan Mandar in Ternate, Saifuddin proved to be a popu-lar ruler. He prevented his officials and his closest councillors from oppressing the common people, and he was known for his liberality. When he received his annual compensation from the Dutch, he retained only a small sum for his household and dispensed the rest among his subjects. Because of his generosity, greater quantities of tribute flowed to him from the outer areas.[55] Once Saifuddin requested 2,000 rijks-daalders worth of cloth, not for himself but to distribute to the bobatos who then gave it to the people "to encourage them in their labors."[56] In this he was acting as any traditional ruler creating and reaffirming bonds with various bobatos through gift giving. Because the flow was constant and generous and the quality of goods exceptional, he was able to maintain a strong center, not through force as in Ternate but through traditional methods. The Company provided the means by which both

Ternate and Tidore could strenthen the position of the ruler, but the method used by each kingdom differed markedly. In Ternate the ruler relied on the Dutch for guns, ships, and men to assist in the war expeditions to subdue his subjects, while in Tidore the ruler used Dutch compensation in the form of valuable products to redistribute in the traditional manner and thereby strengthen ties between the ruler and his subjects.

The Papuan areas became a special focus of Saifuddin's favors. This process was aided by a provision of the 1667 treaty signed between Tidore and the Dutch granting the former exclusive rights to sail into Papuan waters.[57] Saifuddin and most Tidorese knew very little about the Papuans. When Saifuddin was told that the Raja Misool, one of the four kings of the Raja Ampat islands, went annually to collect tribute from the villages of north Seram, he professed ignorance of this and merely assumed that it was an old established custom.[58] He even admitted not knowing how far his territory in the Papuas extended, though he claimed that Gebe and Misool had been subjects of Tidore "since olden times."[59]

As lord of the Papuas he acted quickly when informed that the Dutch had arrested the kapita laut of Misool. He demanded an immediate release and told the Company to punish its own subjects and let him punish his.[60] As a result of the treaty, Saifuddin was expected by the Company to be responsible for all activities in the Papuas, and he now asserted this right. In the past Tidore's rulers were content to rely on local lords to govern the land. The Dutch with their treaty as a "legitimizing" document demanded greater involvement by Tidore's ruler in eliminating "piracy" in his territories, paying compensation for damage done, and punishing the guilty. The financial burden was considered to be heavy, but it was nowhere as onerous as the requirement to punish "guilty" subjects. So oppressive were these demands that Saifuddin complained that "he was bent from bowing to the Company."[61] Nevertheless, he believed that compliance was necessary to retain the friendship of the Dutch and thus maintain Tidore's position in the dualism with Ternate.

Saifuddin was regarded as an expert on Maluku customs, and some of the Dutch Company officials bemoaned his tendency to sermonize and to employ traditional sayings in order to clarify a point. His reference to customary laws and practice to confirm and even legitimize his actions is well grounded in the Tidore belief that the ancestors, as originators of all that was good and useful in the "ordering" of society, were worthy of emulation. This required "remembering" (sonyinga) the ancestors through ritual activities, including the formal narration of history.[62] His active application of Tidore's lore to daily activities was in essence "remembering" the ancestors and thus transforming the mundane into a more socially and sacrally valued undertaking.

One of the ideas in which he strongly believed was the necessity of having four kingdoms in Maluku: Ternate, Tidore, Jailolo, and Bacan. In letters and conversations with the Dutch Governor Padtbrugge, Saifuddin constantly reminded him that in the past there had always been four states in Maluku. To return to this former situation, he urged the Dutch to restore Kaicili Alam to his rightful position as Sultan Jailolo.[63] The reason for this request may have been partially motivated by the desire to weaken Ternate, but a stronger motivation may have been Saifuddin's genuine belief that the troubled situation in Maluku could be corrected only by a restoration of proprieties. The upheavals which eventually saw the intrusion of the Dutch into this world were regarded as stemming from the destruction of the unity of the four. With the demise of the kingdom of Jailolo, the unity of the "four pillars" had been undermined, and with it the former equilibrium and harmony in Maluku.

Saifuddin's concerns may also have been influenced by his own condition. He was diagnosed a leper, but he continued to conduct the business of the kingdom by communicating through the wall of an incense-filled room. Because the Dutch found it increasingly difficult to discuss serious matters in this fashion, they urged the Tidorese to elect Saifuddin's son, Kaicili Seram, to become ruler. Several leading Tidorese saw this request as serving their own best interests and hence attempted to maneuver Seram to a position of greater authority. Saifuddin, however, continued to make decisions on the most important issues, leaving his son to deal with minor matters.[64] In preparation for his death, Saifuddin thanked all his various nonroyal wives and gave leave to all those who had not borne him children to return to their own families. He sent them home with gifts of cloth and assured their continuing high status. By doing this he was able to prevent the uncertain fate of royal widows with no offspring to protect them under a new king. It was remarked among the people that no previous ruler had shown such kindness toward his wives nor brought such joy to the girls' families. This act was typical of Saifuddin throughout his reign, and in the minds of the Tidorese he came to represent the ideal ruler.

Saifuddin's long reign enabled Tidore to maintain its standing in Maluku despite the loss of its Spanish allies. As a result of the 1667 treaty signed with the Dutch, Saifuddin had been able to extend Tidore's authority into the Gamrange and the Raja Ampat Islands. The treaty had also provided Tidore with the same foundations as Ternate to strengthen the center, but the path that Saifuddin took meant that there was less upheaval in Tidore than was the case in Ternate. Sultans Hamzah and Mandar of Ternate had relied principally on the Dutch with their superior firepower and their treaties to strengthen the center and the authority of the ruler. Mandar survived a major rebellion because of the Dutch Company's intervention, and throughout his reign the specter of further interference was ever present. In Tidore, on the other hand, the strengthening of the ruler was achieved in the traditional fashion by an equitable redistribution of wealth. Though it was Dutch compensation which had made possible the Tidore ruler's acquisition of cloth, iron, and other rare products greatly desired by the Maluku inhabitants, it was he who decided to use these desired goods to gain and retain the loyalty of his subjects. Thus at his death Saifuddin had strengthened the position of kingship but had managed to establish a strong bond between the center and the periphery through time-honored methods.

On Balance

The rivalry of the Spaniards and the Portuguese in the sixteenth century, and the Spaniards and the Dutch in the seventeenth, created new ways in which the dualism between Ternate and Tidore could be manifested. Their alliances with the Europeans were calculated in terms of a necessary balance in the dualism, and there was little hesitancy in asking European assistance in the contest to wrest away the other's lands and people. The Europeans were unable to recognize the various manifestations of the dualism and were constantly burdened by the fear of a unified Malukan or Islamic force which would overwhelm their tiny outpost of European civilization. Oblivious to the significance of intermarriages between the royal families of Ternate and Tidore as a way of maintaining the dualism, the Dutch urged that Sultan Mandar not marry the daughter of the Sultan Tidore for fear of the combined strength of the two kingdoms.[65]

European perceptions of the authority which rulers should properly exercise encouraged the strengthening of the Malukan ruler and the center but inadvertently subverted another Malukan dualism between the "stranger-king" and the "lords of the land." This dualism was emphasized in myths and associated with the beginnings of society. While the stranger-king was depicted as possessing some special quality which enabled him to achieve his position of power, it was the lords of the land who were seen as the original landowners who through their women provided the stranger-king access to it. Until the late sixteenth century the importance of the lords of the land was apparent in the maintenance of the Council of State representing the various bobatos in the community. The chief of these was the jogugu whose actual title was literally "Lord of the Land." Sultan Babullah (r. 1570–1583) was the first Ternaten ruler to threaten the balanced relationship because of the greatly strengthened position of the king due to increased trade and the support of Islam. The change was noted in the prominence of two new officials: the syahbandar and the hukum. Nevertheless, the importance of retaining the lords of the land, or bobatos, and the jogugu was still recognized by both Babullah and Said (r. 1583–1606).

The beginning of change seems to have come with Sultan Hamzah (r. 1627–1648), whose long exile in Manila provided him with a Spanish model of kingship and authority. With the help of the Spaniards, he began the process of removing powerful lords in the periphery, the most prominent of whom were drawn from the Fala Raha. His success in tying the periphery closer to the center was matched by his growing dominance over Ternate's bobatos, the principal props of the jogugu. He defied the lords of the land by appointing the jogugu from one of the powerful leaders of northwest Halmahera (from Jailolo, Sahu, or Gamkonora). Under his successor Sultan Mandar (r. 1648–1675), the strengthening of the center was accelerated with the help and encouragement of the Dutch. "Rebellions" in the periphery were suppressed with the help of VOC arms and the Dutch were even asked to serve as governors on the sultan's behalf in Hoamoal and Hitu.

At the time when Ternate was strengthening the center at the expense of the periphery, Tidore underwent a similar change in order to maintain its balance and dualism with Ternate. If the Sultan Ternate received aid from the Dutch, the Sultan Tidore requested the same for his kingdom. The proximity of these kingdoms, and the ease with which the people moved between the two, meant that any new developments in one were quickly copied in the other. There was, however, a difference in Tidore's style and method which was due to the character of Sultan Saifuddin. His knowledge of and respect for Malukan customs were well-known, and he pursued the strengthening of the center with these traditions firmly in mind. While it was necessary to introduce measures to maintain the balance with Ternate, they were always within a framework which was acceptable to the community. Saifuddin was therefore able to achieve the same ends as his Ternaten counterparts but with far less disruption. The preservation of the status of the jojau and the bobatos, representing the powers of the land, during his reign and in subsequent ones may account for the survival of the sowohi kië in Tidore, but not in Ternate. Saifuddin's accomplishments made him a greatly revered ruler in his lifetime and long after his death. Today in a glass picture frame hanging on the wall in the sadly dilapidated former royal residence in Soa Sio in Tidore is the royal genealogical tree. It begins with Sultan Saifuddin depicted as the foundation of all later rulers of Tidore, a portrayal which symbolically captures his crucial role in strengthening kingship with the approval and support of the entire community.

CHAPTER SIX

Father Company and the Malukan Children

ALTHOUGH DUTCH TREATIES and actions assumed the superiority of the Dutch East India Company to Ternate and Tidore, this attitude was not initially shared by the latter. The relationship was regarded as one between brothers, even though it was one of deference of the younger brothers (Ternate and Tidore) to the older brother (the Company). These local kingdoms conducted their affairs as independent entities, and when complying with Company demands they did so on the basis of an equal partnership. This situation, however, was undergoing change as Company activities, especially the introduction of the spice eradication policy in the mid-seventeenth century, required greater commitment from local rulers.

Sultan Mandar Syah of Ternate was the first Malukan ruler to experience the strong intervening hand of the Dutch in Malukan affairs. He owed his throne to the Company and was willing to do what was necessary to retain its support, even if it meant antagonizing powerful members of his own government. His successor took a much more independent stance toward the Company, which was the norm among Ternaten rulers prior to Mandar. But this time the Company was less ready to tolerate opposition because it had become accustomed to a much more pliable Ternaten government under Mandar, and VOC leaders in Amsterdam and Batavia demanded better results from the eradication policy. As the Company came to assert its dominance in local affairs, the Malukan view of an equal relationship as brothers was soon transformed into one of subordination, with the Company as father and Ternate and Tidore as its dependent children. The Dutch were aware of the Malukan perception of the father/child relationship, but they did not fully appreciate that the superior status of a father brought with it paternal obligations. From 1683 until the end of the eighteenth century, a large part of the Company's involvement in Maluku affairs was a consequence of the demands made by its various "children" for assistance, mediation, protection, and solace from their "father." As with all siblings, there was a constant attempt to outdo the other in winning the father's affection, and in this contest for the Company's favor the requirements of the dualistic struggle between Ternate and Tidore were met.

In the decision to conduct the dualism in this fashion, Ternate and Tidore were compelled to enforce the unpopular VOC extirpatie or spice eradication policy in the center and to extend it to the periphery. The hardships imposed on the people by the eradication campaigns, and the inequitable distribution of Company compensation in favor of the ruler, weakened established relationships between the ruler and his bobatos, and between the center and periphery. The older relationships were beginning to be superseded by the new one involving the Father Company and the two children, Ternate and Tidore, represented by their respective rulers.

The Ternate Child

The different paths followed by Ternate and Tidore in strengthening the center in the seventeenth century made the former much more susceptible to Dutch pressure. Sultan Mandar was able to come to the throne and remain in power only because of Dutch intervention. When he died in 1675 he bequeathed to his successor, Kaicili Sibori Sultan Amsterdam (r. 1675–1690), an extensive but politically fragile kingdom. Mandar's decision to give his sons the Dutch names of "Amsterdam" and "Rotterdam" was an acknowledgment of the Company's superiority. Sultan Amsterdam reaffirmed this attitude by openly declaring that "If my father was half a Dutchman, I shall certainly be a whole one."[1] Nevertheless, like his name, Sultan Amsterdam was heir to two different traditions. While assuring the Company of his desire to uphold the treaty, he also fulfilled the ruler's customary role of reestablishing links with the communities in the kingdom. He undertook a royal peregrination to north Sulawesi and the islands to the north, where Ternate's authority was most problematic. His arrival in these lands was marked by ceremonies formalizing their relationship. At Tahulandang the people went head-hunting for the funeral of the late Sultan Mandar, since the taking of heads was a way of transferring the life spirits to the deceased. They also presented him with the traditional tribute of thirteen porcelain plates, two combs, a musket, and a slave.[2] On Sangihe Island the people of the Limau district offered Sultan Amsterdam a belt, a bundle of tobacco, twenty-four large porcelain plates, a small metal cannon, a female slave, and a handkerchief in which was wrapped the ingredients for betel chewing (sirih pinang).

Tabukan, on the same island, gave him another twenty-four large por-celain plates and two gold krisses. In return he distributed Indian cloth and titles of raja ("lord" or "king") to the various local chiefs.[3]

In these peripheral areas the formal exchange of goods was essen-tial for the establishment of a father/child relationship. Though the Company had "presented" these settlements in north Sulawesi and the northern islands to Ternate by means of a European treaty,[4] the links had to be reaffirmed by Sultan Amsterdam in the traditional fashion. The gifts offered in tribute were specifically selected for their symbolic meaning. They signified the submission of all the "child's" possessions to the central lord and "father," Sultan Amsterdam. He in turn con-ferred his royal blessings and spiritual power on the recipients through the distribution of titles and the much-coveted Indian cloth. He realized very quickly that, although some of these areas were at present content with the arrangement, it would be difficult to maintain control over any group which wished to ignore its obligations. He had therefore already decided that he would rely on his special relationship with the Dutch to raise his prestige and, as a last resort, to enforce his will on recalcitrant subjects.[5] To demonstrate his new standing with the Company, Sultan Amsterdam requested a Dutch bodyguard and was given a sergeant, a corporal, and ten soldiers. The Company's reputation had soared since its victory over the kingdom of Goa, once regarded as so invincible that it had earned the nickname "The Cock of the East." Having a personal bodyguard of Dutchmen was a unique honor which considerably enhanced Sultan Amsterdam's reputation among the Malukans. Nev-ertheless, his gratitude toward the Company was mixed with resent-ment at the restrictions imposed on his independence. He expressed considerable regret that his predecessor had agreed to the eradication policy. If the clove trees were still standing, he explained, he would not be in such dire need of money.[6]

Although most of the north Sulawesi settlements reluctantly ac-knowledged Ternate as the center and the sultan as their lord and father, the people of Siau rejected their inclusion in the Maluku family. They had previously been under Spanish control, but in the Bungaya treaty of 1667 the Dutch had made them subjects of Ternate. The islanders resented this decision, and from the outset they were a con-stant source of difficulties for Ternate. In 1677 a combined Ternate-Dutch expedition was sent to force the people to obedience. Sultan Amsterdam himself participated in the fighting and demonstrated his prowess on the battlefield. When he returned to Ternate, he was hon-ored by his people in a celebration feast. The princes and bobatos all came offering Sultan Amsterdam suits of clothes, which he donned two or three per hour and then returned to their owners. By transforming the ordinary clothes into special objects imbued with the sultan's special powers, Amsterdam was reciprocating his subjects' offer of allegiance and tribute. The bobatos also honored him with 1,000 rijksdaalders, which was a major part of their annual share of the Company's compensation for the eradication of spice trees. The presentation, which lasted from midday to late in the evening, was an impressive spectacle of support and honor for Amsterdam.[7] By showing valor in battle, he had demonstrated his right to rule.

Sultan Amsterdam's victory in Siau and the homage paid to him by his bobatos on his triumphal return highlighted the growing strength of the ruler at the center. The Dutch in the seventeenth century had contributed to this development by their readiness to lend their resources and arms to a friendly lord and to safeguard their investment. They understood a powerful ruler and found it more convenient to deal with a single individual instead of an entire council. A king with power could sign treaties, make quick decisions, and be manipulated much more easily than a government operating on the basis of consensus. The Dutch were therefore more than happy to support a strong kingship. With their help both Sultan Hamzah and his successor Sultan Mandar were able to challenge the powerful Fala Raha, which had their own access to substantial resources in the past and had thus served to prevent arbitrary exercise of authority by the ruler. Sultan Amsterdam appreciated the favored position he had inherited from his predecessors, and he used his Dutch compensation to create through gift giving a monopoly of social relationships which could not be matched in the kingdom. He thus contributed to the increasing authority of the ruler and the estrangement from an earlier form of government which emphasized consultation and consensus between the ruler, the council, and the bobatos.

Amsterdam's first major confrontation within his government was with Kaicili Alam, the heir to the defunct kingdom of Jailolo. His presence assured the preservation of the memory of Jailolo's glorious past as part of the four Maluku kingdoms. After the destruction of the kingdom in 1551, the Jailolo royal family was brought to Ternate and continued to represent Jailolo in ceremonies where it was necessary to have the presence of the four pillars. In numerous letters and conversations with the Dutch governors, Sultan Saifuddin of Tidore, an acknowledged expert on the customs and traditions of Maluku, stressed the importance of reestablishing Jailolo and thus restoring the four kingdoms of Maluku.[8] Kaicili Jena, brother of Amsterdam, attributed the flight of people from the royal settlement of Malayu to the effects of the demise of Jailolo which had undermined the unity of Maluku. He argued that in the past the four kings treated one another with respect. Then Ternate, with the help of the Company, had denied Kaicili Alam his right to the Jailolo throne, deprived him of subjects, and forced him to pay allegiance to Ternate. The troubles besetting Ternate, he explained, were the result of this abuse of a traditional arrangement.[9] Even though the conquest of Jailolo had occurred more than a century before, and it had involved the Portuguese and not the Dutch, these details were irrelevant. What was relevant, especially in troubled times, was the belief that there had to be four kingdoms. In Kaicili Jena's explanation to the Dutch, the past and the present were fused. The actors and the times may have changed, but the "truth" remained: Maluku *was* the four kingdoms, and its welfare depended upon their continued existence.

Fearing for his safety the Jailolo prince Kaicili Alam had fled to the Dutch who gave him sanctuary in Fort Orange. The favor shown to an enemy angered Sultan Amsterdam, and to express his displeasure he sent back the rattan baton of authority and royal umbrella which had been presented to him by the Company at his installation.[10] He was later pacified by the Dutch decision to send Alam abroad to prove his loyalty to Ternate by subduing rebels on the islands of Sula, Banggai, and Gapi. To prevent Alam from using the expedition to organize opposition, Amsterdam appointed a second jogugu and a second kapita laut to accompany him.[11] The ease with which Amsterdam could create duplicate positions for Ternate's two most influential offices was clear evidence of his unfettered authority in the kingdom. The Alam problem was scarcely settled when the three most important officials in the land, the Jogugu Baressi, the Kapita Laut Pancola, and the Hukum Marsaoli, fled to Tidore in 1676 to escape from Amsterdam's wrath. Amsterdam responded by abolishing the post of jogugu altogether, justifying this decision by saying that the government would function best with only a sultan and a council composed of sangajis with the eldest serving as leader.[12] In other words, he was proposing a rejection of the jogugu and the bobatos, the lords of the land, in favor of a government ruled totally by the sultan and the sangajis associated with the ruler.

To further strengthen his position at the center, Amsterdam continued a policy begun by his predecessors of resettling whole villages in Ternate to create a greater pool of kolano ngofangare, the "king's people." He planned to transfer the Muslim inhabitants from the north Sulawesi islands of Siau and Sangihe to Malayu because the latter had suffered a steady loss of population.[13] The flight from the royal town had been earlier encouraged by Kapita Laut Reti of Makian and Jogugu Alam of Jailolo. Both these high officials had prudently distributed their followers on Makian and Jailolo under other bobatos so that they would not be summoned to serve Amsterdam directly, a common practice among rulers who wished to maintain control over discontented chiefs. Because of north Halmahera's and Makian's large population and rich resources, Reti and Alam were the greatest threat to

Amsterdam's position. Both entertained the hope of restoring their areas to their former glory free from Ternaten control.[14]

The strains created by the demands of the father/child relationship merely exacerbated Ternate's internal problems. Governor Robertus Padtbrugge regarded it his duty not only to advance the Company's interests but also to promote Christianity among the local inhabitants. So assiduous was he in his pursuit of the latter goal that he quickly antagonized the Malukans, who by the late seventeenth century were becoming increasingly aware of their Muslim identity and links to the wider Islamic world. The Ternaten court sought his removal by sending a list of complaints to Batavia which could be reduced to three principal grievances: he sought to convert the Muslim inhabitants to Christianity; he tried to seize Ternate's lands; and he treated the sultan and his subjects with little respect. The Ternatens also expressed discontent with their general relationship. They accused the Dutch of being too unrealistic in their efforts to destroy the clove trees and too harsh in their confiscation of Ternate's larger boats to prevent external trade. The Dutch were further criticized for being too ready to discourage Muslim teachers from coming to Maluku, while actively pursuing the Christian conversion of the local population.[15]

These complaints reveal the areas where Dutch measures were finally beginning to be felt in Ternate. The Dutch annual payment to the ruler and the bobatos for implementing the eradication policy was never adequate compensation for the loss of revenue from the clove trade. When the Ternatens attempted to supplement their income through trade in other items, they were hampered by another Dutch restriction on the size of vessels allowed to sail westward. As Ternate was forced to extend its spice eradication activities into the periphery, it earned the antagonism of the local inhabitants who viewed these measures as being contrary to the proper functioning of their traditional relationships. Moreover, the Ternaten subjects in the periphery began to suspect that Ternate was relinquishing its overlord position to the VOC because it did not prevent the latter from enforcing a measure to restrict the movement of Muslim teachers in the area. In seeking to please the Company by implementing treaty provisions, the Ternaten leaders were forced to take steps which alienated their own subjects.

It was a situation which could not be sustained, and it led to tensions between the center and the periphery as well as between Ternate and the Company. During a royal visit to Ternate's territories in Banggai and Sula, Sultan Amsterdam's Dutch escort reported to Padtbrugge that they had been abused and insulted throughout the journey. In the trip from Banggai to Sula, Amsterdam had taken off his Dutch clothes and flung them into the sea amidst great cheering and hilarity among his followers. He had then donned Spanish clothes in obvious defiance of the Dutch. When told of this incident, Padtbrugge cited another case at Siau in 1675 where Amsterdam was reported to have given his silver kris secretly to the Spanish captain there and told him: "Captain, this dagger I present as a gift to the king of Spain, and I will keep the sheath for him." The implication of such reports was that Amsterdam would welcome the return of the Spaniards to Maluku, and although the latter incident was suspect because it was related by a Tidorese, Padtbrugge nevertheless conveyed it to Batavia. Padtbrugge also recalled a time when the Dutch refused to advance the compensation payment to Amsterdam, a refusal which had provoked the angry remark: "Then from whom shall I get it? From the Spaniards?"[16]

As both Sultan Amsterdam and Governor Padtbrugge began building their case against the other with Batavia, their relations steadily deteriorated. Amsterdam left letters from Padtbrugge unopened, and rumors were rife that Padtbrugge would order the confiscation of Ternate's cannon. One night Amsterdam returned to Ternate and brought all his bobatos, his women, and his cannon to Jailolo, where he proposed to make his new royal settlement. Padtbrugge suspected Amsterdam's intentions and demanded that he present himself at the Dutch fort. When Amsterdam failed to appear, Padtbrugge summoned Ternate's jogugu, kapita laut, and the Kimalaha Marsaoli to the fort. On their arrival they were arrested and held as hostages by Padtbrugge, who boasted that he had thus seized "the two most important heads and the spokesman of the group." In August 1679 fighting began when the Dutch attempted to enter the royal settlement, and in the ensuing skirmish Amsterdam fled to Toloko and then eventually back to Jailolo.[17]

Because of Padtbrugge's own inclinations, he was quick to focus on the religious factor in the hostilities. Some of the Mindanao boats coming to Ternate reported how a number of Islamic teachers from Banten had been secretly smuggled into the islands to foment revolt against the Dutch. Padtbrugge found it understandable that the Malukans were now talking of a *jihad,* a Muslim holy war, "seeing that from all sides come such a large flood to God's churches, causing the Muslim priests to lose their lucrative source of support and come into disrepute."[18] Like his Iberian predecessors, Padtbrugge viewed Islam as a natural enemy of the Christians and expressed a distrust bred of centuries of anti-Islamic European literature and propaganda.[19] Religion as a principal reason for hostilities was a European perception; for Malukans it was a struggle between two different ways of life—that of the Dutch and that of the Ternatens—for supremacy in Maluku.

Sultan Amsterdam's position as leader of a united Malukan resistance was weakened by the growing momentum for the restoration of

Jailolo as the fourth pillar. Support for this movement reflected an unease and even fear among many Malukans that all was not well with their world. The Portuguese, the Spaniards, and now the Dutch were all symptoms of a general decline caused by the destruction of Jailolo which undermined the unity and wholeness of Maluku. There was a belief that if the four kingdoms could be restored, the situation would improve. Leading the call for the reestablishment of Jailolo was Kaicili Alam, that energetic and able prince of the Jailolo royal family who had been rewarded by Sultan Amsterdam with the post of jogugu of Ternate after his successful expedition to the western lands of Ternate's periphery. His appointment followed a pattern begun earlier in the century when this post was given to powerful sangajis from Halmahera. Areas such as Sahu, Gamkonora, and of course Jailolo itself were fiercely loyal to Alam because of his descent, and he used his position to place many of his followers in positions of influence.

Another thread in the complex web which led to hostilities was Kapita Laut Reti's desire to see an independent Makian. Because of its extensive clove forests, the Dutch had made special provision in the eradication policy for the direct payment of compensation to the various Makian lords. Under Sultan Amsterdam the compensation intended for Makian was kept in Ternate and then redistributed according to his wishes. He was well aware of Reti's ambition to rule over an independent Makian, and so he retained the compensation in order to deprive Reti and the Makian bobatos of the ability to dispense economic favors. Amsterdam's move aroused resentment and inadvertently aided Reti's cause. Many were finally convinced that Sultan Amsterdam had little sympathy for Makian and that an independent kingdom was the only sensible course available.

Padtbrugge sought an assurance from Sultan Saifuddin that Tidore would not support nor give refuge to the Ternatens. Saifuddin was favorably inclined toward the Dutch and persuaded his son Kaicili Seram to withdraw from his earlier determination to ally with Ternate. Tidore acted in character by taking advantage of Ternate's misfortunes to seize its territories. Saifuddin renewed his claims to Gammalamo in Ternate and the half of Makian which had at one time acknowledged Tidore's leadership.[20] When hostilities broke out between Ternate and the Dutch, many Makian inhabitants fled either to Halmahera and settled south of Toseho under the leadership of Reti or else sought protection in Tidore under Saifuddin. The principal reason given for their flight was to escape the perceived exactions and tyrannies of Sultan Amsterdam.

But Ternate did not have to face the Dutch alone. The Jogugu Bacan went to join the Ternatens, while the settlements in north

Halmahera provided the major part of Ternate's fighting force. The greatly feared Tobarus of Halmahera were sent by boatloads to Ternate to roam the forests and prey on Dutch subjects. They were effective because they were so cruel and elusive that their enemies often became demoralized within their own territories. As the Tobarus were replaced from time to time, they were able to maintain constant pressure on the enemy. The Dutch were forced to forbid their subjects from entering the forests, and at nights everyone was moved into fortifications for safety. Through these measures they successfully limited the loss of life, although there were still a few who were ambushed and killed. The Dutch then launched a counteroffensive against the Ternatens in Halmahera and achieved their objective of forcing the recall of the Tobarus to defend their own homes.

The Dutch employed the well-perfected art of using other native kingdoms to do the fighting. Sultan Saifuddin offered his kora-koras, which were then provided with orange flags of the Dutch House of Orange, to proclaim to the Ternatens that the Tidorese had now become Dutch allies.[21] The bulk of the fighting was shared by the Tidorese and the people from the islands north of Sulawesi. When they seized the fortification in Jailolo, both sides fiercely competed with the other for the spoils. The Dutch had earlier prohibited their native allies from keeping captured guns for fear that these weapons would be used against them in the future. But the Tidorese were quick to throw their shields over the cannon to claim them and had to be persuaded to relinquish them to the Dutch. There was always a suspicion that Tidore's part in the war was merely feigned, and the Dutch commented on the greater avidity evinced in the taking of booty than in the actual fighting itself. Nevertheless, it was the participation of the Tidorese and those from the north Sulawesi islands which enabled the Dutch to eliminate all resistance from Halmahera, the center of Ternate's war effort. Sahu, "the strongest post in Maluku," fell to Dutch forces on 8 July 1680 and Gamkonora on 17 July. Weather prevented the Dutch and their allies from going further northward, and so after occupying Sahu's fortress they returned to Ternate.[22]

One of the reasons for the return of the expedition was the difficulties the Dutch faced with Saifuddin. Although he had promised to encourage the people of Makian to return home from their new settlement south of Toseho, he had instead urged them to move to Saketa on the same coast belonging to Tidore.[23] He took advantage of Ternate's troubles to reclaim or seize lands from Ternate, but never urged the destruction of that kingdom. He told the Dutch, "I have commiserated with my son Sultan Amsterdam and father of Maluku that there are only two pillars remaining, since Bacan is now merely a name and Jailolo is no more. This is the reason that I would not gladly see the land of Ternate destroyed." The destruction of either of the remaining two, he warned, would signal the end of Maluku.[24] Padtbrugge's comments regarding the "feigned" battle between the Ternatens and the Tidore were not totally misplaced. Dualism was at the heart of the contest between Ternate and Tidore, and it remained a powerful motivating factor in the relationship. Despite the victory of one over the other, there was never any talk of absorption; and despite European comments on the "hatred" between the two, the frequency of marriage between their peoples and royal families appears to support the belief that sometime in the distant past there may have been an earlier moiety arrangement of a single tribe which later became two separate kingdoms.

In the end the Dutch did not have to rely much on Tidore since internal divisions within Ternate had seriously weakened that kingdom's war effort. Some of the most influential men in the land, including the jogugu, the kapita laut, and the hukum, asked the bobatos who had allied with the Dutch to intervene on their behalf to seek pardon so that the VOC would not destroy their lands. They reported that they were no longer able to rely on the Tobarus, most of whom had returned to the interior of Halmahera to tend their gardens. Sultan Amsterdam, abandoned by most of his own people and accompanied by only a few Tobaru warriors, surrendered to the Dutch on 30 August 1681.[25]

Sultan Amsterdam's reign saw the culmination of the centralizing tendencies promoted by previous Ternaten rulers. As a result of earlier measures, Amsterdam came to believe that the position of kingship was stronger than it really was. He defied his principal officials and the Dutch, thereby alienating two major props to his rule. Moreover, the bobatos resented the untrammeled authority being exercised by Ternaten rulers. In the subsequent war with the Dutch, Sultan Amsterdam was abandoned by many of his people except for the Tobarus. After his defeat the bobatos resumed their positions of prominence in the land with the assistance of the Dutch. Three representatives from the Marsaoli, Tomagola, and the Tomaitu houses of the Fala Raha were made temporary joint leaders of Ternate, and they were assisted by a temporary Council composed of an equal number of Dutchmen and Ternatens.[26]

On 2 July 1682 the Ternatens were informed that Sultan Amsterdam had been pardoned and would be sent back to resume his rule, while his principal supporters would be put to death. This announcement was greeted with disbelief since earlier Dutch justice had been harsh, and the Ternatens had expected Amsterdam to be exiled or even executed. The Fala Raha—particularly the Marsaolis, whose head, the Hukum Marsaoli, had already become accustomed to conducting himself as the new ruler of Ternate—were distressed by the news. When the

Hukum Marsaoli was summoned to Batavia, he was accompanied by a retinue befitting a king. But any hopes which he may have had of being asked to rule Ternate were quickly dashed. The Dutch restored Sultan Amsterdam to the throne after he agreed to a new treaty with the Company. The 1667 Bungaya treaty had acknowledged the Company's special status in Ternate's affairs, and it had respected Ternate's rights as a sovereign state free to negotiate treaty relations with the Company or with any other power. Ternate's rebellion and defeat resulted in a readjustment of the relationship and the signing of a new treaty on 17 July 1683. Ternate became in the eyes of European international law a "vassal" *(leen)* of the VOC based on rights of conquest. Though the terms and the vehicle for this new relationship were couched in a Western European legal framework, the Ternatens acknowledged their new status by now employing the equally solemn and meaningful kinship distinctions of "father" for the Dutch East India Company and "child" for Ternate.[27]

The Ternate government was allowed to rule on behalf of the Company, but the latter removed an earlier guarantee to retain the crown in Sultan Mandar's family. Any royal person was to have equal right to become the Sultan Ternate as long as he met Dutch approval. With Ternate as a vassal kingdom, the Company listed the territories over which Ternate was said to have jurisdiction and hence responsibility for maintaining order. In addition to the areas on Halmahera, which were not subject to dispute, the Company included places whose relations with Ternate had never been secure. The islands of Kayoa, Moti, and Maitara were named, mainly because they had been overlooked when Governor Simon de Cos delineated the boundaries of the Malukan kingdoms which had then been formalized in a treaty between the Malukans and the VOC in 1660. Other areas included by treaty in Ternate's territories in 1683 were the Sula Islands; Gapi (Peling); Tobunku; Tometana (settlements around Lake Matano in southeast Sulawesi), plus a number of other communities in the vicinity; Tibore and Lokea, with Wuna remaining under Butung as agreed upon in a 1677 treaty; Salayar, though it was now governed on behalf of Ternate by the Dutch government based in Makassar; and the entire north Sulawesi as listed in the Bungaya treaty of 1667, with the following exceptions: Gorontalo and Limbotto, which had always chafed under Ternate's overlordship, the Christian settlements on the shores of Tomini Bay, Menado, and the north Sulawesi islands of Tahulandang, Siau, and Sangihe. Other areas formerly listed as Ternate's lands were placed directly under the jurisdiction of the Company. The island of Solor just east of Flores was formally acknowledged as a Company vassal, thereby formalizing a de facto relationship of more than sixty years. Ternate also agreed to give the Company the right to approve the appointments of the sangajis and village heads in Makian and Jailolo, two areas which had been the main source of opposition to Sultan Amsterdam in the recent rebellion.[28]

Since Ternate was now a vassal, the Company no longer felt it necessary to offer any compensation for the implementation of the spice eradication policy. "Through its goodness," however, it agreed to replace the compensation with a smaller annual "subsidy and maintenance" with the understanding that it could be removed at any time. In the new arrangement the sultan was to receive 6,400 rijksdaalders for the maintenance of his court, the council 600, Makian 2,000, and Moti 150.[29] In Ternate's periphery the sultan's representatives were required to consult first with the Dutch Resident before acting on any important matters. Conversely, the sultan's approval had to be sought for any capital punishment in the land and for any Dutch request for kora-koras. The Company even promised to pay for the services of the rowers whenever they were required.[30] The provisions of the treaty were made public on the return of Sultan Amsterdam from Batavia. He was so grateful to the Dutch for restoring him to power that he remained a model vassal until his death in 1690.

The demographic consequences of Ternate's armed opposition to the Dutch were visible throughout the area. Ternate's population was seriously depleted as many fled to safety to Makian, Halmahera, Tidore, and other places away from the fighting. Sultan Saifuddin was the direct beneficiary of this flight, as Dutch accounts speak of "whole villages" moving to Tidore. When Sultan Amsterdam complained to the Dutch, Saifuddin explained that since the people had come without their village heads it was not in contravention of Dutch policy forbidding any principal leader from moving to another area with more than one or two people. Saifuddin argued that since they were simply individuals they had the right to remain in Tidore. It was a long-established practice in Maluku to allow people to come and settle where they wished, and since it did not contravene any article of the treaty signed with the Dutch, he felt no obligation to send the Ternatens back.[31] Makian, too, was heavily depopulated from the war. Before the beginning of hostilities there were an estimated 5,197 inhabitants on the island. Of these some 2,919 had died, and many of the survivors had fled to Tidore.[32] Sultan Amsterdam thus requested and received permission from Batavia to reassemble the remaining population on Makian into the four settlements of Ngofakiaha, Ngofagita, Talapao, and Tabalola so that they would be better able to defend themselves.[33] This move countered an earlier Dutch policy which had forcibly relocated the inhabitants to certain infertile lands under the watchful eye of a Dutch fort.[34]

In the reestablishment of a semblance of order in Maluku,

Padtbrugge introduced measures which he believed would facilitate the Company's control in the area. He encouraged all those living in mountainous areas and on far-off islands to resettle in more accessible locations, and he recommended that the kings go to church and the young be encouraged to attend schools. Among the established local customs which he opposed was the practice of the man following the wife after marriage. To eliminate this "unnatural" tendency, he encouraged the wife to establish the family household in the man's community and even sought, unsuccessfully, to restrict marriage partners to those within one community. Above all he attempted to eliminate blood revenge by enforcing a strict adherence to Dutch laws.[35] These plans encapsulated Padtbrugge's vision of a Dutch-dominated Maluku in which a population properly regulated would be easily brought to Christianity. His hope that kings would go to church was based on the belief generally held by both Muslim teachers and Christian missionaries that, if the ruler embraced a particular religion, the people would quickly follow.

Padtbrugge's attempts to alter native custom were not only intended to undermine "un-Christian" practices, but also had a practical economic basis. In Maluku it was commonplace for men to have wives and blood relationships in many communities. In a region such as Maluku where men spent long periods away from home to raid, to trade, and to collect sago, safe bases among family members were essential. Dangers lurked not only in the dangerous currents, winds, and hidden shoals, but also in the numerous unfriendly groups on isolated islands and coasts. Having family members located at strategic spots guaranteed a safe refuge in a foreign place and enabled an outsider to trade safely as "family." Distrust between groups was endemic in the region, and one of the most effective ways of dispelling it was to take a wife from a local settlement. Matrilocal practice allowed men, especially traders, to leave their wives among their people and to make an annual circumambulation along an established trade route, spending time with each of their wives while plying their trade. The extensive and effective trading network of the Malukans impressed both the Portuguese and the Dutch, who found it difficult to control. By insisting that the Malukans abandon matrilocal practices, Padtbrugge hoped to prevent a trade network which enabled Malukans to continue to sell spices outside the official Dutch system.

He also sought to eliminate blood feuds, which were a common cause of conflict in the region. The Malukans believed that the taking of a human life could be compensated only by the life of a member of the guilty party. It was this practice which Saifuddin, though a stout defender of local traditions, called a "cursed and barbaric custom which was so strong that it had led to the downfall not only of villages but of whole kingdoms."[36] Padtbrugge hoped that by placing all Malukans under Dutch law they would be diverted from pursuing blood revenge. While there may have been resentment at these measures, the Malukans would have acknowledged the propriety of an overlord establishing societal guidelines for its subjects. In the past Ternate and Tidore's expansion had also been characterized by the imposition of their values on the societies which formed their periphery.

The transformation of Ternate into a child of the VOC was reflected in the greater frequency in the use of Dutch names for Ternaten royal children. Sultan Amsterdam named one of his sons "Batavia," and in 1691 a son born of a marriage celebrated as "the most royal in living memory," between Sultan Amsterdam's daughter and Sultan Toloko's son, was given the name of "Outhoorn" for the Dutch governor-general in Batavia.[37] The practice of giving important princes names of Dutch cities and Governors-General was regarded as part of the same process as adopting Dutch dress. Both practices were an external manifestation of an interior transformation resulting from total acceptance of a new overlord. The donning of a new dress and a new name mirrored the change in the inner state. This manner of declaring subordination was not peculiar to Ternate but was shared by other groups in Maluku. When Menado rejected Ternate's overlordship, it replaced all the Ternaten titles for its officials (jogugu, sangaji, and kimalaha) with Dutch military ones (major, captain, sergeant and corporal).[38]

The Company's new role as overlord became quickly apparent. When a new Ternaten salahakan was appointed to Sula Besi, a Dutchman introduced him to the people.[39] A Dutchman with letters from the governor-general in Batavia accompanied a Ternaten envoy sent to summon the heads in the western periphery to attend the sultan's installation.[40] Even the Ternaten ruler himself publicly proclaimed that disobedience to him was disobedience to the Company.[41] By 1696 the Ternate court was able to provide yet another impressive proof of its new inspiration. It welcomed the recently appointed Dutch governor and his wife to a royal dinner which was done totally in the Dutch manner.[42] Not to be outdone, Sultan Fahruddin (r. 1689–1704) of Tidore acknowledged the new status of the Company by appearing in Fort Orange wearing Dutch dress for the occasion.[43] He also ordered for his own use a dinner service consisting of some thirty silver dinner plates, including two large serving platters, thirty forks and spoons, two salt vats, and four chandeliers.[44]

The VOC by the end of the seventeenth century had indeed become, in the words of Sultan Bacan, "like a very large tree with thick leaves in the midst of a flat field where people from near and far come to seek shelter and solace from the searing and frightening times."[45] Ternate, once the most powerful kingdom in Maluku, was now sheltering and prospering under the Company's protective branches. The 1683 treaty between Ternate and the Dutch East India Company marked a major divide in their relations. It altered Ternate's status from an ally to a vassal of the Company—or, in Ternate's view, from a relationship of brothers to one between a father (the VOC) and a child (Ternate).

The Tidore Child

Tidore remained relatively free of direct Dutch interference until the last quarter of the eighteenth century. Over the seventeenth and much of the eighteenth centuries, however, it gradually relinquished its sovereign rights to the VOC. Sultan Saifuddin had signed a treaty as early as 1657 agreeing to the spice eradication policy, which had guaranteed him an annual compensation of 3,000 rijksdaalders and protection against his enemies.[46] This document was reaffirmed in another treaty signed on 29 March 1667, adding a few other conditions which Saifuddin accepted on behalf of the kingdom. Tidore agreed not to admit any foreign (that is, non-Dutch) Europeans or Indians into the kingdom; to show the Dutch governor any correspondence between the Tidore ruler and an outside power; to obtain Dutch Company approval for any new ruler; to accept the Company as a member of Tidore's governing council; and to maintain order among its Papuan subjects so that no more "piracies" would occur. Saifuddin saw in the new treaty a way of maintaining good relations with the Dutch to balance Ternate Sultan Mandar's special status with them. It proved useful when he called upon them to assist in quelling a rebellion among his subjects on the northeast coast of Seram and in the Goram Islands. Much to his chagrin, however, the VOC then proceeded to claim that these lands had been won by right of conquest and that Tidore was exercising jurisdiction on its behalf. And so the situation remained until Saifuddin's death on 2 October 1687. The Dutch Company intervened to place Saifuddin's son, Kaicili Seram, on the throne despite the strong claims of his uncle, Kaicili Goram. On the occasion of Seram's installation as Sultan Hamzah Fahruddin on 31 July 1689, the previous treaties between Tidore and the Company were reaffirmed.[47]

The new treaty was signed only six years after Ternate had become officially a vassal state of the VOC. Both Sultan Amsterdam of Ternate and Sultan Hamzah Fahruddin of Tidore were therefore indebted to the Company for their positions. Not surprisingly, Tidore came to view its relationship with the Dutch in the same way as Ternate, though it had not formally become a vassal state. In 1704 the Company was referred to as "a large tree under which the Tidorese have for many years found security."[48] By depicting the Company as the protector and refuge for Tidore, Tidore was already acknowledging its "child" status. With both Ternate and Tidore accepting their position as "children" to the "father" Dutch Company, the dualistic struggle assumed the form of a sibling rivalry. The transition to this new relationship with the Company had been relatively smooth because the crucial dualism, the local barometer of well-being in the community, had been retained.

In the eyes of the Malukans, the Dutch Company's new status as "father" brought with it responsibilities and obligations to the "children." This became clear in a long-standing dispute between Ternate and Tidore over ownership of sago forests in Toseho. In 1700 Sultan Amsterdam's successor, Sultan Said Kaicili Toloko (r. 1692–1714), asked the Dutch to mediate. When a solution was found, he thanked Batavia in words which expressed his perception of their relationship: "One must indeed acknowledge that the Company deserves the name of father and that we Ternatens are his children. If our father resolves our differences, we as children should not complain but thankfully accept it, for if that is the nature and being of fathers, so should that be for children. If a father lacks something, so would his children; on the other hand, the name of father entails a desire and a responsibility to maintain and nurture his children."[49] While the Dutch East India Company had assumed the powers of an overlord, it had at the same time incurred the ultimate responsibility for the actions of its vassals, a not inconsiderable task in the precariously balanced and complex situation in Maluku. The Company had gained great prestige in its new role as father and overlord, but it had also acquired the onerous obligations of keeping order in its "children's" lands. The "father" could delegate responsibility to the "child," but the outcome was always attributed to the wisdom or folly of the former.

For Ternate and Tidore the new relationship redirected their energies toward fulfilling their duties to the VOC, rather than their obligations to their own "children." It was an especially serious problem for Tidore because its lands were so distant from the center, which made it difficult for the Company to be of any real assistance. Ultimately, the child was beholden to carry out the wishes of the father, and it was the performance of this role, especially with respect to the spice eradication policy, which caused considerable hardship in the periphery. Resentment toward the center grew as demands increased, while obligations were left unfulfilled. Symptomatic of the change was an incident in 1704 when, for the first time in the memory of the local inhabitants of Misool, an envoy from the Sultan Tidore arrived on a Company ship accompanied by a Dutch representative.

Cooperation between the Malukan sultans and the Dutch Company had serious implications for center/periphery relations. Ternate's troubles in 1681 were caused fundamentally by the conflicts between the growing power of the center, reinforced by Company policies, and the periphery. It had been resolved in the center's favor with the restoration of Sultan Amsterdam to the throne of Ternate in 1683, albeit this time under the formal vassalage of the Company. Tidore remained relatively free from difficulties with its periphery until its rivalry with Ternate for the favors of the Company forced it to take steps to match Ternate's activities in its territories.

One of the Company's concerns was the Papuan raks or head-hunting and raiding expeditions, whose traditional routes went southward to the Aru-Kei Islands, Tanimbar, the Seram Laut Islands, Seram, Buru, Ambon, and northward to the Sulas, Banggai, and north Sulawesi. As the Company gained ever more vassals in these areas, it came to see the rak as a threat to its subjects and demanded that the Tidore ruler condemn this practice. Eager to demonstrate his gratitude to the Dutch for his position, Sultan Hamzah Fahruddin Kaicili Seram (r. 1689–1707) delivered the leaders of one particular raid to the Company. The seizure of the Papuan leaders, however, was condemned by the Sangaji Patani. As the acknowledged leader of the Papuans, he felt the injustice of their being punished for activities which were formerly praised and encouraged by the Tidore ruler. He also resented the fact that, contrary to a well-established hierarchy of authority, Tidore was now taking direct action. Previously it had been customary for Tidore to send a lieutenant or some other official to these areas to deliver the sultan's orders, which were then carried out by a leading sangaji from the Gamrange. Now, in the Sultan Tidore's eagerness to please the Dutch and gain an advantage over Ternate, he frequently relied upon his trusted court followers to implement orders in far-off territories. However faithful they may have been to their ruler, they often knew little about local customs or of the interpersonal relationships within these territories. Their activities frequently contributed to the alienation of the periphery from the center.

The disaffection remained close to the surface in Tidore's territories. Although there was no serious trouble during Sultan Hamzah Fahruddin's reign, the accumulation of grievances erupted into rebellion in 1716 under his successor, Sultan Hasanuddin Kaicili Gasea (r. 1708–1728). It began with the refusal by the people of Maba, Patani, and Weda to deliver to the Tidore ruler the annual tribute of tortoise-shell, ambergris, birds of paradise, and slaves. They complained that in former years the Sultan Tidore had been satisfied with a tribute of door-mats, knives (kabilang), and carpets woven from coconut leaves.[50] Then Tidore had requested slaves, and they had complied; now it was demanding gold and ambergris. Despite this burdensome tribute, every man, woman, and child sought to meet their obligations to the Sultan

Tidore. Yet their efforts to satisfy the Sultan Tidore with the requested goods had been rewarded with seizure and punishment. The last complaint was directed to the Sultan Tidore who, in complying with VOC orders to halt all piratical activities, had now begun to seize and punish those who participated in the annual slave raids. Feeling betrayed, the Sangaji Patani quoted the words of the ancestors who had advised: "If those of Tidore were to treat you badly, you should return once again to your Lord of Ternate." And so the decision was made "to follow the Ternaten mountain [that is, the Ternate kingdom] and the Company forever."[51] Despite the considerable strain in the relationship between Tidore and its periphery, the Sangaji Patani's statement revealed a basic understanding among Malukans that Ternate and Tidore represented two complementary parts of a symbolic whole.

Only three of Maba's communities, including the main settlement on Maba Island, decided to remain under Tidore. The other five agreed to support the rebellion and accept the leadership of the Sangaji Patani. The Sangaji Patani, Sangaji Bicoli, and various Maba gimalahas went with their followers from Maba to Gamsungi on Ternate, where they waited until they were summoned by the Sultan Saifuddin Kaicili Raja Laut (r. 1714–1751) of Ternate. Each of the communities in revolt presented the sultan with a male slave to indicate its subservience, and each had received in return a spear and sword as a symbol of the ruler's promise of protection. In addition Saifuddin presented them with a diamond ring, rosary beads, and a blank piece of paper and a pen. According to the Tidore ruler, Saifuddin had then told them: "I have heard that the Sangaji Patani is both a sangaji and an Islamic teacher. I would like you to sign your name on this piece of paper so that all subjects of the Sultan Tidore, upon inspecting it with care and consideration, would come to me because I possess it."

In another version the Ternaten ruler was said to have questioned their motives, demanding as a sign of sincerity that they go to the royal cemetery and offer Koranic prayers at the graves of all the former rulers of Ternate. They did what was asked and the sultan accepted them as his subjects. He then gave them leave to return to Gamsungi to await his orders and honored them with gifts of cloth, two boxes of gunpowder, a hundred shots for small guns, and one hundred and sixty bundles of sago. They in turn gave the sultan five slaves, forty birds of paradise, a piece of ambergris, a small metal cannon, a copper gun, a gold chain, and a porcelain pot worth the equivalent of one slave. Shortly thereafter one of the sangajis from Maba left with a group of his people and settled in Galela, one of Ternate's subject territories in northeastern Halmahera. The move appeared to confirm the Tidore ruler's belief that the rebellion was being supported by Ternate, and he accused Saifuddin of encouraging the Sangaji Patani and his people to seize the tribute from the smaller settlements and preventing others from fulfilling their customary obligations to Tidore.[52]

The incident involving Tidore's rebellious subjects and the Sultan Ternate reveals certain interesting features about Malukan society. The first is the effective use of a symbolic exchange of gifts to establish new relationships and reorder the hierarchy between individuals and states. Without any extensive preliminary negotiations, the exchange of culturally determined objects conveyed precise meanings comprehensible to all. No formal document was required, though the threat of supernatural sanction was ever present. Invoking such sanctions highlights another noteworthy element: the merging of old and new sources of spiritual power. To bind those from Maba and Patani closely to their new patron, they were required to say prayers from the Koran at the graves of the ancestors of the Sultan Ternate. The belief in the ability of the spirits of the ancestors to intervene in the activities of the living was an old idea still prevalent in Maluku society. Added to the efficacy of the spirits of the ancestors was that of the recently introduced source of Islamic wisdom and strength, the Koran. The recitation of Koranic verses at the gravesite of the ancestors combined the two powerful spiritual forces at the disposal of the Sultan Ternate to witness and sanction the momentous occasion.

The ruler's demand that the rebels sign their names on a piece of paper underscores the growing significance of the written word in Malukan society. Writing had been introduced into Maluku only with Islam toward the last quarter of the fifteenth century. Although Islam had begun to spread throughout the region, it had been limited principally to coastal settlements, and even here the religion had not led to a radical transformation of people's lives. As was evident in the swearing of oaths, the strength of local beliefs persisted. The repository of spiritual knowledge was the local priest, who had attained his position through the ability to absorb the wisdom of the community which had been passed down by word of mouth. By contrast, in Islam the source of spiritual knowledge was the written word contained in the Koran. Both the local priest and the Koran as vessels of spiritual power inspired fear and respect—the former by chants employing a secret but efficacious language, the latter by the written page with its lines forming incomprehensible but potent images. The strength of the belief in the written word was reinforced by Dutch treaty practice requiring local leaders to swear upon a written document with all the solemnity ordinarily associated with sacred acts. What the Dutch reported as the signing of names was for the Malukans a reaffirmation of the solemn oath made on the Koran and the graves of the ancestor and completed with the marks or "signs" on paper, much in the way that treaties were prepared with the politically successful and therefore spiritually powerful Europeans.

Despite Sultan Hasanuddin of Tidore's appeals, he was unsuccessful in persuading his Maba and Patani subjects to return voluntarily. He therefore sought VOC help to prevent their serving the Ternaten ruler, not simply because people were a measure of power, but also because it was an admission of Ternate's superiority in the dualism.[53] A principal tactic in this contest was to humiliate the other through enticing the other's subjects and providing haven for them. The dualism was also demonstrated in more obvious ways. In May 1720 the Dutch Company gave a feast to which were invited the sultans of Ternate, Tidore, and Bacan. The aim was to effect a reconciliation between Ternate and Tidore over the question of the Maba and Patani people. From the very outset, however, it was apparent that the meeting was premature. Hasanuddin complained that Ternate's ruler Saifuddin was wearing ash-gray cloth, a color called *lokje*, which the Dutch were told meant "a false heart" in the Ternaten language. To counter this insult Hasanuddin went and changed into a gingham shirt and an old headdress with a stalk of grass stuck in it as a reminder that this was precisely the color shirt which Sultan Amsterdam had worn in 1689 when he sought reconciliation with Sultan Hamzah Fahruddin of Tidore in this very same fortress. On that occasion the latter had refused to see Amsterdam until he had changed into a black shirt, a color which signified "sincerity."[54] In making this point Hasanuddin did not forgo the opportunity to depict Amsterdam as a country bumpkin dressed in old and inappropriate clothes. Through such studied insults familiar to all Malukans, Ternate and Tidore came increasingly to conduct their dualism not on the battlefield but in the grounds of the Dutch fortress.

Since the Dutch believed that the feast held principally to reconcile the two sultans had been a fiasco, they arranged another meeting in the presence of the Dutch commissioner from Batavia, Cornelis Hasselaar. Hasanuddin delivered a letter in Malay explaining that the people of Patani, Maba, and Gebe had begun their rebellion against him on 4 April 1718. He then recounted the cost—both material (3,409 rijksdaalders and 26 stuijvers) and human (providing a list of the lives lost in the fighting)—of the ongoing rebellion. Despite his appeals for assistance, the Company had not prevented his subjects from seeking refuge in Ternate. Hasanuddin blamed this lack of commitment on the Dutch governor in Ternate, whom he accused of being bribed by the Ternatens with two gold chains and two gold armlets, weighing a total of "two kati less three tael," and a fine piece of Indian cloth. Whatever the truth of the allegations, Batavia replaced the governor in order to regain Tidore's trust.[55]

The change of governors was welcomed by Tidore, but this did not alter the primary cause of the difficulties facing the VOC, Ternate, and Tidore: the rebellion in the Gamrange and the Papuan islands. On 3 October 1720, eight Patani kora-koras appeared in Ternate with a letter from the sangajis of Patani and Bicoli, as well as the raja and gimalahas of Waigeu, addressed to Saifuddin of Ternate and the newly appointed Dutch governor. It contained a plea that they be allowed to become subjects of Ternate and the Dutch Company because they no longer could tolerate the Tidore ruler's ill-treatment and onerous tribute.[56] They had already rejected their former lord by joining Ternate's Halmahera subjects in attacks on Tidore's territories. These raids had caused so many deaths that the Sultan Tidore was forced to request extra cloth from the Company for the burial ceremonies. He was therefore given a pack of Guinea cloth, twenty packs of Bengal chits, and four pieces of red bethilles, which he distributed as gifts to the bereaved wives and children so that they would not be displeased with him.[57]

What finally prompted the Dutch to take direct action in the rebellion was the fear of trade disruption. They therefore agreed to send a contingent of Dutch soldiers to accompany a Tidorese punitive expedition to southeast Halmahera in early 1722. The attack on the Patani settlement located on a hill proved successful and resulted in the destruction of the town and all of the fruit trees. Many of the defenders, however, eluded capture. To prevent their seeking refuge in the Ternate territories of Kayoa, Gane, Foya, Kau, and Galela, where their compatriots had gone earlier, the Company demanded that the Sultan Ternate seize any Patanese found in his lands. The victory boosted the spirits of the Tidorese. They were ready to believe rumors that the people of Patani who had rebelled against their leaders now wished to return to the protection of the Sultan Tidore, and that the Papuan islanders who had come to the assistance of the Gamrange had returned home. But the euphoria was short-lived, as reports pieced together provided a picture of a less than successful campaign. It was revealed that when the Tidore force arrived in Patani, the Tidorese were reluctant to take up arms against the rebels and many returned home secretly.[58]

Possession of large numbers of subjects remained a visible measure of a ruler's success and was considered of great importance in the dualism between Ternate and Tidore. Considerable effort was devoted to "stealing" the other's subjects through inducements, raids, or by whatever means available. The Dutch had merely confirmed this practice in 1660 by encouraging both Ternate and Tidore to sign an agreement to allow their subjects to settle wherever they wished.[59] The movements of people between the territories of these two kingdoms therefore continued as in the past, enabling anyone from a ruler to an ordinary villager to seek a new home in another kingdom. But this traditional practice, which was an important part of the Ternate/Tidore dualism and a useful release valve for both these kingdoms, was pinpointed by the VOC as a major cause of conflict. On 6 June 1722, therefore, it forced both rulers to sign an agreement to prevent subjects of one kingdom seeking shelter in another. Anyone found contravening this agreement was to be delivered to the Company for punishment.[60] Despite this agreement there was little change in the situation. Some of the Patani and Maba rebels settled in Galela in Ternaten Halmahera and joined their Galela hosts in thirty boats in a raid on Salawati in 1724.[61]

These raids continued with impunity in 1724–1725 throughout the Seram and Raja Ampat islands. Then in January 1725 the Sangaji Patani arrived late one night on the east coast of Ternate at Toloko with 150 men in two kora-koras. Though Ternate's Sultan Saifuddin urged them to leave, they refused saying that they wanted either to become his or the Company's subjects or to be killed. Although Tidore's Sultan Hasanuddin knew of their arrival, he told the Dutch he was powerless to act because his own people were scattered and too few of them wished to take action. On the Dutch governor's suggestion he approached Saifuddin to ask his cooperation in driving the rebels away in accordance with the agreement between the two kingdoms signed in 1722. But Saifuddin refused to take any action on behalf of the Sultan Tidore which could result in the loss of Ternaten lives. A few days later the rebels left, temporarily resolving the crisis.[62]

Tidore was under severe strain because of the continuing rebellion. What exacerbated the situation was other signs which were seen by Malukans as confirmation of a deep crisis in Tidore society. The first of these was a long drought in 1723, which after six months had depleted Tidore's food supplies. The normally industrious Tidorese were forced to go to Halmahera and buy sago and rice at a high price. With the presence of so many of Tidore's rebel Gamrange subjects in Halmahera, however, even this source of food became threatened.[63] The other sign was a raging smallpox epidemic which devastated Tidore and other communities throughout Maluku. To escape, a large number of people from Ternate and Tidore fled to the safety of the Halmaheran interior. Because of the great number of deaths in his kingdom due to smallpox, Hasanuddin complained that there were scarcely enough healthy men on Tidore to outfit ten kora-koras, which normally required about fifty to seventy men per boat.[64] All of these problems besetting Tidore were interpreted as symptoms of the weakening spiritual power of the sultan and hence his inability to protect his subjects from malevolent human and supernatural forces.

In view of this judgment on Tidore, there was little enthusiasm in the kingdom for a campaign against the rebels. Nor was there any indication that the rebels regarded their actions as being treasonous or extraordinary. On 4 July 1726 some seventeen kora-koras and six other boatloads of Papuans and Patanese appeared before the Dutch fortress and then sailed directly to the royal settlement of Malayu. They marched toward the Sultan Ternate's residence while shouting their "scorn and contempt for their rightful lord [the Sultan Tidore]." Dutch envoys sent to speak to the rebels were told that they wished only to be subjects of the Sultan Ternate or of the Dutch Company "under whose wings they could seek a safe refuge." They explained that in the past they had received this refuge from the Sultan Tidore, but because of his ill-treatment they had abandoned him.[65]

There then followed an unexpected turn of events. One evening the Ternaten bobatos appeared in Fort Orange greatly distressed. They reported how, after Sultan Saifuddin and the principal leaders of the kingdom had eaten and drunk with the rebels on the beach, they had all boarded the rebel boats for a short trip. On their return everyone had disembarked except the sultan. He had then shouted to those on shore: "I cannot leave them and go ashore again before first going to Makian or Ambon. And I do not wish any longer to be the spokesman or slave of the Sultan Tidore." He had then rowed away with the Patani rebels accompanied by only one of his European bodyguards.[66] It was later learned that they had gone first to Makian, then around the islands, and eventually to Kayoa, where the Dutch found him three weeks later. It was a considerable time before the Dutch and the sultan's brothers succeeded in persuading him to return. On the way back to Ternate, he told the Dutch that "he no longer wished to be bothered by the Sultan Tidore and his requests to drive away his unruly Patani subjects." His unwillingness to reject the Patanese as subjects was understandable in terms of Ternate's dualistic contest with Tidore, and he did nothing to dissuade the Patanese from affirming their allegiance to him by the presentation of a substantial tribute consisting of seven Papuan slaves, eight large copper gongs, a small copper gun, two pieces of ambergris weighing five to six catties wrapped in white linen, and a chest with two rattan boxes of tortoiseshell, some silk cloth, a piece of patola four fathoms long, a headband, a piece of goldwork known as *kamaga,* and seven bird of paradise feathers.[67]

Soon after the departure of the rebels, Tidore's Hasanuddin came to the Dutch fort to complain about the whole episode and to seek restititution of his Halmahera subjects who had fled to live in Galela. He further demanded that Saifuddin seize the Ternatens accused of inciting the Patani rebels. The Ternaten sultan could only reply wearily that if the Patani subjects had good intentions toward their overlord, these Ternaten "inciters" would not have been able to cause three hundred of them to abandon the Sultan Tidore.[68] Feeling aggrieved at the Dutch governor's obvious sympathy with Ternate, Hasanuddin appealed directly to the Dutch governor-general in Batavia, "for on whom should we Tidorese place our hope and trust than on the Company, our good friend and mighty father under whose justice we always find shelter?"[69]

The VOC was as eager as Hasanuddin to end the rebellion, mainly because the rebel areas of southeast Halmahera grew spice trees which had not been visited by eradication expeditions since the outbreak of the rebellion in 1716. But there was little it could do short of becoming directly involved in choosing between Ternate and Tidore. The problem was unexpectedly resolved with the sudden death of Sultan Hasanuddin at midnight on 23 May 1728. The Tidore jojau who brought the news took pains to assure the Dutch that although the death was sudden, the sultan had not been murdered. Shortly before his death the sultan had secured the succession of Kaicili Gapi, the son of Sultan Abdul Jalal Mansur who had died in 1708. In keeping with the terms of the treaty signed between Tidore and the Company, the Dutch governor and council met and approved the election, a popular choice that was greeted with "general heartfelt happiness not seen for many years." There was even rejoicing in Ternate, and Sultan Saifuddin appeared genuinely pleased with the change of rulers.[70]

Many Tidorese attributed the troubles to the fact that Hasanuddin had not been of the line of their well-beloved Saifuddin (r. 1657–1687). Kaicili Gapi, on the other hand, was a direct descendant of Saifuddin, which for the Tidorese augured well for the future of the kingdom. He was installed on 14 June 1728 and took the reign name of Sultan Amirulfadli Aziz Muhidin Malikilmannan. In renewing the contract with the Dutch, he relinquished all claims to the hundred Tidore subjects who had fled to Galela and issued a general pardon to the Patani rebels. He then sought to mollify Ternate by renouncing any pretensions to its territories. An agreement was signed between the two kingdoms formalizing these moves and leading to the return of many Tidorese who had fled to Ternate during Hasanuddin's reign. For his part the Sultan Ternate promised to deliver to the Dutch for punishment any of his subjects accused of inciting the rebels. He also pledged to force all Tidore subjects living in Galela to return home and to prevent others from settling in any of his territories.[71] In this way both Ternate and Tidore attempted to outdo the other in demonstrating to the VOC that they were acting as a good ally.

The most important task facing the new Tidore ruler was reconciliation with the rebels. They were cautious at the offer of pardon and agreed to submit only if the following conditions were met: first, that their wives and children, who were brought to Tidore as hostages, be returned safely to them; second, that they retain the offices and privileges which they had held before the rebellion; third, that a Dutch post consisting of a sergeant and a few soldiers be established at Patani to maintain peace; and fourth, that the two chief culprits and cause of the rebellion (a certain Rahim and Sahabat, both Ternatens) be delivered to the Dutch Company for punishment. Sultan Amir agreed to the conditions, even though he had grave misgivings about a Dutch post in Patani. The Company, on the other hand, regarded the request as a great opportunity to prevent the "illicit" spice trade which centered in that region. As a sign of his good faith Amir released the hostages, and the rebels once again swore their loyalty to him as Sultan Tidore.[72]

The formal ceremony of reconciliation took place at about 11 P.M. on 31 July 1728. When the Patanese arrived in Tidore accompanied by the Dutch for security, there were already two boatloads of people from Maba and Weda lying at anchor. At first Amir wished to see the Dutch alone and then meet the rebels the following day. The Dutch, fearing trouble between the Patanese and those from Maba and Weda, persuaded him to arrange a night meeting instead. Late that evening the Patanese went to the royal residence where they were respectfully met at the entrance by the sultan himself and conducted to the main hall. The way was so packed with armed men that only one person at a time could pass. Once inside the sultan asked the Sangaji Patani if he truly wished to submit, to which he replied: "Yes, Lord King. See, I have laid down my arms and submitted." He then fell to the floor, prostrated himself before the sultan, and crawled toward him. One of the Tidore princes tried to kick him aside, but he was restrained by the other onlookers.[73] The sultan bent down, took the sangaji under the arms, and pulled him to his feet. When the sangaji spoke, he told the ruler that he would remain obedient and faithful because he had experienced the goodness of the sultan and the Company. The Tidore bobatos then came and swore their allegiance, followed by the Sangaji Patani and his followers, who bowed down to the ground and called out the Tidorese equivalent of "Long live our lawful king of Tidore." The Sangaji Patani was reinstalled as head over the Papuan islands, and the reconciliation was concluded by a treaty agreed upon by both Tidore and Patani.[74]

The long rebellion revealed the unexpected strength and resilience of Tidore's subjects in southeast Halmahera and the Papuan islands. Despite every effort by Tidore and the Dutch Company, and later even Ternate, to bring an end to the rebellion, the area remained defiant. The distance, the adverse geographical conditions, and the hostile communities were major hindrances to any punitive expedition from the outside. Moreover, the area together had sufficient resources in manpower, boats, and goods to maintain a rebellion almost indefinitely. Its economic and social ties with settlements to the east as far as the coast of New Guinea and to the south to the islands of East Seram provided a secure base of support which could operate independently from Tidore and Ternate. Nevertheless, it continued to link its fortunes to these centers, contributing further to Ternate and Tidore's ongoing dualism.

Strains in the Family

Ternate and Tidore's desire to be regarded by their father, the Company, as exemplary children was motivated by their ongoing dualism. In the effort to outdo the other, both courts were compelled to demonstrate their success in implementing the Company's spice eradication policy. The severity of the physical and economic demands of the policy, however, created strains in the social and political fabric of Malukan society. The result was turmoil, recrimination, and despair, symptoms which Malukans rationalized and eventually solved in the traditional manner.

By the middle of the seventeenth century the oversupply of spices had brought prices down in Europe, and the Company's attempts to obtain from the Malukan rulers guarantees of exclusive delivery of spices were proving a failure. One of the ideas conceived by the Company to remedy the situation was to control supply by destroying all the spice trees in the region except for a few selected places. From 1652 it embarked on a program of limiting the growing of clove trees to Ambon and the nutmeg tree to the Banda Islands. At the very outset the project seemed far too ambitious. There were so many islands on which the clove and nutmeg tree grew wild that a project to destroy all the spice trees except for Ambon and Banda appeared unachievable. In addition to the original home of the clove tree in the islands of Ternate, Tidore, Makian, Moti, and Bacan, it was also found on Halmahera, many of the offshore islands, Hoamoal, Buru, and Ambon. The nutmeg tree grew not only on Banda, but a number of different varieties flourished on islands spread throughout the Malukan region.

In return for agreeing to destroy their spice trees, the Dutch offered to pay an annual compensation to the Malukan rulers and some of the bobatos. The most significant consequence of the compensation was the concentration of wealth in the hands of a few. In determining the sum for compensation, the Dutch had placed greater emphasis on placating the ruler than on seeking an equitable redistribution of income which was being lost throughout the society. The payment of compensation enabled the sultan and those he favored to continue to purchase foreign products and thereby retain their prestige and status in the community. To safeguard this source of prestige goods, they were willing to cooperate, or at least be seen to cooperate, with the Company in undertaking the eradication. They began to use this source of wealth, often partly in the form of Indian cloth, to redistribute among their followers and thus strengthen their position in the community. For the first time the sultan came to possess not only the trappings of a powerful Islamic ruler but also the resources to become one.

As private sales of spices became more difficult because of Dutch restrictions, the ordinary people and those bobatos denied compensation came to be increasingly dependent upon the ruler's largesse. For many the clove had been an ideal product. The clove tree required minimal tending and grew naturally in forests which blanketed the north Malukan islands. Although traders, especially the Europeans, no longer were satisfied with whole branches of cloves picked at random, the local people were willing to invest more time in harvesting the cloves, as well as drying, sorting, and bagging them for export, because the rewards were considerable. The introduction of the eradication policy with its selective compensation removed this reliable source of revenue for the people and most bobatos. As a result of the implementation of this policy, disaffection grew in the kingdom because many bobatos and the ngofagamu, or people of the land, had lost their primary source of income. For the bobatos this meant an inability to obtain prestige items to maintain their status and a growing dependence on the ruler. For the ngofagamu it signaled not only the end of an ideal revenue earner which had made possible the purchase of useful items from the outside world, but also the beginning of the burdensome task of removing the thousands of spice trees found on the islands.

When the actual eradication policy was put into practice, it became obvious that the Dutch had seriously underestimated the enormity of the project. The local inhabitants were regularly organized through their village heads to fell the spice trees under the supervision of Dutch Company officials and soldiers. Although only a few men in a village were usually recruited for such duty, the frequency of the expeditions meant that every adult male was eventually forced to take part. Others in the village had to contribute food, shelter, and transport to carry supplies. One of the problems faced was the hardiness of the spice trees. After a number of years the Dutch came to realize that simply felling the trees and leaving them to rot was ineffective since the fallen ripe fruit seeded and germinated. The laborers were thereafter required not only to fell the trees, some of which were very old and large, but also to dig them out, split the roots, and burn the entire tree and the fruit. It was subsequently found that even burning did not totally destroy all the seeds but simply removed some of the outer shell and hastened the germination process.[75] "Destroying" spice trees was therefore proving to be a far more arduous task than previously envisaged and required long absences from home. The duration and size of these expeditions involved considerable expense and organization, as can be seen by the supplies left behind by the Dutch and local laborers forced to abandon southeast Halmahera halfway through their spice eradication campaign: 8,600 pounds of rice, 2,200 pounds of beans, 313 1/4 pounds of bacon, 140 pounds of butter, 569 1/4 cans olive oil, 294 cans of native vinegar, 1122 1/2 cans of fermented palm wine *(arak)*, 840 pounds of salt, 3,641 pounds of tamarind, 295 containers of sago, 14 pounds of wax candles, 56 cans of coconut oil, 100 pounds of gunpowder, and 50 pounds of bullets.[76]

The apparent lack of success despite these systematic expeditions brought criticism from the VOC directors in Amsterdam. In reply the Dutch governor in Ternate explained:

Your Lordships would find it difficult to comprehend how many [spice trees] there are on most of the islands in this area. If we truly intend to uproot these trees, we must do it with hundreds of men divided into groups and spread out through the forests. For this we must have people who have the desire and inclination to carry out the work since the forests are so thick that a man can barely raise his head. Moreover, they are often full of thorns and bushes which tear to shreds whatever a man is wearing and damage his legs, hands, and face. . . . The places are many, and the uprooting [of spice trees] appears to be nearly an impossible task. It is the most difficult and exhausting work that one can imagine. Sometimes [the spice trees] are so inaccessible that one must push up the [thorny] rattan vines in order to get to them. There is also the danger of breaking a leg. Sometimes the spice trees are surrounded by so many other trees and bushes that one cannot see them. It also requires some knowledge to recognize them and not pass them by. This requires young, strong, and robust individuals who can withstand these rigors on, at times, a simple meal consisting of a piece of bacon and bad rice or some sago. . . . Over half come back sick or incapacitated from these expeditions.[77]

The Dutch persisted by more frequent revisiting of sites, and they eventually succeeded in completely destroying the spice trees in certain areas. The success of this regular visitation was confined to those places within easy reach of Dutch posts. In north Maluku this was mainly Ternate, Tidore, Makian, and Moti, but even on these islands there were sections on the mountains which were difficult to reach. As the years progressed and the more obvious places had been cleared of spice trees, the expeditions were sent to more inaccessible and often dangerous valleys, precipitous cliffs, and malarial interior areas. The hardships suffered on these expeditions is captured in a report by a Dutch official commenting on a recent visit to northern Halmahera:

Because of the height of the mountains and the depths of the valleys, as well as the large quantities of thorny rattans which grow in very thick stands, it is very difficult and unpleasant to get to [the spice trees]. Often we have to crawl on our hands and feet, which results in damage to our hands and so many pricks from thorns that we do not dare to go forward. The difficult paths, swollen rivers, daily rains, and the extreme cold have resulted in only five of the seven soldiers with me at present being able to be used to search for these vexatious plants.[78]

The Malukans, too, complained that the annual eradication expeditions were causing great hardship and poverty. In addition to the backbreaking tasks required of them, any period spent on these campaigns left less time to seek a livelihood elsewhere. Moreover, the experience was often demeaning, since local inhabitants were subjected to abusive and insensitive treatment by Company officials. After weeks of endless trekking through forests, climbing steep mountain slopes, shivering from the cold of a morning fog or sweating in the high humidity of the jungle, and the sheer hard labor required in felling and destroying the trees, the people were paid nothing. Instead, the bobatos were presented with some Indian cloth and perhaps a share of the compensation given to the ruler. There was little direct benefit to the people themselves, and considerable disadvantage in participating in such expeditions. Little wonder, then, that the Dutch complained of attempts by local guides to lead the Dutch away from areas of spice trees, pretending that no trees had been overlooked in previous expeditions.

In this deception the locals were frequently encouraged by Dutch Company servants unfortunate enough to be selected to lead such expeditions. They resented the hardships which they had to endure, and they were often content to take the word of the local inhabitants rather than spend extra days on the exhausting task of combing further difficult areas for spice trees. At first only the numbers of trees felled were listed. But as the Company directors in Amsterdam became more aware of the difficulties of destroying these trees, they required that all reports enumerate both old and young trees, with success being measured by the decreasing numbers of older trees being found. Toward the end of the eighteenth century the Dutch reports had become even more refined, with separate categories for young trees bearing fruit and those not. These highly detailed reports indicated on paper that the Company was at last succeeding in destroying the spice trees in the areas outside Ambon and the Banda Islands. But it became clear that, in distant areas where verification was difficult, reports had been fabricated or the figures exaggerated to please the authorities. So widespread was this practice that it was no longer possible to attribute major discrepancies in numbers from one period to another purely to the natural regeneration of the trees. The unreliability of the reports finally forced one especially conscientious governor to require leaders of these expeditions to swear on the Bible before the Dutch Council that the figures of trees felled, and so forth were accurate.[79] But even such extreme measures were of dubious value since many of the officials would have sworn to anything to escape the hardships involved in the eradication campaign.

The actual cost of these expeditions was so considerable that the policy became a drain on the Company's resources. Despite increasing evidence that the policy had long outlived its usefulness and was a great burden on the local peoples, the Company directors continued to hold to the belief that such expeditions were necessary to maintain high spice prices. The ordinary Malukans had become so impoverished by the policy that they had begun to resort to supplying the immediate needs of the Dutch garrisons and settlements in Maluku to replace the revenue lost from the clove trade. Some, for example, collected the bark of a certain tree which was stripped and twisted to produce wicks. For 4,400 bundles of these wicks they received from the Dutch fifteen packs of cloth worth 2,960 rijksdaalders. Others built lime ovens at various sites and collected coral which was burnt to produce lime used for building fortifications. For such services the Company paid a stuiver and a pound of rice a day to the people of Makian and Guineas cloth to those from Ternate. Tidore supplied all the fish and most of the vegetables and fruit consumed by the Dutch fortress and settlement. In payment the people were able to purchase Indian cloth and other imported items from the Dutch store.[80]

Evidence of the failure of the eradication policy was the existence of new spice routes in areas infrequently visited by Dutch cruisers. The Gamrange in southeast Halmahera became a major collecting point of spices obtained from local forests and from supplies brought without Company knowledge by inhabitants of Tidore and Makian. These spices were then shipped to Keffing in East Seram, where they were exchanged for cloth and other goods. On many occasions the southeast Halmahera traders needed to go no further than the island of Misool, where traders from the western part of the Malay-Indonesian archipelago brought krisses, cloth, broadswords or large hewing knives, and all types of iron and copperwork to exchange for spices, slaves, birds of paradise, and other goods from surrounding islands.[81]

Makassar, Bugis, Javanese, and Malay traders came annually to Keffing to obtain spices and then transport them via different routes to destinations in the west. The Bugis and Makassar traders used the Bay of Tomini to get to Parigi, and then went overland a short distance to Palu. From Palu the spices went to Mandar for transshipment to Makassar or farther west to Banjarmassin. Another route went from Bega on the Bay of Tomini to Dondo near Tolitoli, southward along the east coast of Borneo, and then to the west.[82] It was this route which brought Berau on the northeast coast of Borneo into prominence in the eighteenth century. Traders from East Seram also frequently made the trip through the Papuan islands and to the southeast Halmahera communities of the Gamrange to buy spices. In the last quarter of the eighteenth century the English joined this trade network. On their journey to China using the eastern route, which went through the Dampier

Straits off the west coast of New Guinea, they regularly purchased spices from the Malukans. The French, too, had penetrated the area and took spice trees which they successfully transplanted on the island of Mauritius. In short, the spice monopoly was in tatters, and yet the Company persisted in pursuing its unpopular eradication policy.

For the Malukans the policy had more than simply economic repercussions. By its continuing demands for labor and its annual payment of compensation to the sultan and a favored group of bobatos, personal relationships between the court and the people underwent severe strain. The rulers had relinquished many of their responsibilities to their subjects after the 1683 treaty, establishing the Dutch Company as Ternate's "father." In acknowledging this status of "child" to the Company, Ternate was forced into a position of implementing Dutch directives throughout the kingdom. Such an arrangement was feasible at the center, in the area under the direct leadership of the sultan. In the periphery, however, he had to rely on traditions, perceptions of mutual benefits, and blood relationships to encourage conformity to the center's wishes. Force was contemplated only in exceptional cases, and success in such cases was not always guaranteed. With the new Company overlordship, the Ternaten rulers imposed greater demands on the people which could now be enforced through Dutch arms. Unlike the Malukan kingdoms, the Company was ready to use force and to threaten the center if "order" were not maintained in the periphery. Links between the sultan and the bobatos at the center, and between the center and periphery, were weakened as a result of Ternate's new relationship with the Company. A similar situation confronted Tidore after the long Gamrange-Papuan rebellion of 1716–1728. Although there had been no change in the official relationship, Tidore had become dependent upon Dutch arms to reestablish its position in Maluku. Its desire to retain the goodwill of the Company was strongly motivated by its need to maintain equal status with Ternate in the eyes of the Dutch.

The increasing severity of VOC demands on Ternate and Tidore in the eighteenth century coincided with the period of the Company's greatest financial and military weakness. Distrust, even paranoia, gripped Dutch leaders who saw sinister implications in any alliance between local kingdoms and other Europeans, especially the English. The need to reaffirm the Company's authority throughout the region and to prevent encroachment by other Europeans resulted in the practice of erecting stone pillars with the VOC emblem throughout Maluku. The Company justified the pillars as being in accordance with the European treaty, which had made Ternaten lands "legally" its vassals. After the rebellion in the Gamrange, the Company insisted that Sultan Amir of Tidore have the pillars erected in that area, despite the fact that Tidore was still a sovereign nation.[83] The Company argued that, although it had acted on the sultan's request, it had acquired the lands legitimately through conquest. In addition to the VOC pillars the leaders were presented with a rattan cane with a silver knob on which was embossed the Company's seal. Boundary markers and the symbols of office were established European and Malukan practice, but for the latter they had an added significance because the objects themselves were considered to be repositories of the sacred force associated with an overlord.

The Malukan sultans demonstrated their loyalty to the Dutch in the traditional manner by adopting practices associated with their lord. Sultan Amir counted many of the Dutch officials as his friends, and he acquired a great liking for Dutch beer. When he had drunk too much, he would remove the Tidorese headdress, put on a Dutch wig and hat, and say quite openly: "I have been installed as ruler by the Dutch Company. I want also to do things in the Dutch way." In contrast to the previous ruler who had outfitted his officers with Spanish arms and banners, Sultan Amir provided his officers with Dutch pikes and halberds and a VOC banner. He himself taught his officers how to present arms after being tutored by the Dutch. So encouraged was Governor Pielat by these signs of affection that he wrote to Batavia in 1731 expressing the hope that Sultan Amir, through the adoption of Dutch maxims and customs, would become as "humane" as other Tidore leaders who had undergone the same process. Pielat proudly reported how he had entertained the sultan and the important Tidore princes at his residence and had not served a single "Moorish [that is, Muslim, meaning local] dish," which in Pielat's eyes "demonstrated that this ruler did not hold too strongly to his religion." Of great satisfaction to Pielat was the sultan's transformation of the royal settlement into a much more regulated "Dutch-like city." The town was formerly full of large rocks, among which were scattered "in wondrous fashion" the houses built of sago planks and thatching. Sultan Amir had the rocks removed, the area smoothed over, and houses with fences built along straight streets. To Pielat these measures had greatly improved the island of Tidore and made it a "true gem."[84]

Pielat was typical of the European mood of the time, which differed little from earlier Western European perceptions of lands located on the periphery. The center, and hence the model of civilized behavior, was located in Christian Western Europe. Physical distance from the center correlated with the moral distance from the "measures of humanity," or "civilization," as defined by the center. The belief was that, the more individuals or races came to adopt the various measures, defined outwardly in terms of dress, speech, food, and habitation, the closer they came to being civilized (see Chapter 1). This attitude was alive and well in the early eighteenth century, and Governor Pielat typified it in his depiction of Sultan Amir of Tidore. The latter was beginning to exhibit all the signs of a civilized individual: he wore (on occasion) Dutch clothes; he spoke some Dutch; he ate Dutch food; and he built a town in the Dutch fashion. These were manifestations of a civilized being, hence one whom the Dutch could trust. From Amir's viewpoint, however, he was simply acting in accordance with a Malukan belief that recognition of an overlord required the emulation of all aspects of the latter's world. Since both Pielat and Amir found comfort in the latter's acts, they contributed to an amicable relationship between the Dutch Company and Tidore in these years. Nevertheless, within Tidore there was dissatisfaction in the Council of State with the Company's encroachment on the kingdom's sovereignty and the sultan's neglect of the delegations from Tidore's periphery. These envoys, according to the sultan's critics, were made to wait for hours while Amir consorted with "the young and common sort of people."[85] Opposition to the sultan found expression in the sabotaging of his efforts to implement the Company's spice eradication policy in southeast Halmahera.[86]

By the middle of the eighteenth century the Company was obsessed by the eradication campaign. Official reports are devoted almost exclusively to the results of these expeditions, but interspersed with these reports is evidence of the exacerbation of the conflict between the rulers, supported by the Dutch, and the principal leaders in the land. In 1720 there was a serious challenge to Sultan Saifuddin of Ternate by the jogugu, the sadaha,[87] and the Kimalaha Marsaoli, three highly respected and influential individuals in the kingdom. The sultan accused these officials of a serious crime against the Company, that of "smuggling" spices (the Company's term for trading outside its system). It was a crime which warranted the death penalty, but since the treaty stipulated that this penalty could be imposed only with Company approval, Sultan Saifuddin sought and received permission to carry out the punishment. The decision was greeted with shock and dismay among the Ternatens, and so on the day of the execution Saifuddin requested and received an additional eighty-eight Dutch soldiers to prevent trouble.[88]

Little had changed by 1744 when Saifuddin was challenged by the Kimalaha Tomagola and the Kimalaha Tomajiko, members of two leading Ternaten families. The Dutch governor, who had a right to a seat in the Ternate Council as a result of the treaty of 7 July 1683, invoked article eight to remind the Ternatens that the Company had the final say in the punishment or execution of any councillor accused of a crime. Having made this announcement, the governor then passed sentence exiling one of the kimalahas and depriving all three of their offices and privileges. Saifuddin then took this opportunity to declare that the families of the Tomagola and Tomajiko would never again be allowed to hold office because of their well-known tradition of opposition to the sultan.[89] When the important positions of jogugu in Ternate, salahakan in

Sula Besi, raja in Tobunku, and sangaji of Gamkonora fell vacant, he left the posts unfilled. By not replacing some of the most powerful positions in the land, Saifuddin left these communities leaderless and therefore more amenable to his control. Without the assurance of Company support, he would not have dared to confront such powerful forces within his kingdom nor ignore the custom of consulting the bobatos whenever any momentous decision was being considered.[90]

Makian too came to pose a major threat to Ternate's authority. In March 1742 about 180 Makianese went to Tidore with their leaders and asked to become subjects of the sultan. Their dissatisfaction with Saifuddin stemmed from his contemptuous treatment of their sangajis. In one case he had ordered one of them bound like an ordinary thief; in another he had appointed as sangaji of Ngofakiaha, the principal settlement on Makian, an old, deaf, and blind jogugu who had to be carried everywhere. In a society where any physical or mental imperfection was cause enough for rejection as a suitable candidate for any important office, the appointment of an old and physically impaired jogugu could only be interpreted as a deliberate insult to Ngofakiaha.[91] So intolerable did the situation become that many Makianese, as well as their compatriots who had gone to live in Foya and Gane in Halmahera, went to settle in Tidore under the sultan's protection. The common people went first and were later joined by their leaders, partially to avoid the Company's restriction against heads organizing their people to transfer loyalty from one overlord to another. Despite upheavals caused by natural or man-made disasters which had led to the abandonment of villages, the presence of the leaders provided the spiritual center around which a community could reconstitute itself in a new location. The village heads or bobatos, with links to the community's tutelary deity, became not merely the symbol but the embodiment of the whole group. This is the reason why Saifuddin's actions in Makian were viewed as insulting to the people and interpreted as measures of an oppressive overlord who was no longer interested in maintaining the proper relationships with his subjects.[92]

Those who remained on Makian became direct subjects of the Company in 1745. In the new relationship the Company smoothly assumed the role of overlord and thereby accentuated Saifuddin's abrogation of his responsibilities to his subjects. Instead of the customary thirty-three people who were rotated monthly to perform corvée labor for the Sultan Ternate, they were now organized to supply eight korakoras when required by the Company and to provide all services and supplies for Dutch ships coming to Makian. They were also to gather coral to make lime for the Dutch. Once a direct relationship of "father" and "children" had been established between the Company and the remaining Makian communities, the former noted a greater diligence than before in their performance of spice eradication duties. The Dutch attributed this to the fact that for the first time compensation was paid directly to the people of Makian and not via the Sultan Ternate. Their tasks were now seen as direct services to their Dutch lord, from whom they expected in return economic benefits and protection.[93]

Criticism of Ternate's ruler came also from some of the alifuru groups in Halmahera, including the Tobelos and the Tobarus who were among his most faithful supporters. Their complaint was that Saifuddin was incapable of providing protection against the excesses of the royal princes "who mistreated them, levied unbearable fines, and when they could not pay, sold their children into slavery."[94] In Ternate itself the people described the long period when the positions of jogugu, hukum and Kimalaha Marsaoli were left vacant as a time when they had been "laid bare to all types of abuse from the princes and princesses."[95] Mounting dissatisfaction against Saifuddin ended with the accession of his successor, Sultan Oudhoorn Kaicili Ayan Syah (r. 1752–1755). He worked to reverse the measures introduced by Saifuddin and was praised as "a prince who maintains law and justice and prevents those of the court from committing all manner of extortion, oppression, and tyranny."[96] Among his first acts was to fill the long-vacant posts of jogugu, hukum, and Kimalaha Marsaoli, thus ending a period when the sultan governed almost with no regard for the officials in the land. He was therefore praised as an exceptional ruler who brought reconciliation to many disaffected groups in the kingdom.[97] His brief reign was, however, merely an interlude in an ongoing and older struggle between the ruler and the lords of the land. His successor and younger brother Sultan Amir Iskandar Muda Zwammerdam (r. 1755–1764) resumed the practice of previous rulers by taking an inordinately long time to fill the important position of jogugu.[98]

The strengthening of the ruler and his family was accompanied by a corresponding weakening of the traditional champions of the people. The rise in the incidents of abuse by the royal offspring was a consequence of the growing disparity in power between the sultan, on the one hand, and those officials and bobatos representing the people of the land on the other. The regularity and success with which the Ternate rulers undertook measures to weaken certain officials and the bobatos were a consequence of the new self-confidence among the rulers who were secure in the knowledge that they would be supported by the Company.

The Consequences

The relationship between the Dutch East India Company and Ternate had undergone a qualitative change since 1683, when Ternate was forced to sign a treaty acknowledging its vassal status to the Company. From this period till well into the eighteenth century, Ternate's rulers became less concerned with the proper functioning of their governments and the obligations they had toward their bobatos and subjects than with pleasing the Company and thus assuring continued support. As the position of sultan became much stronger with the assistance of the Company, it became more alienated from the rest of the government. The impunity with which the sultans allowed important posts to remain vacant, to the detriment of the powerful families and to the common people, would not have been tolerated in the past. With the Company as protector and overlord, however, the sense of duty and obligation between the ruler and his people was weakened. Many Ternaten subjects, especially those of the powerful areas of Makian and northwest Halmahera, began to question their relationship with the sultan and to seek to establish direct ties with the Company.

Tidore remained an independent kingdom for much of the eighteenth century. As its dualism with Ternate began to focus on the Company, it came to behave in a similar fashion to Ternate even though it was still a sovereign state. One of the most damaging decisions taken by the Tidore rulers in the eighteenth century was to pursue the Dutch Company's policy of spice eradication in its territories. When it was implemented in southeast Halmahera and the Papuan islands, the people resisted. The stated causes of the rebellion were the brutal and insensitive handling of the local people by the Dutch expedition and the loss of an important source of revenue. Though the Tidore sultan had benefited from a major trade network centered in this area which bypassed the Dutch completely, he was willing to jeopardize the financial benefits of trade to gain the favor of the Company in Tidore's dualistic contest with Ternate. Both kingdoms were eager to demonstrate their readiness and efficiency in the implementation of the eradication policy in their lands, and both responded with all the signs of goodwill to the Company's demands that they punish their "criminal" subjects who had raided its territories. When the Company believed that the root of the troubles between the kingdoms was the frequent movement of subjects from one land to another, the sultans agreed to include a provision in the treaty to prevent such practices. The free flow of people between kingdoms had been useful in the past in serving as a barometer of the state of the dualism between Ternate and Tidore and in helping to defuse serious tensions in each kingdom. The dualism, however, had taken a different turn. In the contest to gain the favor of the Company, the sultans were now willing to implement these measures and sacrifice other established relationships.

Center/periphery ties were weakened by the center's implementation of the VOC's spice eradication program. Although the clove, nut-

meg, and mace were the principal sources of revenue in many peripheral areas, the rulers demanded compliance with the Company's new
economic policy in order to gain favor in the dualism contest. The
periphery's resentment was compounded by the fact that the center
rarely shared with it any portion of the inadequate compensation given
by the Company for the loss of income from the spice trade. The center
was further discredited because of the Company's requirement that rulers be wholly responsible for the acts of their subjects. By the last quarter of the eighteenth century many territories had become VOC possessions as a result of wars. In determining the boundaries of its new vassal
areas in Maluku, the Company sought greater precision regarding Ternate's and Tidore's own lands. For the Dutch this was a useful exercise
for adjudicating future border disputes and for determining under
whose jurisdiction misdeeds had been committed. But for the rulers it
proved a burden because they were forced to become more responsible
for the activities of their subjects in the periphery. The combination of
increased Company lands and subjects, and the obligation of the Malukan kingdoms to preserve the peace throughout their far-flung territories, caused considerable confusion among Ternate and Tidore subjects. In the past these subjects were expected to carry out trade and
raids, whence came the slaves and other tribute items for the courts.
Now, however, these very same demonstrations of loyalty came to be
condemned as hostile acts deserving punishment.

By the last quarter of the eighteenth century, only the dualism
between Ternate and Tidore appears to have survived virtually un-
scathed. Although it was circumscribed by Dutch policies, it retained its
relevance in the form of a contest for the affections of the Company. For
the rest there was a disintegration of established loyalties and the creation of new relationships. A major factor contributing to the undermining of the relationship between the ruler and the lord of the land, as
well as that between the center and the periphery, was the Dutch treaty.
The treaty had made Ternate a formal and Tidore an informal vassal
of the Company or, in Malukan perception, established a relationship
of "father" (Company) to "child" (Ternate and Tidore). The sultans
therefore placed the responsibilities of protecting their subjects and
assuring their welfare in the hands of the Company. The Malukan subjects in the periphery noted this "abandonment" by citing a number of
unreasonable actions by their sultans. Because the relationship was
deemed unilaterally terminated, the subjects felt free to seek another
lord. The movements of people into lands belonging to new overlords
were now interpreted by the sultan as a blatant contravention of a relationship established by treaty. To deal with such "rebellions" the sultans
felt justified in calling upon the Company to uphold the treaty. Once the
Company lent its men, arms, and ships to the sultans, the "rebellious"

subjects found it difficult to find another overlord and in the end were forced to submit to the tyrannies of their old lord. Nevertheless, there were many in the center and the periphery who regarded the disintegration of traditional relationships as symptomatic of the destruction of the unity of Maluku. They now waited for a leader who would restore proprieties and hence harmony in the land.

CHAPTER SEVEN

Nuku and the Restoration

IN THE MALUKAN KINGDOMS links between the center and the periphery gradually weakened as both perceived an abandonment of mutual obligations by the other. A curious situation arose in which the subjects of both Ternate and Tidore asked the Dutch East India Company to be their overlord at the very time that the Company was demanding that Ternate and Tidore maintain a stronger grip on their territories. In the territories there was a growing perception that demands from the center were not being reciprocated with the traditional obligations to the periphery. Ternate and Tidore's reliance on the Company to assume the obligations of overlord resulted in the abandonment of ceremonies and mutual exchanges which were essential for the smooth functioning of the kingdoms. Any demands from the center without these vital cultural ceremonials and exchanges could only be regarded as behavior more becoming of an overlord to a slave rather than to a subject.

It became apparent to many that it was the Company, and not a local kingdom, which was the arbiter in matters of peace and prosperity in Maluku. With growing disillusionment toward Ternate and Tidore, and with Bacan little more than a village, a belief developed among the people that their world was under threat. Social and political upheavals, epidemics, and natural disasters were interpreted as signs of the disharmony in Maluku. Many believed that the troubles were ultimately attributable to the destruction of Jailolo as a kingdom in the mid-sixteenth century. The solution, therefore, was obvious: reestablish the four kingdoms by resurrecting Jailolo and thus restore the unity of Maluku. In such troubled times the people were psychologically prepared for the message of restoration which Nuku, a Tidore royal prince, preached to all disaffected groups in the region.

Beginnings of Disaffection

Jailolo represented to the Malukans the important lost fourth kingdom, the missing element which was at the root of the problems facing their world. In 1551 the unity and harmony of Maluku were considered to have been shattered with the conquest of Jailolo and its absorption into Ternate. Many believed, however, that as long as Ternate and Tidore survived all was well with Maluku. Until the last quarter of the seventeenth century, both kingdoms conducted their affairs in ways which assured the people that proprieties were being maintained. By the eighteenth century, however, the two pillars had come under enormous pressure from the Dutch Company and from their own subjects. The failure of Sultan Amsterdam's rebellion forced Ternate to agree to the European treaty which made it a vassal of the Company. Tidore was not similarly coerced until the late eighteenth century, but it was sufficiently concerned at being disadvantaged vis-à-vis Ternate that it also conducted itself as a child to Father Company.

The decline of the last two pillars was perceived as the cause of the serious problems which came to beset the Malukan world in the eighteenth century. The belief grew stronger that the only way to reverse the process of Maluku's disintegration was to restore the four kingdoms, beginning with the formal reestablishment of the kingdom of Jailolo. In the past various unsuccessful efforts had been made to restore Jailolo, usually at times of upheaval. When the last direct heir of the Jailolo royal family, Kaicili Alam, died in 1684 it appeared that Jailolo was doomed to remain a dependency of Ternate governed by a sangaji. Yet the memory of Jailolo continued to excite the imagination of the Malukans because it symbolized a lost golden past, especially at a time when there was discontent at the state of affairs in Maluku. The restoration of Jailolo thus became a rallying cry promising the end of suffering and the beginning of a new cycle of harmony and peace in Maluku.

In 1765 about 146 people from the settlement of Tomalou on Tidore arrived in Jailolo led by an imam and two khatibs. They wanted to elevate a certain Abu Laif, who claimed direct descent from the Jailolo royal family, to become the new Sultan Jailolo. Toward this end they had gone to Jailolo to prepare the way by seeking the support of the alifuru in that area. Unfortunately for their plans, the alifuru could not be persuaded to give their loyalty to him and fighting erupted between the two groups. The imam and the two khatibs were later seized by the Dutch for inciting a disturbance.[1] This incident would have been interesting but not significant if it had been an isolated event. However, another attempt to restore the kingdom of Jailolo fifteen years later highlighted the strong undercurrent of dissatisfaction in Maluku and the persistent belief that harmony and prosperity would return once Jailolo was again reinstated as one of the four pillars.

The areas which appear to have been especially vulnerable to appeals for the restoration of a golden past were the Gamrange in south-east Halmahera and the Papuan islands. Their growing alienation from their overlord in Tidore had led to a long rebellion which had lasted from 1716 to 1728. Though Papuan myths had encouraged the idea of the west being the source of both wealth and power, their gradual but increasing knowledge of the western kingdoms, and especially of their overlord Tidore, began to dispel this view. Tidore was no longer the sole provider of prestige items such as cloth, iron and copper implements, porcelain, and glass beads. Keffing or even Misool became an even more abundant source of these goods. At the same time that the benefits of the relationship with Tidore were becoming more dubious, the latter began to demand more tribute and the strict implementation of the Dutch spice eradication policy. The end of the rebellion had brought a period of reconciliation, but the alienation remained. With Tidore's abandonment of its responsibilities to the periphery, the latter felt no obligation to comply with demands for tribute. The reaction then was for the overlord to cry "rebellion" and request Dutch assistance to quell it. Joint expeditions composed of soldiers from Tidore, with a complement of musketeers from the VOC, aggravated the situation because they were seen by the periphery as oppressive acts of an uncaring "father" who had abandoned his "children."

In 1761 the Raja Salawati led a force of fifteen hundred Papuans in an attack against Sula Besi, while his son led another eighty kora-koras in a major expedition against Buru. These raids had occurred in defiance of Ternate, the Company, and their overlord the Sultan Tidore.[2] As in 1716–1728, Patani again played a leading role in this rebellion. It was discovered that Salawati's jojau, the mother of Salawati's kapita laut, and many of the Raja Salawati's followers were from Patani.[3] At first the Sultan Tidore declined offers of assistance from the Company and boasted that he was "a great king with an abundance of people." But when he attempted to raise an expedition against the Papuans, he met strong opposition from the various bobatos in Tidore. He therefore turned to the loyal sangajis of Weda and Patani to supply forty kora-koras to battle the rebels.[4]

The Dutch blamed the opposition in Tidore on an influential Javanese family whose members held important posts in the Tidore government. Three brothers held the offices of jojau, kapita laut, and *jurutulis* (the sultan's scribe), while a fourth was based permanently in Maba and Patani where tribute from the Papuan islands was sent for shipment to Tidore. There were in addition thirty to forty children and grandchildren and more than twenty nephews and close relations who were scribes.[5] In a basically oral society such as Maluku's, the ability to write was greatly admired as evidence of the possession of special powers. The written word was accessible to only a select few in the courts among royal scribes or in the villages among local shamans. In both cases the sacred element was present. Though a shaman's memory boards were not writing in a modern sense, the scribbles were nevertheless "read" and formed an important part of the spiritual process. For many court scribes, too, the act of writing was in every sense an act of creation magically causing the deed described to be enacted.[6] With the coming of Islam and Arabic writing, once again writing was seen to be the preserve of a holy few and was in keeping with the earlier experience of spiritually potent individuals possessing the skills to use written materials. The European treaty, consisting of words on paper sworn before the holy books of both the Muslims and the Christians, reaffirmed the Malukan perception of the potency of the written word. In southwest Sulawesi written treaties were preserved with the regalia because they were attributed with powers which could be harnessed for the benefit of the community.[7] As similar reverence for the written word was evident in Maluku, the scribes at court were especially respected and admired.

Since these scribes were principally employed by the court, they had privileged information which could be used to further their own ends or the aims of those whom they supported. The Company therefore suspected that this Javanese family of powerful officials and scribes was behind the refusal of many of the Tidorese to participate in a punitive expedition against Salawati in 1761. But the Dutch ignored a much more basic reason for the opposition. As in 1716–1728, the Tidorese refused to take up arms against the people of the Gamrange and the Papuan islands where family links had been established. Blood ties were always strong in Maluku, and loyalty to the family was of paramount importance. The opposition also reflected the ongoing struggle in Tidore between the sultan and the bobatos. Though the position of sultan had been strengthened considerably by the Europeans, the lords of the land were still able to wield influence among the people. In their struggle the rebellion in the periphery provided an ideal opportunity to undermine the sultan's position.

The Dutch Company was willing to tolerate contraventions of the treaty as long as its overall position in the region was unchallenged. But the atmosphere changed dramatically when the English started to appear in Malukan waters. There was now greater urgency to forestall any crisis which might enable the English to gain a foothold in the area. When Sultan Muhammad Masyud Jamaluddin Syah (r. 1756–1779) became seriously ill, the Dutch forced the Tidore Council to create the office of *raja muda,* or heir apparent, to prevent a succession dispute which could benefit the English. Another preemptive Dutch measure was the removal of all members of the powerful Javanese family from positions of authority in Tidore by 1769. With this family now emasculated and further opposition on the island silenced, the raja muda was encouraged to undertake an expedition against Salawati. The Dutch could no longer allow the periphery territories of either Ternate or Tidore to be too independent from the center because of the presence of the English.

In the campaign against Salawati, the raja muda acknowledged his acceptance of the Company's overlordship by choosing to dress in Dutch clothes and having a bodyguard of Dutch soldiers. Although he was supported by a contingent of warriors from Patani and Gebe, many of their compatriots had sided with the Raja Salawati. The initial attack on the stronghold at Sailolof was only partially successful, but the "rebellion" eventually collapsed because of an epidemic which in fourteen months caused the death of eight hundred defenders. The raja muda saw the unexpected end to the trouble as a sign of divine intervention, calling it a retribution which befell the rebels through his father the sultan's curse. After the surrender he told the assembled crowd of Papuans and Tidorese that, as long as the peace between the Company and Tidore remained in force, there would be no lack of power "to pursue evil subjects with the sword and dislodge them from their hiding places." Even if all the subjects of Tidore were to abandon that kingdom, he continued, the Company would ensure that it was restored to its former glory, just as the Company had done for its friends and allies in the past.[8]

No sooner had the rebellion ended when the area became subject to periodic attacks by strong Iranun fleets from Magindanao. The Iranun were subjects of the Sultan Magindanao and occupied the coastal areas in and around the Pulangi River, Polluc Harbor and Illana Bay, and the inland areas of the large and small Lake Lanao.[9] They became indispensable sailors and warriors of the sultan, and in the eighteenth century they carried out bold raids throughout the archipelago. As Dutch posts in north Sulawesi were especially vulnerable, the Company tried to get both Ternate and Tidore to send kora-koras to ward off their raids. Ternate sent kora-koras manned by the Tobelos, which proved highly effective. Tidore, however, was initially reluctant to become involved. It was reported that a certain Haji Omar was cooperating with the Iranun and had been recently seen in Tidore. Rumors also reached the Dutch of the presence of some 190 Magindanao boats at Maba under the same Haji Omar. Upon investigation it was found that there were only three very large and seventeen smaller Magindanao boats.[10] However, the fear of the Iranun was so great in Maluku that any sighting tended to cause panic among the inhabitants leading to exaggerated reports.

The raids from the southern Philippines had penetrated as far as the Papuan islands. Since it was here that English ships were frequently sighted, the Dutch were convinced that Tidore was involved in some way. In May 1779 Tidore's Sultan Jamaluddin and Raja Muda Kamaluddin Kaicili Asgar, as well as the Sultan Bacan, were seized by order of the Dutch governor. He justified his actions to Batavia by saying that he was implementing secret orders of 1766 to maintain the balance of power between Ternate and Tidore. The decision to make the arrests, he explained, was simply the culmination of a long investigation into the affairs of Tidore and Bacan which had begun in 1758. Both Sultan Jamaluddin and Raja Muda Kamaluddin swore their innocence of the charge of cooperation with the Magindanao raiders, and to pacify the Dutch they even offered to become vassals of the Company and relinquish control over the Gamrange and other areas. Earlier in the century the Company would have eagerly agreed to such an arrangement, but now it was beginning to feel the strains of its financial and military weakness. It believed that local kingdoms were waiting for an opportunity to assist the English in overthrowing the Dutch in the archipelago. Even the new phenomenon of bold and powerful Iranun fleets raiding with impunity throughout the region was regarded as part of a conspiracy to destroy the Company. In this atmosphere of fear, distrust, and despair, Batavia was ready to accept decisions from its officials based oftentimes on nothing but hearsay, thereby alienating the rulers who had once been the Company's greatest supporters.[11]

Unwilling to install another ruler in Tidore who might again challenge the Company, the Dutch governor in Ternate decided to appoint five regents as an interim government until, so he informed the Tidorese, Batavia saw fit to appoint another sultan. The head of the regents was Kaicili Gaijira, a prince of the Tidore royal family, who was assisted by the princess his niece Naicili Hafiatun Nufus. The other four regents represented the spiritual (kali), the pen (hukum), the dagger (jojau), and the fleets (kapita laut).[12] This unusual arrangement was suggested by the governor because of Kaicili Gaijira's lack of experience. He was considered to be a good-natured individual and the most qualified for the throne as the grandson of a famous and greatly respected seventeenth century ruler, Sultan Saifuddin. But his lack of any acquaintance with Dutch customs, or with any of the treaties signed between the Company and Tidore, was regarded by the governor as a serious deficiency. By contrast, he praised Gaijira's fifty-three year old niece, who herself was a descendant of Sultan Saifuddin, knew the contents of all the treaties since the beginning of Dutch presence in Maluku and was greatly loved and revered in Tidore.[13] In structure the government had reverted to a situation of former centuries when it was actually run by a group of elders. To legitimize these changes a treaty was drawn up to which were affixed the seals of the VOC, Ternate, and Tidore. As was the custom, the treaty was read in Ternaten, Tidorese, and Malay, first from the balcony of the governor's residence, then before the Ternaten and Tidorese delegations, and finally throughout both kingdoms.[14]

A well-respected member of Tidore's royal family, Kaicili Nuku, refused to remain under the newly formed government and left Toloa with his followers in 1780 to go to Patani, the site of previous rebellions against Tidore. Somewhere between Weda and Patani he established a temporary base and sent envoys to summon those of Maba, East Seram, and the Papuan islands to join him and those from Magindanao to prepare to retake Tidore. The envoys were also instructed to seek the aid of any Spaniard or Englishman they should meet in these waters.[15] Nuku had his followers load spices on four kora-koras "to accommodate all foreign Europeans, as well as the Mindanao people, whose help and assistance they sought, because . . . the treaties with the Company had expired."[16] Nuku was later proclaimed king over all the Papuan subjects and began a movement to restore Maluku to its former peace and prosperity.

Champion of All Malukans

The VOC refused to recognize Nuku's pretensions and regarded all enmities in the area as simply "piratical activities," which was the official term used to describe any trade or action against Company interests. A Dutch report spoke of "innumerable pirate fleets" manned by those of the Gamrange and the Papuan islands wreaking great destruction everywhere.[17] Among them were also many Tidorese who had accompanied Nuku and now participated in raids on isolated Dutch posts. As time went on there was a note of desperation in Company reports, which spoke of "pirates who are found everywhere and in all seasons," even attacking such distant lands under Company protection as Tabukan, Talaud, and Siau in the north Sulawesi islands. In November and December 1780 the Company, aided by Ternate, attacked Nuku's stronghold in southeast Halmahera. At Weda they found most of the inhabitants had fled to Patani. Maba was destroyed, its fruit trees cut down, and people seized in earlier raids released. But in Patani, the center of resistance, the attack failed because of lack of food and insufficient munitions to lay an effective siege. The defenders were well supplied and occupied a series of nine fortified places one above the other on a mountain slope. The Dutch found it difficult to employ the Halmahera alifuru effectively since they spent much of their time foraging in the woods and mountains for food. The subsequent expedition sent in April 1781 came better prepared and succeeded in burning Patani, releasing 182 captives, and seizing 25 of the principal rebel leaders. By this time, however, Nuku and his followers had already gone to seek a more secure refuge in the Papuan islands.[18]

The Papuan islanders had decided to support Nuku as the legitimate Tidore ruler after being told of Sultan Jamaluddin's exile to Batavia. This news, which was brought to the four Papuan rajas in October 1780, was greeted with silence and obvious distaste, and they refused to swear an oath of allegiance to the Company. From that time on the Papuans gave their full support to Nuku. Their decision to follow Nuku may have been inspired by a strong messianic belief among that group that Koreri, a utopian state reached after the overthrow of the existing social order, was at hand. The seizure by the Dutch of the Papuans' overlord, the Tidore ruler, signaled a radical departure from the norm and prepared the ground for someone like Nuku to appear and be seen as the instrument for the introduction of Koreri.

It is no coincidence that Nuku came to be referred to as Jou Barakati ("Lord of Fortune"), since the Malay word *berkat* (fortune) in its Malukan variations of *barakati* or *barakasi* came to be equated with a future life in Koreri. The term barakati/barakasi is also associated among the Papuan islanders with their word *nanek,* a special force present in the world. It was conceived as something powerful attached to outstanding people, such as shamans and chiefs, and to old people. Their nanek, it was believed, allowed them to confront the obstructive and evil elements present in places and things.[19] Nuku, by taking or being given the title Jou Barakati, was regarded as possessing nanek and became associated with Koreri. By focusing on the messianic messages of Koreri and Jailolo, Nuku was able to appeal to both the Papuan islanders and the north Malukans. In his correspondence with the Dutch he referred to himself purposefully as king of the Papuas and as a scion of the Jailolo royal house, staking claim to legacies which had little substance but immense appeal to the groups concerned.

In June 1781 the Tidore regent Kaicili Gaijira died and his son Kaicili Patra Alam was elected as his successor. On the occasion of his investiture on 17 July 1781 as Sultan Muhammad Mansur Badaruddin, he was required to declare that Sultan Jamaluddin's arrest by the Dutch was just and that the Company had the right to act on behalf of Tidore.[20] Nuku refused to acknowledge the new sultan and claimed that the people continued to give their allegiance to Nuku's brother Sultan Jamaluddin, who had been wrongfully exiled by the Dutch.[21] To illustrate the new ruler's inability to govern, Nuku reported that he had received numerous letters complaining that "the Company now lived among the Tidorese as did the Spaniards in former times, robbing the Tidorese of their homes, their wives, and their children."[22] As a result of the dissatisfaction with the state of affairs in Tidore, two of the five regents appointed by the Dutch fled with their followers to join Nuku. He had solid support within Tidore itself, and he sought to gain further allies by sending separate missions to the coast of Seram, the Seram Laut Islands, Magindanao, the Spaniards in Manila, and the English (most likely at Balambangan, where they had established a post in 1773).[23] Envoys from Magindanao came to Nuku's camp to investigate and were sent home with gifts of a helmet, a gold-knobbed command staff, a silver seal, a flag, a drum, and some gunpowder.[24] The gifts were those associated with sovereignty (the staff, seal, flag, and drum) and with military force (helmet, gunpowder). In this manner Nuku conveyed to Magindanao his acknowledgment of its sovereignty and a request for men to join him in a war.

Nuku remained defiant and escaped capture when expeditions were sent against him in late 1780–1781. Unlike earlier rebellions when the VOC took a rather desultory interest in the events and basically left everything to the native governments, the Company now conducted a campaign against Nuku always with an eye to the growing presence of the English in the region. There was a real fear that Nuku would succeed in gaining English support and threaten Dutch interests in the archipelago. Finally, in late 1781 the Dutch succeeded in defeating Nuku and his supporters among the Gamrange. While Nuku managed to escape to the Papuan islands, the heads of Maba, Weda, and Patani were forced to sign a treaty of submission on 8 November 1781. In article six they were required to do everything in their power to capture Nuku, and in article seven they promised not to "exploit the support and friendship of the Papuans in order to perform evil deeds, but to use all possible means to motivate this nation toward peaceful thoughts and submission to the Company and to their lawful ruler." To prevent their providing any further assistance to Nuku, all the inhabitants of the Gamrange were moved beginning in September 1782 from southeast Halmahera to Payahe on the opposite coast.[25]

The treaty notwithstanding, Nuku was now out of reach of the Dutch and the Gamrange. He had already gone to Salawati where he had reassembled his forces to continue the struggle. Among his strongest supporters was his brother Raja Lukman who had fled Tidore and established his base at Kililuhu on Keffing. In February 1781 Lukman left Nuku in Salawati and returned home to Keffing with twenty kora-koras manned by people from Tidore, East Seram, Patani, and Salawati. He had boasted that with this force, supported by a large Papuan fleet under the command of Nuku himself, he would be soon attacking the Dutch posts in Banda and Ambon. Though the Dutch were on the lookout for the Papuan fleets, they admitted difficulty in overtaking the Papuans on their "incomprehensibly fast boats."[26]

On 11 November 1781 Nuku wrote a letter to the Dutch governor in Ambon in which he called himself "Sri Maha Tuan Sultan Amir Muhammad Saifuddin Syah . . . king of the Papuan areas." In this letter Nuku explained the reason for the rebellion. He, the jojau, the hukum, the bobatos, two gimalahas, a ngofamanyira (a village head), and four hundred Tidorese had gone to the Papuan islands because of their opposition to the Company's decision to exile their ruler Sultan Jamaluddin and appoint Kaicili Gaijira in his place as regent. When Kaicili Gaijira died, he was replaced by his son Kaicili Patra Alam, and no attempts were made to restore the exiled sultan. When this occurred the Tidorese had approached the governor in Fort Orange in Ternate to voice their disapproval of Kaicili Patra Alam as their head. They requested the return of Sultan Jamaluddin or the appointment of either his exiled son Raja Muda Kamaluddin or Kaicili Nuku. The governor refused to pay heed to the requests and provided Patra Alam with guns and ammunition which he then used to attack Toloa in Tidore and burn their homes and possessions. The situation was so desperate that the bobatos brought Nuku to the Papuans where the people proclaimed him sultan.[27]

The Dutch governor in Ambon reported in January 1782 that "Prince Bakanuku" (Nuku) had obtained not only the allegiance of the Papuans but also that of the inhabitants of the north and east coast of Seram, Goram, and even the Christians of Seram's south coast with their interior alifuru. With a vast fleet, including a substantial Tidorese following, Nuku had gone to Hatuana in the northern part of Saparua Island and attacked the Christian villages belonging to the uli lima, the Confederation of Five. His support came from the Muslim settlements of Honimoa in the southern part of Saparua, which formed the uli siwa, the Confederation of Nine.[28] For the local inhabitants their allegiance or antagonism to Nuku attained another dimension based on an old bifurcation of society between the uli lima and the uli siwa. In other areas, too, support or opposition to Nuku often had multilayered significance for the inhabitants, incorporating not only Nuku's messianic appeal but also indigenous cultural elements. Nuku's campaign on the island of Saparua failed dismally, and he narrowly escaped death by swimming to safety.[29]

Even after this setback Nuku managed to attract to his base on the Seram coast a large number of disaffected Tidorese. Soon after Patra Alam was made Sultan Tidore in 1781, there was a revolt among those who supported the exiled heir apparent Kamaluddin. Some three thousand Tidorese gathered at Toloa to demonstrate their opposition to the new sultan, which brought an armed response and the flight of many Tidorese to Nuku.[30] They blamed the Company for the exile of Sultan Jamaluddin and refused to acknowledge Patra Alam who was installed in his place as Sultan Badaruddin. As a result of the Company's direct interference in their choice of ruler, the Tidorese were reported to be harboring an "uncommon hatred" toward the Dutch.[31]

In 1783 the exiled Sultan Jamaluddin died, and the Dutch hoped that the situation in Tidore would improve. They were encouraged by rumors that the Papuans had abandoned Nuku, and so on 1 April 1783 a resolution was passed to send an expedition against him. Tidore was expected to contribute twenty-five kora-koras and a thousand men. To encourage them, a price was put on both Nuku's and Raja Lukman's heads, much in the way that the Portuguese had earlier encouraged the Ternatens against the Tidorese in the sixteenth century.[32] The Dutch Governor Alexander Cornabé also offered a reward of 100 ducatoons and a rattan cane with a gold knob for important chiefs and a silver knob for lesser chiefs who conducted themselves bravely in battle. A large supply of cloth was to be brought along to be used to ransom any captive VOC servants and subjects. After the fleet departed, it was joined by nine kora-koras from Maba, Patani, and Gebe and ten kora-koras from certain Papuan settlements. An assembled fleet of twenty-nine kora-koras and eleven hundred men was thus sent in pursuit of Nuku and Raja Lukman at Kililuhu on Keffing.[33]

The expedition proved to be a total disaster for the Company. The Tidorese and their Gamrange and Papuan allies killed the pro-Dutch Tidore jojau, as well as the Dutch commander and his men, and then seized the fleet and brought it to Nuku. In a letter secretly sent to Sultan Badaruddin on 21 September 1783, the Tidore sangajis, gimalahas, and other heads who had been on the expedition explained why they had defected to Nuku:

We ask forgiveness, but we will not return unless you abandon the Company. If you do not, the land of Tidore will be destroyed because truly the might of your father Nuku in Seram is very great. His followers are many because the kings of the north, the south, and the entire east are assisting your father and sending warriors, all inclined to fight against the Company. . . . O Lord and Great King, be not ashamed. We sangajis and gimalahas will soon be with our Lord. But if our Lord is afraid and continues to follow the Company, that will be very damaging, for we servants would regard this to mean that the land of Tidore and the Company will remain steadfast and loyal in these times. . . . Lord, we place our honor under your foot and trust that everything in the land of Tidore will be in a state of readiness and strengthened, and that the cannon again will be placed in the old fort. Send the Dutch away from Tidore before our arrival, which will be in the month Shawal [September]. Tell the sangajis and gimalahas to prepare their settlements for our coming because we, your twelve servants, will bring with us the Patani people, as well as those of Weda, Gebe, the Papuans, and a group from Ternaten Halmahera, all of whom have an aversion for the Company. There are also some from Seram, Goram, and Onin. With respect to our Lord and King, some of those of Seram and Goram have come under the authority and leadership of your father [Nuku], as have the groups from Onin (from Kubiace [Puat Besi?] and Kasvoye [Kasyu?]), Aru, Tanimbar, Timor, Mosso [?], and Ambon. From the south will come a force of Bugis and Mandarese with more than a hundred boats, from Makassar and Bonerate another hundred boats or more, and from the settlements on Banggai, Pasir, and Butung a further hundred or more boats. There are yet other places which your servants have not mentioned, such as Magindanao, with more than hundred boats, Borneo, and many others in the north, which your servants cannot name with their multitudes, but which Our Lord will witness upon our arrival. In addition there will be fourteen English ships.[34]

The letter reveals the attitudes of the Tidore leaders who had joined Nuku but probably represented a view shared by many in Maluku. There is little question that they regarded Nuku as of higher status than Sultan Badaruddin, referring to Nuku as the Sultan Tidore's "father." There was no resentment toward Badaruddin, but a considerable antipathy toward the Company. The Company's arrest and exile of both the sultan and raja muda of Tidore in 1779, as well as the appointment of a group of five to rule the kingdom, were seen as a gross interference in the affairs of the kingdom. In the past the Company had been content to express its aims and encourage their implementation by native governments, though sometimes with aid from the Company. This arrangement allowed the rulers to appease the Company while still being seen as sovereign lords by their subjects. But the audacious act of arresting and exiling Tidore's ruler and heir apparent upset established conventions and proprieties. Indeed, the Company came to be blamed as one of the causes of the general upheaval besetting Maluku.

Nuku, on the other hand, was regarded as a champion of all Maluku and therefore enjoyed considerable support. The letter implied a "universal" approval for Nuku in speaking of "kings of the north, the south, and the entire east" sending fighting men and ships to him. The enumeration of known areas, as well as those "which your servants cannot name with their multitudes," which the letter claims would send boats and warriors to support Nuku, is in the form of an incantation or a refrain in an oral tale. What was being conveyed was the sense of the entire Maluku world and those on its periphery, including the English, supporting Nuku's just cause. In a more sober assessment of Nuku's strength, the Dutch governor at Ambon estimated that Nuku's following consisted of one hundred Tidorese, six hundred Papuans from the various islands, and about eighty slaves from the north coast of Seram.[35]

Support for Nuku on Tidore was overwhelming, leaving Sultan Badaruddin little choice but to support Nuku and follow the instructions contained in the letter. In mid-October 1783 the Tidorese seized the Dutch forts on their island and murdered all the Europeans stationed there, including the twenty Dutch bodyguards assigned to the Sultan Tidore.[36] Badaruddin and his chief supporter, the Hukum Doi, then declared war on the Company. Nuku was fetched from Bacan, where he had gone with his fleet from his base in Seram. He arrived in Tidore at the head of two hundred boats "bristling with people from all nations." Then on 26 October some seventy kora-koras and small boats, all flying the royal flag upside down, sailed from Tidore and landed on the southern coast of Ternate. The leaders of the fleet assembled on the shore for a conference and then left as suddenly as they had come.[37]

As at the death of a leader when the inversion of the ordinary world is marked by symbolic gestures, the flying of the Tidore royal flag upside down was a clear sign of spiritual upheaval. The old world had passed away, and a new one was being created by Nuku. His survival against huge odds and his ability to attract and retain supporters "from all nations" convinced many people that he had that special quality reserved for those destined for greatness. The disaster which befell the joint punitive expedition sent against him consisting of forces from the VOC, Tidore, and Ternate was seen as a sign confirming Nuku's "prowess," his barakati or mana. Among the Malukans this special character was manifested through spectacular achievements, which had earned Nuku the title Jou Barakati, "The Lord possessing Mana."

Sultan Aharal of Ternate (r. 1781–1796) was shaken by the Tidore gesture and quickly came to Fort Orange to ask for refuge for himself and his family. The Dutch agreed to his request but reprimanded him saying that he should remain behind at the head of his own people. The sultan claimed that, although he had ordered his people to assemble to fight Nuku, only enough people came to outfit thirteen kora-koras. The Dutch later discovered that in fact none of the Ternatens had answered the summons, and those who came were the slaves of the sultan and the princes. After the defeat of Ternate's fleet at the hands of Nuku at Patinti Straits, the Ternatens had a "great fear" of Nuku and began to believe in his mana. Nuku himself contributed to his reputation by sending emissaries to Kau and Sahu to spread stories of his alliance with the English. It was reported that on board the English ships were cannon so large that a man could easily crawl into them and so powerful that they required two vats of powder to fire one of them. Moreover, the cannonballs were reputed to be so heavy that four men were needed to lift a single one. These emissaries also told the Ternatens that Nuku, the English, and "hundreds of native peoples" would destroy the Dutch presence in Ternate, Ambon, Banda, and Makassar.[38]

The Dutch Company decided to punish Tidore for its support of

Nuku. It assembled a joint Ternaten and Dutch expedition which crossed over to Tidore on 1 November 1783. They moved down the east coast of Tidore and faced heavy bombardment from the forts at Tahula, Gammafu, and Cobbo-Cobbo. At the first sign of fighting, some fifty Maba boats crossed over from Halmahera to support the Tidorese. Tahula was taken on 5 November, but Gammafu proved to be more formidable because it was an "extraordinarily strong and barely scalable nest" high on the mountain slopes. The Ternatens and the Dutch were able to subdue it only by using a secret route from the south and surprising the defenders. Many of the men fled to safety, but the women and children sheltering in the fort were massacred by the Ternaten Halmahera alifuru. The people's and sultan's goods stored for safekeeping in the fortification at Gammafu were seized by the invaders, and the looting continued for three days. The royal capital at Soa Sio, described as a "truly most splendid city" as a result of the efforts of Sultan Amir (r. 1728–1756) to make it more like a Dutch town, was seized after heavy fighting which resulted in the burning of the sultan's residence and mosque.

The expedition then continued southward around the island and turned northward on the west side of Tidore burning the settlements of Seli, Tongowai, Gurabati, and Jeppo. Tomalou was the next target, but its strong fortifications kept the invaders at bay until it too fell on 15 November after heavy fighting. A reinforced Ternaten fleet of seventy kora-koras was then sent to Mareku to prevent the escape of Sultan Badaruddin and his officials and to destroy nearby Toloa.[39] On 18 November the Ternatens and the Dutch were preparing to attack Mareku when three of the most prominent leaders of Toloa appeared with their hands placed together in front of their faces in the traditional gesture of greeting and respect. They came asking for forgiveness and offered to surrender. The following day the entire population of Mareku descended from their settlement "without weapons and with a submissive bearing," and were later followed by Badaruddin, his younger brother Kaicili Puasa, and the sultan's wives and family. The Hukum Doi escaped but was later killed in battle and beheaded by the Sangaji Galela.[40] Governor Cornabé in reporting the victory to Batavia wrote with satisfaction that the Tidorese had been so thoroughly castigated that they had "no roof over their heads and so many of their women and friends killed that the spilled European blood had been repaid a hundredfold." All Tidore's food supplies were set alight, and the boats the Tidorese used to fetch food from Halmahera were seized or hacked to pieces. The English claimed that some eighteen hundred Tidorese had been killed in the fighting or had subsequently died of starvation.[41]

The treaty signed between the Dutch Company and Tidore on 17 December 1783 formally placed Tidore on the same level as Ternate as a vassal of the Company according to Western European international law. Cornabé did not name a new sultan because he preferred to have the kingdom ruled by sangajis and gimalahas responsive to his wishes. But Batavia overruled him, explaining that "it would be better for all the people of Tidore to be ruled by a king than by many heads."[42] Nevertheless, article seven of the treaty explicitly left all decisions of importance in the hands of the Dutch governor. New sangajis were appointed and provided with rattan canes with silver knobs, which were the symbols of office given by the Company to its subjects. Though the sangajis were obliged by treaty to deliver all the leading rebels to the Company for punishment, many had already fled while others taken prisoner earlier had been killed by the Ternatens who claimed they were "trying to escape."[43] Despite Badaruddin's attempts to exonerate himself by blaming the war on his officials, he was deposed and arrested by the Dutch, along with many of his princes.

The remaining Tidorese on the island would have preferred Nuku to be their next ruler, but they realized he would be unacceptable to the Dutch. They therefore requested that Kamaluddin, the former heir apparent then living in exile in Ceylon, be returned as their sultan. If Kamaluddin could not be brought back, they asked that any other prince but Patra Alam be appointed because they blamed him for the disasters which had befallen Tidore.[44] The bobatos argued that any of the four princes—Kamaluddin, Mossel, van der Parra, or Hassan— would be acceptable. A new sultan, they explained further, would be necessary to regain the allegiance of the Gamrange and the Papuan islands.[45] The Company took their advice and brought back Kamaluddin to become the next ruler. While large numbers of people from Tidore and its distant territories came to welcome the new sultan back from exile, the Patanese and the Papuan islanders were conspicuously absent. They were still among the strongest supporters of Nuku, and so the Dutch refused to extend to them letters of pardon.[46] On 18 October 1784, Sultan Hairul Alam Kamaluddin Kaicili Asgar was installed as ruler over a land which the Dutch called "a free, indivisible, and nonhereditary vassal of the Company."[47]

With the installation of the new sultan, many Tidorese returned home and refused to leave the island again because of the general turmoil prevailing throughout Maluku. They dared not go to sea to fish nor to make the hazardous expedition to Halmahera to tend their gardens and prepare sago. Even the hewing of wood and the making of lime, which they were required to perform as part of their treaty obligations, were neglected. The Company's decision to detain Sultan Kamaluddin on Ternate to prevent his joining Nuku worsened the situation. The reason the Company gave for this unpopular decision was that the royal residence had been destroyed in the last war, and there had been some dispute whether it should be reestablished at Soa Sio or at Toloa.

Kamaluddin was given a royal residence within walking distance of Fort Orange in Malayu, and he was joined a short time later by large numbers of followers. They came on all types of boats which crammed the shore making it difficult for the Dutch burgers and the Ternaten fishermen to beach their own boats.[48]

The presence of both sultans on one island brought inevitable clashes between the Ternatens and the Tidorese. Ternaten boats would frequently go past the Sultan Tidore's residence without striking their sails as a sign of courtesy. At a feast given by the Dutch for both rulers, Kamaluddin caused great commotion by appearing in the presence of the Sultan Ternate with an unsheathed sword, a sign understood by all to mean that he contemplated war with Ternate. It was common knowledge that Kamaluddin was being urged by his followers to avenge the destruction and the deaths caused by the recent Dutch-Ternaten invasion of Tidore, and so the threat was taken seriously by the Company.[49]

Nuku's support in Tidore continued to grow. It was reported that the Tidore jojau was in secret contact with Nuku and that Kamaluddin himself had confidently asserted that no Tidorese would think of harming Nuku. Despite the Dutch-Ternaten victory in Tidore, the periphery was still in Nuku's hands. It was impossible to sail into Papuan or East Seram waters without Nuku's safe conduct pass, and there were persistent rumors that he was soon to receive English assistance. To counter these rumors the Dutch widely publicized Nuku's failure to gain English support from Bengal. It was later reported by the Dutch post in west coast Sumatra, however, that the English had brought two of Nuku's envoys to meet the English governor-general in Calcutta and that they had safely returned at the end of 1786.[50] English country traders, rather than officials of the English East India Company, were involved in attempting to convince the Company's leaders in Calcutta of the commercial value of supporting Nuku. To Nuku they pretended to be representatives of the Calcutta government.[51]

The Dutch feared that Nuku would provide the English with an opportunity to reestablish a strong foothold in Maluku which had been destroyed by Coen in 1623. Since the mid-eighteenth century English interest in the highly lucrative China trade had led to the exploration of a faster route to China and the discovery of an important passage through the Papuan islands and New Guinea. This new route enabled the English to go from the southern tip of Africa and from India to China, even during the countervailing winds of the northeast monsoon. The route required sailing between the islands of Obi and Seram and then into the Pacific Ocean through the narrow stretch of water between Batanta and Salawati called "Pitt's Strait" (and then "Pitt's Passage" or "Eastern Passage") by the English and Sagewin Straits by the Dutch.

Increased English shipping through Maluku began in the 1760s, and by the 1770s Pitt's Passage was used regularly by those involved in the China trade. But it was only after Thomas Forrest's voyages to Maluku in 1774–1775 that the English realized the possibility of obtaining political advantage in the area because of Nuku's rebellion. Nuku openly styled himself "Sultan over the Papuas and Seram," the two most vital parts of the eastern passage. The English stopped regularly on Seram's north coast to load drinking water, and the straits themselves lay in the heart of the Papuan islands. These Papuan areas, rightfully called the most beautiful pearl of the Sultan Tidore's crown, were firmly in Nuku's hands by the mid-1770s. Nuku's control and his long and successful opposition to the Dutch made him a logical ally of the English.[52]

Nuku's appeal to the Tidorese was at first threatened by the return of Kamaluddin as Sultan Tidore. However, the Company's decision to force Kamaluddin to prove his loyalty by sending an expedition against Nuku simply reaffirmed the latter as the only truly independent leader of the Tidorese. News of the expedition reached Nuku in plenty of time for him to leave his base on the Lamangsai River between Hote and Waru on the northeast coast of Seram and seek safety among his Papuan subjects at Kaipoko on the island of Misool in November 1788. It was initially reported that only ten Tidorese and twenty to thirty slaves accompanied him to Misool, but it was later confirmed that he had received a reinforcement of sixteen boats, including ten junks from Kililuhu on Keffing and Goram.[53] In addition he had the full support of the Raja Onin on the New Guinea mainland and the Raja Salawati. In December 1789 a combined Dutch-Tidore fleet attacked and destroyed Salawati, forcing the people to surrender and swear allegiance to Tidore. A certain Prince Aruwé was then made the new Raja Salawati in February 1790.[54] Nuku was not in Salawati during the attack, nor was he established in any single base. To avoid the Dutch he had adopted the tactic of moving constantly among his followers in the Seram and Papuan islands. On his peregrinations he was accompanied by a strong force from Tidore, East Seram, the Papuan islands, and Tobelo. Another source of support came from the Aru Islands, including Bugis and Balinese settlers, who arrived at Keffing to offer Nuku their assistance.[55] Unlike all previous challenges to the Dutch East India Company, Nuku's was characterized by a wide appeal which crossed all previous political and cultural boundaries.

Toward the end of the eighteenth century, Nuku gained a reprieve from Dutch attack because of the greatly increased Iranun raids on Malukan coastal settlements beginning in the late 1770s. With their large boats outfitted with cannon, the Iranun even successfully attacked some of the smaller European ships. They had become so powerful by the late 1780s that they were said to take little notice of their overlord, the Sultan Magindanao.[56] What worried the Dutch in Maluku was the report that one of the Iranun leaders, a Datu Kiama, had joined another "pirate leader," Haji Omar, who had been in contact with Nuku. The impunity with which the Iranun fleets roamed the seas around Java and Sulawesi made the Company fear an attack on their Maluku posts as had happened in Riau in 1787. Batavia therefore ordered the Dutch governor in Ternate in 1790 to retain all the subjects of the Malukan rulers at home and not send them on any further expeditions against Nuku.[57] This decision enabled Nuku to recover from Dutch attacks and to rebuild his following while the Company was preoccupied with the Iranun threat.

On 12 October 1790 the Dutch Company officials at Amboina interviewed the brother of Sultan Kamaluddin of Tidore, Kaicili Malikuddin, who had been living in exile in Seram. From him they received an abbreviated but revealing account of Nuku's rebellion from the point of view of a Nuku supporter. According to this version Nuku had first fled to Patani where he was declared sultan, and then had left to seek safety in Seram. His move had been prompted by the arrival of a Dutch force sent to punish those followers of Nuku who had killed some people from Loloda. To seek justice, the Kapita Laut Loloda had informed the Dutch of Nuku's whereabouts, thus leading to the expedition. A second Dutch-Tidorese campaign against Nuku had ended with defeat and the death of both the Dutch commander and the Tidore jojau. This victory had so encouraged Nuku that he had gone on the offensive with a sizable fleet, burning Makian and plundering Mareku in Tidore.

As Nuku's successes mounted, his reputation as the lord possessing barakati or mana was enhanced. The Tidorese began flocking to his camp and were joined by others from Maba, Patani, Weda, Tobelo, and the Papuan islands. With a combined fleet of about two hundred boats, Nuku launched an attack on Ternate but failed to dislodge the Dutch from Fort Orange. Some four or five days later the Dutch and their Ternaten allies raised a fleet of two Dutch two-masted sloops, a *pancalang* (a small local sailing vessel), and a hundred Ternaten korakoras and sailed across the narrow strip of water to challenge Nuku on Tidore. At daybreak they had begun firing on the Sultan Tidore's residence and on the boats anchored in the harbor. The sultan and his entire court fled to Tomalou, but returned three days later accompanied by their people. It was then that Malikuddin had taken the opportunity to flee, first to Maidi on Halmahera and then to Misool where he had remained for a year. Since life was difficult on Misool he had moved to the Masiwang River on Seram, which was a whole day's and night's journey from Misool. He had later been invited to settle at Rarakit, where he had remained eking out a living by fishing and selling sago to the people of Goram.[58]

Through further questioning the Dutch learned that Nuku was called "Sultan Tidore" among the ordinary people in Tidore, some Papuans, and those from the Gamrange. Nuku did not arouse the same affection among the princes and many members of the Tidore Council, however, principally because he had favored and rewarded those who had accompanied him. There were five princes who had been with Nuku from the beginning and had been given high posts, and another nine bobatos were also well placed in the government. His large following included those from Tidore, the Gamrange, Geser, Seram Laut, Uring (on Hitu), and the Ternaten subjects from Tobelo. Among the people of Seram, those most inclined toward him were from the settlements of Waru, Kiliha (or Kilitai), Waras-Waras, and some from Keta, Kwaos and Keffing. The people of Kiliwaru were "great friends and supporters of Nuku," and they named him their raja. His greatest backing came from the people of Kililuhu on the island of Keffing, who went regularly to Banda to buy gunpowder, ammunition, and cloth and then traded them to Nuku for tripang or sea cucumber, Papuan slaves, tortoiseshell, and other local goods.

The widespread support which Nuku enjoyed in Maluku was evident in the makeup of his government. The Jojau Bandang, who was second in command, was from Tidore. Next in line were three of Nuku's chief lieutenants, then the three imams, and finally the two hukums—the Hukum Tajuddin from Soa Sio in Tidore and the Hukum Gimalaha from Kampung Jodi. Someone from the Keta settlement on Seram was made syahbandar, an elder from Kilitai the kapita laut, and two individuals from Maba and Geser his scribes. A major responsibility of the scribes was to transmit Nuku's orders to the people on Seram and the surrounding islands which acknowledged his authority. Among his advisors were two people from Maba, the Gimalaha Galela, the Imam Loloda, and someone from Mareku. It was these advisors who appear to have had the task of attempting to persuade others in Tobelo, Maba, Weda, Patani, Seram, and Goram to join Nuku.

Malikuddin further reported that Nuku had spent about a year on Salawati and some other Papuan islands, and a longer time at Rarakit and Waru on Seram. He had then sought refuge in the settlement of Kataloka on Goram, an island surrounded by an extraordinarily large coral reef which made access very difficult. He had settled there under the protection of five thousand fighting men living in fourteen fortified settlements on the island. The people had earlier moved to Manawoka, Kei, and islands further south to escape the annual Dutch tribute-collecting *hongi* expeditions. They had gradually returned once the Dutch discontinued the expeditions during Nuku's presence in the region.[59]

In 1792 Nuku renewed his links with the English East India Company government in India through the English country traders from

Bengal, thereby raising hopes of greater English involvement in Maluku's affairs. It was a sorely needed psychological boost since his following had been decimated by a smallpox epidemic which had been especially severe in Tidore and the Papuan islands.[60] Fortunately for Nuku, the loss was compensated by increasing numbers of Ternaten subjects joining the more than four hundred Galelas, Tobelos, and Tobarus already in his camp.[61] For the people of Maluku the choice was clearcut: Nuku or the VOC. Both the rulers of Ternate and Tidore were virtual hostages to Company policies and were regarded merely as mouthpieces for the Dutch. In 1793 Sultan Kamaluddin of Tidore complained that his subjects, especially those of Patani, no longer obeyed him.[62] As the Ternate and Tidore rulers came to be reduced to mere channels of Company policies, Nuku came to be regarded as the champion of all Malukans whatever their previous allegiances.

Nuku's "Revolution"

Nuku was clearly convinced that the time was ripe for action when he sent envoys to all the Papuan rulers to participate in a "momentous expedition to effect, if it were possible, an unprecedented revolution in the kingdoms of Ternate and Tidore by overthrowing both sultans and making him ruler of both."[63] Nuku himself realized the import of what he proposed by regarding it a "revolution," though the exact term he used is not clear from the Dutch translation. Despite the demise of Jailolo and the impotence of Bacan, the maintenance of the dualism between the remaining two pillars of Ternate and Tidore was seen to be a guarantee of the survival of the world of Maluku. By the late eighteenth century Nuku had sensed the widespread concern that the Dutch East India Company had already undermined if not destroyed the essential dualism of Ternate and Tidore. The Dutch governor in a missive to Batavia proudly commented on the fact that both the sultans of Ternate and Tidore, "under our direction," were friendly toward each other, "which is viewed with amazement by the very old Malukans."[64] What appeared to the governor as a major triumph was viewed with considerable misgivings by the elders of the community. For the latter the spectacle of the rulers of Ternate and Tidore behaving publicly as friends was contrary to the proper performance of their dualism and signaled a breakdown in relationships. It was in this context that Nuku proclaimed his intention to restore the four pillars and hence reestablish proprieties in Maluku.

In 1795 for the first time Nuku's pretensions appeared attainable. Iranun raids were taxing the resources of the VOC, and their successful conquest of the Dutch post in Riau in 1787 had greatly damaged the

Company's prestige in the archipelago. As the standing of the Dutch among the Malukans declined, the reputation of the English rose. Unconfirmed reports flowed into Fort Orange of the establishment of an English post at Dore on the Birdshead in New Guinea and of Nuku's offer to deliver the entire Papuan islands to the English. Rumors of English plans to join Nuku in seizing Ternate were nervously dismissed by the Dutch. They considered it "unthinkable that the English who are our allies [in Europe] would openly conspire with Nuku to do us harm."[65] But the Ternaten royal family was much more ready to believe Nuku than the Dutch. Many Ternate princes and princesses sought permission to go with their families to Batavia because they expected no protection from Sultan Aharal (r. 1781–1796) and were convinced that the Dutch in Maluku would be no match for Nuku and the English. Aharal's reputation had been sullied in the eyes of his subjects because of his intimate association with the Dutch. The ruler of Tobunku, one of Ternate's vassal lords, attributed the weakness of Ternate to the fact that the sultan himself was not of royal blood but a descendant of a Bugis father. Many Galelas and Tobelos who refused to serve him had fled and received refuge in Tobunku, while Banggai showed by frequent rebellion its dissatisfaction with the Sultan Ternate's failure to appoint a new ruler in Banggai in 1784.[66]

On 29 August 1795 a letter from Nuku, using the title "Paduka Sri Sultan Saidul Jihad Muhammad Nabus Amiruddin Syah Kaicili Parang,[67] king of all the settlements and lands which obey me," was sent to Sultan Kamaluddin of Tidore. It read: "I have the honor, Your Highness, to inform you that the English [East India] Company and I are in agreement. I therefore await your intention toward me, and I beseech Your Highness to be not afraid; govern Tidore and its people quietly and with all caution so that no evil can befall you from the Dutch Company as occurred to Patra Alam." The letter went on to ask Kamaluddin to keep the contents a secret from the Dutch as well as from his own councillors. As soon as the English ships were ready, he would inform Kamaluddin "and hope in God's Name that Tidore would act together with him in peace."[68] The Dutch intercepted the letter and used it to force Kamaluddin to write to Nuku urging him to surrender and live the remainder of his life in peace and quiet. By "proper handling" of Nuku, so the VOC directors believed, the rebellion could be brought to a satisfactory end. Nuku quickly dashed any hopes for a quick solution when he told the Dutch that "he had no wish to live in peace and friendship with the Company." Batavia then directed that Nuku be given the northeast coast of Seram as his appanage under the Sultan Tidore and the Company. Because of the futility of such an offer, the Dutch officials in Ternate simply ignored Batavia's directive.[69]

Nuku could reject all peace offerings from the Dutch because he was confident of English support. Once the English had established a post in Dore in 1793, Nuku was able to make frequent contact with the country traders who roamed freely in the Papuan region. These traders quickly learned to fly the red English ensign and not the Union Jack since the Papuans associated the red, white, and blue with the Dutch flag. Nuku was able to obtain cannon, guns, gunpowder, and other war matériel from them, and in 1795 he sent two envoys, one of whom was Kaicili Ibrahim of the Ternate royal family, with an English ship to Bengal to seek further assistance against the Dutch. Though Bengal refused to commit itself, the country traders continued to offer Nuku supplies and a promise of military aid. Nuku's persistence was finally rewarded because of events far removed from Maluku. The Prince of Orange and Stadhouder of the Netherlands, living in exile in London since the Napoleonic invasion of his country, issued what became known as the Kew Letters requesting that the English move into the Dutch overseas territories to prevent their falling into the hands of the French. The English were quick to take advantage of the Letters to move into areas which had long been officially closed to them. So in March 1796 both Ambon and Banda were occupied by the English, raising Dutch fears that the local rulers would soon abandon them. In April 1796 the Dutch claimed to have uncovered a plot between the Ternaten ruler and the English to overthrow the VOC. Acting on this intelligence the Dutch passed a secret resolution dated 29 April deposing Sultan Aharal and replacing him with Kaicili Sarkan (r. 1796–1801).[70]

As soon as Nuku learned of the English seizure of Ambon, he went to join them with a fleet of a hundred boats and three thousand men on 15 May 1796. With his large entourage of a hundred bobatos and princes, Nuku paid a call on the English governor. The latter was impressed by Nuku, whom he described as dignified and well acquainted with European ways and table manners. He was, however, less complimentary about Nuku's boats, which he described as "trifling vessels," though "they go from place to place with great dispatch and can carry a great number of men." The governor could not grant Nuku's immediate request for assistance, but he did offer the hope that, once the English took possession of Maluku, Nuku's branch of the royal family would rule.[71] In that same year Nuku temporarily took control of Jailolo with the help of the English and installed a former Tidore jojau as the new Jailolo ruler. Although the latter was unable to assume control over his kingdom until some time later, he bore the title and was acknowledged as the Sultan Jailolo.[72]

With the installation of the Sultan Jailolo, Nuku symbolically proclaimed to the local inhabitants the restoration of Maluku and the beginning of a new era of peace and prosperity. It seems to have mattered little that the new Sultan Jailolo was a former jojau of Tidore. What was important was the fact that Jailolo had been restored as the fourth pillar in Maluku. Nuku's subsequent activities were intended to preserve the perception that a restoration had occurred. On 21 March 1797 Nuku seized Bacan with the help of the English, and at Gita he sent envoys to the sangaji and gimalaha at Mare and obtained their allegiance. They agreed to go as special emissaries to the Tidore court to demand the surrender of the regalia. The English authorities were wary of providing too much support to Nuku, and so it was left to individual English country traders to continue to supply Nuku with arms for his bid to recapture Tidore.

Nuku's fleet of seventy boats and an English ship arrived at the Tidore royal settlement on 12 April only to learn that Sultan Kamaluddin and his Dutch bodyguard had already fled to Ternate. Later that evening most of the Tidorese who had brought the sultan to Ternate returned secretly to join Nuku. Because the Dutch feared treachery among the Tidorese still remaining on Ternate, they sent the rest back to Tidore leaving Kamaluddin with no followers. Between 25 and 29 April Nuku launched three attacks on Ternate, but even his formidable fleet of 150 boats could not overcome the Dutch Company defenses. The two English ships which were with Nuku did not participate in the fighting and left at the end of the month. Nuku had to be content with maintaining a blockade of Ternate and consolidating his position on Tidore. By December the blockade was taking effect, and the Dutch in Fort Orange were reduced to eating horse, dog, and cat meat to stay alive. Though the Dutch were able to hold out behind their fortifications, the Ternatens deserted their island to seek safety elsewhere.[73]

By the beginning of 1798 the English navy was moving toward closer cooperation with Nuku despite the official policy of noninterference. The English government in Madras wanted no further moves beyond Banda and Ambon, but when William Farquhar became governor of Ambon in January 1799 he regarded an alliance with Nuku and the capture of Ternate as crucial in promoting English interests in Maluku. One of the first positive acts of assistance Farquhar provided Nuku was to exile to Madras both of Nuku's erstwhile allies, Kaicili Ibrahim of Ternate and Raja Muda Zainal Abidin of Tidore. Both had pretensions to the Ternate and Tidore crowns and had begun to defy Nuku openly by seizing the tribute sent to him by the Papuans from the Raja Ampat Islands and the New Guinea coast.[74] The Dutch, meanwhile, had sent envoys to Halmahera to reassemble Ternate's subjects for a counterattack, which came in July and November. On both occasions the invaders were repulsed, and Nuku remained firmly ensconced as the Sultan Tidore at the dawn of the nineteenth century.[75]

The Dutch East India Company was officially absorbed by the

Dutch government at the end of 1799 , and the Company directors were replaced by the Council of Asian Possessions in May 1800. The change-over of authority simply encouraged Farquhar to take direct action in Maluku. On 11 February 1801 the English attacked Ternate but failed to take Fort Orange. With the help of Nuku they tried again on 4 May but were again repulsed. Finally on the third attempt they succeeded, forcing the Dutch to accept a ceasefire on 20 June 1801. Despite the eventual success of the campaign, the English governments in Bengal and Madras both reprimanded those who had initiated it as being con-trary to their instructions. But the deed was done. On 22 June 1801 Farquhar proclaimed Nuku the new Sultan Tidore, and a treaty was signed between the English and Tidore which was quite unlike anything the local kingdoms had ever signed with the Dutch. It stressed the "mutuality of relationship" and had only the vaguest hint of Tidore's dependence on the English. The latter offered protection to Nuku and assured him an annuity of 6,000 Spanish dollars in return for the deliv-ery of spices.[76] Having had time to observe the Dutch spice eradication policy, the English decided it was futile and that even "the entire army of Bonaparte would not be able to complete this task of destruction."[77]

The arrangement for the delivery of spices for a specific compen-sation was an acceptable trade relationship, and there were no demands for the destruction of spice trees. It was the eradication policy of the Dutch treaties which was so greatly resented by the Malukans because the spice trees were the principal source of revenue for the court and the people. In contrast, the terms of the English treaty were much more in keeping with the Malukan idea of creating a mutually beneficial rela-tionship. A definite hierarchy was established with the English as "pro-tector," which in Malukan society was an honored status with great responsibilities and obligations. In return for this protection, the "pro-tected" served their lord in whatever way deemed appropriate. Such a relationship could be severed when one party or the other was seen to be no longer fulfilling its obligations. While the status of the "protector" was high, those "protected" were seen to be crucial in maintaining the high status of their lord. They provided labor to create wealth and num-bers to enhance prestige. There was therefore mutual trust and respect, a feature much more evident in the English document than in any of the treaties signed with the Dutch.

The culmination of Nuku's long rebellion was his installation as sultan, an emotional occasion which Farquhar captured in the following description: "On the 12th November 1801 Newco [Nuku] was solemnly crowned in Fort Orange Sultaun of Tidore an honor which he had been fighting with the Dutch to obtain for twenty years. It must have been an inexpressible satisfaction to the old man sixty-six years of age, perfectly decrepid from persecution and continual hardships, to have still accomplished the darling object of his heart before death and the pleasing reflection will no doubt contribute in a powerful degree to render his latter days a scene of happiness to himself and grateful thanksgiving to the English."[78] Unfortunately for Nuku, the English were not to remain long in Ternate. In the Peace of Amiens of 27 March 1802 they were required to relinquish all areas claimed by the Dutch except for Ceylon. Thus they left Ternate on 23 May and Ambon on 23 June 1803, abandoning Maluku to the Dutch as in 1623.[79]

After the departure of the English, Nuku continued to fly the English flag from the royal settlement of Soa Sio in Tidore in defiance of the Dutch. His independence was further demonstrated in negotiations for a new treaty with the Dutch in 1803. For the first time in many years a Maluku ruler was able to lay down certain conditions for agreement. Nuku demanded that the ruler of Tidore be given an annual subsidy equal to that of the Sultan Ternate, but that the ruler of Tidore be regarded as of higher status. In accordance with this new elevated status, he wanted Makian to be given the choice of belonging either to Ternate or Tidore. Finally, he insisted that the Sultan Jailolo be recognized as an independent lord.[80] While the first two conditions were part of the ongoing struggle for dominance in the dualism, the final condition was an important attempt to restore the four kingdoms in Maluku—Ternate, Tidore, Jailolo, and Bacan. He voiced a deep concern, shared by many in Maluku, that the troubles in the region had been a result of the undermining of the four pillars. With the reestablishment of an independent Jailolo, Nuku and many others believed that the unity and harmony of Maluku would be restored. In addition to presenting these conditions, Nuku also rejected some of the articles proposed by the Dutch because they were contrary to former treaties kept in Tidore's "book."[81]

Governor Willem Cranssen was unwilling to accede to any of the conditions until Nuku confessed his misdeeds against the Dutch, sought forgiveness, and promised to improve his conduct. Nuku complied with Cranssen's requests and expressed his willingness to sign a treaty, such as that concluded with Simon de Cos in 1660 based on equality or, in Malukan convention, a relationship of "brothers." The Dutch thus agreed to the restoration of the title and position of "Sultan Jailolo" and the allocation of the area on Halmahera at Kayosa, south of Dodinga, as his kingdom. Cranssen also agreed to offer Nuku an annual subsidy and to seek Batavia's approval for the condition regarding Makian's choice of overlord. In writing to Batavia, Cranssen secretly advised a delay in meeting Nuku's demands because he believed that Nuku's death was imminent. Relations between Nuku and the VOC grew steadily worse, and a virtual state of war again existed between the two at the time of Nuku's death on 14 November 1805.[82]

Restoration and Innovation

In his lifetime Nuku was known as Jou Barakati, or "Lord of Fortune."
He was one of those rare individuals who spring up in Southeast Asian
history imbued with a certain spiritual quality, an aura which people
recognize and hence follow. It is these figures possessed of mana (or fortune or prowess) who transform the old and provide the basis for a
reconstruction of a new order. Nuku's activities would have been readily comprehensible in Maluku because they followed a well-trodden
path. Ternaten traditions speak of a time when their island was transformed into a dynamic center through the skills and special powers of
one individual appropriately named Guna, a Malay word meaning
"fortune." Again in the late eighteenth century another hero arises to
arrest the decline of the Malukan world. The recognition of his accomplishment is contained in his name: Jou Barakati. In both cases the significance of their deeds is indicated by the honor of being acknowledged
as a person of "fortune." These mana-full individuals therefore form
points in Maluku's past highlighting for the Malukans their significant
historical events. Where both Guna and Nuku were similar was in their
ability to deal successfully with a potential "cosmic" disorder threatening their world and to create a new order. Transformation of the status
quo could occur only through its reaffirmation. By seeking to "restore"
the four pillars and the dualism, symbols of the established order, Nuku
was able to propose the creation of a new unity under the leadership of a
person of mana.

Nuku's struggles coincided with a period in the last quarter of the
eighteenth century when the unity of Maluku was finally shattered by
the exiling of Tidore's Sultan Jamaluddin and the heir apparent Kamaluddin in 1779. With the conquest of Tidore by the VOC and the
deposing of Tidore's ruler, the last true pillar upholding the Malukan
world was undermined. Throughout Nuku's long and successful rebellion, the people were attracted to him because he exhibited the signs of a
unique individual capable of introducing a new cycle of harmony and
prosperity in Maluku. But in pursuing restoration Nuku was compelled
to create new methods and new alliances. In the end Nuku was successful in his task, but the resulting unity was one which was sustained by
his own special qualities. The title by which he was popularly known,
Jou Barakati, bespoke volumes. For the Malukans it was proper that
this individual of prowess, of mana, should be the one to introduce
change in the society. He was in every way a culture hero, an innovator
who strengthened traditions. When he was formally proclaimed ruler in
Tidore in 1801, the people believed that the centuries of strife and suffering brought by outsiders in search of spices could now be reversed
and the world of Maluku once again restored to its former well-being.

Conclusion

Reaffirmation of Malukan History

The story of Maluku is a multilayered one, but the storytellers are almost exclusively European. Based on well-established Classical and Christian theories of the center and periphery, the European representation of the past portrayed the peoples encountered in Maluku as morally and culturally inferior. The Portuguese and Spaniards added their particular refinements upon this underlying assumption by highlighting the struggle against Islam and the contribution of their fidalguia/hidalguía in their glorious overseas enterprise. The young Dutch nation emphasized its technological and economic prowess in its expansion in Asia, while blaming any shortcomings or excesses on its antithesis, the Dutch East India Company. These concerns and cultural assumptions have shaped the European view of Maluku's past.

Different elements have affected the Malukan, and more specifically the north Malukan, perspective. For the Malukans the very core of their history was the mythologizing traditions which posited their unity. This unity is described as a development which occurred on the individual islands, the specific area of north Maluku, and the region known as Maluku. The myths became the basis of a political process which involved the encouragement of "family members" to adopt the dress, titles, language, and religion of a movable "center."[1] The process was never entirely successful, as localized spiritual forces and individual cultural traits proved remarkably tenacious. Nevertheless, within the Maluku family there was an acceptance of the idea of a center and a periphery, both of which were crucial to the maintenance of the unity.

Although these myths are mainly concerned with unity, they also emphasize unique themes. In the story of the creation of island-wide unities, the common theme is the tension between what Sahlins following Dumézil refers to as the "stranger-king" and the "lords of the land."[2] Ternate's tradition leaves no doubt of the foreign origin of the king and his assumption of authority as a result of an auspicious act. But in the process a tension is created between him and the leaders of the original inhabitants, or the lords of the land, represented by the jogugu/jojau and the bobatos. When the Portuguese arrived in Ternate in 1512, the ruler was a primus inter pares governing principally at the sufferance of the lords of the land. Yet his crucial role as arbiter among the bobatos assured his greater prestige which was acknowledged through sartorial and behavioral signs readily understood among the Malukans. Through marriage with women from the bobato families, the use of their women as "milk-mothers," and the dispensing of royal beneficence in the form of prestigious overseas goods, the ruler was able to preserve his unique status and indispensable function in the society.

The tension nevertheless remained in the relationship and was exacerbated by the coming of Islam in the late fifteenth century with its lofty ideas of kingship. The ruler was regarded as the "Shadow of Allah on the Earth" or as the Sufic "Perfect Man." As an Islamic ruler he could appeal to a force which was not dependent on the spiritual and political leaders of the land. With authority emanating from an external origin, the Muslim ruler could begin to create his own hierarchy of power. The new Islamic office of hukum, whose responsibility should be properly that of a religious judicial functionary, was transformed in the late sixteenth and seventeenth centuries into a political post appointed by the ruler as his representative in new overseas territories. The significant sacral duties of the indigenous position of pinate in maintaining the links between the ruler and the lords of the land became increasingly irrelevant as the ruler established new and prosperous relationships with Islam and the Europeans. The pinate was replaced by the syahbandar, an office originating from Muslim Persia, whose primary duties were to oversee international trade in the royal port and to regulate foreign traders on shore. The office of kali, which in Maluku became accepted as the spiritual head of Islam, was institutionalized, relegating to insignificance the previously influential position of the head of indigenous religion, the sowohi kië.

Another factor affecting the relationship between ruler and lords of the land was the Europeans. With their specific ideas of the power and authority of kings, the Europeans reinforced the position of the Malukan ruler already strengthened by Islamic conceptions of kingship. In addition, European spice requirements introduced a fundamental change in local trade which greatly benefited the ruler. A reorganization of the society was necessary for a systematic and regular collection, preparation, storage, and sale of cloves, nutmeg, and mace to the European. Only the ruler as first among equals had the necessary intermediary position to supervise such a reorganization, and so he undertook the task and thereby gained increased prestige from both the

Europeans and the Malukans. As the revenue from the spice trade began to flow to the royal ports, the ruler was able to purchase from the Europeans and other foreign traders items of great demand among his subjects, such as iron, cloth, and arms. The growing reliance of the subjects on the ruler's monopolistic access to these goods gradually provided him with much greater influence in the society than ever before.

The rapid evolution of international trade centered on Ternate enabled the sultan to manipulate his newly found resources to gain the allegiance of pivotal families on the island. To assure himself of their continuing support while defusing any potential challenge at home, the sultan "encouraged" the powerful families of the Fala Raha to organize expeditions in the late fifteenth and early sixteenth centuries to recreate Ternate in lands overseas. The formation of appanages by these families in Hoamoal, Hitu, Buru, Sula Besi, and perhaps even in Gorontalo-Limbotto, was a feature of Ternate's overseas ventures. By the middle of the sixteenth century the sultan had been able to consolidate his position in Ternate and embark on an expansion reflecting the strength of the center, this time led by a new official established for this very purpose, the kapita laut, or admiral of the sultan's fleets.

Tidore and the other Malukan kingdoms also expanded beyond their islands, but they never institutionalized the appanage in the same way as did Ternate, perhaps demonstrating the greater impact of international trade on Ternate than on the rest of north Maluku. Yet Tidore too underwent transformation in its relations with the periphery, although in a different fashion. There is no evidence in Tidore of powerful families posing a challenge to the center or of creating colonies in the periphery. Instead, Tidore appears to have been content to receive acknowledgment of subservience from local lords in the vast area which came to form its territories.

The Bikusagara myth, which delineates the extent of the Malukan world, highlights a second important theme: the proper functioning of center/periphery relations. As the island kingdoms of north Maluku grew wealthier and more powerful as a result of international trade, they began to expand into new areas. To mark their physical and spiritual link to the center, the leaders of these lands adopted its titles, dress, and religion, recreating the periphery in the image of the center. At first only the leaders and selected followers in their settlements made the adjustment. The strength of the local lords of the land and the indigenous religion meant that many on the coast and practically the entire population in the interior retained their original customs. Much of the relationship between the center and the periphery, therefore, continued to be nurtured by traditional means of exchange, both of women and goods.

There was no change in center/periphery relationships until the introduction of the European treaty in the second half of the seventeenth century, which forced the center to make greater demands of its periphery. The treaties identified each kingdom's territories and made the ruler at the center responsible for maintaining the peace in these lands. In the past such a responsibility would have been a normal undertaking of any good ruler. What complicated matters, however, was the treaty definition of piracy, illegal trade, and unlawful deeds, which completely overturned well-established arrangements between the center and the periphery. The raid, which was undertaken for reasons of revenge or ritual, was declared to be an act of "piracy," especially if it occurred in areas which were now regarded as Dutch Company lands or lands under its "protection." The growing list of areas becoming part of the Company as a result of conquest or request made practically any raid an act of hostility against the Company and its allies. There was, however, a "legal" solution according to the treaty, and that was the European conception of "war." It provided the Malukans with an approved means of conducting the raid. The taking of heads and the ceremonial decorating of warboats with the trophies of conflict, which were part of "local warfare" mentioned by European observers in the early sixteenth century, were now part of "European warfare." Though an indigenous practice was preserved through a European mode of warfare, the involvement of the European required many more men and arms than the traditional raid. The result was greater loss of lives, more destruction, and increasing incidents demanding blood vengeance.

Another consequence of the treaty which influenced center/periphery relations in Maluku was the introduction of the spice eradication policy. The rulers of both Ternate and Tidore were eager to outdo the other for favors from the Company by implementing this unpopular policy in their lands. By demanding the destruction of all spice trees in their territories, the rulers of both kingdoms undermined the principal source of revenue for the local bobatos and the ordinary people. Such a measure benefited the sultan even more since Dutch compensation was unequally divided with more than half the sum destined to the ruler alone. Moreover, the Dutch presented him with the total compensation to be divided among the Council and the bobatos. With such discretionary powers, the sultan was able to gain ever greater influence and power over his lords. The impact of such a policy was far more serious in the periphery. Previous relationships founded on mutual duties and obligations were discarded, as more was demanded from the periphery while less was provided by the center in the way of protection or goods. The new Dutch treaty rules had overturned customary relations based on mutual rights and obligations and had introduced those of confrontation and subordination.

A third theme which the myths stress is the unity of a Maluku world symbolized by the maintenance of the "four pillars." The Bikusa-gara myth conceptualizes a Maluku "family" bounded by Banggai-Butung in the west, the Papuas in the east, Loloda in the north, and Bacan in the south. Another myth preserved in old epithets for Ternate, Tidore, Jailolo, and Bacan describes these four kingdoms as forming the world of north Maluku. An earlier myth in the same area lists Moti and Makian, rather than Jailolo and Bacan, as forming the original four. However, this variant is "corrected" in later traditions which describe how the royal house of Jailolo was founded by those of Moti, while that of Bacan was also begun by the royal house of Makian.[3] Each individual kingdom or area had its own separate traditions which describe original kingdoms consisting of either four or five (four with the center forming the fifth) founding villages, or of later kingdoms expanded to form four or five satellite states.[4]

In these myths there is the recurrent theme of the *four* settlements, kingdoms, or areas which form a whole. Based on their ancient Aus-tronesian heritage, the Malukans regarded "four" as an auspicious number symbolizing completeness, order, and harmony. They believed that the survival and well-being of their world depended on the mainte-nance of the "four pillars." It was therefore with apprehension that they witnessed and later remembered the incorporation of Jailolo into Ter-nate in 1551. To allay fears of impending destruction of the unity of Maluku, Ternate retained Jailolo's status as an independent entity and had a member of the Jailolo royal house always present at official and ritual ceremonies. Nevertheless, the enormity of the act remained embedded in the psyche of the people and continued to resurface strongly whenever a serious crisis struck the community. Initial support in north Maluku for Nuku's rebellion in the late eighteenth century came from those who shared his antagonism toward the Dutch, but the rebellion was sustained by those who believed that his promise to restore Jailolo would finally bring peace and harmony to Maluku. The adherence to common myths provided the basis for unity among the groups in Maluku, and the strength of the belief that this unity would continue to survive as long as "the four kingdoms" were preserved became an important motivating principle in the cyclical view of Malu-kan history.

The idea of the survival of the north Malukan world symbolized by the persistence of the four kingdoms was paramount, even though the four kingdoms had ceased to exist since the mid-sixteenth century. The well-being of the whole was believed to be assured by the ongoing dualism between the two most important members of the four: Ternate and Tidore. The presence of dualism in north Maluku is not unique; indeed, it is found in many other eastern Indonesian cultures which have well-developed systems of complementary dual classifications.[5] When the Europeans first arrived in Maluku in the early sixteenth century, they commented on the curious love/hate relationship between these two kingdoms. Likening it to the political and economic rivalries with which they were familiar in Europe, they chose opposing sides and lent their arms and ships to a conflict which became more destructive as the centuries progressed.

The Europeans also transformed the exercise of dualism by enforcing on the Malukans the Western European treaty concept. Unable to pursue traditional areas of dualistic contest for people and lands because of treaty restrictions, Ternate and Tidore were forced to focus their efforts on the contest to win the favor of the Dutch East India Company. The shift in focus of the dualism masked a deeper cleavage between the center and the periphery which became increasingly apparent in the eighteenth century. As Ternate and Tidore devoted their attention to Fort Orange, they also began to expect their "father" the Company to assume the obligations and responsibilities for its Malukan "children" on the periphery. The inability of the sultans in the eighteenth century to extricate themselves from the Company's policies aroused concern among the Malukans that their world was being lost. What was perhaps even more damaging was the local belief that both Ternate and Tidore had become indistinguishable as a result of their relations with the Dutch. The overwhelming perception seems to have been that the dualism was no longer being maintained, and hence the community was being threatened.[6]

The appearance of Kaicili Nuku at this historical juncture is significant because it demonstrates yet again the strength of the traditions of the unity of the Malukan world. He was from the ancient settlement of Tidore's rulers at Toloa, a place regarded with great reverence.[7] In the words of the wise and highly respected storehouse of Malukan lore, Sultan Saifuddin of Tidore, the unity of Maluku was assured as long as the dualism between Ternate and Tidore survived. But by the last quarter of the eighteenth century, there were grave doubts regarding the ability of either Ternate or Tidore to act without the approval of the VOC. Distress at the weakening links between the center and periphery, plus the gradual arrogation of power by the Company, created a groundswell of support for Nuku whose message was the restoration of the four pillars. Among the Papuan islanders Nuku had an added appeal. He was regarded as one possessing special powers (nanek, the equivalent of barakati) which he would use to bring about the golden period known as Koreri. Nuku appeared at a time when Maluku was seen to be disintegrating, and so the people were willing to offer him allegiance as the special "Lord of Fortune" (Jou Barakati) who would again restore normalcy and prosperity to their world. His success against the Company was a source of reassurance to Maluku at the close of the eighteenth century. Through his barakati he had restored the proprieties in Maluku and begun a new cycle of peace and prosperity. The "family" had been reestablished, the conceptual systems preserved, and the "true" tales of Maluku reaffirmed.

Implications for the Study of Southeast Asian Societies

The study of Maluku in the early modern period reveals the importance of myths in early unities. It is generally argued that myths help to explicate and justify current societal arrangements, but they also provide a blueprint for the extension of social, economic, and political relationships. In the sixteenth, seventeenth, and eighteenth centuries, Ternate expanded north and west, while Tidore went south and east in accordance with mythically determined directions and mythically designated lands. Because of the supernatural elements associated with the creation of the Maluku family, relationships perceived to be occurring within the family acquired legitimacy and proved to be more practical, stable, and long-lasting than any political entity. The formation of a unity based on commonly shared myths suited the nature of the geopolitics of Maluku, with its numerous language and ethnic groups located in often inaccessible interiors or isolated islands. As in many eastern Indonesian societies, in Maluku the myths provided the rationale for the flow of women to the numerous groups within the "family," thus assuring an ongoing exchange of goods which helped bind the whole into a functioning economic and political unit.

In Southeast Asia similar cultural entities may have operated where a politically centralized authority would have been ineffective. There is evidence that such a unity existed among the sea and riverine peoples in the archipelago. One of the enduring themes in the folklore of sea peoples is their myth of origin in "Johor," a kingdom which in the past had provided the legitimacy for their activities as well as a market for their products.[8] The absence of major political kingdoms in certain Southeast Asian areas, therefore, did not mean that these societies were any less effective than the Sinicized or Indianized states in other parts of the region. In fact they functioned well in a political, social, and economic arrangement which best suited the conditions of the area. Even among the lowland populations it may be necessary to reassess the nature of apparent "political" control exercised by a "central authority." There may be a greater reliance on the mythologizing process rather than on force of arms or law to assure acquiescence and the successful exchange of goods.

Eastern Indonesia provides examples of cultures which may be more comprehensible as part of an older Austronesian heritage than a more recent Indianized one. A few anthropologists have indicated the Polynesian character of Bali and southwest Sulawesi,[9] but historians have not yet examined historical sources in order to demonstrate or refute such links. As this study has shown, certain features of early modern Malukan society reveal the persistence of older Austronesian ideas. A comparison in this period between Maluku and other parts of more Indianized Southeast Asia may be useful in identifying those aspects of society which were most receptive and those most resistant to outside ideas. It would provide a model for examining what O. W. Wolters has described as the process of "localization" in Southeast Asia.[10] Maluku, for example, typifies many Oceanic societies in the prominence of dualisms. The origin myths reveal the sea/land, earth/ sky, and Upperworld/Lowerworld dualisms which are found throughout the areas inhabited by Austronesian-speakers. The dualism of Ternate and Tidore, and that between the status lineages determined by descent from the "stranger king" and those associated with the indigenous "lords of the land," were two of the more important dualisms which informed the activities of the Malukans. It was the persistence of these two dualisms which provided the historical impetus in Maluku in the early modern period.

Malukan society in this period resembled that of the Pacific Islands in other respects. At a time when many kingdoms in the western half of the archipelago and mainland Southeast Asia were proclaiming the sacred origins of rulers to demonstrate legitimacy, Maluku was still emphasizing individual skills and valor as important royal traits. Another less common but highly desirable trait was a command of local traditions which honored the ancestors through "remembrance." Tidore's Sultan Syaifuddin's command of customs and lore was greatly admired, and he was honored by becoming himself an object of remembrance by later generations who attributed to him the founding of the line of modern Tidore rulers.

While the king was able to win admiration and support through his achievements (and increasingly through his descent), in Maluku as in many Pacific societies moral force and ultimate authority lay with the elders. They did not constitute a formal body, but they were regarded as the repository of the wisdom of the tribe and hence better able than any other to determine what was best for the whole group. So highly esteemed were they that no young man, no matter how high his status and impressive his accomplishment, could enter into this prestigious group.[11] Because of their acknowledged position of respect in Malukan society, they made ideal envoys to undertake delicate missions.

Throughout the history of Maluku in this period, the elders of the community were always present at important ceremonies and gatherings where momentous decisions were made.

In the ideas of kinship, Malukan society again had much in common with the Pacific. Kinship was determined by shared substance, whether it was blood, maternal milk, ritual food, or booty. Because of the scarcity of human and natural resources in Maluku, great care was taken to create kinship bonds which formed the basis for the reallocation of resources. One of the very first acts of a new ruler in Maluku was to obtain at least one royal wife and many other secondary wives from the various parts of his kingdom. Once a child was born to the royal couple, milk-mothers from bobato families throughout the kingdom came to nurse the child, further linking the king to these chiefly families through the shared milk. In the feast to commemorate the birth of the child, raw food and other local products of the land were offered by the people to the ruler. He in turn converted these items to cooked food and foreign prestige objects and redistributed them to the people. Booty taken in raids against hostile nonfamily groups was shared between the ruler and his people. In these acts of reciprocity, links between the ruler as "father" and his people as "children" were reaffirmed.

Malukan and Pacific societies were also similar in the ongoing struggle between rival leaders for the loyalty of their subjects. The contest was fought only infrequently on the battlefield and most often in the public arena, where the rulers could match their wealth and wits against one another. So seriously did the Ternate and Tidore rulers conduct this contest in the seventeenth century, and so evenly matched were Ternate's Sultan Mandar Syah (r. 1648–1675) and Tidore's Sultan Syaifuddin (r. 1657–1687), that the Dutch governor was forced to take extreme steps to appear impartial. At official receptions each ruler would try to insult the other in traditional ways, through the choice of certain colors in their clothing or in the type of dress worn. Whenever the subjects of one sought sanctuary in the lands of the other, much was made of it because people were an important measure of prestige and power.

This study has suggested that Malukan society had been barely touched by Indian or Islamic ideas by the time of the Europeans' appearance in 1512. Early Portuguese accounts are therefore valuable in depicting a community which still retained indigenous features resembling those found in the Pacific and reflecting an ancient Austronesian heritage. During the period from the sixteenth to the eighteenth centuries some of these cultural elements remained, while others underwent a transformation. With the arrival of Islam, "sultanates" were established which appeared similar to those institutions found in the western half of the archipelago. However, there was a difference in

Maluku based on a traditional logic expressed in the myths. Kinship ties determined by shared substances within the mythically prescribed world of Maluku underpinned these "sultanates" and made them more Pacific polities rather than Indianized ones. These observations, based on a study of one specific area over three centuries, suggest that it may be illuminating for historians to reexamine the Southeast Asian past by approaching it not only from India, the Middle East, and Europe, but also from the Pacific.

Finally, it may be worthwhile to reiterate the value of analyzing European sources for the early modern period not only for what they record, but also for what they represent. In the past two decades historians have made impressive strides in the critical analysis and interpretation of Southeast Asian manuscripts. The impetus for this development was the concern to recover the indigenous side of the story and reclaim the study of Southeast Asia from colonial historians. Recent trends indicate that the story of Southeast Asia from a local perspective is indeed established and flourishing. One regrettable consequence of this process, however, has been an attitude that European documents are somehow less legitimate than indigenous records in reconstructing the Southeast Asian past. While only limited numbers of Southeast Asian manuscripts have survived from the early modern period, there is a wealth of material left by European trading companies, officials, and travelers. These have been cataloged in archival collections in Europe and Asia and remain an invaluable repository of information on early modern Southeast Asian societies. But these sources are not simply rich historical mines awaiting the scholar to string together nuggets of "facts" into a chronological sequence. The European material itself is structured and selective, and it requires the same critical examination which is applied to Southeast Asian manuscripts. In its very structure and selectivity the European document offers a distinctive perspective which can illuminate indigenous developments and contribute another dimension to the rich texture which is Southeast Asia's past.

NOTES

INTRODUCTION

1. Chang (ed.), *Food in Chinese Culture*, p. 111.
2. Commelin (ed.), *Begin ende voortgangh*, vol. 1, First Voyage, Neck, p. 30.
3. Buccellati and Bucellati, "Terqa: The First Eight Seasons," p. 54. I am indebted to Dr. Paul Taylor for drawing my attention to this reference.
4. Burkill, *A Dictionary of the Economic Products of the Malay Peninsula*, vol. 1, p. 961.
5. Wolters, *Early Indonesian Commerce*, p. 39.
6. Ptak, "The Northern Trade Route to the Spice Islands," pp. 29, 30.
7. Scott, *Cracks in the Parchment Wall*, p. 47.
8. Cortesão, *Suma Oriental*, vol. 1, pp. 182–189, 214; for an excellent discussion of trade in the Indonesian archipelago in this period, see Meilink-Roelofsz, *Asian Trade and European Influence in the Indonesian Archipelago Between 1500 and About 1630*.
9. Lach, *Asia in the Making*, vol. 1, bk. 1, p. 96.
10. Diffie and Winius, *Foundations of the Portuguese Empire 1415–1580*, pp. 203, 220–248.
11. Clifford, "On Ethnographic Allegory," p. 100.
12. White, *The Content of the Form: Narrative Discourse and Historical Representation;* Iggers and Powell (eds.), *Leopold von Ranke and the Shaping of the Historical Discipline.* See especially Iggers, "The Crisis of the Rankean Paradigm in the Nineteenth Century," pp. 170–179.
13. Collingwood, *The Idea of History*, pp. 231–249.
14. Ricoeur, *Hermeneutics and the Human Sciences*, p. 291.
15. Fischer and Marcus, *Anthropology as Cultural Critique: An Experimental Moment in the Human Sciences.*
16. Clifford and Marcus, *Writing Culture*, p. 109.
17. Sharp, *The Transformation of Bigfoot: Maleness, Power, and Belief among the Chipewyan*, pp. xvi–xvii.
18. Gewertz and Schieffelin (eds.), *History and Ethnohistory in Papua New Guinea*, p. 3.
19. Borofsky, *Making History: Pukapukan and Anthropological Constructions of Knowledge*, p. 186.

20. Baker, "Descent and Community in Tidore," p. 92.

21. Sahlins, "Other Times, Other Customs: The Anthropology of History," p. 520.

22. Adas, *Machines as the Measure of Men: Technology and Ideologies of Western Dominance*, pp. 9, 28.

23. Bellwood, *Prehistory of the Indo-Malaysian Archipelago*, p. 98.

24. Fisher and Marcus, *Anthropology*, pp. 31–32.

25. Eliade, *The Myth of the Eternal Return, or Cosmos and History;* Eliade, *Images and Symbols: Studies in Religious Symbolism*, pp. 67–70; Farriss, "Remembering the Future, Anticipating the Past: History, Time, and Cosmology Among the Maya of Yucatan," p. 574.

26. McDowell, "Past and Future: The Nature of Episodic Time in Bun," in Gewertz and Schieffelin (eds.), *History and Ethnohistory*, pp. 26–39.

27. Sahlins, "Other Times."

28. Farriss, "Remembering the Future," p. 572.

29. Lach, *Asia in the Making*, vol. 1, bk. 1, pp. 96, 152–159.

30. Cortesão, *Suma Oriental*.

31. Pigafetta, *First Voyage around the World;* Transylvanus, *De Moluccis Insulis*.

32. *The Voyage of John Huyghen van Linschoten to the East Indies* (from the Old English translation of 1598).

33. Lach, *Asia in the Making*, vol. 1, bk. 1, p. 169.

34. Quoted in Lach, *Asia in the Making*, vol. 2, bk. 2, p. 144.

35. MacGregor, "Some Aspects of Portuguese Historical Writing of the Sixteenth and Seventeenth Centuries on Southeast Asia," in Hall, *Historians of South-East Asia*, pp. 191–192.

36. Ibid., p. 179.

37. Lach, *Asia in the Making*, vol. 2, bk. 2, pp. 142–143.

38. Ibid., p. 142; MacGregor, "Some Aspects," pp. 179–186; Boxer, *João de Barros, Portuguese Humanist and Historian of Asia*, pp. 138–139.

39. Boxer, *João de Barros*, pp. 140–141.

40. MacGregor, "Some Aspects," pp. 186–187; Harrison, "Five Portuguese Historians," in Philips (ed.), *Historians of India, Pakistan, and Ceylon*, p. 159.

41. "Carta Régia para Matias de Albuquerque, Viceroy of India, 27 Feb. 1595. Livros das Monções, no. 21, in *Boletim da Filmoteca Ultramarina Portuguesa*, vol. 2, p. 319.

42. Harrison, "Five Portuguese," pp. 161–162.

43. Lach, *Asia in the Making*, vol. 2, bk. 2, pp. 138–149.

44. The last two lines refer to the bird of paradise. Because the birds were often sold for their beautiful feathers without their legs, there was a prevalent belief which persisted well into the nineteenth century that these birds lived continually in the air and only fell to earth on their death. Aubertin (trans.), *The Lusiads of Camoens*, vol. 2, canto X, stanza CXXXII, p. 261.

45. Quoted in Lach, *Asia in the Making*, vol. 1, bk. 2, p. 606.

46. Jacobs (ed. and trans.), *A Treatise on the Moluccas (c. 1544)*, pp. 6–20.

47. Sá, *Documentação para a história das missões do padroado português do Oriente*, pp. 192–193, 345–347; Schurhammer, *Francis Xavier: His Life, His Times*, vol. 3, pp. 150–151.

48. Jacobs, *A Treatise*, pp. 70–73.

49. Lach, *Asia in the Making*, vol. 1, bk. 1, pp. 234, 314–315.

50. Brou, "Les statistiques dans les anciennes missions," pp. 361–363.

51. Lach, *Asia in the Making,* vol. 1, bk. 1, pp. 315, 318–319.

52. Ibid., vol. 1, bk. 1, pp. 315–318, 330.

53. Ibid., vol. 1, bk. 1, pp. 289, 331.

54. The issue was finally resolved by the Treaty of Saragossa in 1529, which recognized Portugal's rights to Maluku in return for a payment of 500,000 cruzados.

55. Lord Stanley of Alderley (ed. and trans.), *The First Voyage Round the World by Magellan;* Skelton (ed. and trans.), *Magellan's Voyage:* A Narrative Account [by Antonio Pigafetta] of the First Navigation; Transylvanus, *De Moluccis Insulis.*

56. Lach, *Asia in the Making,* vol. 1, bk. 1, pp. 182–184; Oviedo, *História general y natural.*

57. Gómara, *História general de las Indias,* pp. x–xii.

58. Arasaratnam (ed. and trans.), "Introduction" to *François Valentijn's Description of Ceylon,* pp. 4–10, 16–17.

59. For a discussion on the VOC sources for the study of Indonesia, see Barbara Watson Andaya, *Perak, the Abode of Grace,* pp. 4–6; Leonard Y. Andaya, *The Kingdom of Johor,* pp. 12–15.

60. Eco, *The Name of the Rose,* pp. 23–24.

CHAPTER ONE

1. Glacken, *Traces on the Rhodian Shore,* p. 6.

2. Ibid., pp. 9–12; Friedman, *The Monstrous Races in Medieval Art and Thought,* p. 52.

3. Penrose, *Travel and Discovery in the Renaissance, 1420–1620,* p. 2.

4. Glacken, *Traces,* pp. 112–113.

5. Penrose, *Travel and Discovery,* p. 10.

6. Wittkower, "Marvels of the East: A Study in the History of Monsters," pp. 160–161.

7. Ibid., pp. 161–164.

8. Penrose, *Travel and Discovery,* p. 10.

9. Wittkower, "Marvels of the East," pp. 159, 167–169; Penrose, *Travel and Discovery,* p. 10.

10. Friedman, *The Monstrous Races,* pp. 27–31.

11. Burke, *Popular Culture in Early Modern Europe,* p. 268.

12. In Chapter 8 of Book 16 of the *Civitas Dei,* St. Augustine explained that the Christian had to be guided by Genesis 9:19: "These are the three sons of Noah: and of them was the whole earth overspread." If there were indeed monstrous races, then they must be descendants of Adam and no judgment should be made against them. All of God's creation had a purpose, which was to make one understand the beauty of the whole.

13. Flint, "Monsters and the Antipodes in the Early Middle Ages and Enlightenment," p. 71.

14. It was included in the *Livre de Merveilles* in 1403, the *Nuremberg Chronicle* in 1493, Sebastian Münster's *Cosmographia* in 1544, Richard Hakluyt's first edition of *Principall Navigations* in 1598, and Samuel Purchas's *Purchas his Pilgrimes* in 1625.

15. A sixteenth century miller gained access to the book through his priest

and was thoroughly familiar with its contents. See Ginzburg, *The Cheese and the Worms: The Cosmos of a Sixteenth-Century Miller,* p. 49. The role of churchmen in the spread of literacy was also evident in Protestant countries. The home of the clergyman was an important center of literacy for the community. Koenigsberger, *Early Modern Europe 1500–1789,* p. 249.

16. Another equally significant influence on Columbus's decision to sail westward from Europe was Cardinal Pierre d'Ailly's *Imago Mundi,* which depicted only a narrow stretch of water separating the west coast of Africa from the east coast of India.

17. Moseley, *Travels . . . Mandeville,* pp. 31–32.

18. Ibid., pp. 11–12.

19. Hodgen, *Early Anthropology,* p. 71.

20. Greenblatt, *Marvelous Possessions: The Wonder of the New World,* pp. 22–23.

21. Penrose, *Travel and Discovery,* pp. 3–5, 21–22.

22. Ibid., pp. 6–7.

23. Newton (ed.), *Travel and Travellers,* "Introduction," pp. 13–15.

24. Penrose, *Travel and Discovery,* pp. 15–19.

25. Ibid., pp. 9–10.

26. Hodgen, *Early Anthropology,* pp. 126, 167, 181, 192–196, 276, 278, 288, 345.

27. Todorov, *The Conquest of America,* p. 130.

28. One scholar sees the oceanic division of the Atlantic highlighting the rift between the Old and New Worlds and creating a structural division between "over here" and "over there." Certeau, *The Writing of History,* p. 218. A similar division and rift can be applied to Europe and Asia, with the "Old World" being viewed as "over here" (the "center") and the "New–Old World" being "over there" (the "periphery").

29. For an excellent discussion of the evolution of Western European writing which created this structure of dominance toward the East and the Other, see Campbell, *The Witness and the Other World.*

30. Koenigsberger, *Early Modern Europe,* pp. 251–252.

31. See the case of the heretic miller in Ginzburg, *The Cheese and the Worms.*

32. Newton, "Travellers' Tales of Wonder and Imagination," pp. 4, 165.

33. The Prester John letter is found on pages 175–178 in Ross, "Prester John and the Empire of Ethiopia." See also pp. 174, 179–182, 192–193; Rogers, *The Quest,* pp. 78–79, 94–95.

34. Phelan, *The Millennial Kingdom of the Franciscans in the New World,* p. 48; Lach, *Asia in the Making,* vol. 1, bk. 1, p. 319.

35. Ricard, *The Spiritual Conquest of Mexico,* pp. 34–35.

36. Phelan, *The Millennial Kingdom,* p. 12.

37. Landini, "The Historical Context of the Franciscan Movement," in Iriarte de Aspurz, *Franciscan History: The Three Orders of St. Francis of Assisi,* p. 570.

38. Iriarte de Aspurz, *Franciscan History,* pp. 303–304; Boxer, *The Church Militant and Iberian Expansion 1440–1770,* pp. 77–78.

39. Boxer, *The Church Militant,* pp. 78–81.

40. Ibid., p. 81.

41. Latourette, "Three Centuries of Advance AD 1500–1800," section 3 in *A History of the Expansion of Christianity,* pp. 22, 37–38, 303.

42. Diffie and Winius, *Foundations,* p. 212.

43. Ibid., p. 47.

44. Lach, *Asia in the Making,* vol. 1, bk. 1, pp. 229-230.

45. Ibid., vol. 1, bk. 1, pp. 230-239, 247-251, 319, 329.

46. Ibid., vol. 1, bk. 1, pp. 263-264.

47. Speaking of the Malukans, Galvão writes: "There are among them many courageous and valiant knights. While fighting they call their names, as happened in that story: 'Gaula! Gaula! I am Amadis [of Gaula]!' " Jacobs, *A Treatise,* p. 171.

48. Lach, *Asia in the Making,* vol. 2, bk. 2, pp. 78-79.

49. Lynch, *Spain Under the Habsburgs,* vol. 1 Empire and Absolutism 1516-1598, pp. 14-15, 20; Pierson, *Philip II of Spain,* p. 71.

50. Elliott, *Imperial Spain 1469-1716,* p. 54.

51. Stradling, *Europe and the Decline of Spain: A Study of the Spanish System, 1580-1720,* pp. 29-30.

52. Rafael, *Contracting Colonialism: Translation and Christian Conversion in Tagalog Society Under Early Spanish Rule,* pp. 116-117.

53. Parry, *The Spanish Seaborne Empire,* pp. 123-124.

54. Phelan, "Prebaptismal Instruction and the Administration of Baptism in the Philippines during the Sixteenth Century," pp. 24-25.

55. Lopez and Alfonso (eds.), *The Christianization of the Philippines,* Document V, pp. 264-265.

56. Spate, *The Spanish Lake,* pp. 90-95. This controversy over jurisdiction in Maluku exercised the legal minds of both nations, giving later historians a goldmine of information to maintain an ongoing debate on the subject. See, for example, Mota (ed.), *A viagem de Fernão Magalhães e a questão das Malucas.* It is a collection of articles on the subject of the Maluku Controversy, which was the result of the "Second" Luso-Hispanic Colloquium on Overseas History.

57. Nowell, "The Loaisa Expedition and the Ownership of the Moluccas," pp. 325-336; Ciríaco Pérez-Bustamante, "La expedición de Ruy López de Villalobos a las islas del Pacífico," in Mota (ed.), *A viagem,* pp. 613-626; Gómara, *História general de las Indias o "Hispania vitrix,"* pp. 183-184; Gonzalo Fernandez de Oviedo, *História general y natural de las Indias,* pp. 226-239, 261-302.

58. Vlekke, *Evolution of the Dutch Nation,* pp. 58-59, 109-110, 170-173.

59. Diffie and Winius, *Foundations,* pp. 210-211.

60. Vlekke, *Evolution,* pp. 14-15.

61. Boxer, *Dutch Seaborne Empire,* pp. 24-25.

62. Ibid., p. 90. But one distinguished historian refutes the view that the Dutch were truly advocating an open seas policy. He attributes the success of Dutch capitalist activity to an "elaborate and extensive system of protection," which had more in common with medieval and Renaissance ethos than with modern mercantilist behavior. Schama, *The Embarrassment of Riches: An Interpretation of Dutch Culture in the Golden Age,* p. 341.

63. Boxer, *Dutch Seaborne Empire,* p. 225; Taylor, *The Social World of Batavia: European and Eurasian in Dutch Asia,* chap. 3.

64. Boxer, *Dutch Seaborne Empire,* p. 184.

65. Zumthor, *Daily Life in Rembrandt's Holland,* p. 296.

66. Geyl, *The Netherlands in the Seventeenth Century,* vol. 2 (1648-1715), p. 181.

67. Ibid., p. 100.

68. Boxer, *Dutch Seaborne,* p. 50.
69. Geyl, *The Netherlands,* vol. 2, p. 182.
70. Vlekke, *Evolution,* p. 187.
71. Geyl, *The Netherlands,* vol. 2, p. 185.
72. Sainsbury (ed.), *Calendar of State Papers Colonial Series, East Indies, China and Japan 1617–1671,* p. 105.

CHAPTER TWO

1. No such difficulty seems to have been faced by the Chinese, who used the term *kun-lun* to refer to the inhabitants in the Southeast Asian region. Wolters, *Early Indonesian Commerce,* Chap. 1, passim. The unity of the region was also evident in Arab and Indian sources which talked of those inhabiting the "lands below the winds." In more recent times there has been a recognition of the shared cultural heritage which has contributed to a sense of unity even in an area as large as Southeast Asia. Coèdes in his *Indianized States of Southeast Asia* was the first to advance the argument of a cultural unity of Southeast Asia, a theme which is the subject of Reid's *Southeast Asia in the Age of Commerce.*

2. No. 73, "Apostolado," in Sá, *Documentação para a história das missões do padroado português do Oriente. Insulíndia,* vol. 2, p. 493.

3. Couto, *Da Asia,* vol. 11, p. 167.

4. Argensola, *Conquista de las islas Malucas,* p. 8.

5. Quoted in Fraassen, "Ternate, de Molukken en de Indonesische Archipel," vol. 1, p. 24. A fourteenth century Javanese poem, the *Nagarakrtagama,* contains the first known evidence of the use of the term "Maluku" to refer to the clove-producing islands.

6. In this regard Maluku is unlike the situation in Celebes/Sulawesi where the concept of a united island appeared to be a European rather than a local creation. See Henley, "The Idea of Celebes in History," pp. 8–10.

7. Castles, "Statelessness and Stateforming Tendencies Among the Batak Before Colonial Rule," in Reid and Castles (eds.), *Pre-Colonial State Systems in Southeast Asia,* pp. 67–76.

8. Baker, "Descent and Community in Tidore," pp. 10, 55–56.

9. Eliade, *Images and Symbols: Studies in Religious Symbolism,* p. 40.

10. Baker, "Descent," pp. 52, 119–120, 334–335, 338–339.

11. Valentijn, *Oud en Nieuw,* vol. 1, pp. 282–283.

12. Bellwood, *Man's Conquest of the Pacific, The Prehistory of Southeast Asia and Oceania,* p. 238.

13. Holt, *Art in Indonesia: Continuities and Change,* p. 24.

14. Hasan, *Maloko Kië Raha,* p. 6.

15. For a recent discussion of this concept of a "merit-full" individual, or of a person of "prowess," see Wolters, *History, Culture, and Region in Southeast Asian Perspectives,* pp. 6–8, 100–104.

16. For an excellent discussion of the concept, see Shore, "Mana and Tapu," in Howard and Borofsky (eds.), *Developments in Polynesian Ethnology,* pp. 137–173.

17. Andaya and Andaya, *A History of Malaysia,* pp. 50–55.

18. Barros, *Da Asia,* Dec. III, Liv. V, Cap. VI, vol. 6, p. 327.

19. Jacobs, *A Treatise on the Moluccas,* p. 83. There is a striking similarity

between this tale and that found in the Indian epic, the *Mahabharata*. In the latter there is a king named Sagara who has two wives but is childless. Through his devotion to Shiva his wives become pregnant, with one giving birth to a son and the other to some type of gourd. The king is about to cast away the gourd when a voice stops him and instructs him to take it home and preserve it with care. In time from each seed of the gourd comes forth a son. (The tale is from the Vana Parva, Section CVII, quoted in Mackenzie, *Myths from Melanesia and Indonesia*, p. 357.) The inspiration for the Maluku tale may have come from India, with the Buddhist Pali title of a monk, "Bhikku," attached to the name Sagara. However, the focus on the four and the sacred rattan are clearly of indigenous (Austronesian) origin.

20. Eliade remarks that the story of the severing of communications between humans and the gods because of some "ritual" fault is a well-known mythical theme. Eliade, *Images*, pp. 40–41. An example closer to Maluku comes from southwest Sulawesi in the Bugis epic, the *I La Galigo*. The rainbow linking the Upperworld and Earth is withdrawn, and seven generations suffer turmoil and disorder before the gods send someone to govern Earth once again. As in Maluku a special individual "finds" these new rulers who restore order. Andaya, "Kingship-*Adat* Rivalry and the Role of Islam in South Sulawesi," pp. 22–25.

21. For examples of this theme, see Chap. 4 of Ras, *Hikajat Bandjar*.

22. Mus, *India Seen from the East: Indian and Indigenous Cults in Champa*, pp. 13–14.

23. Alkire, "Concepts of Order in Southeast Asia and Micronesia," pp. 484–493.

24. Zainal Abidin bin Farid, "Filsafat hidup 'Sulapa appaka' orang-orang Bugis-Makassar (Pandangan hidup 'segi empat')," pp. 2–17.

25. Leeden, "The Raja Ampat Islands: A Mythological Interpretation," in Masinambow (ed.), *Halmahera dan Raja Ampat sebagai Kesatuan Majemuk*, p. 228.

26. Baker, "Descent," p. 15.

27. Fox, "Introduction," in Fox (ed.), *To Speak in Pairs: Essays on the Ritual Languages of Eastern Indonesia*, p. 26.

28. The role of Tidore as wife-giver to Ternate may reflect Tidore's ritual superiority to Ternate. Even to this day Tidore is the home of the sowohi, the sacred leader of the indigenous religion and of customary law *(adat)*. He resides in a special Fola Sowohi (House of Adat). People from all parts of Maluku still come to consult him on various matters, often to do with local spirits or the efficacy of traditional remedies for both physical and psychological ills. In the past he was associated with the ruler's sacred regalia. During the time of the sultanate, it was the sowohi who was entrusted with the task of cutting the hair of the ruler's crown. This was a crown of hair which grew mysteriously as a sign of the spiritual potency of the ruler. Trimming the hair was thus a dangerous task which could only be done by an individual possessed of great spiritual power. Now that there is no longer a Tidore sultan, the hair on the crown no longer grows. Personal communication from Abdul Wahab Togubu, head of the Cultural Section in the Office of Education and Culture, Soa Sio, Tidore, 24 Dec. 1987.

29. Jacobs, "New Sources," Letter 5, p. 236.

30. Jacobs, *A Treatise,* p. 115.

31. Rebelo, *Informação,* text 1 (1561), p. 297.

32. The European market for Malukan spices in the 1490s was about 250,000 ponds (1 pond = 1.09 pounds avoirdupois), but by about the 1620s the market was about 1.4 to 1.5 million ponds. See Wake, "The Changing Patterns of Europe's Pepper and Spice Imports, ca 1400–1700," pp. 393–395.

33. Colín, *Labor Evangélica. Ministerios apostólicos de los obreros de la Compañiá de Jesús,* new ed. vol. 3, p. 41.

34. Jacobs, *A Treatise,* pp. 112–113.

35. In the original formulation of the conception of "raw" and "cooked," or "nature" and "culture," Lévi-Strauss demonstrates through an analysis of American Indian myths from Latin America the mediatizing function of fire through cooking, thereby transforming both the raw product and the human consumer. Lévi-Strauss, *The Raw and the Cooked,* p. 336.

36. In this regard north Maluku differed from the situation in the Hawaiian Islands in the eighteenth century described by Marshall Sahlins. In Hawaii the rulers were quick to place taboos on highly desired foreign goods and on products sought by Europeans in order to reinforce their already strongly hierarchical position in society. See Sahlins, *Historical Metaphors and Mythical Realities,* pp. 43–46. In Maluku in the sixteenth and seventeenth centuries, the Europeans and Islamic teachers provided the means by which the rulers were able to establish the distinction between themselves and their people.

37. Valentijn, *Oud en Nieuw,* pp. 288, 291.

38. Jacobs, *A Treatise,* p. 85.

39. Cortesão, *Suma Oriental,* p. 213.

40. Jacobs, *A Treatise,* p. 87.

41. Ibid., pp. 86–87.

42. Ibid., pp, 102–103.

43. Holt, *Art in Indonesia,* pp. 274–275, 307–314; Pigeaud, *Javaansche volksvertoningen,* pp. 489–492.

44. Carta de Rui Gago a El-Rei, Malucas, 15 de Fev. de 1523 in Sá, *Documentaçao,* vol. 2, p. 160.

45. Boon makes a similar point with regard to the choice of words which Pigafetta decided to collect during his voyage: "Pigafetta wrote as Magellan voyaged: circularly. In crossing from the Old World to the New and back to the Old, he probably saw and heard according to conventions less like linguistic empiricism and more like great chains of being." Boon, *Affinities and Extremes: Crisscrossing the Bittersweet Ethnology of East Indies History, Hindu-Balinese Culture, and Indo-European Allure,* p. 11.

46. Transylvanus, *De Moluccis Insulis,* p. 127.

47. Pigafetta, *First Voyage Around the World,* pp. 65, 71; Skelton (ed. and trans.), *Magellan's Voyage: A Narrative Account* [by Antonio Pigafetta] *of the First Navigation,* p. 117.

48. Argensola, *Conquista,* p. 8.

49. Pigafetta, *First Voyage,* p. 65; Lord Stanley of Alderley, *The First Voyage Round the World by Magellan.* pp. 124–125.

50. In some Polynesian societies these special individuals were regarded as little inferior to the priests themselves. See Oliver, *Ancient Tahitian Society,* vol. 1,

p. 71. In the archipelago there arc also examples of people able to foresee the future being regarded as possessing luck or fortune. Daeng Menambun, one of the five Bugis brothers who came to change the history of the Malay Peninsula in the eighteenth century, was inspired by a dream which foretold their fate in the Malay world. See Andaya and Matheson (eds. and trans.), *Tuhfat al-Nafis (The Precious Gift)*, pp. 52-53.

51. Febvre, *The Problem of Unbelief in the Sixteenth Century*, p. 441.

52. Jacobs, *A Treatise*, p. 85.

53. A term derived from Syrian through Arabic to indicate a Muslim clergyman. But in Maluku the term was used loosely to indicate any religious teacher or even a foreign Muslim.

54. Jacobs, *A Treatise*, p. 123.

55. Fox, "Introduction" in Fox (ed.), *To Speak*, p. 27.

56. See, for example, Castanheda, *História do descobrimento e conquista da India pelos portugueses*, vol. 2, pp. 599-600.

57. Jacobs, *A Treatise*, p. 123.

58. Ibid., p. 103.

59. The betelnut was from the areca palm (*Areca catechu*, Linn.) and is chewed as a stimulant together with the leaf of the pepper vine (*Piper betle*, Linn.) and crushed lime. It was a sign of courtesy and respect to offer betel to guests before any business was transacted. The areca palm is found in India, Southeast Asia, and the Pacific as far as western Micronesia and the Santa Cruz Islands.

60. Pigafetta, *First Voyage*, pp. 65, 72.

61. Jacobs, *A Treatise*, p. 153; Pigafetta, *First Voyage*, pp. 71, 74-76.

62. Jacobs, *A Treatise*, p. 143.

63. Ibid., pp. 106-107.

64. Ibid., pp. 143-144; Kooijman, *Tapa in Indonesia*, pp. 189, 414, 427; Shore, *"Mana* and *Tapu,"* pp. 150, 152.

65. Sahlins, *Islands of History*, pp. 85-86.

66. Jacobs, *A Treatise*, pp. 107-109.

67. Rodgers, *Power and Gold*, pp. 48, 63, 79-80.

68. Jacobs, *A Treatise*, p. 113.

69. Ibid., p. 131.

70. Ibid., pp. 132-133.

71. Rebelo, *Informação sobre as Malucas*, text 2, Sá, *Documentação*, vol. 3, p. 355.

72. "Legende en geschiedenis van Ternate," pp. 310-311.

73. Dumézil as discussed in Sahlins, *Islands of History*, p. 90.

74. Rebelo, *Informação*, text 1, p. 294; Jacobs, *A Treatise*, p. 115.

75. Pigafetta, *First Voyage*, p. 68.

76. Commelin, *Begin ende voortgangh*, First Voyage, Neck, vol. 1, p. 34.

77. Errington, *Meaning and Power in a Southeast Asian Realm*, chap. 8.

78. Jacobs, *A Treatise*, pp. 103-105, 121.

79. Andaya, *The Heritage*, pp. 57, 315.

80. Jacobs, *A Treatise*, p. 123.

81. Oliver, *Ancient Tahitian*, p. 148.

82. Jacobs, *A Treatise*, pp. 105, 307.

83. Ibid., p. 105.

84. Ibid., p. 151.

85. Rebelo, *Informação,* text 1, p. 291.

86. The Spanish, Portuguese, and Dutch practice of erecting stone pillars with their coats of arms to proclaim their "discovery" and "possession" of lands in Maluku was treated by the local inhabitants in much the same way as their own markers. In the seventeenth century they showed their displeasure at the Dutch and their "gods" by destroying the pillars containing the VOC seal which had been erected in various parts of Maluku.

87. Mus described the lands of monsoon Asia as possessing a particular belief in the deity of the soil which came to be the basis for a territorial and a dynastic principle within a small area. The furthest limit of adherents to a particular deity of the soil defined the territorial boundaries of a group, while the individual who "discovered" the material presence of the deity of the soil and was the first intermediary between the deity and the community became the founder of the family of local lords. See Mus, *India Seen from the East,* pp. 15–17.

88. The precision of a single word to refer to a specific type of activity is not unusual in local languages where a particular act may be commonplace. Another example is in Malay where there are a number of specific terms to refer to sitting in different positions on the floor. In the central Philippine islands of the Visayas a seventeenth century Jesuit missionary illustrated the richness of the local language by explaining that there were different words used for washing separate parts of the body and between twenty to thirty distinct words for "taste" which "distinguish the drinkable from the eatable, the fruits from the meat, the words from the sentences, . . . sound from the senses." Alcina, "The Muñoz Text of Alcina's History of the Bisayan Islands (1668)," Part 1, bk. 3, pp. 13–15.

89. Leeden, "The Raja Ampat Islands," pp. 220–224.

90. Grimes, "The Return of the Bride: Affiliation and Alliance on Buru," p. 14.

91. Sá, *Documentação,* p. 355.

92. Jacobs, *A Treatise,* p. 113.

93. Rebelo, *Informação,* text 1, p. 289.

94. Jacobs, *A Treatise,* pp. 113, 151. This custom appears similar to that in Pacific societies where a stimulant was prepared from the root of the shrub *Piper methysticum,* which was chewed and mixed with water to make the Fijian *yaqona* and the Polynesian *kava.* In Fiji, Tonga, and Samoa, kava drinking became a ritual accompanying important events which involved high-ranking individuals. It has been suggested that there is a division between those peoples who chewed betel and those who drank kava. If this is the case, then Maluku may be somewhere in the transition area between these two types. Bellwood, *Man's Conquest,* p. 139.

95. Baker, "Descent," p. 67.

96. In this period the various villages and towns, including the royal settlement, were divided into soas. Each of these soas was under a bobato who appears to have been the head of a large extended family group which composed the soa. For an anthropological explanation of the functioning of the soa in Ternate, see Fraassen, "Ternate," especially pp. 183–186.

97. Baker, "Descent," p. 52.

98. Mus, *India Seen from the East,* pp. 14–15.

99. Jacobs, *A Treatise,* p. 369. The Spanish reference comes from Colín, *Labor Evangélica,* vol. 3, p. 39.

100. Clercq, *Bijdragen tot de kennis der residentie Ternate,* pp. 280, 324.

101. VOC 1240, Memorie van Overgave, Simon de Cos, 23 May 1662, fols. 796, 807.

102. Valentijn lists these four families as composing the Fala Raha, which seems to accord with contemporary sources in this period; Valentijn, *Oud en Nieuw,* vol. 1, p. 241. A 1682 report by Governor R. Padtbrugge also mentions these four families as forming the Fala Raha; VOC 1376, Memorie van Overgave, R. Padtbrugge, 31 Aug. 1682, fol. 265. In other sources the three which are always mentioned are the Tomagola, the Tomaitu, and the Marsaoli. It is the fourth member which is in dispute and a subject of controversy among present-day Ternatens. See the discussion on the Fala Raha in Fraassen, "Ternate," vol. 1, pp. 193–210.

103. Valentijn, *Oud en Nieuw,* vol. 1, p. 241.

104. Personal communication, Husain Mahifa, ex-Head Kelurahan Gurabunga, Tidore, 25 December 1987.

105. Jacobs, *A Treatise,* pp. 74–75.

106. Ibid., pp. 74–75.

107. Ibid., pp. 74–75. Galvão may have been exaggerating when he claimed that even children of six or seven years old had a say in decision-making. Wisdom was believed to be cumulative, making the elders the fount of knowledge.

108. Ibid., pp. 74–77.

109. Ibid., p. 183.

110. Ibid., pp. 153–159.

111. Baker, "Descent," pp. 302–304.

112. Cortesão, *Suma Oriental,* vol. 1, p. 216.

113. Jacobs, *A Treatise,* p. 141.

114. Ibid., pp. 137–139.

115. Burnell (ed.), *The Voyage of John Huyghen van Linschoten to the East Indies,* vol. 2, p. 82.

116. An early seventeenth century account of the Franciscans in Asia, which was based on reports sent from the brethren in the field in Maluku in the sixteenth century, had this to say about the rare bird: "There also exist in these islands some very beautiful birds which the natives call 'birds of the gods *(pássaros de Deus).'* The reason is not only that they are very beautiful . . . but they never set foot on land until they die." Trindade, *Conquista espiritual do Oriente,* vol. 1, p. 45.

117. Burnell (ed.), *The Voyage of John Huyghen van Linschoten to the East Indies,* vol. 1, p. 118.

118. Willer, "Aanteekeningen omtrent het Noorder-Schiereiland van het Eiland Halmahera," p. 345.

119. Jacobs, *A Treatise,* pp. 133, 137, 143–145, 255.

120. Ibid., pp. 107–109.

121. Ibid., pp. 105–107, 139.

122. Commelin (ed.), *Begin ende voortgangh,* vol. 1, First Voyage, Neck, pp. 30–40.

123. The process is one which Lévi-Strauss describes as the transformation of "raw"/nature into "cooked"/culture. By accepting the validity of these origin myths, the particular group becomes socialized/acculturated to the conception of a single world of Maluku. Lévi-Strauss, *The Raw,* p. 336. See note 35 above.

CHAPTER THREE

1. Valentijn, *Oud en Nieuw,* pp. 230, 239.

2. Rumphius, *Ambonsche Landbeschryving, 1679,* pp. 244–247.

3. Jacobs, *A Treatise,* p. 102.

4. Fraassen, "Ternate," vol. 1, p. 194.

5. See Article 17 of the Bungaya treaty in Stapel, *Het Bongaais Verdrag,* pp. 242–243.

6. VOC 1376, Memorie van Overgave, R. Padtbrugge, 31 Aug. 1682, fols. 260v–262r.

7. Ptak, "The Northern Trade Route to the Spice Islands," pp. 29–31.

8. VOC 1345, Papers of R. Padtbrugge on his journey through Maluku, 1 Aug. 1678 to 8 March 1679, fols. 222–223.

9. VOC 1727, Description of Maluku , Pieter Rooselaar, 11 June 1706, fols. 904–906.

10. VOC 1794, Memorie van Overgave, Jacob Claaszoon, 14 July 1710, fols. 55–56.

11. VOC 1345, Papers of R. Padtbrugge on his journey through Maluku, 1 Aug. 1678 to 8 March 1679, fols. 282–287.

12. VOC 1727, Description of Maluku, Pieter Rooselaar, 11 Jan. 1706, fol. 907.

13. VOC 1376, Memorie van Overgave, R. Padtbrugge, 31 Aug. 1682, fol. 322r.

14. VOC 1794, Memorie van Overgave, Jacob Claaszoon, 14 July 1710, fols. 51–54.

15. Rumphius, *D'Amboinsche Rariteitkamer,* p. 205.

16. Ibid., fols. 214–215.

17. Abdul Razak Daeng Patunru, *Sedjarah Gowa,* p. 24.

18. VOC 1428, Memorie van Overgave, J. Lobs, 5 Oct. 1686, fol. 145v.

19. Ibid. , fol. 145v.

20. Ibid., fol. 202.

21. Ibid., fols. 203–204.

22. VOC 1345, Papers of R. Padtbrugge on his journey through Maluku, 1 Aug. 1678 to 8 March 1679, fols. 208–209.

23. VOC 1727, Description of Maluku, Pieter Rooselaar, 11 June 1706, fols. 742, 767, 908–911; VOC 1376, Memorie van Overgave, R. Padtbrugge, 31 Aug. 1682, fol. 322r.

24. The following account of Ternate's territories is extracted from VOC 1376, Memorie van Overgave, R. Padtbrugge, 31 Aug. 1682, fols. 790–804; VOC 1428, Memorie van Overgave, J. Lobs, 5 Oct. 1686, fol. 151r–155r.

25. VOC 1240, Memorie van Overgave, Simon de Cos, 23 May 1662, fol. 792.

26. Cortesão, *Suma Oriental,* pp. 217–218.

27. Carta Lebe huçem, rey de Macquiem, pera o senhor governador das Indias del-rei de Portugal (1518), in Sá, *Documentação,* vol. 1, p. 114.

28. VOC 1376, Memorie van Overgave, R. Padtbrugge, 31 Aug. 1682, fol. 281r.

29. VOC 1240, Memorie van Overgave, Simon de Cos, 23 May 1662, fol. 793.

30. Ibid., fols. 793–794.

31. Platenkamp, "Myths of Life and Image in Northern Halmahera," p. 149.

32. Laarhoven, "Lords of the Great River: The Maguindanao Port and Polity During the Seventeenth Century," p. 174.

33. VOC 1675, Secret Missive Ternate to Batavia, 20 Sept. 1703, fol. 178.

34. VOC 1662, Report on the Patani eradication campaign, 11 July 1702, fol. 497.

35. VOC 1690, Daily Register by Hofman in the mission to Gebe, 25 Aug.– 28 Nov. 1703, fol. 233.

36. VOC 1662, Report on the Patani eradication campaign, 11 July 1702, fol. 497.

37. VOC 1727, Description of Maluku, Pieter Rooselaar, 11 June 1706, fols. 924–925.

38. In a trip from Gebe to Patani in January 1988, our fishing boat stopped at Mor, which appeared to be a thriving, well-populated village. To my surprise they explained that they all came from Patani and only spent a few months of the year in Mor to tend their gardens and harvest them from time to time.

39. VOC 1727, Description of Maluku, Pieter Rooselaar, 11 June 1706, fol. 924; VOC 1662, Report on the Patani eradication campaign, 11 July 1702, fol. 498.

40. VOC 1727, Description of Maluku, Pieter Rooselaar, 11 June 1706, fol. 926.

41. VOC 1727, Mission to the Papuan islands, 17 June 1705, fols. 486–487, 493–495.

42. VOC 1727, Description of Maluku, Pieter Rooselaar, 11 June 1706, fols. 917–918.

43. Ibid., fols. 915–921.

44. Bellwood, *Prehistory of the Indo-Malaysian Archipelago,* pp. 120–121, 128.

45. Kamma, *Koreri: Messianic Movements in the Biak-Numfor Culture Area,* p. 8.

46. "Ringkasan kisah perjalanan ke Irian Barat dalam tempu 7 bulan 77 hari," typed manuscript in the Department of Education and Culture, Soa Sio, Tidore, p. 3; "Susunan pemerintahan sultan dan pemerintahan umum pada daerah kesultanan Tidore," quoted from the *Buku Sejarah Jou Barakati and the Silsilah Keturunan Sultan.* Typed manuscript in the Department of Education and Culture, Soa Sio, Tidore, p. 1.

47. Kamma, *Koreri,* p. 215.

48. The term "Papuan language" itself is imprecise, and linguists prefer to speak of it as a non-Austronesian language. In this book the term "Papuan" is retained to highlight an acknowledged cultural distinction between groups.

49. Kamma, "De verhouding tussen Tidore en de Papoese eilanden in legende en historie," pp. 366, 368; Kamma, *Koreri,* p. 8.

50. VOC 2099, Report on the transporting of the Patanese to Tidore, 5 Aug. 1728, fol. 970.

51. "Hubungan antara Tidore dengan Irian Barat," typed manuscript in the Department of Education and Culture, Soa Sio, Tidore, pp. 10–11.

52. Kamma, "De verhouding," p. 541. In this version the unity of the group is stressed.

53. "Ringkasan kisah," pp. 3–9.

54. Haga, *Nederlandsch-Nieuw Guinea en de Papoesche Eilanden: Historische Bijdrage, 1500–1883,* vol. 1, pp. 21, 25, 27.

55. Kamma, "The Incorporation of Foreign Culture Elements and Complexes by Ritual Enclosure Among the Biak-Numforese," p. 61.

56. Ibid., p. 75.

57. Ibid., pp. 76–78.

58. Ibid., p. 80.

59. Kamma, *Koreri,* p. 95.

60. Ibid., p. 66.

61. VOC 1345, Papers of R. Padtbrugge on his journey through Maluku, 1 Aug. 1678 to 8 March 1679, fol. 701.

62. Story told by the Kepala Desa Patani, Salahuddin Faruk at Kapaleo, Gebe, on 9 January 1988.

63. Adelaar, "Malagasy Culture-History: Some Linguistic Evidence," forthcoming.

CHAPTER FOUR

1. The November date is recorded in a later compilation of Albuquerque's letters. Correia says that they embarked for Maluku on 1 December, while Galvão and Castanheda say they left Melaka in January. Cortesão, *Suma Oriental,* p. lxxx.

2. In some documents he is called Bayansirullah.

3. Sá, *Documentação,* vol. 1, pp. 405–407; Cortesão, *Suma Oriental,* vol. 1, p. lxxxi.

4. Barros, *Da Asia,* vol. 5, p. 593, Dec. III, Liv. V, Cap. VI.

5. Argensola, *Conquista,* p. 13.

6. Sá, *Documentação,* vol. 1, p. 86, "Carta do Rei de Ternate a El-Rei D. Manuel."

7. Ibid., pp. 119–120, Carta do Rei de Ternate ao Capitão de Malaca [1520?].

8. Pigafetta, *First Voyage,* p. 65; Lord Stanley , *The First Voyage,* pp. 124–125.

9. Barros, *Da Asia,* vol. 5, pp. 618–619, Dec. III, LIv. V, Cap. VII.

10. Jacobs, *A Treatise,* p. 21; Lima Felner, *Subsidios,* p. 112.

11. Sá, *Documentação,* vol. 1, p. 163, Carta de Rui Gago a El-Rei, 15 Feb. 1523.

12. Barros, *Da Asia,* vol. 5, p. 610, Dec. III, Liv. V, Cap. VII; Schurhammer, *Die zeitgenössischen,* p. 9.

13. Castanheda, *História,* p. 594; Barros, *Da Asia,* vol. 7, pp. 249–250, Dec. IV, Liv. II, Cap. XX.

14. Oviedo, *História,* p. 266.

15. Sá, *Documentação,* vol. 1, p. 263, Carta de Pedro de Monte Maior a El-Rei, 14 Jan. 1533.

16. Pérez-Bustamante, "La expedición," in Mota (ed.), *A viagem,* pp. 613–626; Oviedo, *História,* pp. 239, 266–289; Lopez and Alfonso (eds.), *Christianization,* document V, pp. 262–265.

17. Barros, *Da Asia,* vol. 7, pp. 244–246, Dec. IV, Liv. IV, Cap. XIX.

18. Ibid., p. 248, Dec. IV, Liv. II, Cap. XX.

19. Although the four traditional Papuan kingdoms of the Raja Ampat islands in later reports refer to Waigeu, Misool, Waigama, and Salawati, these Portuguese sources may be recording an early tradition where Gebe was still a powerful kingdom with links to the Sawai groups in southeastern Halmahera.

20. Sá, *Documentação,* vol. 1, p. 162, Carta de Rui Gago a El-Rei, 15 Feb. 1523; Barros, *Da Asia,* vol. 8, p. 130, Dec. IV, Liv. VI, Cap. XIX.

21. Barros, *Da Asia,* vol. 5, p. 614, Dec. III, Liv. V, Cap. VII.

22. Castanheda, *História,* vol. 2, p. 607.

23. Ibid., pp. 597–598.

24. Sá, *Documentação,* Carta de Vicente Da Fonseca a El-Rei, 8 Dec. 1531, vol. 1, p. 230.

25. Argensola, *Conquista,* p. 35.

26. Castanheda, *História,* vol. 2, pp. 637–638; Couto, *Da Asia,* vol. 11, p. 249, Dec. IV, Liv. VIII, Cap. VI; Argensola, *Conquista,* p. 36; Jacobs, *A Treatise,* p. 223.

27. Barros, *Da Asia,* vol. 8, pp. 133–139, Dec. IV, Liv. VI, Cap. XXII; Castanheda, *História,* vol. 2, pp. 660–663.

28. Castanheda, *História,* vol. 2, pp. 655–656, 660–662.

29. Ibid., vol. 2, p. 721.

30. Ibid., p. 722.

31. Jacobs, *A Treatise,* pp. 222–225.

32. Barros, *Da Asia,* vol. 8, pp. 146–150, Dec. IV, Liv. VI, Cap. XXIV; Castanheda, *História,* vol. 2, pp. 719–720.

33. Sá, *Documentação,* vol. 1, pp. 253–257, "Carta do Rei de Geilolo ao Imperador Carlos V," 1 March 1532.

34. Ibid., vol. 3, Rebelo, *Informação,* Text 2, pp. 473–474.

35. Ibid., p. 367.

36. Ibid., vol. 1, Carta de Tristão de Ataide a El-Rei, 20 Feb. 1534, pp. 292–294.

37. Castanheda, *História,* vol. 2, p. 688; Argensola, *Conquista,* p. 61.

38. Sá, *Documentação,* Carta de Tristão de Ataide a El-Rei, 20 Feb. 1534, vol. 1, p. 298.

39. Argensola, *Conquista,* p. 38.

40. Schurhammer, *Francis Xavier,* p. 161.

41. Sá, *Documentação,* vol. 1, Outra carta de Tristão de Ataide a El-Rei, D. João III, pp. 342–343.

42. Schurhammer, *Francis Xavier,* vol. 3, pp. 163–164.

43. Jacobs, *A Treatise,* pp. 224–225.

44. Castanheda, *História,* vol. 2, p. 750.

45. Jacobs, *A Treatise,* pp. 231–251.

46. Argensola, *Conquista,* p. 62.

47. Jacobs, *A Treatise,* pp. 323–325.

48. Ibid., pp. 298–299.

49. Castanheda, *História,* vol. 2, pp. 905–906.

50. Schurhammer, *Francis Xavier,* vol. 3, p. 157.

51. Castanheda, *História,* vol. 2, p. 907.

52. Jacobs, *A Treatise,* p. 299.

53. Argensola, *Conquista,* p. 70; Castanheda, *História,* vol. 2, p. 906.

54. Jacobs, *Documenta,* vol. 1, Letter from Francis Xavier to Rome, Cochin, 20 Jan. 1548, p. 40.

55. Schurhammer, *Francis Xavier,* vol. 3, p. 151; Sá, *Documentação,* vol. 1, Carta de Jordão de Freitas a El-Rei D. João III, 13 Feb. 1545, pp. 438–441.

56. The Portuguese in the sixteenth century used the term *canarin* to refer to the Konkani people of Goa. Burnell and Yule, *Hobson-Jobson,* p. 154.

57. Schurhammer, *Francis Xavier,* vol. 3, pp. 157–160.

58. Copia auténtica do testamento de D. Manuel, rei de Ternate, 30 June 1545. Fundo Geral, caixa 61, no. 17, Biblioteca Nacional Lisboa, fol. 46v; Couto, *Da Asia,* vol. 13, pp. 448–452, Dec. V, Liv. X, Cap. X.

59. Couto, *Da Asia,* vol. 14, pp. 22–23, Dec. VI, Liv. I, Cap. IV; "Carta de D. João de Castro, sendo Governador da India, para El-Rei D. João III, 16 Deç. 1546," in Sanceau, *Cartas,* pp. 224–227; Schurhammer, *Francis Xavier,* vol. 3, pp. 157–160, 192, 198; Villiers, "De um caminho," p. 30.

60. Schurhammer, *Francis Xavier,* vol. 3, p. 153; Wicki, "Gesang," p. 147; Rhodes, *Rhodes of Viet Nam,* p. 69; Borges, *Métodos,* pp. 165–166, 170.

61. Jacobs, *Documenta,* vol. 1 (1542–1577), Fr. Jerónimo de Olmedo SJ to Jesuits College of Goa, Ambon, 12 May 1571, pp. 627–628; and Fr. Fernando Alvares SJ to Jesuits of Goa College, Bacan, 20 April 1570, pp. 578–579.

62. Jacobs, *Documenta,* Fr. Nicolau Nunes to Jesuits of Goa College, Tolo, 2 Jan. 1570, p. 564; Jacobs, *Documenta,* vol. 1, Fr. Fernando Alvares SJ to Jesuits of Goa College, Bacan, 20 April 1570, p. 579.

63. Ibid., vol. 1, Fr. Fernando Alvares SJ to Jesuits of Goa College, Bacan, 20 April 1570, p. 578.

64. Wicki, "Gesang," p. 147.

65. Franciscan historians attribute the conversion of New Spain to the children; one even entitled a chapter of his book, "How the Conversion of the Indians Was Done Through Children." The Franciscans were noted for their conversion of young people, especially the sons of chiefs, who were then expected to bring the gospel to their elders. See Ricard, *Spiritual Conquest,* pp. 99–101; Iriarte de Aspurz, *Franciscan History,* pp. 320, 326. Music was so effective in the Americas that people came from far and wide just to listen to the music of the organ or learn tunes which the missionaries had put to the Christian prayers and rituals. Franciscans remarked on the way that the Mexicans used to gather in groups and spend the hours singing the prayers. Borges, *Métodos,* pp. 165–166, 170.

66. Jacobs, *Documenta,* vol. 1, Francis Xavier to Jesuits in Rome, Cochin, 10 May 1546, pp. 13–14.

67. Schurhammer, *Francis Xavier,* vol. 3, pp. 153–154.

68. Jacobs, *Documenta,* vol. 1, Letter from Luis Frois, Goa, 14 Nov. 1559;

vol. 1, p. 423, Letter from Marcos Pancudo, Ternate, 12 Feb. 1564, pp. 290–291.

69. Ibid., Letter from Pero Mascarenhas, Ternate, Dec. 1563–Feb 1564, p. 486; ibid., Letter from Melchior Nunes, Cochin, 20 Jan. 1566, p. 432.

70. Ibid., vol. 1, Letter from Pero Mascarenhas, Ternate, March–April 1564, pp. 436–437.

71. Argensola, *Conquista,* pp. 38–39; Schurhammer, *Francis Xavier,* p. 161.

72. Jacobs, *Documenta,* vol. 1, Letter from Pero Mascarenhas, Ternate, 10 Feb. 1564, pp. 412–413.

73. Ibid., vol. 1, Report on the Mission Work of the Jesuits in the East, Evora, Sept. 1561, p. 323, fn. 2.

74. Although the numbers appear small, Maluku was very well served and was considered one of the larger of the Jesuit communities abroad.

75. Jacobs, *Documenta,* vol. 2 (1577–1606), Report of the Visitation to Maluku by Fr. António Marta, Tidore, April 1588, pp. 250–255.

76. Ibid., Juan de Beira to Ignatius Loyola, Ternate, 13 Feb. 1550, p. 78, fn. 11.

77. While in Sahu in 1987, I had the opportunity of meeting a number of Tobarus who had been moved to permanent settlements from their home area further north in Ibu. We were discussing various aspects of the history and the customs of the Tobarus when one of them remarked that it was a pity that this particular headman could not be there since he was the authority on the subject. They said that I had to go north to see him. Then, as we talked, this man appeared, apparently having just arrived after walking through jungle paths for several days, which is common among the Tobarus even today. This impressed my Bacan companion who said, "It is the way of the Tobarus; they can do things without our knowing how they do it. Did you see how he just appeared when we needed him?"

78. A detailed account of the campaign is provided in "Exposição de Bernadim de Sousa, Capitão da fortaleza de Maluco, 13 June 1551," in *Gavetas,* vol. 2 , pp. 784–786.

79. Couto, *Da Asia,* vol. 15, pp. 295–324, Dec. VI, Liv. IX, Cap. X; Jacobs, *Documenta,* vol. 1, Juan de Beira to Ignatius Loyola, Ternate, 13 Feb. 1550, vol. 1, p. 78, fn. 11.

80. Tiele, "De Européers," vol. 28, p. 418.

81. Valentijn, *Oud en Nieuw,* vol. 1, p. 353.

82. Sousa, *Capitães,* p. 227; Jacobs, *Documenta,* vol. 1, Fr. Jerónimo de Olmedo, Ambon, 2 June 1570, p. 592. One tradition says that his body was dismembered, hung up for all to see, salted, and then thrown into the sea. Argensola, *Conquista,* pp. 76–77; Couto, *Da Asia,* vol. 18, pp. 213–214, Dec. VIII, Cap. XXVI.

83. Sá, *Documentação,* vol. 4, Antonio Bocarro, "História de Maluco no tempo de Gonçalo Pereira Marramaque e Sancho de Vos," March, 1636, pp. 210–211.

84. Ibid., p. 211; Couto, *Da Asia,* vol. 18, p. 263, Dec. VIII, Cap. XXXI.

85. Jacobs, *Documenta,* vol. 1, Fr. Jerónimo de Olmedo to Jesuits in Goa, Ambon, 2 June 1570 p. 590.

86. Ibid., vol. 1, Fr. Jerónimo de Olmedo to Jesuits in Goa, Ambon, 12 May 1571, pp. 627–628; ibid., vol. 1, Fr. Nicolau Nunes' General Survey of Maluku, Goa, 4 Jan. 1576, pp. 690–691; ibid., vol. 1, Fr. João de Mesquita to Rome, Melaka, 30 Dec. 1573, p. 648.

87. Ibid., vol. 2, Fr. Mateus Lopes to unknown Jesuit [in Europe?], Macao, 29 Nov. 1578, pp. 28–9; ibid., vol. 1, Fr. Jerónimo de Olmedo to Jesuits in Goa, Ambon, 12 May 1571, p. 625.

88. Ibid., vol. 1, Fr. Nicolau Nunes' General Survey of Maluku, Goa, 4 Jan. 1576, p. 689.

89. Jacobs, "New Sources ," pp. 227–8; Argensola, Conquista, pp. 93–95.

90. Jacobs, Documenta, vol. 1, Fr. Francisco Dionísio to Rome, Cochin, 25 Jan. 1577, pp. 705–706; Sousa, Capitães, pp. 229–230; Valentijn, Oud en Nieuw, vol. 1, pp. 357–358.

91. Argensola, Conquista, p. 95; Tiele, "De Europëers," vol. 28, p. 456, vol. 29, p. 161.

92. Valentijn, Oud en Nieuw, vol.1, p. 358.

93. Ibid., p. 359; Argensola has a list of all the islands in Conquista, pp. 81–82. The tradition of "seventy-two islands" seems to have been some local perception of innumerable islands, since no one ever provides precisely the seventy-two claimed to have been under Babullah.

94. Jacobs, Documenta, vol. 2, Fr. Jerónimo Rodrigues to Fr. Provincial Rui Vicente, Tidore, Feb. 1579, p. 39.

95. Ibid., Fr. António Marta to D. Gomez Perez Dasmariñas, Tidore, July 1591, p. 308.

96. The idea of controlled collection of statistics is a recent one. As discussed in the Introduction, missionaries in this period described their activities for the edification of the brotherhood and the Christian communities in Europe. Citing of tens of thousands and even hundreds of thousands of converts fulfilled the desire for edification rather than for statistical accuracy. Brou, "Les statistiques dans les anciennes missions," p. 361.

97. Jacobs, Documenta, vol. 2, Fr. António Pereira to Fr. Claudio Acquaviva, Manila, 24 June 1594, pp. 398–400.

98. Ibid., vol. 2, Fr. António Marta to Fr. Provincial in Goa, in Tidore, April 1588, p. 257.

99. Temple, World Encompassed, p. 87.

100. Ibid., pp. 66–72.

101. VOC 1254, Memorie van Overgave, Anthony van Voorst, April 1665, fol. 1199.

102. Archivo General de India (AGI), Seville, Patronato Real 46, Ramo 18, Carta de Pedro Sarmiento: Relación de las fuerzas, poder y artillería que tiene el Rey de Terrenate en su Reyno, 30 April 1584.

103. VOC 1240 (1663), Memorie van Overgave, Simon de Cos, 23 May 1662, fol. 795.

104. Couto, Da Asia, vol. 20, pp. 506–507, Dec. X, Cap. IV.; Tiele, "De Europëers," vol. 29, p. 180.

105. Argensola, Conquista, pp. 67–68.

106. Colín, Labor Evangélica, vol. 3, p. 41; Tiele, "De Europëers," vol. 29,

pp. 182–184. In the sixteenth century the Ottoman Turkish ruler responded to appeals for help against the Portuguese from the Sultan Aceh by sending fire-arms and gunners. The Turks who were mentioned by the Spaniards may have been part of the Turkish contingent sent to Aceh. The Turks had developed considerable skill in the manufacture and use of cannon and muskets and were an asset to the Muslim kingdoms in the archipelago. Reid, "Sixteenth Century Turkish Influence in Western Indonesia," pp. 396–397.

107. Argensola, *Conquista,* pp. 188–190.

108. Ibid., p. 255.

109. Commelin, *Begin ende voortgangh,* vol. 1, First Voyage, Admiral Neck, p. 34.

110. Ibid., p. 33; Tiele, "De Europeërs," vol. 30, p. 148.

111. Commelin, *Begin ende voortgangh,* vol. 1, First Voyage, Neck, p. 34.

112. Iria, "As ilhas Molucas," in Mota (ed.), *A viagem,* Document 21, Letter from the King of Portugal to the viceroy of India, 15 Feb. 1603, p. 710.

113. Guerreiro, *Relação,* vol. 2, pp. 127–128, 305–308; Argensola, *Conquista,* p. 350.

114. Temple, *World Encompassed,* pp. 66–72.

115. Argensola, *Conquista,* pp. 358–376.

116. Ibid., pp. 380, 382.

117. AGI, Patronato Real 47, Ramo 21, Relación de lo sucedido en las islas del Maluco desde 3 de Mayo de 1606 . . . hasta 31 de Mayo de 1607, fols. 8v–9r.

118. AGI, Patronato Real 47, Ramo 13, Copia del recado que Acuña dió al dicho Cachile Samaroe, rey de Tidore, sobre los pueblos de Macquen, Ternate, 2 May 1606.

119. AGI, Patronato Real 47, Ramo 14, Copia del recado que Acuña dió al rey de Bacan, 2 May 1606.

120. AGI, Patronato Real 47, Ramo 14, Carta del rey de Bacan, Sultan Alauddin al de España, pidiendole favor y ayuda contra el de Terrenate su enemigo, 26 April 1606.

121. AGI, Patronato Real 47, Ramo 16, Carta de Don Pedro de Acuña sobre la conducta y persona del Ruy Percira, Sengaji, 2 May 1606.

122. Argensola, *Conquista,* pp. 380–381.

123. AGI, Patronato Real 47, Ramo 21, Relación de lo sucedido en las islas del Maluco desde 3 de Mayo de 1606 . . . hasta 31 de Mayo de 1607, fol. 2v.

124. Argensola, *Conquista,* pp. 387–388.

125. AGI, Patronato Real, Ramo 21, Relación de lo sucedido en las islas del Maluco desde 3 de Mayo de 1606 . . . hasta 31 de Mayo de 1607, fols. 4r–5r.

126. Ibid., fols. 8v–9r.

127. Argensola, *Conquista,* p. 393.

128. Castanheda, *História,* vol. 2, p. 90, Liv. V, Cap. LIV.

129. Diffie and Winius, *Foundations,* p. 361; Sá, *Documentação,* vol. 1, Carta dos moradores de Ternate a El-Rei D. João III, Ternate, 20 Feb. 1546, p. 475.

130. Moseley, *Travels,* pp. 11–12.

131. That the syahbandar position had arisen out of the pinate function seems to be corroborated by a Dutch report in 1681 of a Ternaten official known

as the "syahbandar pinate." VOC 1361, Ternate to Ambon, 9 May 1681, fol. 271r.

132. In van Fraassen's discussion of the kapita laut of Ternate, he has assumed that the title was in use earlier in the sixteenth century. Fraassen, "Ternate," vol. 2, pp. 444–445.

133. Argensola, *Conquista,* p. 346.

134. Pastells, *História,* in Torres y Lanza, *Catálogo,* pp. clxxxi, 46.

CHAPTER FIVE

1. Argensola, *Conquista,* p. 393.

2. This is a phrase used by James Fox, who bases his observations on anthropological essays on eastern Indonesian societies. He suggests the need to alter the idea of dualism as "a thing in itself" to one of "a particular mode of perception and action." Fox, "Models and Metaphor," in Fox (ed.), *The Flow of Life,* p. 333.

3. Tiele, "De Europeërs," vol. 32, p. 56.

4. Pastells, História, vol. 5, pp. clxx–clxxi.

5. Tiele, "De Europeërs,"vol. 32, pp. 69–71.

6. Commelin (ed.), *Begin ende voortgangh,* vol. 2, 13e Journaal, p. 66.

7. Tiele, "De Europeërs," vol. 32, pp. 71, 100–101; Valentijn, *Oud en Nieuw,* vol. 1, p. 371.

8. "El Maestre de Campo Juan de Esquivel daba cuenta a la Audiencia de Manila de la toma de Macquién," in Pastells, *História,* vol. 6, pp. xxxvii–xxxviii.

9. Tiele, "De Europeërs," vol. 32, pp. 101–103.

10. Colenbrander (ed.), *Coen. Bescheiden,* "Vertoogh van de staet der Vereenichde Nederlanden in de quartieren van Oost-Indien, 24 Nov. (21 Sept.) 1623," vol. 4, p. 581.

11. Tiele, "De Europeërs," vol. 35, pp. 271–273.

12. Colenbrander, *Coen. Bescheiden,* Letter from Batavia, 22 Aug. 1617, vol. 4, p. 260.

13. Perez, "Los Franciscanos," pp. 225, 430–431; Colenbrander, *Coen. Bescheiden,* Letter from Batavia to Patria, 5 Aug. 1619, vol. 1, pp. 449–450; Tiele, "De Europeërs," vol. 35, pp. 299–300.

14. Perez, "Los Franciscanos," pp. 623–626.

15. "Koxinga," or Cheng Ch'eng-kung, led the Ming resistance to the Manchus in Fukien in 1647. After he was pushed out of China, he fled to Taiwan and seized it from the Dutch. It became his headquarters, and it was from here that he posed a threat to the Spaniards in the Philippines.

16. Perez, "Los Franciscanos," p. 653.

17. Tiele, "De Europeërs," vol. 32, p. 105.

18. Colenbrander, *Coen. Bescheiden,* "Vertooch," vol. 4, p. 582.

19. Heeres and Tiele, *Bouwstoffen,* vol. 1, pp. 225–226.

20. Ibid., vol. 1, pp. 230–231.

21. Ibid., vol. 2, p. 40.

22. Ibid., vol. 2, p. Lii.

23. Colenbrander, *Coen. Bescheiden,* vol. 5, Batavia to Patria, 9 Nov. 1627, pp. 42–43.

24. Ibid., p. 41; Valentijn, *Oud en Nieuw,* vol. 1, pp. 414–415; Heeres and Tiele, *Bouwstoffen,* vol. 2, pp. 120–121.

25. Colenbrander, *Coen. Bescheiden,* vol. 5, Batavia to Amsterdam, 3 Nov. 1628, p. 121; Heeres and Tiele, *Bouwstoffen,* vol. 2, pp. 136–137; Fraassen, "Ternate," vol. 1, p. 85; *Dagh-Register Batavia,* 1624–1629, pp. 378–379.

26. Valentijn, *Oud en Nieuw,* vol. 1, pp. 419.

27. Colenbrander, *Coen. Bescheiden,* vol. 5, Batavia to Amsterdam, 3 Nov. 1628, p. 138; Heeres and Tiele, *Bouwstoffen,* vol. 2, p. 176; Fraassen, "Ternate," vol. 1, p. 85; Valentijn, *Oud en Nieuw,* vol. 1, pp. 419, 426; *Dagh-Register Batavia,* 1631–1634, p. 377.

28. Heeres and Tiele, *Bouwstoffen,* vol. 2, pp. 283, 292.

29. *Dagh-Register Batavia,* 1631–1634, p. 377.

30. In the sources there is occasionally a mention of the greater antiquity of the old capital of Mareku to the royal settlement named Soa Sio. In Baker's study of present-day Tidore, he noted a distinction in the Tidore language between a Mareku and a Soa Sio dialect. According to his informants, this was due to two different periods of migration to the island. It appears that the political conflict between these two settlements masked older and deeper divisions in Tidore society. Baker, "Descent," p. 37, fn. 9.

31. Valentijn, *Oud en Nieuw,* vol. 1, p. 441; Heeres and Tiele, *Bouwstoffen,* vol. 3, pp. 128–129.

32. Valentijn, *Oud en Nieuw,* vol. 1, p. 442.

33. Heeres and Tiele, *Bouwstoffen,* vol. 3, p. 209.

34. Ibid., p. 216.

35. Riedel, *De sluik- en kroesharige rassen,* pp. 402, 460.

36. Valentijn, *Oud en Nieuw,* vol. 1, p. 444.

37. The word to define that special quality of unusual individuals with a supernatural gift of authority is *hpon* in Burmese, *pon* in Thai, and *sakti* or *keramat* in many archipelago languages. Although the Dutch source does not provide the local Ternaten term, the translated word conveys the same idea. In a seventeenth century Dutch translation of the Ayudhya chronicles, the Dutch used precisely the same term *geluk* to translate an unrecorded Thai word to indicate the special qualities of the founder of the Ayudhya dynasty. See Vliet, *The Short History,* p. 65.

38. Heeres and Tiele, *Bouwstoffen,* vol. 3, pp. 396–397.

39. Ibid., pp. 399, 447.

40. Andaya, *The Heritage of Arung Palakka,* p. 27; Abdurrahim and Wolhoff, *Sedjarah Goa,* p. 50.

41. Valentijn, *Oud en Nieuw,* vol. 1, p. 448.

42. Ibid., pp. 481, 487–489.

43. Ibid., p. 457.

44. Stapel, *Het Bongaais Verdrag,* p. 243.

45. VOC 1301, Translation of a Malay letter from Gov. Francx to the kings of Gorontalo and Limbotto, dated 15 March 1674, fols. 262r–v; VOC 1301, Menado to Batavia, 28 Jan. 1674, fols. 401r–v; VOC 1301, Menado to Batavia, 25 Feb. 1674, fols. 408v–409r.

46. VOC 1240, Memorie van Overgave, Simon de Cos, 23 May 1662, fols. 788–794.

47. VOC 1246, Ternate to Batavia, 5 May 1664, fol. 1177; Fraassen, "Ternate," vol. 1, p. 85.

48. VOC 1240, Memorie van Overgave, Simon de Cos, 23 May 1662, fol. 794.

49. Jacobs, "New Sources," Letter 5, D. Julião de Noronha, Cap. Tidore to Felipe I of Portugal, Tidore, 9 July 1597, p. 237.

50. Ibid., Letter 7, Portuguese soldiers and civilians of Tidore to Francisco Tello, Gov. of the Philippines. Tidore, 30 May 1599, p. 249.

51. AGI, Patronato Real 47, Ramo 13, Copia del recado que Acuña dió al dicho Cachile Samaroe, rey de Tidore, sobre los pueblos de Macquien, Ternate, 2 May 1606.

52. VOC 1243, Ternate to Batavia, 20 Aug. 1662, fols. 1202–1203, 1206.

53. VOC 1264, Ternate to Batavia, 20 April 1667, with "Treaty of 29 March 1667 between Tidore and Admiral Speelman on behalf of the VOC," fols. 8r–10r; Heeres and Stapel, *Corpus Diplomaticum,* vol. 2, Treaty between Tidore and the VOC, 29 March 1667, pp. 102–104.

54. VOC 1345, Daily Register Ft. Orange, 24 Sept. 1678, fol. 48.

55. VOC 1236, Ternate to Batavia, 7 May 1661, fol. 365.

56. VOC 1336, Daily Register Ft. Orange, 10 June 1678, fol. 719.

57. VOC 1264, Treaty between Tidore and the VOC, 29 March 1667, fol. 38.

58. VOC 1267, Ternate to Batavia, 30 April 1668, fol. 56r.

59. VOC 1345, Daily Register Ft. Orange, 24 Sept. 1678, fol. 42.

60. VOC 1318, Daily Register Ft. Orange, 8 Nov. 1675, fol. 679r.

61. VOC 1359, Ternate to Batavia, 31 Aug. 1680, fol. 143r.

62. Baker, "Descent," p. 121.

63. VOC 1338, Ternate to Batavia, 26 April 1678, fol. 166v.

64. VOC 1336, Daily Register Ft. Orange, 26 April 1678, fols. 553–554.

65. Valentijn, *Oud en Nieuw,* vol. 1, pp. 457, 470.

CHAPTER SIX

1. VOC 1311, Ternate to Batavia, 13 March 1675, fol. 141r.

2. VOC 1310, Report of the visit of Sultan Amsterdam to his kingdom by Paulus Harkszoon, 19 Aug. 1675, fols. 457v–458r.

3. Ibid., fols. 464v, 468v.

4. Andaya, "Treaty Conceptions," pp. 275–295.

5. VOC 1336, Daily Register Ft. Orange, 1 Jan. 1678, fols. 163–164; 28 Feb. 1678, fol. 374.

6. VOC 1318, Daily Register Ft. Orange, 5 June 1676, fol. 740r.

7. VOC 1336, Daily Register Ft. Orange, 28 Feb. 1678, fols. 374–376.

8. VOC 1338, Ternate to Batavia, 26 April 1678, fol. 166v.

9. VOC 1336, Daily Register Ft. Orange, 26 April 1678, fols. 535–536.

10. VOC 1320, Ternate to Batavia, 29 Aug. 1675, fols. 106r–107r.

11. Ibid., fol. 107r.

12. VOC 1318, Daily Register Ft. Orange, 5 June 1676, fol. 740r; VOC 1345, Daily Register, letters . . . from a trip of the Governor of Maluku with His Highness Amsterdam . . . beginning 1 Aug. 1678 and ending 8 March 1679, fol. 187.

13. VOC 1345, Daily Register, Letters from a trip of the Governor of Maluku . . . , 1 Aug. 1678 to 8 March 1679, fols. 762, 770.

14. VOC 1347, Ternate to Batavia, 31 Aug. 1679, fol. 264v.

15. VOC 1359, Ternate to Batavia, 31 Aug. 1680, fols. 143r–144v.

16. VOC 1347, Ternate to Batavia, 31 Aug. 1679, fol. 242r.

17. Ibid., fols., 248r–249r.

18. Ibid., fols. 244r–v, 278v.

19. In the Middle Ages, Muslims were commonly described as a race of dogs, and in one painting illustrating St. Augustine's two centers of human-kind, one of the two great families of nations is depicted with black skin, dog's head, and wearing clothes associated with Islam. Friedman, *The Monstrous Races,* pp. 63, 67.

20. VOC 1347, Ternate to Batavia, 31 Aug. 1679, fol. 253r.

21. VOC 1359, Ternate to Amboina, 12 July 1680, fols. 133r, 134r.

22. VOC 1359, Ternate to Batavia, 31 Aug. 1680, fols. 140r–141v.

23. Ibid., fol. 141v.

24. VOC 1345, Report by Andries Oloffsz on his visit to Tidore and Makian, 22 June 1679, fol. 447.

25. VOC 1361, Dutch letter to Sultan Syaifuddin, 23 Aug. 1681, fols. 355v–356r.

26. VOC 1376, Ternate to Batavia, 31 Aug. 1682, fol. 167r; VOC 1361, Ternate to Batavia, 30 Aug. 1681, fol. 339r.

27. Heeres and Stapel, *Corpus,* vol. 3, pp. 304–319.

28. Ibid., pp. 304–314.

29. Ibid., p. 316.

30. VOC 1428, Memorie van Overgave, Jacob Lobs, 5 Oct. 1686, fol. 145v.

31. VOC 1366, Daily Register Ft. Orange, Report of Envoy Oloffsz to Tidore, 4 Sept. 1680, fol. 50.

32. VOC 1375, Daily Register Ft. Orange, 12 Aug. 1682, fol. 419.

33. VOC 1428, Ternate to Batavia, 5 July 1686, fol. 93v.

34. VOC 1428, Memorie van Overgave, Jacob Lobs, 5 Oct. 1686, fol. 158r.

35. VOC 1376, Memorie van Overgave, R. Padtbrugge, 31 Aug. 1682, fol. 287r.

36. VOC 1375, Report on the killing of a Tidorese by a Ternaten alifuru, 17 Dec. 1681, fols. 236–237.

37. VOC 1437, Ternate to Batavia, 20 June 1687, fol. 177v; VOC 1622, Ternate to Batavia, 14 Sept. 1699, fol. 481.

38. VOC 1461, Instructions for H. J. Steenkuyler, Dutch head at Menado, 18 July 1689, fol. 460r.

39. VOC 1514, Daily Register Ft. Orange, 12 Aug. 1691, fols. 47r–v.

40. VOC 1516, Letter from Ternate Council to Sula, etc., dated 18 Dzulhij-jah 1102 [13 Sept. 1690], fols. 507v–508r.

41. VOC 1595, Ternate to Batavia, 28 May 1697, fol. 24.

42. VOC 1579, Ternate to Batavia, 20 Sept. 1696, fol. 426.

43. VOC 1595, Ternate to Batavia, 28 May 1697, fol. 8.

44. VOC 1556, Letter from Sultan Tidore and Council to Batavia, 18 Dzulhijjah 1105 [11 July 1693], fol. 588r.

45. VOC 1579, Letter from Sultan Bacan to Batavia, 5 June 1696, fol. 344.

46. Heeres and Stapel, *Corpus,* vol. 2, pp. 102–104.

47. VOC 1637, Agreement between the Company and Tidore, 15 May 1700, fols. 83–84; Heeres and Stapel, *Corpus,* vol. 3, pp. 499–500.

48. VOC 1690, Ternate to Batavia, 17 June 1704, fol. 47.

49. VOC 1637, Sultan Ternate to Batavia, 21 July 1700, fols. 76–77.

50. VOC 1979, Letter from Patani leaders to the Sultan Ternate, 3 Oct. 1720, fol. 98.

51. Ibid., fols. 98–99.

52. VOC 1960, From the Daily Register of Commissioner Cornelis Hasselaar, Letter from Sultan Tidore, received in Ternate 26 April 1720, fols. 83–88.

53. VOC 1960, Memorie van Overgave, Commissioner Hasselaar, 26 April 1720, fol. 404.

54. VOC 1960, Daily Register of Commissioner Hasselaar, 29 May 1720, n.p.

55. VOC 1960, Daily Register of Commissioner Hasselaar, under date 31 May 1720, n.p.

56. VOC 1979, Letter from Patani leaders to the Sultan Ternate and the Dutch government, 3 Oct. 1720, fols. 97–98.

57. VOC 1979, Letter from Tidore ministers to the Dutch governor, 14 Nov. 1720, fols. 105–106, 110.

58. VOC 1979, Ternate to Batavia, 14 Sept. 1722, fol. 106; Letter from Sultan Tidore in Patani, 8 Feb. 1722, fols. 148–150; VOC 1995, Memorie van Overgave, Hensius, 31 May 1723, fol. 141.

59. VOC 2012, Ternate to Batavia, 13 Sept. 1724, fol. 119.

60. VOC 1995, Hasselaar's report on problems in Ternate and Tidore, 31 May 1723, fol. 199.

61. VOC 2012, Ternate to Batavia, 13 Sept. 1724, fols. 431–432; VOC 2029, Ternate to Batavia, 12 June 1725, fols. 15–17.

62. VOC 2029, Ternate to Batavia, 12 June 1725, fols. 22–23.

63. VOC 1995, Memorie van Overgave, Hensius, 31 May 1723, fols. 139–140.

64. VOC 2029, Ternate to Batavia, 13 Sept. 1725, fols. 24, 34; VOC 2029, Ternate to Batavia, 12 June 1725, fol. 44.

65. VOC 2050, Ternate to Batavia, 12 Sept. 1726, fol. 477.

66. Ibid., fols. 482–483.

67. Ibid., fols. 483–493; VOC 2050, Letter from Sultan Tidore to Gov.-Gen. in Batavia, 12 Nov. 1726, fols. 648–650.

68. VOC 2050, Ternate to Batavia, fol. 500.

69. VOC 2050, Letter from Sultan Tidore to Gov.-Gen. in Batavia, 12 Nov. 1726, fol. 654.

70. VOC 2099, Ternate to Batavia, 31 May 1728, fols. 11–15.

71. VOC 2099, Ternate to Batavia, 30 June 1728, fol. 75; VOC 2099, Secret Resolution, 10 May 1728, fol. 275; VOC 2191, Memorie van Overgave, Gov. Pielat, 9 June 1731, fols. 1004–1007.

72. VOC 2099, Ternate to Batavia, 9 Sept. 1728, fols. 813–820.

73. The prostration ceremony was followed by all tribute missions to Tidore. In these missions those delivering the tribute would crawl on all fours in the

central throne room and approach the seated ruler. They then came and grasped the ruler's big toe on his right foot as a sign of obeisance. This is what was intended here, but a Tidore nobleman obviously saw the rebellion as not deserving pardon.

74. VOC 2099, Report on the Patanese in Tidore, 5 Aug. 1728, fols. 957–970.

75. VOC 2344, Ternate to Batavia, 20 Sept. 1735, fol. 91.

76. VOC 2344, Report of goods abandoned by spice eradication expedition to Maba, Weda, and Patani in September 1732, fol. 455. An Amsterdam pound was equivalent to 494 grams or 1.09 pounds avoirdupois.

77. VOC 1428, Ternate to Batavia, 5 Oct. 1686, fols. 109v–110r.

78. VOC 1608, Ternate to Batavia, Report on the spice eradication expedition to Halmahera, 14 July 1697, fol. 344.

79. VOC 2191, Memorie van Overgave, Pielat, 7 June 1731, fol. 1049.

80. VOC 1336, Daily Register Ft. Orange, under date 16 August 1677, Letter from Sultan Amsterdam, fol. 17.

81. VOC 2237, Ternate to Batavia, 11 Sept. 1732, fols. 62–65.

82. VOC 2162, Ternate to Batavia, 28 Sept. 1730, fols. 114–115.

83. VOC 2099, Ternate to Batavia, 31 May 1728, fol. 7.

84. VOC 2191, Memorie van Overgave, Pielat, 7 June 1731, fols. 1028–1029.

85. Ibid, fols. 1021–1023.

86. VOC 2237, Letter from Gov. Ternate to Dutch Sergeant in Tidore, 17 March 1732, fols. 959–961.

87. In 1718 the Dutch described this office as "keeper of the treasury and governor of everything *(schatbewaarder en bestuurder van alles)*" and in another place as "stadhouder or governor and treasurer *(stedehouder en tresourier)*." VOC 1910, Ternate to Batavia, 21 Sept. 1718, fol. 54; VOC 1926, Ternate to Batavia, 16 Sept. 1719, fol. 29.

88. VOC 1960, Daily Register of Commissioner Hasselaar, under date 9 Aug. 1720, n.p.

89. VOC 2628, Resolution of the Dutch Council in Ternate, 12 March 1744, fols. 321–327.

90. VOC 2740, Memorie van Overgave, Gov. Blokland, 28 Aug. 1749, fol. 425.

91. VOC 2567, Daily Register Ft. Orange, under date 30 March 1742, fols. 1249–1250.

92. VOC 2628, Letter from the village heads in Makian to Gov. Lelivelt in Ternate, 17 Sawal 1156 [4 Dec. 1743], fols. 208–211.

93. VOC 2649, Ternate to Batavia, 13 Sept. 1745, fols. 137–145.

94. VOC 2717, Ternate to Batavia, 11 May 1748, fol. 51.

95. VOC 2882, Memorie van Overgave, J. Elias van Mijlendonk, 20 July 1756, fols. 85–86. Complaints against the many penurious and oppressive royal progeny were common throughout the archipelago in these centuries. For an example of this in Malay history, see B. Andaya, "The Role of the *Anak Raja* in Malay History," pp. 162–186.

96. VOC 2798, Ternate to Batavia, 8 Sept. 1752, fols. 34–35.

97. VOC 2779, Ternate to Batavia, 15 Sept. 1751, fol. 597.

98. VOC 2693, Ternate to Batavia, 30 May 1759, fols. 72–73; VOC 3022, Ternate to Batavia, 30 June 1761, fols. 81–83.

CHAPTER SEVEN

1. VOC 3186, Secret papers, Report on the interrogation of two Tidorese, 7 June 1766, fol. 218; VOC 3181, Resolutions of the Dutch Council in Ternate, 23 Oct. 1765, fol. 5.

2. VOC 3022, Resolutions of the Dutch Council in Ternate, 11 Sept. 1760, fol. 3; VOC 3022, Ternate to Batavia, 31 Aug. 1761, fols. 17–27.

3. VOC 3248, Secret papers, Resolutions of the Dutch Council in Ternate, 25 Jan. 1768, fol. 113.

4. VOC 3022, Ternate to Batavia, 30 June 1761, fol. 86.

5. VOC 3186, Ternate to Batavia, 31 July 1766, fols. 5–6.

6. The process in Java is described by Berg, "The Javanese Picture of the Past," in Soedjatmoko (ed.), *An Introduction,* pp. 89–90.

7. Cense, "Eenige aantekeningen," p. 47; Andaya, *The Heritage of Arung Palakka,* p. 112.

8. VOC 3357, Daily Register, Hemmekans on his mission to the Papuas, under date 24 Aug. 1771, n.p.

9. Laarhoven, "Lords of the Great River," in Kathirithamby-Wells and Villiers (eds.), *The Southeast Asian Port and Polity,* p. 170.

10. VOC 3529, Secret papers, Ternate to Batavia, 13 Aug. 1778, fols. 319–340.

11. VOC 3556, Secret papers, Ternate to Batavia, 29 May 1779, fols. 4–12.

12. VOC 3551, Ternate to Batavia, 12 June 1779, fol. 28.

13. VOC 3556, Secret papers, Ternate to Batavia, 12 June 1779, fol. 19.

14. VOC 3551, Ternate to Batavia, 12 June 1779, fols. 30–31.

15. Haga, *Nederlandsch-Nieuw Guinea,* vol. 1, p. 299.

16. VOC 3603, Secret papers, Ternate to Batavia, 22 May 1781, fols. 5–6.

17. Ibid., fols. 5–6; VOC 3556, Secret papers, Secret advice, Ternate to Batavia, 29 Sept. 1779, fol. 101.

18. VOC 3603, Secret papers, Ternate to Batavia, 22 May 1781, fols. 15, 18–27; ibid., fols. 104–105.

19. Kamma, "The Incorporation," p. 70. See also Kamma, *Koreri,* passim.

20. Haga, *Nederlandsch-Nieuw Guinea,* vol. 1, pp. 299–300.

21. VOC 3603, Secret papers, Resolutions, Report of the Secretary of the Police in Ternate, 20 Oct. 1780, fol. 37.

22. Ibid., fols. 35–36.

23. Ibid., fol. 36.

24. Haga, *Nederlandsch-Nieuw Guinea,* vol. 1, pp. 301–302.

25. VOC 3622, Ternate to Batavia, 28 Sept. 1782, fol. 273; ibid., Resolution of the Dutch Council in Ternate, 8 Nov. 1781, fol. 138.

26. VOC 3602, Secret papers, Ambon to Batavia, 20 Sept. 1781, fols. 9–11.

27. Katoppo, *Nuku,* Appendix from Ambon Archives, pp. 237–239.

28. Fraassen, "Ternate," vol. 2, pp. 465–467; Knaap, "Kruidnagelen en Christenen," pp. 11–13.

29. VOC 3628, Secret resolutions, Ternate to Batavia, 15 April 1782, fols. 186–187.

30. VOC 3671, Ternate to Batavia, 10 Sept. 1784, fols. 68–69.

31. Ibid., 28 Sept. 1782, fol. 16.

32. Barros, *Da Asia,* vol. 6, p. 319, Dec. III, Liv. VIII, Cap. IX.

33. VOC 3676, Ternate to Batavia, 14 Sept. 1783, fols. 87–89.

34. VOC 3677, Secret resolutions, Ternate to Batavia, under date 28 Sept. 1783, Letter from twelve sangajis, gimalahas, and heads of Seram to the Sultan Tidore, fols. 2–4.

35. VOC 3764, Secret papers, Ambon to Ternate, 10 Oct. 1783, n.p.

36. VOC 3677, Secret papers, Banda to Ternate, 31 Dec. 1783, n.p.

37. VOC 3676, Secret papers, Ternate to Batavia, 8 March 1784, fols. 206–218.

38. Miller, "The Moluccas," p. 30.

39. Though today Toloa is located south of Mareku, contemporary Dutch sources clearly state that Toloa was "below" Mareku. This description accords with traditions in Mareku which describe the existence in the past of two settlements in Mareku: one on the slopes of the mountain and the other on the coast. The relationship between these settlements is interesting because in the past both fielded rival candidates for the Tidore royal house. Even when the royal residence was moved to Soa Sio sometime in the seventeenth century, Toloa-Mareku continued to retain their prestige and remained the seat of the family of the rulers and many of the important court officials.

40. VOC 3677, Secret papers, Resolution of 14 Feb. 1784, Report by Hemmekan on the expedition to Tidore, fols. 192–202.

41. VOC 3676, Secret papers, Ternate to Batavia, 8 March 1784, fols. 250–251; Miller, "The Moluccas," p. 30.

42. Miller, "The Moluccas," p. 31.

43. VOC 3676, Secret papers, Ternate to Batavia, 8 March 1784, fol. 250.

44. Ibid., fols. 281–282.

45. VOC 3676, Secret papers, Ternate to Batavia, 10 Sept. 1784, fol. 284.

46. VOC 3705, Secret papers, Ternate to Batavia, 15 Sept. 1785, fol. 74.

47. Haga, *Nederlandsch-Nieuw Guinea,* vol. 1, p. 311.

48. VOC 3705, Secret papers, Ternate to Batavia, 15 Sept. 1785, Secret resolution of 30 April 1785, fol. 80; Ternate to Batavia, 15 Sept. 1785, fols. 77–78.

49. VOC 3731, Ternate to Batavia, 15 Sept. 1786, fol. 21; VOC 3763, Secret missive Ternate to Batavia, 15 July 1787, fols. 97–103.

50. VOC 3763, Secret papers, Ternate to Batavia, 6 Sept. 1787, fols. 143–144, 185–186.

51. Wright, *The Moluccan Spice Monopoly,* pp. 29–30.

52. Miller, "The Moluccas," pp. 41–48; VOC 3653, Secret papers, Mission to Amboina, 7 April 1783, fol. 58; VOC 3815, Secret papers, Ternate to Batavia, 6 Sept. 1788, fol. 212.

53. VOC 3910, Secret papers, Amboina to Batavia, 28 Sept. 1789, fols. 14–16.

54. VOC 3912, Secret papers, Resolution of the Dutch Council in Ternate, under date 30 Dec. 1789, fols. 50–51; under date 22 Feb. 1790, fol. 79.

55. VOC 3910, Secret papers, Amboina to Batavia, 30 Sept. 1790, fols. 2–3.

56. VOC 3815, Secret papers, Ternate to Batavia, 7 Aug. 1788, fols. 123–124.

57. VOC 3910, Secret papers, Ternate to Batavia, 38 Sept. 1790, fols. 53–55.

58. VOC 3943, Secret papers, Police report from Amboina, Interview with Kaicili Malikuddin, brother of Sultan Kamaluddin of Tidore, 12 Oct. 1790, fols. 31–33.

59. Ibid., fols. 36–38.

60. Miller, "The Moluccas," p. 57.

61. VOC 3966, Secret papers, Ternate to Batavia, Sept. 1792, fol. 81.

62. Oost-Indische Comité (OIC) 90, Secret papers, Ternate to Batavia, 18 Sept. 1793, section 23.

63. Ibid., section 23.

64. Ibid., 10 May 1794, section 20.

65. OIC 91, Secret papers, Ternate to Batavia, 25 July 1795, n.p.

66. Ibid., 16 Sept. 1795, sections 5, 6, 9.

67. A genealogical list compiled by the Department of Education and Culture in Soa Sio in Tidore based on the "Buku sejarah Jou Barakati dan Silsilah Keturunan Sultan yang disesuaikan dengan Buku Tembaga dan Buku Sejarah Permulaan Islam Ket. Prof. Dr HAMKA" gives Nuku's title as: Nuku Muhammad Nil Mab-Us Amiruddin, Kaicil Peperangan (Jou Barakati).

68. OIC 91, Secret papers, Ternate to Batavia, 16 Sept. 1795, sections 49, 50.

69. Ibid., section 51; Ternate to Batavia, 29 April 1796, section 21.

70. Ibid., 29 April 1796, sections 64, 68; 13 May 1796, section 34; Katoppo, *Nuku,* Lampiran V, p. 248.

71. Miller, "The Moluccas," pp. 57–80.

72. Leirissa, "The Idea of a Fourth Kingdom," pp. 1, 13–14.

73. Miller, "The Moluccas," pp. 84–89; Haga, *Nederlandsch-Nieuw Guinea,* vol. 1, pp. 365–372.

74. Miller, "The Moluccas," pp. 90–117.

75. Haga, *Nederlandsch-Nieuw Guinea,* vol. 1, pp. 377–385.

76. It is estimated a Spanish dollar was worth about 5 shillings or a little less. See Wright, *The Moluccan Spice Monopoly,* p. iv.

77. Katoppo, *Nuku,* p. 38.

78. Farquhar to Madras, 1 Jan. 1802, quoted in Miller, "The Moluccas," p. 149.

79. Miller, "The Moluccas," p. 176; Haga, *Nederlandsch-Nieuw Guinea,* vol. 1, p. 413.

80. Miller, "The Moluccas," p. 191.

81. Katoppo, *Nuku,* Lampiran IXa, p. 260. The "book" referred to the practice of preserving the treaties and letters in a special book, which was regarded with great reverence and whose contents were known to a select few. One of the Tidore princesses became the principal assistant to the regent Kaicili Gaijira in 1779 because of her intimate knowledge of all the treaties ever signed with the Dutch—in other words, with the contents of the "book." VOC 3556, Secret papers, Ternate to Batavia, 12 June 1779, fols. 18–19.

82. Miller, "The Moluccas," pp. 192–193, 202; Haga, *Nederlandsch-Nieuw Guinea,* vol. 2, p. 432; Katoppo, *Nuku,* Lampiran XIIIa, p. 274.

CONCLUSION

1. A useful point is made by Ellen when discussing central places in central Maluku. He suggests that "centers" should be seen as spaces, rather than points, and that the locus of trade and political power may move temporarily to the periphery or within the center itself. See Ellen, "Environmental Perturbation," p. 54.

2. Sahlins, "The Stranger-King," pp. 73–103.

3. Hasan, "Maloko Kië Raha," p. 5.

4. Hasan, "Maloko"; Mustafa Ishak, "Sejarah Kesultanan Bacan," p.10. Similar stories can be found in the Raja Ampat Islands and in the other kingdoms in Maluku.

5. Fox, "Introduction," in Fox (ed.), *To Speak in Pairs*, p. 26. On dualism in eastern Indonesia see also the important pioneering work of van Wouden, *Sociale structuurtypen in de Groote Oost*. It was translated into English in 1968 by R. Needham as *Types of Social Structure in Eastern Indonesia*. A more recent collection of articles from 1980 on dualism in eastern Indonesia can be found in Fox (ed.), *The Flow of Life*.

6. The disquiet of the Malukans at the turn of events in the late eighteenth century was expressed in general terms and focused on Maluku's welfare. The depth of concern at these developments may have also reflected an older, deeper cultural prescription of maintaining a dualism to avoid stasis in the society. For an excellent discussion on this theme, see Errington, *Meaning and Power*, p. 272.

7. Toloa's special place in Tidore society is acknowledged in traditions which attribute to it the origins of the sacred art of iron forging in Maluku. See Kamma and Kooijman, *Romawa Forja*, p. 24.

8. Sopher, *The Sea Nomads*, pp. 239–290; Andaya, "Historical Links," pp. 34–51.

9. Boon, *The Anthropological Romance of Bali;* Geertz, *Negara;* Errington, *Meaning and Power*.

10. Wolters, *History, Culture, and Region*, pp. 53–55.

11. Jacobs, *A Treatise*, p. 113.

Glossary

alifuru: A general term used for non-Christian and non-Muslim interior inhabitants of Maluku.

Ambon Quartier: a general term used by the Dutch to refer to the islands of Buru, Ambelau, Manipa, Kelang, Boano, Seram, Seram Laut, Nusalaut, Honimoa (on Saparua), Oma (on Haruku), and Ambon.

baileu: A permanent or temporary roofed structure open on four sides used for receptions of distinguished guests or for public meetings.

barakati/barakasi/berkat: "Fortune", in the Papuan islands associated with the concept of Koreri, the future golden age. See also under *guna*.

bobato: "That which gives order"; hence a traditional leader of a *soa* identified with the forces of the land; a "lord of the land."

casado: A Portuguese term which means literally "married"; used to refer to those Portuguese men married to local women.

casis: A word of Syrian origin used by the Portuguese to refer to a Muslim religious teacher or scholar of Muslim law. In Maluku it was also loosely applied to scribes, mosque officials, and even to Islamic saints.

country trader: A term used for private European traders involved in the port-to-port trade east of the Cape of Good Hope. Because of the dominance of the English in this trade in the eighteenth century, the term became practically synonymous with "English" country trade.

dachin: A Chinese-designed balance consisting of a lever with unequal lengths which moves on a fulcrum.

East Seram: A common Dutch usage for the eastern end of Seram and the off-shore islands, including the Goram and the Seram Laut archipelagoes.

extirpatie: "Eradication," the term used to describe a policy in which the Dutch East India Company forced the Malukans to uproot all spice trees outside Ambon and Banda in return for compensation to the ruler and the more important officials in the land. See also *recognitie penningen*.

Fala Raha: "The Four Houses" in Ternate, which in this period referred to the Tomagola, Tomaitu, Marsaoli, and Limatahu families.

fidalguia: A Portuguese word meaning nobles, nobility, people of rank; equivalent to the Spanish *hidalguía*.

Gamrange: "The Three Settlements," a general name for the settlements of Maba, Patani, and Weda in southeast Halmahera. In this period it was often extended to include the island of Gebe.

gimalaha: The Tidore title for a village or district head, equivalent to the Ternaten *kimalaha.*

guna: A Malay word meaning "fortune," used with individuals to indicate their possession of a special quality found only in those destined for greatness; a common term associated with those of "prowess," those who become culture heroes. See also *mana.*

hidalguía: A Spanish words meaning nobles, nobility, people of rank; equivalent to the Portuguese *fidalguia.*

hukum: Properly "law or judgment," but in Maluku the term was applied in different ways in the early modern period. Initially it refered to an Islamic judicial official and later became a prestigious position in the north Malukan courts. The term was also used for certain officials who served as representatives of the sultans in outlying territories.

imam: "Model" or "exemplar." A leader in prayer chosen because of age, social leadership, and knowledge of Islam, principally of the Koran.

jogugu: A shortened version of the Ternaten *kolano magugu.* The title is the equivalent of the "lord of the land," and its holder was regarded to be more powerful than the sultan in the sixteenth century. In subsequent centuries it lost its authority as the representative of the forces of the land and hence its links to the *bobatos* as leaders of the communities. Instead it became dominated by the sultan and closely linked to the court. See also *kolano magugu.*

jojau: The Tidorese equivalent of the Ternaten *jogugu.*

juanga: The largest type of *kora-kora* with four banks of fifty paddlers on each side and another hundred men on the platform in the boat itself. See also *kora-kora.*

jurutulis: A scribe.

kaicili: A north Malukan title used exclusively for princes.

kalaudi: The official entrusted with implementation of the important annual symbolic exchange and any preparations necessary for court banquets. It was also the title of the Ternaten official who governed Taliabu in the Sula Islands on behalf of the Sultan Ternate.

kali: The principal Muslim official in the land.

kapita laut: "Captain of the Seas," a title used by the leader of the sultan's fleets. It became one of the most important officials in the kingdom, and in Ternate it came to rival the position of the *jogugu.*

khatib: An Islamic religious functionary who usually delivers the sermon on Friday services; a secretary.

kië: The term for "mountain," but which in time came also to mean "island," or "kingdom," depending on the context. Since these northern Malukan islands were basically peaks of mountains, and communities were identified with island unities, it is possible to see how the word evolved in meaning.

kimalaha: The Ternaten title of a village or district head.

kolano: The Malukan term for ruler, most probably derived from the Javanese

Klono (Klana), who is described in the Panji tales as the king from overseas and the worthy adversary of the Javanese rulers.

kolano magugu: Ternaten for "the lord who holds the land/kingdom in his hands," or the title of the lord of the land. The title was shortened in daily usage to *jogugu,* from *jou* meaning "lord" and *gugu* "to grasp (as a clump of earth) in one's hand."

kolano ngofangare: "The king's people" or personal subjects of the ruler. They were his personal bodyguards and were entrusted with working the ruler's own lands and furnishing him and his family with all the necessities of life.

kora-kora: A Malukan double-outrigger vessel. Two and sometimes three rows of floats were attached to the beams where additional paddlers sat. An ordinary *kora-kora* was manned by fifty to seventy men, while the largest could hold some two hundred. See also *juanga.*

Koreri: The concept held by Biak and the Raja Ampat Papuan islanders of a future golden age.

leen: "Vassal state," a term used by the Dutch East India Company in its treaties with Malukan kingdoms to indicate their political subordination to the Dutch.

madihutu: Genuine or true, in the sense that something is original and hence genuine. A tale would be *madihutu* because it is perceived as original and true.

mana: An ancient Austronesian concept often associated with Pacific Island societies to refer to those individuals favored by the gods; see also *guna.*

mestizo: "Mixed," a term applied to offspring of unions between two different racial groups. In Maluku the reference to a Chinese *mestizo* was to the offspring of a marriage between a Chinese and a local person.

momole: A local north Malukan title given to a person of proven war ability and often associated with heads of early communities.

naga: A serpent associated with Indian and Southeast Asian ideas of fertility and the deity of the soil.

naicili: A north Malukan title for princess.

nanek: Among Raja Ampat islanders it is that special quality in the world which attaches itself to outstanding people, such as shamans, chiefs, and old people. It is this quality which enables these favored individuals to confront difficult and hostile forces present in places and things. See also *barakati* and *guna.*

ngofagamu: "The people of the Land," the ordinary people.

ngofamanyira: Title of the head of a village or a *soa.*

ngofangare: See under *kolano ngofangare.*

pinate: A sixteenth century Ternaten official whose function was to oversee the annual ceremonies of symbolic exchange which reaffirmed the bonds between the people and the ruler.

raja muda: "Young ruler," the heir-apparent.

rak: Papuan raids or head-hunting expeditions.

recognitie penningen: "Payment for acknowledged service," the compensation paid to the rulers and selected officials in Maluku for undertaking the policy of *extirpatie,* the eradication of spices. See also *extirpatie.*

sadaha: A court official who is described in Dutch sources as having the duties of both keeper of the treasury and governor.

salahakan: The title given by the Ternaten sultan to the governor of the Sula Islands. The position was held mainly by the Tomaitu family, though there was a short period in the late seventeenth century when it was given to the Tomagola family.

sangaji: A Malukan title derived from the Javanese *sang,* an honorific, and *aji,* meaning "king." It was awarded by the sultan to the most important *kolanos,* who continued to govern their own domains while acknowledging the sultan's superior political position. It was also used for heads of important settlements.

sembahyang: To show respect and honor to a lord or an individual by placing the palms of the hands together and raising them to one's forehead.

sirih pinang: A preparation of betel leaf, areca nut, gambier and lime which is chewed, producing a mild narcotic effect. It was traditionally offered to guests as a sign of courtesy and welcome.

soa: The smallest sociopolitical unit in a settlement under a local leader; wards or quarters within a village.

soa sio: "The Nine Soas," equivalent to the *uli siwa* or the Confederation of Nine in the Ambon Quarter, refers in this period to the royal settlements in both Ternate and Tidore. The *soa sio* was linked to the royal family, hence its important role in the selection of rulers. Their association with the court led to the later use of the term to distinguish the Muslim Ternatens of the main island from the Ternaten subjects in the periphery, especially the alifuru of Halmahera.

sonyinga: Tidorese term meaning "remembering" the ancestors through specific ritual activities. It is a significant concept based on the belief that the ancestors, as originators of all that is good and useful in the ordering of society, are worthy of emulation.

sowohi kië: "Guardian of the mountain/land/kingdom." The most important pre-Islamic religious functionary in the land with close links to the *jogugu/ jojau.*

suanggi: An evil nocturnal ghost.

syahbandar: A Persian-derived title meaning "Lord of the Port". The function of the *syahbandar* in Maluku was to oversee international trade and the foreign traders in the port.

ulama: Muslim religious scholars.

utusan: The ruler's representative in the periphery.

WORKS CITED

ARCHIVAL SOURCES AND UNPUBLISHED MANUSCRIPTS

Alcina, Francisco Ignacio. "The Muñoz Text of Alcina's History of the Bisayan Islands (1668): Part 1, Books 3 & 4." Preliminary translation by Paul S. Lietz, Loyola University, 1960.

Algemeen Rijksarchief te Den Haag. The material for the seventeenth and eighteenth century history of Maluku comes principally from the Koloniaal Archief (Colonial Archives) of the VOC (Dutch East India Company). The papers sent from Batavia were collected and bundled by years and given a VOC number. These were termed the "Overgekomen Brieven en Papieren" (Letters and Papers Sent [from Batavia]) and contained monthly missives from Dutch outposts plus special reports. The most valuable were the "Memories van Overgave" (Reports on the Transfer of Authority) from an outgoing to an incoming governor. The reports consulted were those from the years since the early seventeenth century when the VOC began sending letters from Maluku until the end of the eighteenth century when the Company was taken over by the Dutch government. The letters were then sent by the Oost-Indische Comité (OIC) beginning in 1793 and focus on the activities of Nuku and the English until the end of the century.

Arquivo Nacional da Torre do Tombo in Lisbon. Selected documents from the *Corpo Cronológico*.

Archivo General de Indias (Casa de India) in Seville. Documents Legajos 34–49, Patronato Real, from the bundles called "Maluco o Especiería 1518–1619."

Bibliotéca Ajuda de Lisboa. *Papeis de Castro, D. João III*. Selected documents from Sections 50-V-31 and 50-V-33.

Bibliotéca Nacional Lisboa. "Copia auténtica do testamento de D. Manuel, rei de Ternate. 30 June 1545." Fundo Geral, caixa 61, no. 17. Ms. 201, nos. 90, 149; Ms. 206, nos. 174–5; Ms. 207, no. 151.

Boletím da Filmotéca Ultramarina Portuguesa. 4 vols. Lisbon: Centro de Estudos Históricos Ultramarinos. Microfilmed documents from the *Livros das monções* in Goa, and from the Arquivo General de Simancas in Spain.

Cunha Rivara, J. H. da (ed.). *Arquivo Portuguez-Oriental.* 8 vols. Nova Goa: Imprensa Nacional, 1857–1877.

Documentação Ultramarina Portuguesa. Lisbon: Centro de Estudos Históricos Ultramarinos, Vols. 1–2, 1960, 1962.

Gavetas da Torre do Tombo. 12 vols. Lisbon: Centro de Estudos Históricos Ultramarinos, 1960–1977.

Hasan, Abdul Hamid. "Maloko Kië Raha." Typed manuscript, Ternate, 1979.

"Hubungan antara Tidore dengan Irian Barat." Typed manuscript in the Department of Education and Culture, Soa Sio, Tidore.

Ishak, Mustafa. "Sejarah Kesultanan Bacan." Hand-typed manuscript held by author in Labuha, Bacan.

Leirissa, R. Z. "The Idea of a Fourth Kingdom in Nineteenth Century Tidorese Maluku." December 1983.

Ramos-Coelho, José de (ed.). *Alguns documentos da Arquivo Nacional do Torre do Tombo, acerca das navegações e conquistas portuguesas.* Lisbon, 1892.

"Ringkasan kisah perjalanan ke Irian Barat dalam tempu 7 bulan 77 hari." Typed manuscript in the Department of Education and Culture, Soa Sio, Tidore.

"Susunan pemerintahan sultan dan pemerintahan umum pada daerah kesultanan Tidore." From the manuscripts *Buku Sejarah Jou Barakati and the Silsilah Keturunan Sultan.* Typed manuscript in the Department of Education and Culture, Soa Sio, Tidore.

PUBLISHED SOURCES

Abdul Razak Daeng Patunru. *Sedjarah Gowa.* Makassar: Yayasan Kebudayaan Sulawei Selatan dan Tenggara, 1967.

Abdurrahim and G. J. Wolhoff. *Sedjarah Goa.* Makassar: Yayasan Kebudayaan Sulawesi Selatan dan Tenggara, n.d.

Adas, Michael. *Machines as the Measure of Men: Technology and Ideologies of Western Dominance.* Ithaca: Cornell University Press, 1989.

Adelaar, K. A. "Malagasy Culture-History: Some Linguistic Evidence." In J. E. Reade (ed.), *The Indian Ocean in Antiquity.* London/New York: Kegan Paul International, forthcoming.

Alkire, William H. "Concepts of Order in Southeast Asia and Micronesia." *Comparative Studies in Society and History* 14, (4) (1972), pp. 484–493.

Andaya, Barbara Watson. *Perak, the Abode of Grace.* Kuala Lumpur: Oxford University Press, 1979.

———. "The Role of the *Anak Raja* in Malay History: A Case Study from Eighteenth Century Kedah." *Journal of Southeast Asian Studies* 7 (Sept. 1976), pp. 162–186.

Andaya, Barbara Watson, and Virginia Matheson (eds. & trans.). *Tuhfat al-Nafis (The Precious Gift).* Kuala Lumpur: Oxford University Press, 1981.

Andaya, Barbara Watson, and Leonard Y. Andaya. *A History of Malaysia.* London: Macmillan, 1982.

Andaya, Leonard Y. *The Heritage of Arung Palakka: A History of South Sulawesi (Celebes) in the Seventeenth Century.* The Hague: Martinus Nijhoff, 1981.

————. "Historical Links Between the Aquatic Populations and the Coastal Peoples of the Malay World and Celebes." In *Historia*. Kuala Lumpur: Department of History, University of Malaya, 1984.

————. *The Kingdom of Johor: Economic and Political Developments*. Kuala Lumpur: Oxford University Press, 1975.

————. "Kingship-*Adat* Rivalry and the Role of Islam in South Sulawesi." *Journal of Southeast Asian Studies* 15 (1) (March 1984), pp. 22–42.

————. "Treaty Conceptions and Misconceptions: A Case Study from South Sulawesi." *Bijdragen tot het Taal-, Land-en Volkenkunde* 134 (1978), pp. 275–295.

Anderson, Gerald H. (ed.). *Studies in Philippine Church History*. Ithaca: Cornell University Press, 1969.

Arasaratnam, Sinnapah (trans. and ed.). "Introduction" to *François Valentijn's Description of Ceylon*. London: Hakluyt Society, 1978.

Argensola, Bartolomé Leonardo de. *Conquista de las islas Malucas*. Madrid: Imprenta del Hospicio Provincial, 1891.

Aubertin, J. J. (trans.). *The Lusiads of Camoens*. 2 vols. London: K. Paul Trench, 1884.

Baker, James Norm. "Descent and Community in Tidore." Ph.D. thesis, University of Michigan, 1988.

Barros, João de. *Da Asia, dos feito que os Portugueses fizeram as conquista e descubrimento das terras, e mares do Oriente*. 9 vols. Lisbon: Imprensa Nacional, 1777–1778.

Bellwood, Peter. *Man's Conquest of the Pacific: The Prehistory of Southeast Asia and Oceania*. Auckland: Oxford University Press, 1978.

————. *Prehistory of the Indo-Malaysian Archipelago*. Sydney: Academic Press, 1985.

Berg, C. C. "The Javanese Picture of the Past." In Soedjatmoko (ed.), *An Introduction to Indonesian Historiography*. Ithaca: Cornell University Press, 1965.

Biros, Nicole. "Commentaire sur le livre de la Conquête des îles Maluques (1609) de Bartolomé Leonardo de Argensola." Thesis (D.E.A.), Paris III, 1984.

Blair, Emma, and James Robertson. *The Philippine Islands, 1493–1803*. 55 vols. Cleveland: A. H. Clark and Co., 1903–1909.

Blussé, Leonard. *Strange Company: Chinese Settlers, Mestizo Women and the Dutch in VOC Batavia*. Dordrecht: Foris Publications, 1986.

Bocarro, Antonio. "História de Maluco no tempo de Gonçalo Pereira Marramaque e Sancho de Vos. March, 1636." In Sá, *Documentação*, vol. 4.

Boon, James A. *Affinities and Extremes: Crisscrossing the Bittersweet Ethnology of East Indies History, Hindu-Balinese Culture, and Indo-European Allure*. Chicago/London: University of Chicago Press, 1990.

————. *The Anthropological Romance of Bali, 1597–1972: Dynamic Perspectives in Marriage and Caste*. Cambridge: Cambridge University Press, 1977.

Borges, Pedro. *Métodos Misionales en la Cristianización de América*. Madrid: Departamento de Misionología Española, 1960.

Borofsky, Robert. *Making History: Pukapukan and Anthropological Constructions of Knowledge*. Cambridge: Cambridge University Press, 1987.

Boxer, C. R. *The Church Militant and Iberian Expansion, 1440–1770*. Baltimore: Johns Hopkins University Press, 1978.

———. *The Dutch Seaborne Empire*. London: Penguin, 1965.

———. *João de Barros, Portuguese Humanist and Historian of Asia*. New Delhi: Concept Publishing Company, 1981.

Brou, A. J. "Les statistiques dans les anciennes missions." *Revue d'Histoire des Missions* (Sept. 1929), pp. 361–384.

Brown, C. C. "The Malay Annals." *Journal of the Malaysian Branch of the Royal Asiatic Society* (Feb. 1953).

Buccellati, Giorgio, and Marilyn Kelly Buccellati. "Terqa: The First Eight Seasons." *Les annales archéologiques arabes syriennes: Revue d'archéologique et d'histoire* 32, (2) (1983), pp. 46–67.

Burke, P. *Popular Culture in Early Modern Europe*. New York: New York University Press, 1978.

Burkill, I. *A Dictionary of the Economic Products of the Malay Peninsula*. 2 vols., London: Crown Agents for the Colonies, 1935.

Burnell, Arthur Coke (ed.). *The Voyage of John Huyghen van Linschoten to the East Indies*. Vol. 1. London: Hakluyt Society, 1885.

Burnell, Arthur Coke, and Henry Yule. *Hobson-Jobson*. New Delhi: Munshiram Manoharlal Publishers Pvt. Ltd., 1979. (Originally published in 1903.)

Campbell, Mary B. *The Witness and the Other World: Exotic European Travel Writing, 400–1600*. Ithaca: Cornell University Press, 1990.

Castanheda, Fernão Lopes de. *História do descobrimento e conquista da India pelos portugueses*. 2 vols. Porto, 1979.

Castles, Lance. "Statelessness and Stateforming Tendencies Among the Batak Before Colonial Rule." In A. Reid and L. Castles (eds.), *Pre-Colonial State Systems in Southeast Asia*. Kuala Lumpur: Royal Asiatic Society, 1973.

Cense, A. A. "Eenige aantekeningen over Makassaars-Boeginese geschiedschrijving." *Bijdragen tot het Taal-, Land-en Volkenkunde* 107 (1951), pp. 42–60.

Certeau, Michel de. *The Writing of History*. Translated by Tom Conley. New York: Columbia University Press, 1988.

Chang, K. C. (ed.). *Food in Chinese Culture: Anthropological and Historical Perspectives*. New Haven: Yale University Press, 1977.

Clercq, F. S. A. de. *Bijdragen tot de kennis der residentie Ternate*. Leiden: E. J. Brill, 1890.

Clifford, James. "On Ethnographic Allegory." In James Clifford and George E. Marcus (eds.), *Writing Culture*. Berkeley: University of California Press, 1986.

Colenbrander, H. T. (ed.). *Jan Pietersz. Coen. Bescheiden omtrent zijn bedrijf in Indië*. vols. 1–5. The Hague, 1919–1923.

Colín, Francisco, SJ. *Labor Evangélica. Ministerios apostólicos de los obreros de la Compañía de Jesús*. 3 vols. New edition by P. Pablo Pastells, SJ. Barcelona: Impr. y litografía de Henrich y Compañía, 1900–1902.

Collingwood, R. G. *The Idea of History*. New York: Galaxy Books, 1956.

Commelin, I. (ed.). *Begin ende voortgangh van de Vereenighde Nederlantsche Geoctroyeerde Oost-Indische Compagnie*. Amsterdam: Theatrum Orbis Terrarum, 1970. Reprint of 1646 edition.

Coolhaas, W. Ph. *Bescheiden*. See under Coen, J. P.

Cortesão, Armando (ed. & trans.). *The Suma Oriental of Tomé Pires*. 2 vols. London: Hakluyt Society, 1944.

Couto, Diogo do. *Da Asia, dos feito que os Portugueses fizeram as conquistas e descubrimento das terras, e mares do Oriente*. 15 vols. Lisbon, 1778–1788.

Dagh-Register gehouden int Casteel Batavia vant passerende daer ter plaetse als over geheel Nederlandsts-Indië, 1624/29–1682. The Hague: Martinus Nijhoff, 1887–1931.

Dalgado, Sebastião Rodolfo. *Glossário Luso-Asiatico*. 2 vols. Coimbra, 1919–1921.

Dassen, M. *De Nederlanders in de Molukken*. Utrecht: W. H. Van Heiningen, 1848.

Diffie, Bailey W., and George D. Winius. *Foundations of the Portuguese Empire 1415–1580*. Minneapolis: University of Minnesota Press, 1977.

Eco, Umberto. *The Name of the Rose*. London: Harcourt Brace Jovanovich, 1984.

Eliade, Mircea. *Images and Symbols: Studies in Religious Symbolism*. New York: Sheed & Ward, 1969.

——. *The Myth of the Eternal Return, or Cosmos and History*. Princeton: Princeton University Press, 1974.

Ellen, R . F. "Environmental Perturbation, Inter-Island Trade and the Relocation of Production Along the Banda Arc; or Why Central Places Remain Central." In Tsuguyoshi Suzuki and Ryutaro Ohtsuka (eds.), *Human Ecology of Health and Survival in Asia and the South Pacific*. Tokyo: University of Tokyo Press, 1987.

Elliott, J. H. *Imperial Spain 1469–1716*. London: Macmillan, 1969.

Errington, Shelly. *Meaning and Power in a Southeast Asian Realm*. Princeton: Princeton University Press, 1989.

Farriss, Nancy M. "Remembering the Future, Anticipating the Past: History, Time, and Cosmology Among the Maya of Yucatan." *Comparative Studies of Society and History* 29 (1987), pp. 566–593.

Febvre, Lucien. *The Problem of Unbelief in the Sixteenth Century: The Religion of Rabelais*. Cambridge/London: Harvard University Press, 1982.

Fischer, Michael M. J. and George E. Marcus. *Anthropology as Cultural Critique: An Experimental Moment in the Human Sciences*. Chicago: University of Chicago Press, 1986.

Flint, Valerie I. J. "Monsters and the Antipodes in the Early Middle Ages and Enlightenment." *Viator: Medieval and Renaissance Studies* 15 (1984), pp. 65–80.

Fox, James J. "Introduction." In Fox (ed.), *The Flow of Life: Essays in Eastern Indonesia*. Cambridge: Harvard University Press, 1980.

——. "Introduction." In Fox (ed.), *To Speak in Pairs: Essays on the Ritual Languages of Eastern Indonesia*. Cambridge: Cambridge University Press, 1988.

Fraassen, Ch. F. van. "Ternate, de Molukken en de Indonesische Archipel." 2 vols. Ph.D. thesis, University of Leiden, 1987.

Friedman, John Block. *The Monstrous Races in Medieval Art and Thought*. Cambridge: Harvard University Press, 1981.

Geertz, Clifford. *Negara: The Theater State in Nineteenth Century Bali.* Princeton: Princeton University Press, 1980.

Gewertz, Deborah, and Edward Shieffelin (eds.). *History and Ethnohistory in Papua New Guinea.* Sydney: University of Sydney Press, 1985.

Geyl, Pieter. *The Netherlands in the Seventeenth Century.* 2 vols. London: Benn, 1964.

Ginzburg, Carlo. *The Cheese and the Worms: The Cosmos of a Sixteenth-Century Miller.* Translated by John and Anne Tedeschi. Baltimore: Johns Hopkins University Press, 1980.

Glacken, Clarence J. *Traces on the Rhodian Shore: Nature and Culture in Western Thought from Ancient Times to the End of the Eighteenth Century.* Berkeley: University of California Press, 1967.

Gómara, Francisco López de. *História general de las Indias o "Hispania vitrix."* New edition, Barcelona, 1965.

Greenblatt, Stephen. *Marvelous Possessions: The Wonder of the New World.* Chicago: University of Chicago Press, 1991.

Grimes, Barbara Dix. "The Return of the Bride: Affiliation and Alliance on Buru." M.A. thesis. Australian National University, 1990.

Guerreiro, Fernão. *Relação anual das coisas que fizeram os padres de Companhia de Jesus nas suas missões do . . . Tidore, Ternate, Ambóino, Malaca . . . nos anos de 1600 a 1609.* 2 vols. Coimbra: Inprensa da Universidade, 1930–1931.

Haga, A. *Nederlandsch-Nieuw Guinea en de Papoesche Eilanden: Historische Bijdrage, 1500–1883.* 2 vols. Batavia: W. Bruining & Co., 1884.

Harrison, J. B. "Five Portuguese Historians." In C. H. Philips (ed.), *Historians of India, Pakistan, and Ceylon.* London: Oxford University Press, 1961.

Heeres, J. E. and F. W. Stapel (eds.). *Corpus Diplomaticum Neerlando-Indicum.* 6 vols. The Hague: Martinus Nijhoff, 1907–1955.

Heeres, J. E. and P. A. Tiele. *Bouwstoffen voor de geschiedenis der Nederlanders in den Maleischen archipel.* 3 vols. The Hague: Martinus Nijhoff, 1886–1895.

Henley, David. "The Idea of Celebes in History." Working Paper 59. Clayton, Victoria: Centre for Southeast Asian Studies at Monash University, 1989.

Hodgen, Margaret. *Early Anthropology in the Sixteenth and Seventeenth Centuries.* Philadelphia: University of Pennsylvania Press, 1964.

Holt, Claire. *Art in Indonesia: Continuities and Change.* Ithaca: Cornell University Press, 1967.

Howard, Alan, and Robert Borofsky (eds.), *Developments in Polynesian Ethnology.* Honolulu: University of Hawaii Press, 1989. See under Borofsky.

Iggers, Georg G. "The Crisis of the Rankean Paradigm in the Nineteenth Century." In Georg C. Iggers and James M. Powell, *Leopold von Ranke and the Shaping of the Historical Discipline.* Syracuse: Syracuse University Press, 1990.

Iriarte de Aspurz, Lazaro. *Franciscan History: The Three Orders of St. Francis of Assisi.* Chicago: Franciscan Herald Press, 1979.

Jacobs, Hubert (ed.). *Documenta Malucensia.* 3 vols. Rome: Jesuit Historical Institute, 1974–1984.

———. "New Sources for the History of Portuguese Maluku 1575–1605, Letters of the Captains." *Erste Reihe, Aufsätze zur Portugiesischen Kulturgeschichte.* Munster, 1980.

————— (ed. & trans.). *A Treatise on the Moluccas (c. 1544) . . . of António Galvão.* Rome: Jesuit Historical Institute, 1970.

Kamma, F. Ch. "The Incorporation of Foreign Culture Elements and Complexes by Ritual Enclosure Among the Biak-Numforese." In P. E. de Josselin de Jong and Erik Schwimmer, *Symbolic Anthropology in the Netherlands.* The Hague: Martinus Nijhoff, 1982.

—————. *Koreri: Messianic Movements in the Biak-Numfor Culture Area.* The Hague: Martinus Nijhoff, 1972.

—————. "De verhouding tussen Tidore en de Papoese eilanden in legende en historie." *Indonesië* 1 (1) (July 1947), pp. 361–370, 536–559; *Indonesië* 2 (1948–1949), pp. 177–188, 256–275.

Kamma, F. Ch., and Simon Kooijman. *Romawa Forja: Child of the Fire.* Leiden: Brill, 1973.

Katoppo, E. *Nuku: Perjuangan Kemerdekaan di Maluku Utara.* Jakarta: Penerbit Sinar Harapan, 1984.

Kimble, George H. T. *Geography in the Middle Ages.* London: Methuen & Co., 1938.

Knaap, Gerrit. "Kruidnagelen en Christenen: De Verenigde Oost-Indische Compagnie en de Bevolking van Ambon 1656–1696." Ph.D. thesis, Utrecht University, 1985.

Koenigsberger, H. G. *Early Modern Europe 1500–1789.* New York: Longman, 1987.

Kooijman, Simon. *Tapa in Indonesia.* Bishop Museum Bulletin 234, Honolulu: Bishop Museum, 1972.

Laarhoven, Ruurdje. "Lords of the Great River: The Maguindanao Port and Polity During the Seventeenth Century." In J. Kathirithamby-Wells and John Villiers (eds.), *The Southeast Asian Port and Polity: Rise and Demise.* Singapore: University of Singapore Press, 1990.

Lach, Donald F. *Asia in the Making of Europe.* 5 vols. Chicago: University of Chicago Press, 1965–1970.

Landini, Lawrence C. "The Historical Context of the Franciscan Movement." In Lazaro Iriarte de Aspurz, *Franciscan History: The Three Orders of St. Francis of Assisi.* Chicago: Franciscan Herald Press, 1979.

Latourette, Kenneth S. *A History of the Expansion of Christianity.* Section 3: "Three Centuries of Advance AD 1500–1800." London: Harper & Brothers, 1947.

Leeden, A. C. Van der. "The Raja Ampat Islands: A Mythological Interpretation." In E. K. M. Masinambow (ed.), *Halmahera dan Raja Ampat sebagai Kesatuan Majemuk.* Jakarta: Lembaga Ilmu Pengetahuan Indonesia, 1987.

"Legende en geschiedenis van Ternate." *Tijdschrift van het Binnenlandsch Bestuur* 51 (1917), pp. 310–320.

Lévi-Strauss, Claude. *The Raw and the Cooked: Introduction to a Science of Mythology.* Translated by John and Doreen Weightman. Vol. 1. New York: Harper & Row, 1969.

Lima Felner, Rodrigo José de. *Subsidios para a história da India portugueza.* Lisbon, 1848.

Lopez, Rafael, and Felix Alfonso, Jr. (eds.). *The Christianization of the Philippines.* Document V. Manila: Historical Conservation Society, 1965.

Lord Stanley of Alderley (ed. and trans.). *The First Voyage Round the World by Magellan.* London: Hakluyt Society, 1874.

Lynch, John. *Spain under the Habsburgs.* Vol. 1 Empire and Absolutism 1516–1598. Oxford: B. Blackwell, 1986.

McDowell, Nancy. "Past and Future: The Nature of Episodic Time in Bun." In D. Gewertz and E. Schieffelin (eds.), *History and Ethnohistory in Papua New Guinea.* Sydney: University of Sydney Press, 1985.

MacGregor, I. A. "Some Aspects of Portuguese Historical Writing of the Sixteenth and Seventeenth Centuries on Southeast Asia." In D. G. E. Hall, *Historians of South-East Asia.* London: Oxford University Press, 1961.

Mackenzie, Donald A. *Myths from Melanesia and Indonesia.* London: Gresham Publishing Company, 1930.

Manusama, Z. J. "Hikayat Tanah Hitu." Ph.D. thesis, University of Leiden, 1977.

Masinambow, E. K. M. (ed.). *Halmahera dan Raja Ampat sebagai Kesatuan Majemuk.* Jakarta: Lembaga Ilmu Pengetahuan Indonesia, 1987.

Meilink-Roelofsz, M. A. P. *Asian Trade and European Influence in the Indonesian Archipelago Between 1500 and About 1630.* The Hague: Martinus Nijhoff, 1962.

Miller, W. G., "The Moluccas Under the British." M.A. thesis, University of Hull, 1974.

Morga, Antonio. *Sucesos de las Islas Filipinas.* 2 vols. Mexico, 1609. In E. Blair and J. Robertson, *The Philippine Islands.* Cleveland: A. H. Clark and Co., 1907.

Moseley, C. W. R. D. (ed. & trans.). *The Travels of Sir John Mandeville.* London: Penguin, 1983.

Mota, A. Teixeira da (ed.). *A viagem de Fernão de Magalhães e a questão das Malucas.* Lisbon, 1975.

Mus, Paul. *India Seen from the East: Indian and Indigenous Cults in Champa.* Translated and edited by David Chandler and Ian Mabbett. Melbourne: Monash Centre for Southeast Asian Studies, 1975.

Newton, A. P. "Travellers' Tales of Wonder and Imagination." In A. P. Newton (ed.), *Travel and Travellers of the Middle Ages.* London: Routledge & Kegan Paul 1949. (First published 1926.)

Nowell, Charles E. "The Loaisa Expedition and the Ownership of the Moluccas." *Pacific Historical Review* 5 (1936), pp. 325–336.

Oliver, Douglas L. *Ancient Tahitian Society.* Vol. 1: Ethnography. Honolulu: University of Hawaii Press, 1974.

Oviedo, Gonzalo Fernandez de. *História general y natural de las Indias.* Madrid: Impr. de la Real Accademía de la história, 1959.

Parry, J. H. *The Spanish Seaborne Empire.* London: Hutchinson, 1966.

Pastells, Pablo, SJ. *História general de Filipinas.* In D. Pedro Torres y Lanza, *Catálogo de los documentos relativos a las Islas Filipinas.* Vol. 5. Barcelona, 1929.

Penrose, Boies. *Travel and Discovery in the Renaissance, 1420–1620.* Cambridge: Harvard University Press, 1967.

Perez, P. Lorenzo. "Los Franciscanos en las Malucas y Celebes." *Archivum Franciscanum Historicum* 6 (1913), pp. 45–60, 198–653, 681–701.

Pérez-Bustamante, Ciríaco. "La expedición de Ruy López de Villalobos a las islas del Pacífico." In A. Mota (ed.), *A viagem*. Lisbon, 1975.

Phelan, John L. *The Millennial Kingdom of the Franciscans in the New World*. 2nd ed. Berkeley: University of California Press, 1970.

―――. "Prebaptismal Instruction and the Administration of Baptism in the Philippines during the Sixteenth Century." In Gerald H. Anderson (ed.), *Studies in Philippine Church History*. Ithaca: Cornell University Press, 1969.

Pierson, Peter. *Philip II of Spain*. London: Thames and Hudson, 1975.

Pigafetta, Antonio. *First Voyage Around the World*. Manila: Filipiana Book Guild, 1969.

Pigeaud, Th. G. Th. *Javaansche volksvertoningen: bijdrage tot de beschrijving van land en volk*. Batavia: Volkslectuur, 1938.

Platenkamp, J. D. M. "Myths of Life and Image in Northern Halmahera." In Henri J. M. Claessen and David S. Moyers (eds.), *Time Past, Time Present, Time Future: Perspectives on Indonesian Culture*. Dordrecht: Foris Publications, 1988.

Ptak, Roderich. "The Northern Trade Route to the Spice Islands: South China Sea-Sulu Zone-North Moluccas (14th to Early 16th Century)." *Archipel* 43 (1992), pp. 27–56.

Rafael, Vicente L. *Contracting Colonialism: Translation and Christian Conversion in Tagalog Society Under Early Spanish Rule*. Ithaca: Cornell University Press, 1988.

Ras, J. J. *Hikajat Bandjar*. The Hague: Martinus Nijhoff, 1968.

Rebelo, Gabriel. *Informação sobre as Malucas*. In A. B. de Sá, *Documentação*, vol. 3. Lisbon, 1955.

Reid, Anthony. *Southeast Asia in the Age of Commerce, 1450–1680*. Vol. 1. New Haven: Yale University Press, 1988.

―――. "Sixteenth Century Turkish Influence in Western Indonesia." *Journal of Southeast Asian History* 10, (3) (Dec. 1969), pp. 395–414.

Rhodes, Alexandre de. *Rhodes of Viet Nam: The Travels and Missions of Father Alexandre de Rhodes in China and Other Kingdoms of the Orient*. Translated by Solange Hertz. Westminster, Md.: Newman Press, 1966.

Ricard, Robert. *The Spiritual Conquest of Mexico*. Translated by Lesley Byrd Simpson. Berkeley: University of California Press, 1966.

Ricoeur, Paul. *Hermeneutics and the Human Sciences*. Cambridge: Cambridge University Press, 1987.

Riedel, Johan Gerard Friedrich. *De sluik-en kroesharige rassen tusschen Selebes en Papua*. The Hague: Martinus Nijhoff, 1885.

Rodgers, Susan. *Power and Gold*. Jewelry from Indonesia, Malaysia, and the Philippines from the Collection of the Barbier-Müller Museum in Geneva. Geneva: Barbier-Müller Museum, 1985.

Rogers, Francis M. *The Quest for Eastern Christianity: Travel and Rumor in the Age of Discovery*. Minneapolis: University of Minnesota Press, 1962.

Ross, E. Denison. "Prester John and the Empire of Ethiopia." In A. P. Newton (ed.), *Travel and Travellers of the Middle Ages*. London: Routledge and Kegan Paul, 1949.

Rumphius, G. E. *Ambonsche Landbeschryving, 1679*. Edited by Z. J. Manusama Jakarta: Arsip Nasional Republik Indonesia, 1983.

————. *D'Ambonsche Rariteitkamer.* Amsterdam: François Halma Boekverkoper, 1705.

Sá, Artur Basílio de. *Documentação para a história das missões do padroado português do Oriente. Insulíndia.* Vol. 2. Lisbon: Agencia Geral do Ultramar, Divisõ de Publicacões e Biblioteca, 1955.

Sahlins, Marshall. *Historical Metaphors and Mythical Realities: Structure in the Early History of the Sandwich Islands Kingdom.* Ann Arbor: University of Michigan Press, 1981.

————. *Islands of History.* Chicago: University of Chicago Press, 1985.

————. "Other Times, Other Customs: The Anthropology of History." *American Anthropologist* 85, (3) (Sept. 1983), pp. 517–544.

————. "The Stranger-King; or, Dumézil Among the Fijians." In Sahlins (ed.), *Islands of History*, pp. 73–103.

Sainsbury, W. Noel (ed.). *Calendar of State Papers Colonial Series, East Indies, China, and Japan 1617–1621.* London: Longmans, 1870.

Sanceau, Elaine. *Cartas de D. João de Castro.* Lisbon, 1955.

Schama, Simon. *The Embarrassment of Riches: An Interpretation of Dutch Culture in the Golden Age.* Berkeley: University of California Press, 1988.

Schurhammer, Georg, SJ. *Francis Xavier: His Life and Times.* Vol. 3, Indonesia (1545–1549). Translated by M. Joseph Costelloe, SJ.) Rome: Jesuit Historical Institute, 1980.

————. "Novos documentos para a história das Molucas no tempo de S. Francisco Xavier." *Broteria* 16 (1932).

————. *Die zeitgenössischen Quellen zur Geschichte Portugiesisch-Asiens und seiner Nachbarländer . . . zur Zeit des HL. Franz Xaver (1538–1552).* Rome: Jesuit Historical Institute, 1962.

Scott, William Henry. *Cracks in the Parchment Wall.* Quezon City: New Day Publishers, 1982.

Sharp, Henry S. *The Transformation of Bigfoot: Maleness, Power, and Belief Among the Chipewyan.* Washington: Smithsonian Ethnographic Inquiry Service, 1988.

Shore, Bradd. "Mana and Tapu." In Howard and Borofsky (eds.), *Developments in Polynesian Ethnology.* Honolulu: University of Hawaii Press, 1989.

Silva Rego, Antóno da. *Documentação para a história das missões do padroado portugûes do Oriente. India.* 12 vols. Lisbon, 1947–1958.

Skelton, R. A. (ed. & trans.), *Magellan's Voyage: A Narrative Account [by Antonio Pigafetta] of the First Navigation.* New Haven: Yale University Press, 1965.

Soedjatmoko (ed.). *An Introduction to Indonesian Historiography.* Ithaca: Cornell University Press, 1965.

Sopher, David E. *The Sea Nomads: A Study Based on the Literature of the Maritime Boat People of Southeast Asia.* Singapore: Singapore National Museum, 1965.

Sousa, Esther de. *Capitães Portugueses nas ilhas Molucas.* Lisbon: Centro de Estudos Ultramarinos, 1980.

Spate, O. H. K. *The Spanish Lake.* Canberra: Australian National University Press, 1979.

Stapel, F. W. *Het Bongaais Verdrag.* Groningen/The Hague: J. B. Wolters Uitgevers Mij., 1922.

Stradling, R. A. *Europe and the Decline of Spain: A Study of the Spanish System, 1580–1720.* Boston/London: G. Allen & Unwin, 1981.

Taylor, Jean Gelman. *The Social World of Batavia: European and Eurasian in Dutch Asia.* Madison: University of Wisconsin Press, 1983.

Taylor, Paul Michael. *The Folk Biology of the Tobelo People: A Study in Folk Classification.* Washington: Smithsonian Institution Press, 1990.

Temple, Richard Carnac. *The World Encompassed and Analogous Contemporary Documents Concerning Sir Francis Drake's Circumnavigation of the World.* London: Argonaut Press, 1926. (Reprinted from the 1628 edition.)

Thomaz, Luís Filipe, FR. "Maluco e Malaca." In A. Mota (ed.), *A viagem.* Lisbon, 1975.

Tiele, P. A. "De Europeërs in den Maleischen archipel." *Bijdragen van het Taal-, Land-en Volkenkunde* 25 (1877), pp. 321–420; 27 (1879), pp. 1–69; 28 (1880), pp. 261–338, 395–482; 29 (1881), pp. 153–215; 30 (1882), pp. 141–242; 32 (1884), pp. 49–118; 35 (1886), pp. 257–355.

Todorov, Tzvetan. *The Conquest of America.* Translated by Richard Howard. New York: Harper Torchbooks, 1984.

Torres y Lanza, D. Pedro. *Catálogo de los documentos relativos a las Islas Filipinas existentes in el Arquivo de Indias de Sevilla.* 10 vols. Barcelona, 1925–1934.

Transylvanus, Maximilianus. *De Moluccis Insulis.* Manila: Filipiana Book Guild, 1969.

Trindade, Frei Paulo da. *Conquista espiritual do Oriente.* 2 vols. Lisbon, 1954.

Urdaneta, Andres de. "Relación del viaje de la Armada del comendador García de Loaisa a las islas de Especiería o molucas en 1525, y sucesos acaecidos en ellas hasta el de 1536 . . ." In Isacio R. Rodriguez, *História de la Provincia Agustiniana del Santíssimo Nombre de Jesus de Filipinas.* Vol. 13. Manila: Arnoldus Press, 1978.

Valentijn, François. *Oud en Nieuw Oost-Indiën.* 2 vols. Amsterdam: J. C. van Keesteren & Zoon, 1862.

Villiers, John. "The Cash-crop Economy and State Formation in the Spice Islands in the Fifteenth and Sixteenth Centuries." In J. Kathirithamby-Wells and John Villiers (eds.), *The Southeast Asian Port and Polity.* Singapore: University of Singapore Press, 1990.

———. "De um caminho ganhar almas e fazenda *: Motives of Portuguese Expansion in Eastern Indonesia in the Sixteenth Century." *Terrae Incognitae* 14 (1982), pp. 23–39.

Visser, Leontine E. "Mijn Tuin is Mijn Kind: Een antropologische studie van de droge rijstteelt in Sahu (Indonesië)." Ph.D. thesis, University of Leiden, 1984.

Vlekke, B. H. M. *Evolution of the Dutch Nation.* New York: Roy Publishers, 1945.

Vliet, Jeremias van. *The Short History of the Kings of Siam.* Edited by David K. Wyatt, translated by Leonard Y. Andaya. Bangkok: Siam Society, 1975.

Wake, C. H. H. "The Changing Patterns of Europe's Pepper and Spice Imports, ca 1400–1700." *Journal of European Economic History* 8, (2) (Fall, 1979), pp. 361–403.

White, Hayden. *The Content of the Form: Narrative Discourse and Historical Representation.* Baltimore: Johns Hopkins University Press, 1987.

Wicki, Josef (ed.). *Documenta Indica.* 14 vols. Rome: Jesuit Historical Institute, 1948–1979.

———. "Gesang, Tänze und Musik im Dienste der alten Indischen Jesuiten-missionen (ca. 1542–1582)." *Missionskirche im Orient.* Immensee, 1976.

Willer, T. J. "Aanteekeningen omtrent het Noorder-Schiereiland van het Eiland Halmahera." *Indisch Archief* 1 (1) (1849), pp. 343–398.

Wittkower, Rudolf. "Marvels of the East: A Study in the History of Monsters." *Journal of the Warburg & Courtald Institutes* 5 (1942), pp. 159–197.

Wolters, O. W. *Early Indonesian Commerce.* Ithaca: Cornell University Press, 1967.

———. *History, Culture, and Region in Southeast Asian Perspectives.* Singapore: Institute of Southeast Asian Studies, 1982.

Wouden, F. A. E. van. *Types of Social Structure in Eastern Indonesia.* Translated by R. Needham. The Hague: Martinus Nijhoff, 1968.

Wright, H. R. C. "The Moluccan Spice Monopoly, 1770–1824." *Journal of the Malayan Branch of the Royal Asiatic Society* 11 (4) (1958).

Yule, Henry, and Arthur Cole Burnell. *Hobson-Jobson.* See under Burnell.

Zainal Abidin bin Farid. "Filsafat hidup 'Sulapa appaka' orang-orang Bugis-Makassar (Pandangan hidup 'segi empat')." *Bingkisan* 2 (Aug. 1969), pp. 2–17.

Zumthor, Paul. *Daily Life in Rembrandt's Holland.* London: Macmillan, 1961.

Index

ABOUT THE AUTHOR

LEONARD Y. ANDAYA received his Ph.D. in Southeast Asian history from Cornell University and is currently professor of history at the University of Hawaii at Manoa. Among his recent publications are *The Heritage of Arung Palakka: A History of South Sulawesi (Celebes) in the Seventeenth Century* and *A History of Malaysia* (co-author Barbara Watson Andaya).

Production Notes

Composition and paging were done on the
Quadex Composing System and typesetting
on the Compugraphic 8400 by the design
and production staff of University of
Hawaii Press.

The text typeface is Baskerville and the
display typeface is Goudy Old Style.

Offset presswork and binding were done by
The Maple-Vail Book Manufacturing Group.
Text paper is Writers RR Offset,
basis 50.